AF210029

Hither Shore

Interdisciplinary Journal
on Modern Fantasy Literature

Jahrbuch der
Deutschen Tolkien Gesellschaft e. V.

Tolkien's *On Fairy-stories*

Interdisziplinäres Seminar der DTG
1. bis 3. Mai 2015, Aachen

Herausgegeben von:
Thomas Fornet-Ponse (Gesamtleitung),
Thomas Honegger, Julian T.M. Eilmann

SCRIPTORIUM OXONIAE

Bibliografische Information
der Deutschen Bibliothek

Die Deutsche Bibliothek verzeichnet diese
Publikation in der Deutschen Nationalbibliografie;
detaillierte bibliografische Daten sind im
Internet über http://dnb.ddb.de abrufbar.

ISBN 978-3-9818313-0-6

Hither Shore, DTG-Jahrbuch 2015
veröffentlicht im Verlag »Scriptorium Oxoniae«

Deutsche Tolkien Gesellschaft e. V. (DTG)
E-Mail: info@tolkiengesellschaft.de

Scriptorium Oxoniae im atelier für TEXTaufgaben e. K.
Brehmstraße 50 · 40239 Düsseldorf · Germany
E-Mail: rayermann@scriptorium-oxoniae.de

Hither Shore, Gesamtleitung: Thomas Fornet-Ponse
E-Mail: hither-shore@tolkiengesellschaft.de

Vorschläge für Beiträge in deutscher oder englischer Sprache (inklusive
Exposé von ca. 100 Wörtern) werden erbeten an o.g. E-Mail-Adresse.

Abwicklung: Susanne A. Rayermann, Düsseldorf
Layout/Design: Kathrin Bondzio, Solingen
Umschlagillustration: Anke Eißmann, Herborn
Druck und Vertrieb: Books on Demand, Norderstedt

Inhalt

Note

Reviews / Rezensionen

Preface

Following recent conferences which addressed specific topics such as adaptations or nature and landscape in Tolkien's whole oeuvre, the 12th Tolkien Seminar of the German Tolkien Society DTG focused on one single text again. Even though *On Fairy-stories*, Tolkien's academic treatise on fantasy, has certainly exerted its influence, articles that are analysing its theories and concepts systematically and across disciplinary borders are rare. The text was thus analysed from many different angles in May 2015 in Aachen.

Apart from basic and concrete deliberations on interpreting Tolkien's theses, discussions ranged from his possible and verified precursors (e.g. Chesterton) and innovation, (Romantic) poetology, the understanding of secondary creation, the implicit epistemology as well as the possible heterotopic character of Faërie to the explanatory potential of different elements of the theory, for example Faërie as a conceptual framework for the blending of different narrative spaces. Supplementing these theoretic deliberations from the "nether regions of concretion" are articles on the responsible use of power, on (roleplaying-) games as a different story-telling medium, musicals and how elements of his theory can be applied to Tolkien's own narrative works.

The large number and diversity of articles as well as the animated discussion during the conference have revealed the potential of Tolkien's deliberations as part of a theory of fantasy and for further academic examination, so that further discussions are hopefully emerging from this publication. Apart from the articles from the Seminar, the book includes several reviews on recent secondary literature.

In closing, I would like to thank Prof. Dr. Wenzel and his team at RWTH Aachen, Julian Eilmann and the Tolkien AG study group of the local secondary school Inda-Gymnasium as well as Walking Tree Publishers for their kind support in generating a successful Seminar. Further thanks are due to all authors, co-editors, Marie-Noëlle Biemer for translations and corrections of English texts as well as the publisher's team Susanne A. Rayermann and Kathrin Bondzio. As in previous years, without all these people this volume of *Hither Shore* could not have been completed.

Thomas Fornet-Ponse

Vorwort

Nach den verschiedenen Seminaren der Vorjahre, die sich einer speziellen Thematik wie Adaptionen oder Natur und Landschaft im Gesamtwerk Tolkiens gewidmet haben, stand beim 12. Tolkien Seminar der Deutschen Tolkien Gesellschaft wieder ein einzelner Text im Mittelpunkt der Diskussionen: *On Fairy-stories*, Tolkiens wissenschaftliche Studie über die Phantastik. Da es diesem Text zwar nicht an Einfluss mangelte, wohl aber an Arbeiten, die die dort vorgestellten Annahmen und Konzepte systematisch und interdisziplinär untersuchen, wurde er im Mai 2015 in Aachen aus vielen unterschiedlichen Perspektiven in den Blick genommen.

Diskutiert wurde neben grundlegenden und konkreten Überlegungen zur Interpretation der Thesen Tolkiens bezüglich seiner möglichen und nachweisbaren Vorläufer (u.a. Chesterton) und Innovationen, der (romantischen) Poetologie, dem Verständnis von Zweitschöpfung, der impliziten Erkenntnistheorie sowie dem möglichen heterotopen Charakter von Faërie auch das Erklärungspotential verschiedener Theorieelemente, beispielsweise Faërie als begrifflicher Rahmen für das „Blending" verschiedener Erzählräume. Eine Ergänzung aus den „Niederungen der Konkretion" zu solchen eher theoretischen Überlegungen bilden Beiträge zum verantwortlichen Umgang mit Macht, zu (Rollen-)Spielen als anderen Erzählmedien oder dem Musical bzw. Tolkiens eigenen narrativen Werken unter der Fragestellung, ob und inwiefern sich dort die Elemente seiner Theorie überprüfen lassen.

Die große Anzahl und die Diversität der Beiträge sowie die anregenden Diskussionen während des Seminars haben deutlich das Potential der Überlegungen Tolkiens im Rahmen einer Theorie der Phantastik und der weiteren wissenschaftlichen Auseinandersetzung mit ihnen gezeigt, sodass sich aus diesem Band hoffentlich anschließende Diskussionen ergeben. Neben den Beiträgen zur Seminarthematik gibt es wieder einige Rezensionen zur neueren Sekundärliteratur.

Abschließend ist für ein erfolgreiches Seminar herzlich Prof. Dr. Peter Wenzel und seinem Team von der Rheinisch-Westfälischen Technischen Hochschule Aachen, Julian Eilmann und der Tolkien AG des Inda-Gymnasiums, Aachen, sowie dem Verlag Walking Tree Publishers für die freundliche und tatkräftige Unterstützung zu danken. Ferner danke ich sehr allen Beitragenden, den Mitherausgebern, Marie-Noëlle Biemer für die Übersetzungen und Korrekturen englischer Fassungen sowie schließlich unserem Verlags-Team Susanne A. Rayermann und Kathrin Bondzio. Wie in den Vorjahren gilt: Ohne sie alle wäre auch dieser Band von *Hither Shore* nicht erschienen.

Thomas Fornet-Ponse

Derived from and Flowing into Reality:

Faërie as a Conceptual Framework for the Blending of Story Rooms

Timo Lothmann & Janek Scholz (Aachen)

> ye shall show forth your powers in adorning this theme, each
> with his own thought and devices   (S 3)

1. Introduction

In his seminal essay *On Fairy-stories*,[1] Tolkien assumes the term *Faërie* to be non-definable due to its elusiveness and its range beyond text. He reaches, however, to point out effectively the importance of *Faërie* as a concept which functions as a mental and cultural Überbau for the construction of story worlds. Taking this as a starting point, we want to shed light on the concept from different perspectives. In the event, it is manifested that Tolkien does not only stand in a discourse tradition, but that his views on *Faërie* are largely consistent with, and even anticipate, modern theoretical approaches that deal with the complexities of the author's and the reader's mind. Among these approaches, the cognitive framework of blending theory (according to Fauconnier et al.) will be focused on in particular as a tool to come closer to an assessment of the nature of *Faërie* and its functional range. Accordingly, our paper is organised along the hypothesis that blend stability is a prerequisite for the interconnection and elaboration of narrative elements we will call story rooms. With respect to Tolkien, we claim that his *Faërie* concept is in line with the view of it as a playground that serves as a vast input space for the creation of coherent story worlds.

2. Tolkien in the Discourse Tradition

In his attempt to delineate *Faërie* in FS, Tolkien dissociates the term from ill-conceptions prevalent at his time. Rather, he recurs to the semantics of early English uses by Gower and Spenser in whose 14-16c writings *Faërie* denotes a magical world or creature of a diverse imaginary kind. Tolkien sees himself in exactly this discourse tradition which, according to him, not only deserves, but

---

1   Here, we rely on the 2014 version of FS as it comprises the text editions of 1939, 1947, and 1964.

requires a conservative revival. It is, thus, no coincidence that Tolkien's Elves remind us of Spenser's "Faerie knights" from *The Faerie Queene* (cf. Spenser I, Intr., 14). Further inspiration in terms of tying in with a storytelling tradition Tolkien found, among others, in Sidney, Coleridge and MacDonald, whose influence can only be highlighted in brief here.

In *The Defence of Poesie* (1595),[2] Sidney defines writing as a divinely in-spired creation of new realities beyond nature—which Tolkien takes up and refines into the concepts of *sub-creation* and *Secondary World*. In accordance with this, *Secondary Belief* can be chiefly linked to Coleridge's well-known "willing suspension of disbelief" postulate from *Biographia Literaria* (1817) as a constitutive of narrative faithfulness as well as to "secondary imagination" as an abstract impulse for any writing creativity (cf. Coleridge chs. XIII-XIV). Ultimately, in Tolkien's reworking of these ideas on creating story worlds that readers can indulge in, it is the customary apprehension of reality that Tolkien wants to challenge by raising our awareness of things *Faërie*. It was particularly MacDonald in *The Fantastic Imagination* (1895) who opted for a consistency of law in story creation for credibility reasons. This, again, informs Tolkien's *inner consistency of reality* which, in turn, determines the *Secondary Belief* and, ultimately, conditions *Enchantment* (cf. e.g. FS 52). Tolkien, in his eclectic outline of a theoretical framework for his own writings, follows MacDonald's conception of imagination as a powerful actor within all of us.[3] With regard to *Faërie*, it is implicit in Tolkien's remarks in FS that he, consequentially, seeks to conceive of *Faërie* as a cover term for an entity that is not of this world. It is an entity that fuels imagination, which then sparks our immersion into a story. In cognitive terms, it is *Faërie* that promotes story-related constructs of the mind.

We seek to establish further theoretical link-ups to Tolkien in order to show that the discourse tradition he is in can be extended beyond his lifetime. We will touch on Huizinga's game theory, Benjamin's conception of *awaking*, and the so-called spatial turn. It is fruitful, however, to elaborate on the cognitive blending perspective first.

3. Blends and Emergent Meaning

Conceptual blending is a basic mental operation for meaning construction. It operates along the mapping of abstract mental spaces, which are connected to culturally shaped frames.[4] This may be best explained with the help of an example: "*Last night I dreamt I had a dispute with Gandalf and Charlemagne.*"

---

2   Cf. Sidney 9-11. See also Wood 99.
3   Cf. MacDonald. On his influence on Tolkien, cf. Bergmann; Fisher.
4   Cf. Fauconnier; Fauconnier/Turner; Schneider. The theoretical framework is presented in simplified form here.

If somebody tells you this, and if the utterance is considered meaningful by the speaker and you in a particular context, both speaker and you make use of a cognitive blending process. In the event of this quasi-automatic process, the *real-I* (i.e. the speaker), the *dream-I, Gandalf,* and *Charlemagne* constitute different mental input spaces (all highlighted in bold above) that are mapped and shape a blend. Into this blend, knowledge from the input spaces is projected. With respect to our example, this means that indeed Gandalf, Charlemagne, and "I" can have an actual dispute in a reality constructed in the individual mind. This includes characteristics of the (fictitious or non-fictitious) persons involved, their clothing, their behaviour, etc.[5] Such dynamic blends can be elaborated, i.e. can be run creatively and serve as a potential input for new blends. This meaningfulness beyond a single context is called emergent meaning, which, if shared, has a cultural effect. This effect represents the intrinsic power of blends that can be exploited for story creation in general.

What are workable blends in a Tolkien story world context? We may justifiably consider blends as assemblies that are constructed from 'real' (i.e. in Tolkien terms: primary world) and 'fictional' (i.e. in Tolkien terms: *Faërie*) inputs. These seemingly opposing conceptual realities can be operationalised as dynamic spaces of meaning negotiation, open to be developed further, for instance by the story author. A prime condition for a reader's immersion into the author's blend offer is blend stability. A factor that fosters blend stability along the narrative development is a consistent logic (e.g. the laws of gravity apply, or Gandalf acts in accordance with his motivation), which includes *Faërie* logic (e.g. there is a dragon, or Gandalf can wield magic). Further, the author's and readers' widely sharing input spaces adds coherence to a story that may originate in the author's mind, but that acquires meaning beyond, namely in the individual reader's mind. The bridge between author and reader is the mutual agreement on the workability of the respective input spaces made accessible via language.

We may think of Númenor, for instance, as a blend in terms of Atlantis and the actual island depicted in *The Silmarillion*. And how about "The Song of Eärendil"? The blend works as the reader may combine songs and poems from his/her actual sphere of life with the function of the song in LotR I (227-230). The more knowledge the reader adds to the input spaces, for instance the song's actually being a hybrid of old and modern English poetry styles including alliteration, metre, etc., the more the reader can "bring" to the blend. In a similar process, we may consider Lórien as a world-within-world construction—it

---

5   The blend relies on partial mappings of the input spaces, i.e. there is a selection of particular highlights on the basis of shared and individual (cultural) knowledge. In other words, if you had not read H or LotR, nor watched the film adaptations, several features of the full potential of the *Gandalf* input space would be missing in your blend that the speaker has initiated when telling about his dream in the first place.

may remind us of a fairy land, or an Arcadia, within a hostile world in LotR.[6] The notorious ring itself constitutes a blend. In the form of a material anchor[7] it combines its being a common object with powers that stem from *Faërie*. This latter blend, and its stability, for instance, is of particular importance throughout the story. In constructing the blends, or in attempting to do so, the reader tries to crack the blends that the author may have had in mind during the writing process by incorporating diversified knowledge in the meaning-making process. Different readers will come to different blend constructions. Yet, considerable overlap given, readers can, for instance, discuss effectively about "their" reading(s) of the story.

Story narration, 'fantastic' or not, relies on blends.[8] The author of a story creatively provides input spaces and lets story characters act within the ensuing blend. If the reader of the story can re-enact this mental processing (which shows via language) him/herself to a considerable degree, immersion may ensue. We will have a closer look on blends and immersion in the following by applying these terms to *Faërie*, thus widening our understanding of the Tolkienian concept.

4. The Faërie Space and Story Rooms

From the cognitive perspective outlined above it follows that in story works such as H and LotR, the narrated *Secondary World* is, on its most abstracted level, a blend of *Faërie* and *Primary World* input.[9] From this blend, in turn, may stem emergent meaning which affects the *Primary World* again. It is this interplay that Tolkien wants to draw our attention to when he states that in the author's creation, or in his words *sub-creation*, of the *Secondary World*, this *Secondary World* is derived from the *Primary World* as well as flowing back into it (cf. FS 77). Indeed, it is the readers' shared cultural background with the author that facilitates their access to the blends and, eventually, renders them successful. Moreover, the more experience readers have with secondary story worlds, the higher is the potential of blends of the abovementioned kind to feed back into

---

6   Cf. the reference to the Celtic Tír-na-nOg in Flieger (184).
7   On behalf of material anchors in blends, cf. the applications of the theoretical framework in Dancygier (to novels) and Lothmann/Hützen (to gameplay).
8   Fauconnier/Turner assume complex double-scope blends (i.e. the merger of clashing input spaces such as described here) to be the crucial potential for meaning establishment and meaning negotiation in general. As such, they are available to all human beings.
9   In this context, the *Primary World* is the world that surrounds both author and readers in the first place. It is the non-fictional world of their everyday life spheres, including common uses of language, other cultural experiences, and physical laws. There is more than one *Primary World*, depending on the perspective: "The Primary World, Reality, of elves and men is the same, if differently valued and perceived" (FS 63).

the *Primary World*. After all, *Primary* and *Secondary World* are intertwined and neither polar nor isolating. Tolkien claims their inseparability to be used as a tool that is longed for in order to come to a better understanding of our (primary-world) human self. As Sandner (137) concisely puts it,

> [the] longing for Faërie, then, is not a 'blind' yearning for a trans-cendental world, simply beyond or above the 'real', but rather offers integration, or reintegration, with the world itself, with 'real woods' and the natural world... The promise of Faërie for Tolkien is a return to the world from which we have become estranged.

While the conception of a *Primary World* appears rather straightforward, *Faërie* still deserves explanation. In the event, conceptual metaphors of space and journey have proved helpful.[10] We categorise *Faërie* as a multidimensional, abstract and dynamic universe that consists of the entire potential of non-primary-world input spaces. The tapping of these for the generation of story blends is, from the author's perspective, confined by his/her sub-creational skill. On this basis, story narration can be seen as a journey through rooms (cf. Fig. 1). By the writing activity, the author unveils, illuminates, furnishes and re-furnishes rooms step by step as the storyline proceeds. Via language, conceptualisations are thus imparted to the reader, who can, ideally, pick those up to serve as a story walkthrough.

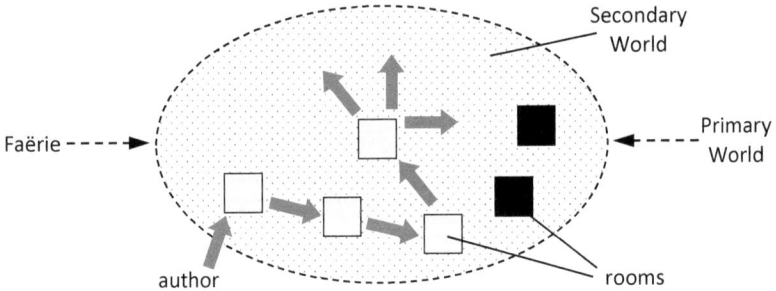

Fig. 1: Narration as a journey through rooms

Idiomatically speaking, the journey is the reward. The story world is widely unexplored at first by both author and reader.[11] You may compare it to Bilbo's journey in *The Hobbit* itself—the story world grows successively larger and,

---

10   For details of Conceptual Metaphor Theory, cf. e.g. Lakoff/Johnson.
11   In this respect, cf. Zgorzelski (137) and Tolkien himself: "At about that time we had reached Bree, and I had then no more notion than they [i.e. the Hobbits] had of what had become of Gandalf or who Strider was" (TL 9).

thus, particular events out of innumerable potential events form the rooms which are interconnected by the story path that the author has laid out and which the reader follows.

Rooms and paths constitute the *Secondary World* as a gestalt. The author does not have to describe every minute detail—the reader will add non-explicit parts to imagine connected rooms, thus building conceptual coherence on the basis of the loci highlighted by the author. However, the abstract story rooms described above remain dynamic. Differing conceptualisations are possible from reader to reader, and even the individual may re-conceptualise path and rooms when, for instance, reading the story for a second time. The path that links the rooms may be continued individually, for instance if the reader experimentally and selectively develops the story beyond the original author (as in fanfiction or film adaptations) and hence turns into an author him/herself, or it may be discontinued altogether, for instance if the reader stops forming story-related blends because of their lacking *inner consistency*.[12] Hence, emergent meaning can be differently contextualised. In doing so, low blend integrity leads to decompression, i.e. a lack of motivation to mentally maintain the *Secondary World*.

Again, with respect to Tolkien's story framework, *sub-creation* can be seen as an original, culturally framed blending activity that, if effective, employs *Faërie* not only as a mere blend source, but also for creating the (mental) reality of *Enchantment*. An author should strive to induce story readers to achieve this state of mind of *Enchantment* as a chief goal of the writing enterprise on the one hand (cf. FS 64), and reader immersion on the other. In an integrative model centred on author and reader, Tolkien's framework underlying story writing brings together *Primary World*, *Secondary World*, *sub-creation*, *Secondary Belief*, and *Enchantment* (cf. Fig. 2).

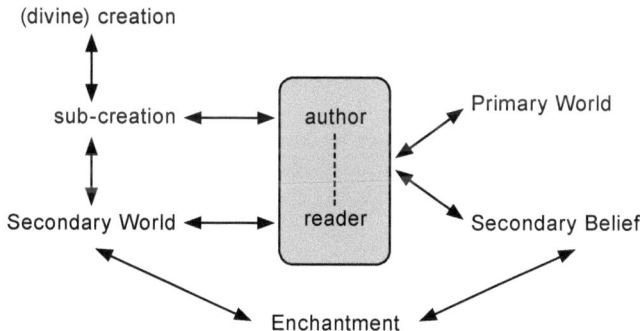

Fig. 2: Author and reader in Tolkien's story framework

---

12 "You... believe it, while you are, as it were, inside. The moment of disbelief arises, the spell is broken" (FS 52).

The author performs sub-creation, thus celebrating and filtering divine creation,[13] and shapes a *Secondary World* which is attempted to be summoned in the reader via language. The mind of the reader may enter this *Secondary World*, and if author and reader (of the same story) may largely share *Secondary Belief*, they are likely to invigorate and to keep up the effect of *Faërie* together. Readers may become story authors, while authors (usually) are also story readers. Both are rooted in the *Primary World*, yet they can tap *Faërie* which, in the event, shines through in story-building blends for which *Faërie* and the *Primary World* are constitutive input sources. *Enchantment* may follow from the co-occurrence of *Secondary World* and *Secondary Belief* as well as blend stability. From the cognitive perspective and in line with Tolkien, *Enchantment* is the utmost proof of *Faërie* impact, and thus of the power of blends.

As hinted at in chapter 3, a plethora of examples can be identified that contribute to the *inner consistency of reality* in Tolkien's stories. We selected instances from nature and cosmology conceptualisations to highlight their potential for the reader to be immersed on the one hand, and their availability for *Faërie* on the other.

> (1) *with the wolves of the wild, in the snows under Caradhras*
> (LotR II 662)
> (2) *The White Tree has grown from the fruit of Nimloth the Fair*
> (S 349)

There are wolves (cf. (1)), eagles and horses which readers can immediately relate to from their *Primary World* experience—so they should with cabbage, carrots, or trees (cf. (2)). All these fauna and flora instantiations occur, among many others, in S, H, and LotR. These lend themselves well to be, from a *Primary World* perspective, incorporated easily into the conceptual shaping of the *Secondary World*. As soon as the reader encounters Wargs, Gwaihir, Shadowfax or Ents along the story path, however, our blends require *Faërie* input to assess them. While these latter entities do portray features of *Primary World* wolves, eagles, horses, and trees, the author has, by dint of *Faërie*, assigned additional or modifying individual fantastic features to them which can be exploited along the narrative journey (cf. Fig. 1).[14]

> (3) *Snowstorms on January the twelfth*   (LotR I 282)
> (4) *Down west sinks the Sun*   (LotR I 118)
> (5) *Innumerable stars, faint and far*   (S 44)

---

13 Religious motivations for Tolkien's story framework have been excluded from the discussion here.

14 For instance, genealogy is applied to explain distinct powers of beings, which includes animals (Shadowfax) and plants (The White Tree).

In a similar vein, there are natural phenomena such as storms, snow (cf. (1), (3)), a cycle of seasons, sunrise/sunset (cf. (4)), or a starry firmament (cf. (5)). As trivial as this may seem, these primary-world elements set the consistent story landscape which is, likewise open to *Faërie*. The transcendent, elusive Undying Lands in Arda's West, for instance, depend more on *Faërie*. The blends that construct this locus strongly rely on elements beyond the spheres of mortals and their perception of the world. As sketchy as these elements are depicted in S and LotR, the Undying Lands constitute a story room which is not fully illuminated by the author's words. Their timelessness stands in contrast to the blends that are more shaped by primary-world elements such as the concept of time as a river (cf. LotR I 379)[15] or the monthly units on a year's calendar (cf. (3)). With respect to stars, the Menelmacar star constellation (cf. S 45) can be seen as an appropriation of the Orion star constellation from a primary-world perspective, while *Faërie* has it that one of the immortal Valar, Varda, had the ability to arrange it in the way it appears in the story (cf. S 44).

Blends of *Primary World* and *Faërie* are frequent, systematic, and occur to different input degrees. They include laws from both input universes that are conceptually amalgamated in writing and reading. Further domains in this respect that are worthwhile investigating in detail elsewhere are *technology* and *language*. Here, we may just hint at the pseudo-medieval weaponry, the concept of knighthood (among the Rohirrim) or means of transportation in LotR. With respect to language, Tolkien sees himself as acting as a mediator when, in his conceptual logic, translating LotR from the *Faërie* language Westron into primary-world English (cf. LotR A 1107),[16] thus linking both universes in his writing activity and making blends possible to be run by the readers, as these blends are now triggered via a language they are familiar with.

So far, we have dealt with conceptual blending. In what follows, we intend to show that Tolkien's understanding of the *Secondary World* finds its analogies in several other schools of thought from the 1930s until today.

5. Huizinga, Benjamin and the Spatial Turn

It has been claimed that reading is a process of filling the gaps which an author has left, consciously or unconsciously. From this traditional literary studies perspective (cf. e.g. Iser) there is a perpetual back-and-forth in the readers mind. This may have given rise to consider the (mental) reading activity

---

15 With respect to conceptual metaphors as gateways to the narrative plot, cf. Sullivan and in particular Vaeßen/Lothmann. For other examples, e.g. of natural phenomena in LotR, cf. Zgorzelski.

16 Cf. L 131 (143): "Behind my stories is now a nexus of languages..."

as a form of gameplay.[17] In 1939 the Dutch anthropologist Johan Huizinga defined play and playful elements in games as a constituent of civilisation and an engine for the development of our cultural achievements, including the war domain, law, poetry, philosophy, art and knowledge in general (cf. ibid.). While his views can be deemed Eurocentric and his usage of *play* and *game* lack distinctiveness as technical terms, his work was and still is an inevitable reference for game studies. In a vein comparable to Tolkien's, he defined *play* as a longing to understand life, i.e. to confirm our cosmic existence (cf. ibid. 12), and qualified it as a possible way to escape from reality as it is imposed on us in order to try out different models of dealing with our lives. When considering Tolkien's notion of escapism (cf. FS 73), the conceptual link to Huizinga becomes apparent. The back-and-forth process, which means also the in-betweenness meanwhile, is a major characteristic of games as it is of stories. However, this threshold between (primary-world) reality and episteme[18] is strongly restricted and structured by rules and frames.

Again, if disbelief arises (cf. footnote 14), the whole illusion collapses. In this respect, a cheat, who violates the rules of the game or who may skip several story chapters when reading, may still maintain the illusion. A grinch, however, who consciously spoils the game or refuses to enter the story world altogether, does not. The latter cannot achieve *Enchantment* (in Tolkien's understanding of it), he even avoids it. Finally, he may keep others away from a eucatastrophic experience. But it is this *eucatastrophe* (cf. FS 75) that gives us consolation and hope and brings us closer to an answer to the question whether the illusion is real. Only by *Enchantment*, i.e. when we are noticeably benefiting from the multiple options of this playground, we are able to reach a higher state of mind. Thus, in Huizinga, there is a strong plea for becoming aware of the positive effects of games and playful elements therein—as there is in Tolkien's FS.[19]

With regard to a higher state of mind, Walter Benjamin and his ideas on dreams and awaking from the 1930s suggest themselves. According to Tolkien, *Enchantment* is a mind state in which *Primary* and *Secondary World* are interconnected to such a degree that we are enabled to see things more clearly. Benjamin's *awaking* (cf. ibid. 490) is a state that connects two different conditions of our mind, namely reality (or *Primary World*) and dream. Benjamin states that during the process of waking up, our mind is not preset by conventions

---

17 Playing a game, as well, can be considered a back-and-forth process. This can be traced, for instance, in the etymology of the modern English word *play*, which is historically cognate to Middle Dutch *pleyen* meaning *to dance*.

18 Here, *episteme* is used in the sense of 'that what shapes the perception of knowledge and discourse'.

19 Cf. Huizinga (21-23): "In der Sphäre eines Spiels haben die Gesetze und Gebräuche des gewöhnlichen Lebens keine Geltung. [... Es ist eine] zeitweilige Aufhebung der 'gewöhnlichen Welt'... Mit dem Ende des Spiels ist aber seine Wirkung nicht abgelaufen; es wirft vielmehr auf die gewöhnliche Welt da draußen seinen Glanz..."

any more, we can actually remember our dream and everything we did in the dream world seems perfectly normal to us. Hence, *awaking* can be defined as a situation in which the *Primary World* is surpassed and a longing arises for the world how it can be (according to the dream). These new perspectives on reality gained by the person who awakes can be seen as the emergent meaning of a successful blending process. In Benjamin's view, the status between reality and dream in *awaking* makes us feel closer to the answer to questions concerning the real and the non-real. This at the same time diminishes our sensation of the world's strangeness as *awaking* means remembering the things that already happened, but which we were yet unaware of (cf. ibid. 491).

Benjamin defined *awaking* not only as an individual process, but as a social phenomenon. In this line of argument, he calls on us to awake, i.e. to perceive reality differently.[20] However, he is aware that dreams are only accessible to others via language. We will never be able to capture the dream completely, because once we try to express and communicate it, its fascination wanes.[21] The dream, thus conceptualised as a world beyond our words, has characteristics similar to *Faërie*.

In Benjamin's *Arcades Project*, he takes the concepts of dream and awaking a step further. An individual, he suggests, can also experience the world beyond in *arcades* (i.e. *Passagen* in the German original). He exemplifies this by referring to metropolitan shopping arcades where another, secondary world becomes visible. In these seemingly endless and mirror-clad rooms, our orientation is bewildered. We perceive an ensemble of fragments from the present, the past and, potentially, the future. The effect is similar to that of *awaking*: we are enchanted, i.e. we are mazed and amazed at the same time, by entering a *Secondary World* with all its inherent options revealed to us all of a sudden (cf. ibid. 524-527). This arcades imagery corroborates that space metaphors are a main conceptual tool in coming to terms with *Secondary Worlds*.

Over the past centuries space was generally conceived of as a given which humans can make use of, but cannot conceptually re-shape. Only after World War II, the conceptualisation of space as a bounded entity started to break up. This development is promoted in the so-called spatial turn, a paradigm change in the social and cultural sciences that gained first impact in the 1980s. In this perspective, persons' identities are not empty containers to be filled with the

---

20 Cf. Benjamin (1020): "Diesen durchaus fluktuierenden Zustand eines zwischen Wachen und Schlaf jederzeit vielspältig zerteilten Bewußtseins hat [... man] vom Individuum aufs Kollektiv zu übertragen".

21 Cf. ibid. (161): "Langeweile ist ein warmes graues Tuch, das innen mit dem glühendsten, farbigsten Seidenfutter ausgeschlagen ist. In dieses Tuch wickeln wir uns, wenn wir träumen. Dann sind wir in den Arabesken seines Futters zuhause. Aber der Schläfer sieht grau und gelangweilt darunter aus. Und wenn er dann erwacht und erzählen will, was er träumte, so teilt er meist nur diese Langeweile mit."

traditions and conventions of the place the persons happened to be born in, but are coined by experiences of migration through real (i.e. cities or countries) and imagined places (cf. e.g. Soja). In Tolkien's words from several decades earlier, this means that we enter and experience a *Primary* and a *Secondary World*. We have pointed out (cf. chapter 4) that such an experience is a journey that presupposes blends. The thresholds between *Primary World*, *Secondary World*, and *Faërie* are particularly interesting. It is a major concept of the spatial turn that thresholds exist, for instance, between the now and the then. Wandering between those 'empty spaces' is an expression of our search for lost things. In the event, the construction of space is a social process. The empty places may become our world and language serves as the key to those.[22] We remember the world how it was or how it can be (cf. Benjamin above) and try to compensate the felt loss by taking over as much as possible from the search into our corporeal reality. The *Secondary World* lends itself as an imagined space with influences on the real world, including the shaping of the identity of the individual who opts to go beyond conventionalised views.[23]

6. Conclusion

We have presented Tolkien as a cultural forerunner with challenging views which find their expression in FS. His call for fairy stories for a broad audience finds its origins in an English storytelling tradition. He claims fairy stories to be valuable beyond common assumptions. What is more, his approach is consistent with the cognitive approach of blending theory which has been emphasised here. Tolkien postulates *sub-creation* as an essential cultural activity that finds its expression in stories, which we have described as a successful journey through story rooms blended from primary-world and *Faërie* inputs. These blends require stability so that coherent narration can develop. With respect to the spatial turn framework, we found links to Tolkien in the imagined places being comparable to *Secondary Worlds*, created by the combination of the

---

22 Here, Bhabha's concept of *Thirdspace* is worth mentioning. In postcolonial contexts, Bhabha examined situations of change and transition from one system of values and conventions to another. In the interim a *Thirdspace* is opened up where values and conventions can be negotiated anew, thus combining familiar, well-known ideas with new visionary ones. Again, the key to the success of such a *Thirdspace* is language, because only with the help of language, negotiation can take place and can be made recourse to; cf. Rutherford.

23 If such applies to a whole group, a so-called Global Ethnoscape (cf. Appadurai ch. 3) might develop, which unifies people from all over the world who are interested in sharing the same knowledge or experiences. The Tolkien fandom may serve as an example: Middle Earth as a *Secondary World* influenced LotR readers to such a degree that it became not only a reality, but a part of their (in-group) cultural identity. For an overview of the spatial turn as a cultural turn, cf. Bachmann-Medick.

experiences humans make during journeys through reality and imagination. Hence, empty places may become our world when we use language effectively. It is Tolkien's plea to make such worlds via language and that we need to be aware of what is hidden. He calls on us to gain a clear view[24] and, by this, to rethink our lives as individuals; cf. FS (146):

> We say we know things, but: we laid hands on them, acquired them and thus ceased looking at them.

Moreover, if deliberate, a social and cultural effect may accrue from the awareness process. With this strong desire to make positive use of in-between spaces Tolkien stands in line with other researchers of his time, such as Huizinga and Benjamin. From their perspective, *Faërie* has parallels in playground and dream scenarios.

Faërie is more than text and it can only be summoned in blends, which are ideally shared by author and recipient. It is an "Otherworld beyond the five senses" (Flieger/Anderson 85), the longing for which can be described as a fundamental human desire for the world itself. Here, we wanted to present *Faërie* as an appeal to keep mental rooms open so that stories can ever continue and, thus, can affect authors and readers in a beneficial way.

Bibliography

Appadurai, Arjun. *Modernity at Large: Cultural Dimensions of Globalization.* University of Minnesota Press, 1996

Bachmann-Medick, Doris. *Cultural turns: Neuorientierungen in den Kulturwissenschaften.* Reinbek bei Hamburg: Rowohlt, 5th ed. 2014

Benjamin, Walter. *Das Passagen-Werk.* 2 Vols. Rolf Tiedemann (Ed.). Frankfurt a.M.: Suhrkamp, [c1935] 1983

Bergmann, Frank. "The Roots of Tolkien's Tree: The Influence of George MacDonald and German Romanticism upon Tolkien's Essay *On Fairy Stories.*" *Mosaic* 10/2 (1977): 5-14

Coleridge, Samuel T. *Biographia Literaria.* Tapio Riikonen et al. (Eds.). *Project Gutenberg*: E-book 6081. [1817] 2013 http://www.gutenberg.org/files/6081/6081-h/6081-h.htm#link2HCH0014 (27/02/2015)

Dancygier, Barbara. *The Language of Stories: a Cognitive Approach.* Cambridge et al.: Cambridge University Press, 2012

Fauconnier, Gilles. *Mappings in Thought and Language.* Cambridge et al.: Cambridge University Press, 1997

---, & Mark Turner. *The Way We Think: Conceptual Blending and the Mind's Hidden Complexities.* New York: Basic Books, 2003

---

24 Cf. FS (67): "We need... to clean our windows".

Fisher, Jason. "Reluctantly Inspired: George MacDonald and the Genesis of J.R.R. Tolkien's 'Smith of Wootton Major'." *North Wind* 25 (2006): 113-120

Flieger, Verlyn. "Faërie." *J.R.R. Tolkien Encyclopedia: Scholarship and Critical Assessment.* Ed. Michael Drout. New York et al.: Routledge, 2007, 183-185

---, & Douglas A. Anderson. "Editors' Commentary." *Tolkien On Fairy-stories.* London: HarperCollins, expanded ed. 2014, 85-121

Huizinga, Johan. *Homo ludens. Vom Ursprung der Kultur im Spiel.* Hamburg: Rowohlt, [1939] 1994

Iser, Wolfgang. *Die Appellstruktur der Texte: Unbestimmtheit als Wirkungsbedingung literarischer Prosa.* Konstanz: Universitätsverlag, 1972³

Lakoff, George, & Mark Johnson. *Metaphors We Live by.* Repr., Chicago et al.: University of Chicago Press, 2011

Lothmann, Timo, & Nicole Hützen. "Bringing Tolkien to the Table: Blending and Conceptual Metaphor in the Board Game Adaptations *Der Herr der Ringe* and *Der Hobbit*." *Hither Shore* 10 (2013), 2014: 146-158

MacDonald, George. "The Fantastic Imagination." *The Complete Fairy Tales.* [n.p.]: Digireads. com, [1895] 2009, 5-8

Rutherford, Jonathan. "The Third Space: Interview with Homi Bhabha." *Identity: Community, Culture, Difference.* Ed. ibid. London: Lawrence and Wishart, 1990, 207-221

Sandner, David. "'Joy beyond the Walls of the World': The Secondary World-Making of J.R.R. Tolkien and C.S. Lewis." *J.R.R. Tolkien and His Literary Resonances: Views of Middle-earth.* Eds. George Clark et al. Westport et al.: Greenwood Press, 2000, 133-145

Schneider, Ralf. "Toward a Cognitive Theory of Literary Character: The Dynamics of Mental-Model Construction." *Style* 35 (2001): 607-640

Sidney, Philip. *The Defence of Poesie.* Ed. Wolfgang Clemen. Heidelberg: Winter, [1595] 1950

Soja, Edward W. *Thirdspace: Journeys to Los Angeles and Other Real-and-Imagined Places.* Cambridge et al.: Blackwell, 1996

Spenser, Edmund. *The Faerie Queene.* London et al.: Longman, [1590] 1990

Sullivan, Karen. "One Metaphor to Rule Them All? 'Objects' as Tests of Character in *The Lord of the Rings*." *Language and Literature* 22 (2013): 77-94

Tolkien, John R.R. "Tree and Leaf". In ibid. *Tree and Leaf, Smith of Wootton Major, The Homecoming of Beorhtnoth Beorhthelm's Son.* London: Allen & Unwin, 2nd impr. 1977, 7-102

---. *The Letters of J.R.R. Tolkien.* Ed. Humphrey Carpenter et al. London et al.: Allen & Unwin, 1981
    http://faculty.smu.edu/bwheeler/tolkien/online_reader/TolkienLetters131.pdf (11/02/2015)

---. *The Hobbit: or There and Back Again.* New York: Ballantine Books, rev. ed. 1982

---. *The Lord of the Rings.* London: HarperCollins, 1995

---. *The Silmarillion.* London: HarperCollins, ill. ed. 2008

---. *Tolkien On Fairy-stories.* Eds. Verlyn Flieger & Douglas Anderson. London: HarperCollins, expanded ed. 2014

Vaeßen, Julia, & Timo Lothmann. "Do You Read Me? Metaphor as a Pathway to the Conceptualisation of Literary Identity." *International Journal of Literary Linguistics* 3, 2014, 1-18
    http://www.ijll.uni-mainz.de/index.php/ijll/issue/viewIssue/6/4 (23/07/2015)

Wood, Tanya C. "Is Tolkien a Renaissance Man? Sir Philip Sidney's 'Defense of Poesy' and J.R.R. Tolkien's On Fairy-stories." *J.R.R. Tolkien and His Literary Resonances: Views of Middle-earth.* Eds. George Clarke et. al. Westport et al.: Greenwood Press, 2000, 95-108

Zgorzelski, Andrzej. "A Fairy Tale Modified: Time and Space as Syncretic Factors in J.R.R. Tolkien's Trilogy." *Zeitschrift für Literaturwissenschaft und Linguistik* 92 (1993): 126-140

Human-stories or Human Stories?

Renée Vink (Hilversum)

Discussing the escape function of fairy tales in the chapter 'Recovery, Escape, Consolation' of his essay *On Fairy-stories* (FS) Tolkien remarks that the deepest desire of humans is "the Great Escape: the Escape from Death". The standard phrase concluding many a fairy story, 'and they lived happily ever after' seems to confirm this. The protagonists have been saved: the Prince wakes Snow White from her glass coffin; Gretel saves Hansel from being eaten; Little Red Riding Hood and her grandmother are cut alive from the wolf's belly. All these characters escape imminent or even actual death.

The English ending seems to suggest they have also escaped permanent death. In German the stock phrase at the end merely says that the characters 'lived happily until the end of their life/days'; in Swedish they 'lived happily in all their days', and in my native Dutch they 'lived on long and happily'. Life unending does not come into the picture in these languages.[1]

The English phrase suggests more. At least, Tolkien does by immediately contrasting Death with its opposite, Deathlessness. Noting that the fairy stories celebrating the escape from death are man-made he adds that "the Human-stories of the elves are doubtless full of the Escape from Deathlessness". He goes on to say that the deathlessness which seems so desirable to mortals would ultimately turn out to be a burden, if achieved (FS § 97). This would explain why the Elves focus on the opposite.

Did Tolkien believe in Elves writing "Human-stories"? Or was he merely playing with words here? The first question is difficult to answer, even if we consider the essay as a whole. He never actually claims that fairies exist, yet he keeps referring to things like elvish craft, elvish enchantment, "Faërian Drama" (FS § 70-76), etc. as though their existence is a given. But I will leave this aside for now. The answer to the second question, whether Tolkien was playing with words, obviously has to be: yes. Tolkien replaced deathless fairies with mortal men and Death with its opposite, Deathlessness.

A clever trick. And once again, the English language is behind it. In Dutch, German, Danish and Swedish Tolkien could not have performed it. In Dutch, the word for fairy story is *sprookje*, meaning 'little oral story', in German

---

1   At the Seminar at Aachen 2015, I was reminded that the German ending is often followed by the stock phrase: *und wenn sie nicht gestorben sind, dann leben sie noch heute* (and if they didn't die, they are still alive today), a phrase also found in Dutch (*en als ze niet gestorven zijn dan leven ze nu nog*) and Swedish (*och är de inte döda, så lever de än idag*). However, this hardly suggests the protagonists will live forever—Sat least, I never interpreted it that way even as a child.

Märchen, meaning 'little tale, report', in Danish *eventyr*, literally 'adventure' (exactly the thing Bilbo did not like but then embarked on anyway), and in Swedish *folksaga*, 'popular oral story'. Confronted with Tolkien's trick, the Dutch translator evaded the word-play and translated the sentence as: 'The stories of the Elves about Humans are doubtless full of the Escape from Immortality'. I do not know wether the German, Danish or Swedish translators made similar moves, but I would not be surprised, if they had. None of these languages have any fairies in their words for fairy tales. However, the French 'conte de fées' does—and that, of course, is the origin of the English term fairy story.

Back to Tolkien's essay. After the introduction, the first full chapter begins with the question "What is a fairy-story?" (FS § 3). Having argued that the first meaning given in the OED, 'a story about fairies', is too narrow Tolkien posits that in "normal English usage" the term means a story about 'Fairy', or as he spells it:

> Faërie, the realm in which fairies have their being. Faërie contains many things besides elves and fays, and besides dwarfs, witches, trolls, giants, or dragons: it holds the seas, the sun, the moon, the sky, and the earth, and all things that are in it: tree and bird, water and stone, wine and bread, and ourselves, mortal men, when we are enchanted. (FS § 10)

Well said and evocative though this is, it also seems somewhat manipulative: to my best knowledge in normal English usage a fairy is a being, not a location (in fact Tolkien admits this by consistently spelling it as *Faërie* when he is referring to the latter). But as a non-native speaker, I have to give Tolkien the benefit of the doubt. After all, he is correct in pointing out that these stories are about more than fairies alone—if we look at the best known collection, the Brothers Grimm's *Kinder- und Hausmärchen*, it turns out these are hardly about fairies at all. They are filled with dwarfs, giants, witches, evil stepmothers, various talking animals, kings and their daughters, and enchanted objects—but fairies?

So, if fairy stories are stories about the realm of Faërie, the Dutch translation is erroneous: 'the Human-stories of the Elves' would not be stories that Elves told about humans, but stories taking place... where? In 'the province of Men', 'the human realm', or even 'Humanitie', to keep the analogy with Faërie as close as possible? Whatever we pick, said realm then would contain human beings instead of fairy tale beings. But at the end instead of 'us, mortal men when we are enchanted' we would get 'the deathless elves, when they are...'—well, maybe we would need the opposite here as well, so: 'the deathless elves, when they are disenchanted'?

Bear with me for a while; this is not just trickery or juggling words. That might be the case, if there were no stories of the Elves to investigate. But if we go along with Tolkien, as we like to do, and we treat the subject as though the Elves are somewhere out there, crafting story and drama, we would have to pretend that such stories existed. Which was precisely what Tolkien did when he set out to write his *Books of Lost Tales*. Just in case not everyone is familiar with the story, I will give a brief sketch.

On one of his voyages the Anglo-Saxon mariner Ælfwine (*aka* Eriol) happened upon the Straight Path leading up and away from our round world to the Undying Lands. Eventually, he came to Tol Eresseä. The Elves living there told him the stories now found in the earlier volumes of *The History of Middle-earth*. Originally, this would have made him our source for the mythology of Arda: in due time, these tales were to have been passed on to Ælfwine's many descendants, ultimately ending up with J.R.R. Tolkien. Later, things took a different turn, but this was still the plan when Tolkien gave his lecture *On Fairy-stories* in 1939. At that time, what we know now as the Ainulindalë, the Valaquenta and the Quenta Silmarillion were essentially elvish texts. The most important one for my present purpose is the latter, plus the writings attached to it in some way. Now the question arises: do any of the stories found in these texts qualify as 'Human-stories of the Elves, full of the Escape from Deathlessness'?

These stories would have to meet at least five criteria. In the first place, seen from a Legendarium-internal point of view they have to be of elvish origin. That is, elvish authorship must be mentioned, or else be plausible, based on characteristics found in the texts. In the second place, humans and their realm must play some kind of role in them, or they wouldn't be human-stories. It is not necessary for the Elves to know any humans personally, though; after all, humans are able to imagine Elves and/or immortals without ever having met any in the flesh. The third criterion is that deathlessness is pre-ordained and not a choice—but that is the case for all Elves in Tolkien's Legendarium, of course. The fourth would be that at least one character in such a human-story attempts to escape from it, whether successfully or not. And fifth and last, if I am on the right track regarding the opposition 'enchantment in fairy-stories' versus 'disenchantment in human-stories', the disenchantment would be a criterion, too.

Let us further take a broad view of the 'Escape from Deathlessness', allowing it to refer to all Elves who could be claimed to have either made the attempt to escape, or actually managed to do so. In chapter 10 of the Quenta Silmarillion we read that Eru appointed the Elves "not to die in Eä" (S 88). Meanwhile, "with anguish in the[ir] hearts", they are doomed to live in the world "until it's whole, evil-aroused story is complete", as Tolkien writes (L 246). It seems reasonable to believe that this is at least one of the reasons behind the wish to escape deathlessness.

The first Elf who seeks this escape, however, does not do so because she has seen too much evil for too long a time, but because she is exhausted. I am referring to Míriel, mother of Fëanor. Having given birth to him she was so weary that "she yearned for release from the labour of living". After she had laid herself to rest in the gardens of Lórien, "her spirit indeed departed from her body and passed in silence to the halls of Mandos" (S 63f). As Elves do not leave Arda after death, passing to the Halls of Mandos is not dying in the sense in which humans die. So this cannot be a viable way to escape deathlessness; it cannot work. However, Tolkien makes explicitly clear that it was a very serious attempt. As he writes in a letter:

> In the Elvish legends there is a record of a strange case of an Elf (Míriel mother of Fëanor) that tried to die, which had disastrous results, leading to the 'Fall' of the High-elves. The Elves were not subject to disease, but they could be 'slain': that is their bodies could be destroyed... But this did not lead naturally to 'death': they were rehabilitated and reborn... But Míriel wished to abandon being.   (L 286)

Did Míriel want to cease existing because she was disenchanted with life? Possibly. It does seem as though she was unable to enjoy life any longer, and she was certainly unwilling to live on[2].

In any case, the legend of Míriel does not qualify as a 'Human-story'. It is set entirely in the Undying Lands and there is no reference to humans—and not merely because Man had not yet appeared, for the Elves had been told about Men, as the next example will show. Could this legend work as a human-story of the Elves, if it dates from after the first contact between Elves and mortal Men in Middle-earth, perhaps as a reinterpretation of a past event by someone who had it from hearsay? It probably could, if it is indeed a story and not an historical account; note that Tolkien calls it a 'legend' in his letter. One of the definitions of 'legend' according to the *Merriam-Webster Dictionary* is "a story from the past that is believed by many people but cannot be proved to be true"[3]. Did some Elf of Middle-earth, knowing Fëanor's mother passed away in Aman but nothing else, and also knowing about death in childbirth by mortal women, spin this kind of yarn around her? Impossible to prove, of course.

---

2   In Mandos she found healing and after Finwe's death she wished to return to life again. Finwë agreed to remain in Mandos in her stead, but nothing indicates this is an (attempt to) escape from deathlessness. He offered to stay 'out of pity' for Míriel (MR 248f).

3   http://www.merriam-webster.com/dictionary/legend

So far the Legendarium-internal point of view. Míriel first enters the Legendarium in 'The later Quenta Silmarillion', which Christopher Tolkien dates to 1951 (MR 141)—remarkably late for something that had such momentous consequences. This legend obviously postdates both the year of the lecture and the publication year of FS (1939 and 1947, respectively), and the letter stating that she "wished to abandon being" was written in 1958. More importantly, by the time he wrote the letter, Tolkien had decided that the *Silmarillion* matter was not an Elvish text, but "two stages removed from a true record", handed on by the Númenoreans and the Men of Middle-earth, "blended and confused with their own Mannish myths" (MR 401, 370). This would stress its legendary—as opposed to historical—character.

Of course, then the question arises, if the legend of Míriel's 'death-wish' can still be considered a story of the Elves once it has passed through the minds and hands of mortal lore-masters.[4] As Verlyn Flieger asked while dealing with the matter of the Elder Days (Flieger 45ff): "Whose myth is it?"

On to the second case now, which may seem more far-fetched. After the Kinslaying at Alqualondë, the rebellious Noldor are subjected to the Doom of the Noldor, also known as the Prophecy of the North. I quote from it: "though Eru appointed to you to die not in Eä, and no sickness may assail you, yet slain ye may be, and slain ye shall be" ... "Then," so the story goes on, "many quailed; but Fëanor hardened his heart" (S 88). Some Noldor turn back; the majority goes on and many of them do indeed die, notably the leaders, first and foremost Fëanor himself. As in the case of Míriel, there are no humans around yet in this story. The Prophecy is present in Tolkien's Legendarium from the *Book of Lost Tales I* onwards (167f), but the wording "slain ye shall be" dates from after the publication of FS[5]—just like the idea of Míriel wanting to abandon being. It could easily be an original elvish story, elaborated on by a human editor.

Basically, the Noldor who persist in their rebellion after the Prophecy are choosing death. Of course, this is not the same as trying to escape from deathlessness. Nevertheless, in this context Fëanor's choice of words while addressing the Noldor in Tirion is interesting. One might say that he is disenchanted with life in the Blessed Realm: blessed though it was, this is where his mother died on him and his father was murdered. He claims the Elves are "cooped here in

---

4   In 'The Shibboleth' of Fëanor', written in the late 1960s, Míriel does not pass away after giving birth to him: he grows old enough to be counselled by her before she dies, and her wish to die is much more outspoken than in *The Silmarillion* (published 1977), though the cause is still weariness after giving birth to Fëanor (PM 333f). Here, she is explicitly called 'obstinate'.

5   The pre-essay Quenta Silmarillion has: "For this [the Kinslaying at Alqualondë] the Noldor should taste death more often and more bitterly than their kindred" (*The Lost Road*, 237). Also, in BLT 1 those who return after the Prophecy still end up with Mandos (168).

a narrow land" whereas "in Cuiviénen... wide lands lay about, where a *free* people might walk"[6]. In Aman "the Valar would hold them captive so that Men might rule in Middle-earth". And among his final, rousing words we find the exhortation: "Say farewell to *bondage!*" (S 82f). In other words, the Noldor in general and Fëanor in particular are certainly making an escape here, and it is an escape towards death. It is no coincidence that they are leaving the *Undying* Lands. Even mortal men briefly appear in this context of escape, though Fëanor has no inkling of what their mortality means. Still, if this qualifies, it is a qualified qualification, so to speak, as the Noldor do not seem to be deliberately trying to escape from deathlessness. For Fëanor, though, the death he did not specifically pursue seems to have been as permanent as it gets for an Elf: according to *The Silmarillion* his spirit has not "left the halls of Mandos" (107).

Example three dates, again, from after the publication of *On Fairy-stories*. It is set in the mortal lands of Middle-earth, so we are firmly in human territory now. Like Míriel's case this one concerns a single Elf: Finrod's youngest brother, Aegnor. His unhappy love story forms the conclusion of the "Athrabeth Finrod ah Andreth". He loves a mortal maiden, Andreth, and she loves him, but for various reasons—all voiced by his brother, but let us assume Finrod's assessment of his position is correct—he feels he cannot marry her. Ironically, Aegnor dies before Andreth, slain in the Dagor Bragollach. While he is still in the flesh, Finrod predicts that "for thy sake now he will not wish to return..., sitting in the House of Mandos in the Halls of Awaiting until the end of Arda" (MR 324f). The reason is not hard to guess. Aegnor is disenchanted with a world in which his beloved Andreth is no longer alive. Remaining in the Halls of Mandos is the best escape from deathlessness he can manage, and his way to prove his solidarity with Andreth.

This time it seems more likely we are dealing with a human-story of the Elves. The encounter between Elvenkind and Mankind has taken place and the Elves have discovered that Man is mortal, that a limit has been set to his life-span, and that he will leave Arda upon death. They call this mortality "the Gift of Ilúvatar", a gift which according to *The Silmarillion* "even the Powers shall envy" (42) as time wears on. Now Finrod discovers that many mortals see it very differently, as a curse rather than as a gift, and he gets to hear a number of other new things as well. His surprise suggests an elvish viewpoint. But the passion, bordering on fanaticism, with which Andreth defends her point of view, could point towards the editorial presence of a human. When Tolkien changed tack regarding the provenance of the tales of the Elder Days, he may have realised that the introduction of death as a curse would profit from the intervention of a mortal editor.

---

6   Italics here and elsewhere in this paragraph mine.

The former seems predominant, though, and not just because the conversation is said to have been "recorded in the ancient lore of the Eldar" (MR 304) or because the Elf has the last word. The surprise, namely regarding the background of human mortality, is mostly on Finrod's side. Whatever food for speculation Andreth gets, seems wasted on her, though she learns a few new things, too. But what does it mean that Aegnor's decision to remain in Mandos is not presented as questionable—that an elvish narrator considers his kind of death the next best thing when the real thing is unattainable? Or are we dealing with a mortal editor who applauds Aegnor's 'solidarity' with Andreth and does not consider the separation of body and spirit (*hröa* and *fëa*) unnatural, like an Elf would (MR 339)? One can only speculate.

By now, it will be clear that I am discussing these stories in the chronological order in which the underlying events occur in the Legendarium. So my next example will be easy to guess. It is the first of the two examples mentioned, though not discussed, in Flieger's *Interrupted Music*:

> How many of the 'human stories' of Tolkien's Elves truly make an issue of this 'escape'? Two come to mind—the story of Beren and Lúthien and the parallel story of Aragorn and Arwen, in both of which an Elf escape from 'deathlessness'.   (Flieger 46)

The latter will be discussed as fifth and last story, but first it is Lúthien's turn. Her case is more complex and differs from the previous ones. If anyone in Tolkien's Legendarium is an escape artist, it is Lúthien Tinúviel. And unlike the characters in my previous examples, she truly achieves the escape from deathlessness.

In brief, the textual history of her tale is as follows: In the *Book of Lost Tales II* Beren is an Elf, and the issue of Lúthien becoming mortal never arises. The 'Lay of Leithian' in *The Lays of Beleriand* is unfinished; in the brief outline for the ending of the lay, Lúthien is stated to have become mortal, but Tolkien does not elaborate on it. The story, including the choices Mandos puts before her, is told in full for the first time in the *Lost Road* version of the Quenta Silmarillion. Christopher Tolkien provides a relative chronology:

> When QS came back from the publishers on 16 December 1937, my father began immediately... on "a new story about Hobbits", and I do not think that after that time he extended the narrative of the Quenta Silmarillion any further.   (LR 293)

Which suggests that the story of Beren and Lúthien dates from before December 1937. As *On Fairy-stories* was first written in 1939 and already contained the remark about the human-stories of the Elves (FS 241), Tolkien may have had this particular tale in mind when he wrote this remark. It is worth noting that this first case of an escape from deathlessness in the development of his Legendarium, and the only one dating from before he began to write LotR, is a successful one.

The title 'Lay of Leithian' also provides food for thought. The Sindarin word *Leithian* means 'release from bondage', Tolkien tells us, but what is being released, and from which bondage? The lay suggests that it is the Silmaril Beren cut from the Iron Crown: "[T]he hope of Elvenland,/ the fire of Fëanor, light of morn/ before the sun and moon were born,/ thus out of bondage came at last,/ from iron to mortal hand it passed" (LB 362). Is this meant as a positive counterpart to Fëanor's 'farewell to bondage', his misguided belief that the Undying Lands are a prison, and that escaping them will lead to the recovery of 'his' jewels? This is not improbable, but it is tempting to think that *leithian* also refers to Lúthien's escape from deathlessness. Release from bondage and escape are not so dissimilar and in any case the result is the same: freedom. In the case of an Elf becoming mortal, it means being no longer bound to the world.

The story is chockfull of images of captivity and imprisonment: Gorlim, ensnared and held by Sauron; the tree-house where Thingol puts his daughter to prevent her from following Beren (and from which she escapes like an inverted Rapunzel by letting her hair grow and using it as a rope—definitely a fairy tale reference); Nargothrond, where she is locked up because Celegorm wants to marry her against her wish; the dungeon of Tol-in-Gaurhoth, where Sauron imprisons the company of Finrod and Beren, and which only the latter leaves alive; and Angband, the stronghold of Morgoth, which is one huge prison filled with enslaved orcs and captured slaves. From these various places of confinement Lúthien or Beren, or both together, escape, prefiguring their next and greatest 'prison break', from Mandos. Beren escapes from actual death and Lúthien from the deathlessness that would have separated her from her lover until the end of Arda. And ultimately, they are freed from the *confines*[7] of the world (S 187)—one should think Tolkien did not choose this word randomly. In short, this is the ultimate escape story. What is also interesting is that Tolkien twice inverts the myth of Orpheus trying to claim Eurydice from Hades: first by changing the genders of the two lovers, then by making the escape successful.

The two did not live happily ever after, or even long and happily in the German, Dutch or Scandinavian way[8]. So this is definitely not a human fairy tale. After their return to Middle-earth from the Houses of the Dead Lúthien and

---

7   Italics by the author.
8   At some point, it was Tolkien's idea to have them live long after their return from Mandos (LR 307), and in 'The Tale of Years' they die 38-40 years afterwards (WJ 346-351). In other texts, however, the date of their death is left uncertain, and according to Christopher Tolkien, this should have made it to the 1977 *Silmarillion* (LR 307). The idea that the Silmarilli shortened Lúthien's life is found from BLT II onwards, for the last time in version C of the Annals in 'The Tale of Years' (WJ 348).

Beren would be 'without certitude of life or joy' (S 187), and though Aragorn's song of Tinúviel states they passed into the woods 'singing and sorrowless' (LotR, Bk I, Ch. XI), this sounds less positive than 'happily'. They die before their time: "The Silmaril hastened their end; for the flame of the beauty of Lúthien as she wore it was too bright for mortal lands" (S 236). They seem to have passed away together, yet the conclusion of the story leaves a feeling of melancholy, a tinge of the disenchantment which no human-story of the Elves can do without, apparently.

This certainly applies to the final example, the tale of Aragorn and Arwen in Appendix A to LotR. Before I go on, though, I will briefly touch on two more cases. The first concerns an Elf seeking death: Maedhros, son of Fëanor. It is true that on discovering the Oath of Fëanor has been vain and his right to the Silmarilli is void (S 254), he wants to die. But he believes his lot would be Everlasting Darkness. "Who shall release us?" he asks his brother Maglor, referring to the Oath of Fëanor. We may be able to think of an answer, but to Maedhros the question is obviously rhetorical, given his further actions. And if he did not even believe release was possible from the bondage of the Oath, he would hardly have expected that escaping life would solve his troubles, as the Everlasting Darkness would still await him in death. The best guess would be that, unable to let go of the Silmarilli, Maedhros wanted to be free from the physical and mental torment that living had become to him. Moreover, this is no human-story. Humans do not come into it; the story has no need of them.

The second case is Elros, the brother of Elrond. Both were half-elven and they were offered a choice to which race they wanted to belong. Basically, they had to choose between mortality and deathlessness. This is the chief difference between Men and Elves and the only one demanding a choice at all: you cannot be half mortal. The example of Elrond's children suggests that anyone who postpones this choice does not die, which would mean that Elros managed to escape from deathlessness when he decided to be a mortal Man. On the other hand, Elros was never fully Elvish to begin with and the Half-Elven are a special case. But we do not really know their 'default' status: are they mortal or not? Moreover, Elros is a very secondary character. His background, his choice and his future as King of Númenor are given, but the Legendarium tells no real story about this character beyond these basic facts—neither a fairy story nor a human-story of the Elves.

The children of Elrond, though, are a different matter. On to the tale of Aragorn and Arwen. Like her foremother Lúthien, Arwen renounces the life of the

Eldar[9]—which she owes to the fact that she is Elrond's daughter. And for the same reason the man she loves is doomed to die and she does not want their fates to be sundered. We can see a shift of focus here, as her mortality is the foreordained consequence of tying her fate to that of a mortal man. As Aragorn does not die before his time, there is no moving scene in Mandos, and compared to Lúthien Arwen seems to slip almost imperceptibly into mortality. She does not appear to age the way mortals do; it even looks as though she remains the same until Aragorn dies. It is explicitly stated that she did not grow weary of the world in the 120 years they were married.

She also differs from Lúthien in that we get to see her reaction to her own mortality. It is predominantly negative: "I must... abide the Doom of Men," she says. Not 'will' or 'shall', but *must*, as though she would refuse, if it was up to her. She changes her mind about Men, understanding now why they rebelled against mortality and concluding that "if this is indeed, as the Eldar say, the gift of the One to Men, it is bitter to receive." In the end she leaves the city of men to die alone. "[T]he light of her eyes was quenched, and it seemed to her people that she had become cold and grey" (LotR, Appendix A). Reaching abandoned Lórien, she lays herself down to die.

To call this death suicide seems a bridge too far, but as Arwen has been granted the gift to lay down life of her own free will, the difference is hard to tell. It is more likely that she dies of grief and loss, though. This is at best an escape from the deathlessness that would have condemned her to grieve until the end of Arda. But we are even further removed from happiness than at the end of the tale of Beren and Lúthien. To say Arwen is disenchanted with mortality seems an understatement.

Interestingly, the disenchantment *follows* Arwen's loss of deathlessness, instead of contributing to the wish for it. If an Elvish storyteller would want to caution an elvish audience against escape from deathlessness—the way a human storyteller would caution against the quest for it—, he certainly could have done a worse job. However, the author of this story is not an elf. He is a mortal. This is fictionalised history written by Barahir, grandson of Faramir (LotR, Prologue). I call it fictionalised: it is difficult to imagine that Barahir was present during this last, highly private conversation of Aragorn and Arwen, or

---

9   At the Tolkien Seminar in 2015, Thomas Honegger gave a summary of this tale (see else-
     where in this volume) that could also apply to the Middle-English narrative poem *Sir
     Orfeo*, which Tolkien translated. *Sir Orfeo* is of course a fairy tale version of the Ancient
     Greek Orpheus myth; earlier we saw how Tolkien inverted its tragic ending in the 'Lay
     of Leithian' (see above). It looks as though he wrote variations on both versions of the
     story, making the tragic version happier and the happy version more tragic than it seems
     at first.

that he witnessed her death. In fact, 'Barahir' merely seems a thin disguise for J.R.R. Tolkien. The conceit that he was only translating and editing old texts had to be sustained, but here it is not particularly convincing. So, the person who presents this interesting case of elvish disenchantment with the escape from deathlessness turns out to be a mortal. This is not a human-story of the Elves at all.

Flieger's question whose myth this is, reasserts itself. The question can be approached from two different angles: a narrative and an authorial one. The first has already been touched upon: these were originally Elvish legends that Tolkien decided had become "influenced by contact and confusion with the myths, theories and legends of Men" (MR 390, n. 17).

We also know that the tale of Aragorn and Arwen is not Elvish at all. How about that of Beren and Lúthien? Does this qualify as a human-story told by Elves? Is the account of their premature deaths, absent from any version of the 'Lay' and related in a later, separate chapter of *The Silmarillion*, an addition? And if so, when and by whom? Maybe it is a human fairy story after all, ending happily with Beren's escape from death because Lúthien makes a sacrifice on his behalf?

And what about Míriel, who didn't stay dead but found a kind of closure in the gardens of Lórien? Or Aegnor, who did stay dead but who may possibly meet Andreth again in Arda renewed, if Finrod is to be believed? Probably not even close reading of all the available texts would provide answers to these and similar questions. Especially not as Tolkien changed his mind about the nature and textual history of his Legendarium and tended to revise his texts often and meticulously. The original narrators of the stories remain elusive, even if they are, say, Rumil or Pengoloð—who are hardly more than names anyway. And the human editors and authors are just as elusive, even if they are, say, Barahir grandson of Faramir, who also is no more than a name.

Which leaves us with the translator-editor, or, to abandon the conceit, J.R.R. Tolkien. In his essay he mentioned the human-stories of the elves as being full of the escape from deathlessness. He thought, perhaps, that he had put one such story in his Legendarium, the tale of Beren and Lúthien. But the escape from deathlessness itself falls curiously flat. What makes us, mortal readers, happy, is that Lúthien's love moves someone believed to be immovable, that the dead man lives again, be it only for a while, that the boy gets his girl and the girl gets her boy. That is how the Mannish editor aka Tolkien liked it and also how we, the readers, like it.

The other tales discussed in this paper are not about true escape attempts either. There is a strong undercurrent of disenchantment, but it has little to do with world-weariness. Míriel is severely weakened in body and spirit by the birth of her son. Fëanor c.s. are not trying to die so much as striving after what they think is freedom (among other things), and if this means death, so be it. Aegnor has no desire to be reborn or re-embodied[10] in a world from which his beloved Andreth has departed.

None of these stories convince us that deathlessness or immortality can become an ordeal. The *Star Trek Voyager* episode "Death Wish"—a human-story of the Q, so to speak—does a better job in showing why an immortal would wish to die than Tolkien's examples of Elves wanting to be dead. It also does a better job of showing the immortal's satisfaction at the prospect of dying, the bewilderment of some of the mortals and their gradual insight into the burden that deathlessness has become to him.

This is probably because it was not the point Tolkien wanted to make; such a death-wish reeks of suicidality. And indeed, Q actually does commit suicide after he has become mortal: it was never his intention to *live* as a mortal—he merely wanted to die. It is obvious, however, that Tolkien considered it wrong for mortal men to want to escape death at the end of their natural lives (see the 'Akkalabêth'), as opposed to escaping from premature death. It was ordained by Ilúvatar that men should leave the world and Elves should not. So maybe he also considered Elvish attempts to escape deathlessness less than commendable except under extraordinary circumstances, "for some high purpose of doom", to put it with Finrod Felagund (MR 324).

In Tolkien's essay the two kinds of escape are contrasted. So when he adds "Few lessons are taught more clearly in [fairy-stories] than the burden of… immortality, or rather endless serial living" (FS § 97), wouldn't it stand to reason that he would at some point try to show the opposite is also true: that the escape from deathlessness also has a downside: the bitterness of leaving? Though mortal himself, the wise teller of Arwen's story obviously knew this, whether we call him Barahir or Tolkien. And he knew it because he was mortal.

It is also possible that the escape from deathlessness in these stories does not work very well because the opposite hardly seems to happen either. Only one person in Tolkien's Legendarium has possibly been granted the life of the Eldar, namely Tuor. In the *Silmarillion*, this is a mere rumour: "It was sung" (245). By whom? By the mortals through whose hands the Elvish legends were passed on, and who just possibly engaged in wishful thinking? In an unsent letter Tolkien remarks: "[I]t is supposed (not stated) that he as an unique exception receives the Elvish limited 'immortality'"; a page further on, however, this

---

10   In the appendix to the 'Athrabeth', Tolkien rejected the notion of rebirth and definitively changed it to re-embodiment, which he also called rehousing (MR 361-366).

suddenly seems to be a fact (L 193, 194). The overall impression is that Tolkien does not want Tuor's fate to be certain in his Legendarium[11].

What could we learn from all this? Despite Flieger's assessment, I would say that Tolkien perhaps wrote a single, true human-story of the Elves: the one predating his essay. It is the only one that works, as Lúthien escapes deathlessness. However, even this is a hybrid, so to speak. Beren's temporal escape from death also makes it resemble a mortal fairy story, at least in the 'continental' sense. For various reasons, none of the other candidates really qualify. Did the Professor, trying to create other elvish human-stories after writing his essay, realise at some point that mortals cannot really tell such tales? After all, he also abandoned the idea that the matter of the Elder Days he had 'translated' was purely Elvish, postulating mortal storytellers and editors through whose hands and minds everything passed.

In the end, all this talk of elvish enchantment and Faërian Drama and Elves making up human-stories is interesting, but also a little whimsical. In his essay Tolkien acts quite convincingly as though he believes in the existence of Elves and in his Legendarium he even tries to write as though he is one. But though he makes a fairly good job of it he never quite succeeds. Writing about the escape from deathlessness, he remains a mortal man who knows in his heart of hearts that writing what you know works best, that 'dying happily ever after' does not exist and that the human-stories of the Elves can never be fairy tales.

---

11 The Elves visiting Númenor could have confirmed Tuors Elvish status, which might have suggested to the disgruntled Númenoreans that it was possible for mortals to achieve 'deathlessness'. Tolkien, however, did not give them even that much of an excuse for their invasion of Valinor: Tuor does not come up in any version of the Akkallabêth.

Bibliography

Carpenter, Humphrey, Ed. *The Letters of J.R.R. Tolkien.* London: Allen & Unwin, 1981

Flieger, Verlyn. *Interrupted Music.* Kent OH: Kent State University Press, 2005

Grimm, Jakob & Wilhelm. *Kinder- und Hausmärchen.* 1812-1857, various editions and translations

Tolkien, J.R.R. *The Lord of the Rings.* London: Allen & Unwin 1954-5

---. *The Silmarillion,* London: Allen & Unwin, 1977

---. *The Book of Lost Tales I. The History of Middle-earth I.* London: George Allen & Unwin, 1982

---. *The Lays of Beleriand. The History of Middle-earth III.* London: George Allen & Unwin, 1984

---. *The Lost Road and Other Writings. The History of Middle-earth V.* London: Unwin Hyman, 1987

---. *Morgoth's Ring. The History of Middle-earth X.* London: HarperCollins, 1994

---. *The War of the Jewels. The History of Middle-earth XI.* London: HarperCollins, 1995

---. *Tolkien. On Fairy-stories.* Expanded edition, with commentary and notes. Ed. Verlyn Flieger & Douglas A. Anderson. London: HarperCollins, 2008

http://www.merriam-webster.com/dictionary/legend (accessed 21-01-2015)

Theorists of Sub-creation
before Tolkien's *On Fairy-stories*

Gerard Hynes (Dublin)

J.R.R. Tolkien's essay *On Fairy-stories* has become an important reference point for critics of fantasy literature, folklore, children's literature, and more recently transmedial world-building (see James/Mendlesohn 1; Zipes 160-168; Hunt 269-273; Wolf 23-25). One of the concepts developed in that essay which has proven most attractive to critics is the idea of "sub-creation". Tolkien coined this term to describe the artistic production of fictional environments, from landscapes to entire universes, which induce literary or ironic belief in the audience while that audience is engaging with them (what Tolkien called "Secondary Belief" (FS 59n)). Tolkien's legendarium has subsequently provided the canonical example of a "sub-created" fictional world. In John Clute's words, Tolkien "gave final definitive legitimacy to the use of an internally coherent and autonomous Land of Faerie as a venue for the play of the human imagination" (Clute 952).

Though Tolkien's term describes the construction of imaginary worlds, it is not precisely synonymous with the term "world-building", derived from science fiction.[1] The words "create", "creation", and "creativity" may be shopworn today—the subject of TED talks and business courses—but for centuries the act of creation was restricted to God and the application of the term "creator" to human invention was a risky and daring metaphor. Tolkien's term deliberately retains this theological core: human artistry is a direct reflection of divine artistry since "we are made in the image and likeness of a maker" (FS 66).

Thus sub-creation is both subordinate and secondary to divine creation. This connection between divine and human creativity is essential to Tolkien's thinking, and while the term "sub-creator" may be original to Tolkien, the concept has a rather longer history, one worth exploring.

---

1   *The Oxford Dictionary of Science Fiction* defines world-building as "the creation of an imaginary world and its geography, biology, cultures, etc., especially for use as a setting in science fiction or fantasy stories, games, etc." and dates the first recorded use to R.A. Lupoff's *Edgar Rice Burroughs: Master of Adventure* (1965) (Prucher 270). The term was however used as early as 1920 for the thinking out of hypothetical worlds with different physical laws (see Eddington 160).

1. Coleridge and MacDonald: The Established History of Sub-creation

As is well-known, Tolkien invented the terms "sub-creator" and "sub-creation" out of dissatisfaction with the critical terminology available to him to discuss the techniques and effects of fantasy: a terminology inherited from Samuel Taylor Coleridge and George MacDonald (see FS 98, 107). This familiar prehistory of *On Fairy-stories* (see Bergmann, Milburn, Seeman) is, however, worth briefly recounting to establish the meaning of sub-creation for Tolkien. In his *Biographia Literaria*, Coleridge had used the terms "willing suspension of disbelief" and "poetic faith" (169) to describe the hoped-for audience reaction to the "supernatural" or "romantic" elements in his and Wordsworth's *Lyrical Ballads*. Tolkien believed this placed excessive emphasis on the audience rather than on authorial skill:

> What really happens is that the story-maker proves a successful "sub-creator". He makes a Secondary World which your mind can enter. Inside it, what he relates is "true": it accords with the laws of that world. You therefore believe it, while you are, as it were, inside... suspension of disbelief is a substitute for the genuine thing.   (FS 52)

Though arising out of a disagreement with Coleridge, sub-creation did not involve an outright rejection of Coleridge's thought, or his terminology, but a development of them. As mentioned, sub-creation implies creation of a secondary and derivative nature, dependent upon a primary Creator and act of creation. In this regard it can be compared with Coleridge's concepts of Primary and Secondary Imagination, described as such:

> The Imagination then I consider either as primary, or secondary. The primary Imagination I hold to be the living power and prime agent of all human perception, and as a repetition in the finite mind of the eternal act of creation in the infinite I AM. The secondary Imagination I consider as an echo of the former, co-existing with the conscious will, yet still as identical with the primary in the kind of its agency, and differing only in degree, and in the mode of its operation. It dissolves, diffuses, dissipates, in order to recreate.   (Coleridge 175)

Primary Imagination is the subliminal arrangement of sense experience into perception and understanding, while Secondary Imagination is the specifically artistic use of imagination to re-create the world for artistic ends. For Coleridge, we are like God firstly in perceiving and knowing and only secondarily in making and inventing. Secondary Imagination, the artistically productive one, is only an echo. Tolkien disagreed. At least when writing about sub-creation, he seems to treat the creative side of the imagination, which Coleridge relegated to a secondary position, as, in fact, our primary resemblance to God. Rather than privileging perceiving over making, Tolkien puts the perception of images as merely the first step in artistic sub-creation.

As well as Coleridge, Tolkien also had George MacDonald in mind when writing *On Fairy-stories*. In his essay "The Imagination: Its Functions and its Culture", MacDonald wrote:

> The imagination is that faculty which gives form to thought…
> It is, therefore, that faculty in man which is likest to the prime
> operation of the power of God, and has, therefore, been called
> the creative faculty, and its exercise creation. Poet means maker.
> We must not forget, however, that between creator and poet lies
> the one unpassable gulf which distinguishes… all that is God's
> from all that is man's.   (MacDonald 2)

MacDonald was emphatic that human making and divine creation must not be conflated and suggested reserving the term "creation" for divine acts or, at most, for certain "daring" symbolic expressions (2). Having warned his readers, MacDonald then writes, however:

> The imagination of man is made in the image of the imagination
> of God. Everything of man must have been of God first; and it
> will help much towards our understanding of the imagination
> and its functions in man if we first succeed in regarding aright
> the imagination of God, in which the imagination of man lives
> and moves and has its being.   (MacDonald 2f)

MacDonald's essential argument is, first, that human imagination can be attributed to, and is derived from, the imagination of the divine creator but, second, that there is equally an unbridgeable ontological gulf between a self-existent Creator and a dependent, and created, human maker. Both of these ideas have parallels in *On Fairy-stories*. In MacDonald's other essay "The Fantastic Imagination", he further develops this argument:

> Man may, if he pleases, invent a little world of his own, with its
> own laws; for there is that in him which delights in calling up new
> forms—which is the nearest, perhaps, he can come to creation.

> When such forms are new embodiments of old truths, we call them products of the Imagination; when they are mere inventions, however lovely, I should call them the work of the Fancy: in either case, Law has been diligently at work.   (MacDonald 314)

MacDonald went on to emphasise the importance of establishing these "laws" of the imagined world, the world-defaults as it were, and the responsibility of the author to keep to them if the world is to engage the audience's belief:

> His world once invented, the highest law that comes next into play is, that there shall be harmony between the laws by which the new world has begun to exist; and in the process of his creation, the inventor must hold by those laws. The moment he forgets one of them, he makes the story, by its own postulates, incredible. To be able to live a moment in an imagined world, we must see the laws of its existence obeyed. Those broken, we fall out of it. The imagination in us, whose exercise is essential to the most temporary submission to the imagination of another, immediately, with the disappearance, of Law, ceases to act.
>   (MacDonald 314f)

This matches point-for-point with Tolkien's account of sub-creation: the world being created is defined by coherence, the reader is inside it while enchanted and is ejected once disenchanted (FS 52).

The only significant difference between Tolkien's thoughts here and those of MacDonald is that MacDonald's description of "the temporary submission to the imagination of another" puts the emphasis on the audience, as was the case in Coleridge, rather than the author, as is the case in Tolkien (see Bergmann 13). To summarize, Tolkien and MacDonald are in agreement on two key points: the closest humanity can come to creation is in the construction of imaginary worlds, and for these imaginary worlds to induce belief they must be coherent and internally consistent.

Although Tolkien's theory of sub-creation may have its acknowledged immediate sources in Coleridge, George MacDonald—as well as in Romanticism more widely—it also, however, has important precedents, and possible sources, going back much further. As scholars have already situated sub-creation in a Romantic context, I will not discuss Romanticism here (see Eilmann, *Song* and Eilmann, *World* as well as *Hither Shore* VII: "Tolkien und Romantik"). Instead I will examine some earlier precedents in late medieval and early modern writings for the idea of artist as "sub-creator". This is not to claim that these earlier writers who compared artists to God operated in a continuous literary or philosophical tradition or were necessarily direct sources for Tolkien's thought,[2] but rather to situate him in a historical and theoretical context, allowing his similarities with his predecessors as well as his innovations to become more apparent.

2. The Prehistory of Sub-creation

An examination of sub-creation should however begin, as Tolkien would have, with philology. The *Oxford English Dictionary* derives the verb "create" from classical Latin *creāt-*, past participle stem of *creāre*, "to procreate, (of males) to beget, (of females) to give birth, (of God, Nature, etc.) to bring into being, to produce, to bring about, cause, to appoint."[3] It ultimately derives from the Proto-Indo-European stem **ker-* "to grow" (cf. cereal), hence "to cause to grow" (Watkins 42). In classical Latin a *creātor* could be so named for creating the world, founding a city, fathering a child, or appointing an official (Lewis/Short 478). The closest Old English equivalent to *creāre* is *scieppan* "to shape, form; to create", from Proto-Germanic **skapjan* and ultimately from Proto-Indo-European **(s)kep* "to cut, scrape, hack" (Watkins 80). This gives us *Scieppend* "the Creator" and *gesceaft* "creation" (Bosworth/Toller 509).[4] It is worth noting that several of the Old English words for the world as God's creation are compounds of verbs denoting shaping and making with adjectives denoting age and originality, e.g. *ealdgeweorc* "ancient work", *frumheowung* "first formation" (see Roberts et al., i, 701), indicating an analogy between this earlier divine work and later, human works. In both Latin and Old English then, there was an implicit connection between divine and human creativity. This is understandable given that analogues for God's activity must be drawn from observation of human activity.[5]

Scippend survived into Middle English, but the OED records that by the 16th century *sceop* (by then spelled *shope*), though still used of God's act of creation, primarily had the weaker sense of "to shape, form" and by the 17th century no longer distinguished divine, as opposed to human, creation. While *scieppan* lost its connection to God, "create" entered English almost entirely

---

2   Plato, Aquinas and Sidney are the only figures here discussed whom Tolkien is known with certainty to have read (see Hammond/Scull i, 37, 70 and Milbank 27 n38).

3   All citations from OED are from http://www.oed.com/ (accessed 16 July 2015).

4   *Scieppan* also gives us the rare and possibly poetic term *handgesceaft* (found in *Genesis* B l. 455) for a work wrought by hand.

5   On a related note, Jakob Grimm connected *scop* 'poet' to *scieppan* and *Scieppend* (Grimm i, 407–8; iii, 900). Modern consensus is, however, against this etymology. The OED connects *scop* to Old High German *scoph* and Old Norse *skop*, both of which imply 'derision' or 'mocking' (compare the Modern English word '*scoff*'). Julius Pokorny traced *scop* to PIE **skeub-* 'to shove' while he traced *scieppan* to **(s)kĕp-* 'to cut, cleave' (Pokorny i, 930f, 955). More research is needed to discover Tolkien's thoughts on this etymology.

restricted to references to God. The first recorded use of "creator" in English is from the life of Thomas Becket in the *Early South-English Legendary* (early 14th century), "heo bad him þane wei gon... / For-to serui is creatour" (Horstmann 111). Interestingly, this is a work with which Tolkien would have been familiar (see Shippey 270f, 327, 394). The verb "create" also appeared in the 14th century, first recorded in Chaucer's *Parson's Tale*, "And al be it so that God hath creat alle thynges in right ordre" (Benson X (i), 218). In the 15th century, "create" could be used of human agents only with the restricted meaning of "to invest (a person) with a particular function or character, or with a title of nobility" or "to bring into legal or official existence", for example, "creating" a duke or a council. Human and divine creativity had become linguistically sundered in English and would only be reconnected in the 16th century.

To turn from language to literature, philosophy, and theology, the comparison of divine creative action with human artistry has an equally long history. In the *Timaeus* Plato suggested that the demiurge was like a human craftsman; they both look to the eternal, unchanging forms for the pattern from which they will make (*Timaeus* 28a-29b). The *Bible* provided images of God as potter (Ps 2:9; Is 29:16; Rom 9:21) or measuring the heavens like an architect (Ps 104:2; Job 9:8; Is 40:22). In the 13th century, Bonaventure compared God's satisfaction with nature to a sculptor's satisfaction with his work (see Camille 34). Thomas Aquinas compared God to an architect designing a house when discussing the possibility of Platonic "Ideas" in the divine mind:

> *Sicut similitudo domus praeexistit in mente aedificatoris. Et haec potest dici idea domus; quia artifex intendit domum assimilare formae quam mente concepit. Quia igitur mundus non est casu factus, sed est factus a Deo per intellectum agente... necesse est quod in mente divina sit forma, ad cujos similitudinem mundus est factus; et in hoc constit ratio Ideae.*

> [The form of the house already exists in the mind of the architect. This can be called the idea of the house; because the architect intends to make the house to the pattern of the form which he has conceived in his mind. Now since the world is not made by chance, but is made by God acting as an intellectual agent... there must be in the divine mind a form, to the likeness of which the world is made; and that is what we mean by an Idea.]

> (ST Ia. q.15 a.1)[6]

---

6   Translation from the Blackfriars edition of the *Summa Theologiae*. All other translations, unless noted, are my own. I wish to thank Julie Le Blanc and Sarah Kuenzler for assistance with them.

There is however a significant difference between claiming "God is like a human artist" and "a human artist is like God"; a difference scholastic writers strongly emphasised. While Aquinas considered an architect an appropriate analogy for God as Creator, he insisted the likeness was not exact. There was a qualitative difference between divine creation and human making (ST Ia. q.45 a.8); creation was an action reserved for God alone (ST Ia. q.45 a.5). Bonaventure asserted that "the soul can make new compositions but it cannot make new things" (Camille 35) and actively distanced human artistry from that of God, writing: "the work of the supreme artist is more excellent than any human art could be" (Camille 35). Though Hugh of St Victor also called God "the supreme artist", he presented human artistry as an appropriation and adulteration of God's creation; a second-order copying of nature (Camille 35, 37). The connection between divine creation and human making was in the 13th century still largely a one-way metaphor, and one which reflected negatively on human artistic ambitions.

A change began with the advent of humanism and the general increase in the social standing of the artist in the Renaissance. E.N. Tigerstedt has identified the 15th-century Florentine humanist Cristoforo Landino as the first person to explicitly claim that the human artist is a creator analogous to God (Tigerstedt 456). In his commentary on Dante's *Commedia*, Landino wrote:

> *Ed e' Greci discono poeta da questo verbo "poiein", el quale è in mezo tra creare, che è proprio di Dio quando di niente produce in essere alcuna cosa, e fare, che è degl'uomini in ciascuna arte quando di materia e di forma compongono. Imperò che, benché el figmento del poeta non sia al tutto di niente, pure si parte dal fare e al creare molto s'appressa. Ed è Idio sommo poeta, ed è el mondo suo poema.*
>
> [And the Greeks say "poet" from the verb "poiein", which is halfway between "to create", which is particular to God when out of nothing he brings forth something into being, and "to make", which applies to men when they compose with matter and form in any art. For this reason, although the fiction of the poet is not entirely out of nothing, it nevertheless departs from making and comes very near to creating. And God is the supreme poet, and the world is His poem.]   (Landino i, 142)

As can be seen however, Tigerstedt oversimplifies; Landino does not actually equate God and the human artist. Divine creation is still defined as creation *ex nihilo*, while human poetry works from pre-existing material. But Landino does give poetry an intermediate position between creation and mere making. His etymology of the word "poet" strongly links human and divine creativity and his metaphor of God as supreme poet serves not to denigrate human poetry but to connect it to the act of creation. As a consequence, human-authored poems become analogous to the world-as-poem created by God, just as Tolkien saw sub-creations corresponding to the created world.

The comparison of human artists to God became even more open as the Renaissance progressed, with the figure of the *divine artist* becoming a trope of panegyric material (see Emison 3-19). From Michelangelo to Titian, *divino* became an epithet to which the most successful artists could aspire, and the connection with God found its way into artists' own writings. Albrecht Dürer, while grumbling that kings once used to reward artistic talent, claimed that such talent was:

> ein geleichformig Geschopf nach Gott. Dann ein guter Maler ist inwendig voller Figur, und obs müglich wär, dass er ewiglich lebte, so hätt er aus den inneren Ideen, davon Plato schreibt, allweg etwas Neus durch die Werk auszuggiessen.
> [a creation like God. For a good painter is internally full of figures, and if it were possible that he live forever, he would have from the inner ideas, of which Plato writes, always something new to pour out in his works.]   (Lange and Fuhse 297f; cf. 127)

This image makes the human artist a reproduction in miniature of the Neoplatonic deity, which adds a new dimension to Dürer's famous Christ-like self-portrait. Leonardo da Vinci too recognised:

> *la deità, ch' a la scientia del pittore, fa che la mente del pittore si transmutta in una similtudine di mente divina, imperoche con libera potesta discorre alla generatione di diverse essentie, di varii animali, pante, frutti, paesi, campagne, ruine di monti, loghi paurosi e spaventevoli, ...et anchora lochi piaccevoli.*
> [that divinity, which exists in the knowledge of the painter and transforms the mind of the painter into a likeness of the divine mind, for with freedom he speaks of the generation of different beings, animals, plants, fruits, landscapes, fields, the ruins of mountains, places terrifying and fearful, ...and even pleasant places.]   (Ludwig i, 126 § 68)

The artist can produce not only works comparable to nature but "*infinite più che quelle, che fa natura*" [infinitely more than those which nature produces] (Ludwig i, 180 §133), though there are still limits on artistic ability in Leonardo's thought. Although he called the artist "*signore e Dio* [lord and god]" of the world he forms in paint or marble, Leonardo seems to have deliberately avoided the terms *creare* and *creazione* in favour of *generare* and *generazione* (see Panofsky 188 n3). He also insisted that imaginative works must have a basis in reality even if they were in a fantastic mode. He wrote that the imagination must relate to reality as the shadow relates to the body that cast it (Ludwig i, 4 § 2) and if the artist wishes to depict monsters they should be built up from observation of living animals (Richter 292f § 585). This could be compared with Tolkien's claim that fantasy is founded on a recognition of fact but not a slavery to it (FS 65).

For the Italian Mannerist painter Federico Zuccari (1540-1609), the idea in the artist's mind is a "*Scintilla della Divinità* [a spark of the divine mind]" (Zuccari 162). This grants the artist an almost god-like ability:

> *Così havendo per sua bontà, & per mostrare in picciolo ritratto l'eccelenzia dell'arte sua divina, creato l'uomo ad imagine, & similtudine sua, quanto all'anima... quasi un secondo Dio, volle anco dargli facoltà di formare in se medesimo un Dissengo interno intelletivo... & in oltre acciocchè con questo Dissegno quasi imitando Dio, & emulando la Natura, potesse produrre infinite cose artificiali simili alle naturali, & col mezo della Pittura, & della Scoltura, farci vedere in Terra nuovi Paradisi.*
> [Because of his goodness and to demonstrate in a small portrait the excellence of his divine art, having created man in his image and likeness with regard to the soul... almost a second God, he wanted to give him the ability to form in himself an inner intellectual design... so that with this design, almost imitating God and matching Nature, he could produce an infinite number of artificial things resembling natural ones, and by means of painting and sculpture make visible new paradises on Earth.]
> (Zuccari 162)

By sharing in God's ability to know the Platonic "Ideas", the artist can give them physical form in works of art just as God does in the creation of nature. This actually allows the artist to add new things to the world of created nature, a claim similar to Tolkien's comment on "the effoliation and multiple enrichment of creation" through sub-creation (FS 79). The claims of Dürer, Leonardo and Zuccari are certainly grandiose but none of them simply equates themselves with God. They "imitate" God, or are "like" God, but are still essentially different.[7]

---

7   The differing implications of the term sub-creation for literature and the visual arts, in terms of the construction of imaginary worlds, is too large an issue to be adequately addressed here.

Turning from art back to poetry, and from Italy to England, Sir Philip Sidney's *Apology for Poetry* (published 1595) is the next relevant text. Building up to his famous claim that poets produce "another nature", Sidney traced the etymologies of the terms for poet in Welsh, Latin, and Greek, connecting poets to both prophecy and craftsmanship (Sidney 98f). He claimed that all other arts are subject to Nature—measuring it, recording it, learning from it—but poetry is unique in going beyond nature:

> Only the poet, disdaining to be tied to any such subjection, lifted up with the vigour of his own invention, doth grow in effect into another nature, in making things either better than Nature bringeth forth, or, quite anew, forms such as never were in Nature... Nature never set forth the earth in so rich tapestry as divers poets have done... Her world is brazen, the poets only deliver a golden.
> (Sidney 99f)

Sidney counters the claim that poetry is either "wholly imaginative" (i.e. exists only in the imagination) or merely imitative of Nature, by describing how the poet makes manifest an "Idea" or "fore-conceit of the work", not itself dependent on Nature (101). He then pre-empts criticism of this comparison of human "wit" and Nature's efficacy by assigning honour to "the heavenly Maker of that maker" (101). Here the second "maker" is Nature, not the human poet. God creates Nature, which then produces rivers, trees, flowers, etc. through a secondary creative power (159 n16). In Sidney's thought, Nature itself is a sub-creator. Poets, however, can go beyond Nature because their "wit" gives them knowledge of perfection, the perfection Creation would have had when God first made it. Nature, as a result of the Fall, does not produce the perfection of original Creation, hence Sidney calls it "second nature" (101). (The apparent immunity of human artists to the effects of the Fall may be a result of Sidney's Neoplatonism outweighing his Protestantism.) In poetry, Sidney claims: "with the force of a divine breath he bringeth things forth far surpassing her [Nature's] doings" (101). Following the description of the poet working from the Platonic "Ideas" just mentioned, this claim brings the poet close to God's creative powers, and places them above Nature, which can only reproduce creation on a debased level. This is a much more Neoplatonic position than Tolkien takes in *On Fairy-stories*. Far from seeing the poet as a jealous rival of nature, Tolkien described the story-teller as nature's "lover not her slave" (FS 69) and in his discussion of "Recovery" claimed that fantastic sub-creation could renew our appreciation for the mundane world (FS 69).

Following Sidney, the idea that poets create new natures, or secondary worlds, seems to have become critical commonplace in English letters. John Donne, Sir William Temple, and Alexander Pope mention it in passing without any sense that the metaphor is original or daring. Donne calls poetry "a counterfeit creation, [which] makes things that are not, as though they were" (Donne iv, 87). Temple wrote: "The Names given to Poets, both in Greek and Latin, express the same Opinion of them in those Nations: The Greek signifying Makers or Creators, such as raise admirable Frames and Fabricks out of nothing" (Temple iii, 74). Though Temple uses the phrase "out of nothing", he proceeds to write of poets being inspired by the celestial fire of God (iii, 74), which again posits a divine source. Pope's *Essay on Criticism* is explicit about world-creation: "So when the faithful pencil has design'd / Some bright idea of the master's mind, / Where a new world leaps out at his command" (ll. 484-486). This is much closer to claiming that poets create outright than Sidney was prepared to go. But, to my knowledge, none of these three writers developed the idea further.

M.H. Abrams, however, identified a substantial change in the concept in the 18th century, especially in the writing by Joseph Addison (Abrams 274). In *The Spectator* (No. 419), Addison claimed that in those kinds of writing which John Dryden called "the Faerie way of Writing" (i.e. fantasy), the poet "quite loses sight of Nature, and entertains his Reader's Imagination with the Characters and Actions of such Persons as have many of them no Existence, but what he bestows on them" (No. 419: Bond iii, 570). The audience is led "into a new Creation", for "Poetry addresses itself to the Imagination, as it has not only the whole Circle of Nature for its Province, but makes new Worlds of its own" (No. 419: Bond iii, 571, 573). He goes on to claim that poetry "has something in it like Creation. It bestows a kind of Existence... It makes additions to Nature, and gives a greater variety to God's Works" (No. 421: Bond iii, 579). While Sidney's "golden world" is, implicitly, our world returned to its original perfection and wonder, Addison's is an independent second world— "valid in itself, and only analogous to the one we owe to God" (Abrams 275). As Abrams views it, critics coming after Addison drew a radical conclusion from the analogy of poet and Creator:

> The poem of the marvellous is a second creation, and therefore not a replica nor even a reasonable facsimile of this world, but its own world, sui generis, subject only to its own laws, whose existence (it is suggested) is an end in itself.   (Abrams 278)

The rivalry with "nature' seen in several of the earlier writers is potentially resolved or transcended here by severing the connection between the created world and the sub-created world. Addison's emphasis is on originality (see Pask 1). He praised Shakespeare for those moments when he most departed from Primary World sources:

> It shews a greater Genius in Shakespeare to have drawn his Caly-
> ban, than his Hotspur or Julius Cæsar: The one was to be supplied
> out of his own Imagination, whereas the other might have been
> formed upon Tradition, History and Observation.
> 　　　　　　　　　　　　　　　　　　(No. 279: Bond ii, 586f)

For Addison, the more fully fictive the character, the greater the writer's originality (Pask 40). Here Addison is in agreement with Tolkien's claim that fantasy
is not less but more sub-creative than mimetic fiction (FS 60).

　　Addison's writings may be usefully contrasted with those of his contemporary
the Earl of Shaftsbury. In his *Characteristics* (1711) he praised:

> The man who truly and in a just sense deserves the name of poet
> and who as a real master... can describe both men and manners...
> Such a poet is indeed a second *Maker*; a just Prometheus under
> Jove. Like that sovereign artist or universal plastic nature, he forms
> a whole, coherent and proportioned in itself, with due subjection
> and subordinacy of constituent parts... The moral artist... can thus
> imitate the Creator.　　　　　　　　　　　　　　(Cooper i, 136)

Here the analogy of poet and creator is repeated but the emphasis is not on the
creation of the world but on the creation of man. Unlike Addison's regard for
fantasy, Shaftsbury advocated fiction which dealt with the actions of convincing and lifelike characters, mocking the romances and travel narratives of
his day for their exaggerated contents (Cooper i, 222). This is a reminder that
sub-creation need not imply fantasy—a secondary world is not necessarily a
separate fantasy world, but can be any narrative world, however mundane—
something implicitly recognised by Tolkien when he comments on the relative
sub-creativity of fantastic and mimetic fiction (FS 60).

　　Like Tolkien, Shaftsbury stresses the coherence and internal logic of the sub-
creation, though here in the psychology and actions of an individual character
rather than a world's consistency. Sub-creation may find its fullest expression
in the construction of imaginary worlds but any artistic production, from
Niggle's leaf to characters as complex as Emma Bovary or Leopold Bloom, is
a sub-creation if we take Tolkien's term in the wider sense he repeatedly used
in his letters, where he described the elves as sub-creators and Morgoth as a
fallen sub-creator (L 146).

3. Conclusion

The idea of sub-creation was not wholly original to Tolkien, but neither was Tolkien merely a derivative thinker. He, and the writers before him, all claimed that sub-creation did not occur *ex nihilo*, that there was always a reliance on some pre-existing source, whether this was the materials of the primary world or ideas accessed from God. For them, human creativity worked upon an already existing basis. These writers do, however, differ as to how far human artistry can depart from the default realities of the primary world. Leonardo would have an art based upon observation, while Addison would allow imagination to leave the primary world behind. While some critics (for example Saler 156) have claimed that Tolkien's account of "secondary worlds" makes them completely autonomous from the everyday "primary world", Tolkien's position is actually more nuanced. He argued that Fantasy could potentially be considered a higher form of art than mimetic fiction as the "inner consistency of reality" is more difficult to achieve "the more unlike are the images and the rearrangements of primary material to the actual arrangements of the Primary World" (FS 60). This comes shortly after the curious sentence: "That the images [in Fantasy] are of things not in the primary world (if that is possible) is a virtue not a vice" (FS 60). Tolkien's parenthetical question would seem to imply that fantastic creatures and worlds are already present *in potentia* in the primary world, though quite how this would be the case is left unclear. One possible solution is to connect this claim to Tolkien's treatment of fantastical things as "rearrangements" of the primary world. Green faces, blue moons, red dragonfire are built from realignments of the categories of the everyday world, not invented from thin air (FS 41). Tolkien's clear wish to maintain a strong connection with the primary world is evinced by his repeated assertions in his letters that Middle-earth was our world in a fictional time period (L 239) and by the great difficulties he caused for himself by trying to make Middle-earth scientifically accurate (such as the interminable problems of the flat earth and the formation of the sun and moon (see Noad)).

Tolkien also differed from some of these writers in his consideration for "Nature". Zuccari, Sidney and Addison saw human artists as either rivalling or bypassing nature, while Tolkien saw the potential for sub-creation to inspire renewed wonder for the world he always called the *primary* world. Some of these writers—Dürer, Zuccari, Sidney—saw the connection between artist or poet and God as residing in the artist's access to the divine ideas. Tolkien located it instead in the artist's own created nature. This is implicitly a much more egalitarian account of artistic ability, with sub-creation a potential ability of all of us rather than the prerogative of an inspired artist. Something else which is distinct about Tolkien, though he does not stress it in *On Fairy-stories*, is the collaborative nature of sub-creation—whether we think of the Valar cooperating in the making of Arda or the collaboration of elves and dwarves in the making of Menegroth. While all of these writers discussed what the artist can do alone, Tolkien went on to explore what artists do together.

All of the writers who developed ideas comparable to sub-creation were cautious, no matter how much they praised human creativity, not to merely equate it with divine creation *ex nihilo*. They were anxious about quite how far the analogy could be taken. Repeatedly poetry is described as "like" an act of creation, the poet "almost" God. To actually equate the poet with God would have been theologically dangerous during much of the period surveyed. Tolkien was similarly concerned not to push the analogy from metaphor to open identification. His position is codified in the term he chose for artistic invention: *sub*-creation. Artistic creation is not only a limited repetition of God's act of creation but is always defined against and dependent upon that act. Human creativity is not only a reflection of divine creativity but arises from our own creation by God.

Although the title of this essay calls the figures discussed here "theorists of sub-creation", in truth, George MacDonald is the only one who comes close to Tolkien in terms of actually working out a coherent theory of sub-creation. For the others, it is a striking metaphor but not a central aspect of their thought. The depth of Tolkien's engagement with the metaphor throughout his career is what makes him an innovative and important thinker, but it is only by situating him in such a context that this importance may be seen.

Bibliogrgaphy

Abrams, M.H. *The Mirror and the Lamp: Romantic Theory and the Critical Tradition.* New York: W.W. Norton, 1958

Aquinas, St Thomas. *Summa Theologiae.* Ed. Thomas Gilby, 61 vols. London: Blackfriars, Eyre & Spottiswoode, 1964-1974

Benson, Larry. D. (Ed.). *The Riverside Chaucer.* Oxford: Oxford University Press, 1988

Bergmann, Frank. "The Roots of Tolkien's Tree: The Influence of George MacDonald and German Romanticism Upon Tolkien's Essay *On Fairy-stories*". *Mosaic* 10.2 (1977): 5-14

Bond, Donald F. (Ed.). *The Spectator*, 5 vols. Oxford: Clarendon Press, 1965

Bosworth, Joseph and T. Northcote Toller (Eds.). *An Anglo-Saxon Dictionary.* Oxford: Oxford University Press, 1898

Camille, Michael. *The Gothic Idol: Ideology and Image Making in Medieval Art.* Cambridge: Cambridge University Press, 1989

Carpenter, Humphrey (Ed.). *The Letters of J.R.R. Tolkien.* London: HarperCollins, 1995

Clute, John. "Tolkien, J.R.R.". *The Encyclopedia of Fantasy.* Eds. John Clute & John Grant. London: Orbit, 1999: 950-955

Coleridge, Samuel Taylor. *Biographia Literaria: or Biographical Sketches of my Literary Life and Opinions.* Ed. George Watson. Dutton: Everyman, 1975

Cooper, Anthony Ashley. *Characteristics of Men, Manners, Opinions, Times, etc.* Ed. J.M. Robertson, 2 Vols. London: Grant Richards, 1900

Donne, John. *The Sermons of John Donne.* Eds. George R. Potter & Evelyn M. Simpson, 10 vols. Berkeley: University of California Press, 1953-1962

Eddington, A.S. *Space, Time and Gravitation: An Outline of the General Relativity Theory.* Cambridge: Cambridge University Press, 1920

Eilmann, Julian. "Sleeps a Song in Things Abounding: Tolkien and the German Romantic Tradition". *Music in Middle-earth.* Eds. Heidi Steimel & Friedhelm Schneidewind. Zurich/Jena: Walking Tree Publishers, 2010: 167-184

---. "Romantic world building: J.R.R. Tolkien's concept of sub-creation and the Romantic spirit". *From Peterborough to Faëry: The Poetic and Mechanics of Secondary Worlds.* Eds. Thomas Honegger & Dirk Vanderbeke. Zurich/Jena: Walking Tree Publishers, 2014: 37-56

Emison, Patricia A. *Creating the Divine Artist: Dante to Michelangelo.* Leiden: Brill, 2004

Grimm, Jacob. *Teutonic Mythology.* Trans. James Steven Stallybrass, 4 vols. London: W. Swan Sonnenschein and Allen, 1880-1888

Hammond, Wayne G., and Christina Scull (Eds.). *The J.R.R. Tolkien Companion and Guide*, 2 vols. London: HarperCollins, 2006

Horstmann, Carl (Ed.). *The Early South-English Legendary, or, Lives of Saints*, Early English Text Society, o.s. 87. London: Trübner, 1887

Hunt, Peter. *Children's Literature*, Blackwell Guides to Literature. Oxford: Blackwell, 2001

James, Edward, and Farah Mendlesohn (Eds.). *The Cambridge Companion to Fantasy Literature.* Cambridge: Cambridge University Press, 2012

Landino, Cristoforo. *Scritti critici e teorici.* Ed. Roberto Cardino, 2 vols. Rome: Bulzoni Editore, 1974

Lange, K., and F. Fuhse (Eds.). *Dürers Schriftlicher Nachlass.* Halle: Max Niemeyer, 1893

Lewis, Charlton T., and Charles Short. *A New Latin Dictionary.* Oxford: Clarendon Press, 1891

Ludwig, Heinrich (Ed.). *Leonardo da Vinci, Das Buch von der Malerei*, 3 vols. Vienna: Wilhelm Braumüller, 1882

MacDonald, George. *A Dish of Orts: Chiefly Papers on the Imagination and Shakspere* [sic]. London: Sampson Low, Marston & Company, 1895

Milbank, Alison. *Chesterton and Tolkien as Theologians: The Fantasy of the Real.* London: T&T Clark, 2008

Milburn, Michael. "Coleridge's Definition of Imagination and Tolkien's Definition(s) of Faery". *Tolkien Studies* 7 (2010): 55-66

Noad, Charles E. "On the Construction of 'The Silmarillion'". *Tolkien's Legendarium: Essays on The History of Middle-earth.* Eds. Verlyn Flieger & Carl F. Hostetter. Westport CT/London: Greenwood Press, 2000: 31-68

Oxford English Dictionary www.oed.com (accessed 16 July 2015)

Panofsky, Erwin. *Renaissance and Renascences in Western Art.* New York/London: Harper and Row, 1972

Pokorny, Julius. *Indogermanisches etymologisches Wörterbuch*, 2 vols. Tübingen/Basel: Francke Verlag, 1994

Pope, Alexander. *The Major Works.* Ed. Pat Rogers. Oxford: Oxford University Press, 2006

Prucher, Jeff (Ed.). *Brave New Words: The Oxford Dictionary of Science Fiction.* Oxford: Oxford University Press, 2007

Pask, Kevin. *The Fairy Way of Writing: Shakespeare to Tolkien.* Baltimore MA: Johns Hopkins University Press, 2013

Plato. *Timaeus, Critias, Cleitophon, Menexenus, Epistles*. Ed. R.J. Bury. Cambridge MA: Harvard University Press, 1999

Richter, Jean Paul (Ed.). *The Literary Works of Leonardo Da Vinci*, 2 vols. London: Sampson Low, Marston, Searle & Rivington, 1883

Roberts, Jane, et al. (Eds.). *A Thesaurus of Old English*, 2 vols. London: King's College London Centre for Late Antique and Medieval Studies, 1995

Saler, Michael. *As If: Modern Enchantment and the Literary History of Virtual Reality*. Oxford: Oxford University Press, 2012

Seeman, Chris. "Tolkien's Revision of the Romantic Tradition". *Proceedings of the J.R.R. Tolkien Centenary Conference* 1992. Ed. Glen Goodknight. Milton Keynes: The Mytho-poetic Press, 1995: 73-83

Shippey, Tom. *The Road to Middle-earth*, rev. ed. London: HarperCollins, 2005

Sidney, Philip. *An Apology for Poetry; or The Defence of Poesy*. Ed. Geoffrey Shepherd. Manchester: Manchester University Press, 1973

Temple, William. "Of Poetry". *Critical Essays of the Seventeenth Century*. Ed. J.E. Spingarn, 3 vols. Oxford: Clarendon Press, 1908-1909

Tigerstedt, E.N. "The Poet as Creator: Origins of a Metaphor". *Comparative Literature Studies* 5.4 (Dec. 1968): 455-88

Tolkien, J.R.R. *Tolkien On Fairy-stories: Expanded Edition*. Eds. Verlyn Flieger & Douglas A. Anderson. London: HarperCollins, 2008

Watkins, Calvert. *The American Heritage Dictionary of Indo-European Roots*, 3rd ed. Boston/New York: Houghton Mifflin Harcourt, 2011

Wolf, Mark. J.P. *Building Imaginary Worlds: The Theory and History of Subcreation*. New York: Routledge, 2012

Zipes, Jack. *Breaking the Magic Spell: Radical Theories of Folk and Fairy-Tales*, rev. ed. Lexington KY: University Press of Kentucky, 2002

Zuccari, Federico. *Scritti d'arte di Federico Zuccaro*. Ed. Detlef Heikamp. Florence: L.S. Olschki, 1961

Ein Kessel voller Geschichten und eine Bananenschale

Wilhelm Kuehs (Klagenfurt)

These

Wir leben aus dem Mythos heraus, und unser Sein ist tief verstrickt mit den Erzählungen, die aus den Archetypen geboren werden. Diese Erkenntnis hat sich im 20. Jahrhundert allmählich gebildet und ist von Forschern wie C.G. Jung (*Traum* 254) und Joseph Campbell (*Hero* 3ff) systematisch in ein theoretisches Kleid gefasst worden. Tolkien wird als Wegbereiter und Vorläufer dieser Bewegung bis heute verkannt. Mit diesem Aufsatz versuche ich zu zeigen, wie Tolkien mit *On Fairy-stories* am Ende der 1930er Jahre sich der Angelegenheit aus der Richtung der Literaturwissenschaft nähert. Dieser Zugang wurde lange Zeit ignoriert, und erst jetzt scheint es an der Zeit, Tolkiens Anregungen aufzugreifen und sie mit den Forschungsergebnissen der letzten Jahrzehnte abzugleichen.

Der Mythos steht im Zentrum unseres Lebens. Jeder von uns ist in eine Vielzahl von Geschichten, die wir als Ausfaltung des Mythos verstehen können, verwoben und bezieht seine Integrität, die Sicherheit seines Seins aus der Verwurzelung im Mythos (Campbell, *Mythology* 6). Der Mythos ist also die Matrix sowohl unseres Selbstverständnisses als auch unserer Kultur.

Wenn wir C.G. Jungs Theorie folgen, dann müssen wir feststellen, dass der Einzelne, das Subjekt eine je einzigartige Zusammenstellung und Aktualisation der kollektiven Psyche ist und dass aus dieser kollektiven Psyche die Mythen hervordringen und sich durch uns zu Erzählungen, zu alltäglicher Geschichte ausformen (Jung, *Persönlichkeit* 40).

In *On Fairy-stories* äußert Tolkien eine sehr ähnliche Position. Nur dass er diese nicht wie Jung und seine Nachfolger über das Psychische begründet, sondern über die Sprache. »History resembles ›Myth‹, because they are both ultimately of the same stuff« (FS 47). Der Stoff, das sind die Archetypen. Die Form, in der uns sowohl Mythos als auch Historie gegenübertritt, ist die Erzählung.

Mythos und Sprache

Wir wollen uns dem Mythos zunächst auf jener Spur annähern, die Tolkien selbst verfolgte. Als Philologe schien ihm der Zusammenhang von Sprache und Mythos evident. In »A Secret Vice« zeigt Tolkien, inwieweit Mythologie und Sprache einander entsprechen. Er begründet hier seine eigene Arbeitsmethode.

Um eine Sprache zu erschaffen, muss man gleichzeitig auch eine Mythologie kreieren (SV 210). So sind viele Teile des Tolkien'schen Universums entstanden. Aus der Leidenschaft für die Sprache und dem kreativen Drang, immer neue Details in Lexik und Grammatik zu entwickeln, erwuchs die Notwendigkeit, eine Mythologie zu entwerfen, um die Sprache in einer Semiosphäre zu verankern.

Damit wendet sich Tolkien gegen eine sehr dominante Lehrmeinung seiner Zeit. Was Max Müller 1897 als »disease of language« (Müller 68) bezeichnet, nämlich die Neigung der Sprache, sich über die Wirklichkeit zu legen und die eigentlichen Phänomene zu überdecken, sieht Tolkien weniger als Krankheit oder Problem, sondern vielmehr als Funktion der Sprache, die notwendigerweise immer Erzählungen hervorbringt.

Max Müller versucht zu zeigen, wie mythologische Erzählungen aus der Fehlinterpretation von Metaphern erwachsen (Müller 71). Die Götter seien ursprünglich nichts weiter gewesen als Allegorien für Naturphänomene. Durch die Fehlinterpretation der Metapher hätten sich die Begriffe von den Naturphänomenen auf die Allegorien verschoben, und so seien etwa der Blitz und der Donner zu Zeus geworden (Müller 74f).

Was Max Müller hier als Krankheit der Sprache zu fassen versucht, ist ein Generierungsprinzip der Mythologie, das wir mit den Mitteln der Semiotik und der Kulturanthropologie schärfer fassen können, als es Müller möglich war.

Im Grunde sind wir hier mit zwei Fragestellungen konfrontiert. Wie kommt es, dass Menschen Naturphänomene personifizieren? Und wieso scheint die Sprache diese Mythologisierung der Welt zu begünstigen?

Auf die erste Frage geben Alfred Schütz und Michael Tomasello interessante Antworten. Alfred Schütz geht in seiner Generalthese der reziproken Perspektiven davon aus, dass wir einander nur verstehen können, weil wir annehmen, der andere würde die Welt genauso interpretieren wie wir selbst (Schütz, Luckmann 341). Zu dieser Auffassung gelangen wir, weil wir unsere Selbstauslegung auf den anderen übertragen und dabei feststellen, dass wir zu einem funktionierenden intersubjektiven Verständnis kommen. Diese Übertragung der Selbstauslegung ist uns laut Tomasello nur möglich, weil wir über die Gabe der Empathie verfügen. Tomasello zeigt in seiner Arbeit, dass Kinder ab dem neunten Lebensmonat geteilte Aufmerksamkeit entwickeln. Unter geteilter Aufmerksamkeit (joint attention) verstehen wir mit Michael Tomasello die Fähigkeit, den anderen als intentionales Subjekt wahrzunehmen und sich gemeinsam mit ihm auf ein Objekt oder eine Aufgabe hin auszurichten. Aus einer dyadischen Beziehung von Subjekt zu Subjekt wird eine triadische Beziehung von Subjekt zu Subjekt zu Objekt, wobei die beiden Subjekte ihre Intentionalität und Aufmerksamkeit hinsichtlich des Objektes teilen (Tomasello 62).

Wir erfahren nun also von Kindheit an die anderen Menschen als intentionale Subjekte und sind daher geneigt, diese Eigenschaften per Analogie auch auf andere Wesen und Entitäten zu übertragen. Durch die Jahrtausende während Koevolution haben wir auch Hunden diese Fähigkeit angezüchtet, sich in uns einfühlen zu können (Horowitz 161f). So werden wir auch in der Kommunikation mit unseren Vierbeinern in unserer Weltsicht bestätigt, und es scheint geradezu zwingend, dass wir die Generalthese der reziproken Perspektiven auch auf andere Entitäten unserer Mitwelt übertragen. Der Mann, der mit seinem Auto redet, und die Frau, die ihren Computer auffordert, endlich zu funktionieren, verhalten sich nicht anders, als unsere Vorfahren, die einen Baum um Verzeihung baten, bevor sie ihn zu Brennholz verarbeiteten.

Darüber kann man sich lustig machen, wie das Max Müller und seitdem viele getan haben. Tolkien aber kritisiert Müller scharf und wirft ihm vor, hier eine ideologische Position einzunehmen. Er führt Müllers Argument ad absurdum, indem er sagt: »You might as well say that thinking is a disease of the mind. It would be more near the truth to say that languages, especially modern European languages, are a disease of mythology« (FS 41).

Vom Wort zur Erzählung

Wie so oft schafft es Tolkien auch hier, mit einer geradezu akrobatischen Denkbewegung eine neue Perspektive auf die Frage zu eröffnen. Indem er die Sprache als Krankheit der Mythologie bezeichnet, dreht er nicht nur den Argumentationszusammenhang, sondern auch die hierarchische Struktur um. Der Mythos geht nicht aus der Sprache hervor. Es ist genau andersherum. Die Sprache ist vom Mythos abhängig, und der Mythos ist der Geburtsort der Sprache.

Tatsächlich ist die Sprache eine notwendige Folge des Mythos. Der Mythos drängt zum Ausdruck und findet diesen unter anderem im Medium der Sprache. Man kann sogar so weit gehen, die Sprache als komplexestes und flexibelstes Ausdrucksmittel des Mythos zu bezeichnen, ohne dabei andere Medien zu vergessen. Wir wollen hier aber bei der Sprache als ausgezeichnetes Medium bleiben und uns kurz dem Zusammenhang von Sprache und Mythos widmen.

Wie gesagt, sieht Tolkien Sprache und Mythos als zwei ineinander verschränkte Funktionen: Eine bestimmte Mythologie benötigt eine bestimmte Sprache.

Wie man sich das vorstellen kann, lässt sich leicht an der berühmten Anekdote über den ersten Satz des *Hobbit* zeigen. Als Tolkien den Satz »In a hole in the ground there lived a hobbit« auf ein leeres Blatt Papier schrieb, hatte er keine Ahnung, wer oder was ein Hobbit ist (L 215). Im Appendix F von *The Lord of the Rings* liefert Tolkien dann eine Etymologie des Wortes. Es soll von hobytla herstammen, und das bedeute so viel wie hole-builder (LotR 1104). Dieses altenglische Kunstwort (Shippey 61) verbindet den Begriff »Hobbit« mit einem ganz bestimmten Ausschnitt aus der Enzyklopädie unserer Kultur und setzt damit einen Prozess der Semiose in Gang.

Wie Algirdas Greimas sagt, steckt hinter jedem paradigmatischen Ausdruck ein Skript, das dieses Sem beschreibt (Greimas, *Actants 174*). Umberto Eco sieht in diesem Skript ein erzählerisches Programm, das sich geradezu unweigerlich entfaltet, wenn wir auf eine semantische Einheit stoßen (Eco, *Lector* 21). Bei einem Begriff wie »Fischer«, den Greimas als Beispiel verwendet, eröffnet sich jedem Subjekt ein je eigenes Erzählprogramm, das aber einen denotativen Kern besitzt. Wir verfügen über einen Nuklearen Inhalt (NI) des Sems »Fischer«, der uns sagt, woran wir einen Fischer erkennen (Eco, *Schnabeltier* 162f). Bei genaue-rer Betrachtung sehen wir, dass dieser NI vor allem eine Erzählung über die Tätigkeit des Fischens enthält. Das Aussehen des Fischers, sein Handwerkszeug und vieles andere sind auslöschbare Eigenschaften. Wir können sie also beiseite lassen, ohne die Identifikation unseres Begriffs zu gefährden. Die Erzählung aber können wir nicht streichen, denn dann versagt unsere Erklärung, und wir erfahren nicht, was wir uns unter einem Fischer vorzustellen haben.

Besonders schön und eindringlich demonstriert Charles Sanders Peirce, wie sich aus einem Begriff eine Geschichte entfaltet, wenn er uns zeigt, wie wir etwas über das seltsame Metall Lithium wissen können. Peirce sagt, nur eine Erzählung darüber, wie wir das Metall gewinnen und wozu wir es verwenden, bringt uns zu einer ausreichenden Kenntnis über das kulturelle Objekt, das wir »Lithium« nennen (C.P. 2.330).

Nun verhält es sich mit dem Hobbit ganz ähnlich wie mit dem Lithium. Stellen wir uns vor, wir hätten noch nie etwas von einem Hobbit gehört. Für die Anwesenden dürfte das eine recht schwierige Übung sein, aber lassen sie es uns versuchen. Wenn wir also eine Zeitreise machen könnten, zurück zu jenem Tag, an dem Professor Tolkien etwas gelangweilt und vermutlich auch ein bisschen genervt in seinem Zimmer saß und auf ein leeres Blatt kritzelte, dann könnten wir ihn fragen, was denn ein Hobbit sein soll.

Wahrscheinlich hätte Tolkien zu erzählen begonnen, und in Wirklichkeit tat er das ja auch. Das erste Fragment der Erzählung umfasst beinahe das gesamte erste Kapitel des *Hobbit* und enthält schon im Wesentlichen die Aktantenstruktur und die Isotopien, die am Ende den ganzen Roman bestimmen werden (Rateliff 3ff).

Ein Topf voller Geschichten

Dieses Erzählen setzt einen Prozess in Gang, den ich den Austausch von kulturellen Mustern nennen möchte. Nur auf dem Weg des Erzählens, mittels der Semiose, können wir Intersubjektivität und damit Einigkeit über die Bedeutung von kulturellen Mustern herstellen, und nur über diesen Prozess des Austausches lässt sich Gemeinschaft herstellen.

Bedeutung in Form von potentiellen Erzählungen lagert sich durch den Prozess der kooperativen Semiose, des gemeinsamen Aushandelns von Wirklichkeit in der Semiosphäre ab und ist über Texte im weitesten Sinn immer wieder aufrufbar und kann auf diesem Weg aktualisiert werden.

Was in der Semiosphäre als Muster abgelegt ist, begegnet uns als Erzählungen. Diese Erzählungen nehmen über die Jahrzehnte und Jahrhunderte eine bestimmte Form an. Sie werden sozusagen auf eine archetypische Struktur hin angeglichen. Das ist es, was Tolkien meint, wenn er sagt, dass wir alle in einem Kessel voller Geschichten landen. Dort kochen unsere Erzählungen vor sich hin und verlieren ihre individuellen Details, werden immer mehr zu abstrakten kulturellen Mustern. Um es erzähltheoretisch zu sagen: Aus den ausgefalteten Plots werden wieder Fabeln. Wir neigen dazu, von der konkreten Erzählung zu abstrahieren und sie auf ihre Fabel zurückzuführen. Von dieser Fabel aus ist es meistens ein Leichtes, auf den zugrunde liegenden Mythos und auf die beteiligten Archetypen zu schließen.

Tolkien führt das an mehreren Beispielen aus. Unter anderem zeigt er, wie sich das Märchen von der Gänsemagd an Bertha Breitfuß (eigentlich Bertrada die Jüngere) geheftet hat (FS 45). Bertha, die Mutter Karls des Großen, soll ähnlich wie das Mädchen im Märchen von einer Magd zunächst um ihre Hochzeit betrogen worden sein. Als sie dann endlich Königin wurde, hing ihr noch eine zweite archetypische Geschichte an, und zwar jene von der furchtbaren Mutter. Ihr breiter Fuß, der manchmal auch als Gänsefuß bezeichnet wird, rückt sie in die Nähe der beiden unheimlichen Göttinnen Percht (Simrock 219/Petzold 39) und Thrud.

Vielleicht noch stärker als bei König Artus (FS 46) scheint die archetypische Struktur der Erzählung die historische Person zu überlagern und macht aus der Mutter Karls des Großen eine Inkarnation der Großen Göttin.

Was ist es aber, was uns in diesen Kessel der Geschichten hineinzieht und uns in das Schema einer überpersonalen Erzählung presst, und zwar sowohl als Persona, also wie wir den anderen erscheinen, als auch als Ego und Selbst?

Die Antwort hat mit einer Bananenschale zu tun und führt uns zunächst scheinbar sehr weit weg von unserem eigentlichen Thema. In einer für ihn so charakteristischen Denkbewegung dreht Tolkien an der herkömmlichen Argumentationskette, die da besagt, dass sich eine bestimmte Geschichte an eine bestimmte Person heftet. Als Beispiel wählt Tolkien eine Slapstickszene, in der der Erzbischof von Canterbury auf einer Bananenschale ausrutscht (FS 45).

Diese Geschichte erhält ihre Komik vor allem durch etwas, das man mit barocken Rhetorikern allgemein als Fallhöhe bezeichnet, und damit ist bekanntlich nicht unbedingt der zurückzulegende Weg zwischen Hintern und Boden gemeint, sondern die Diskrepanz zwischen der sozialen Stellung der Person und dem Missgeschick. Auslöser dieser Szene ist aber nicht der Erzbischof, sondern die Bananenschale. Der Erzbischof könnte hier hundertmal entlang spazieren und nichts Seltsames würde sich ereignen. Erst wenn die Bananenschale da am Boden liegt, kann sich ein Skript entfalten. Die Bananenschale ist also für diese Szene mindestens ebenso entscheidend wie der Erzbischof, ja noch viel entscheidender. Denn statt des Erzbischofs könnte auch gern irgendein anderer Würdenträger auftreten. Tolkien hat also völlig recht, wenn er sagt:»I think it would be nearer the truth to say that the Archbishop became attached to the banana skin...« (FS 46).

Womit haben wir es hier zu tun? Drei Komponenten bestimmen diese Szene. Die Bananenschale, der Erzbischof und der Umstand, dass es in unserer Kultur als komisch gilt, wenn einer hochgestellten Person ein Missgeschick widerfährt. Mit Erving Goffman können wir sagen, dass diese drei Elemente einen Frame definieren (Goffmann 27ff).

Ein Frame ist eine Kontur rund um ein Geschehen. Gregory Bateson, auf den der Begriff zurückgeht, definiert den Rahmen als eine »Klasse oder Menge von Mitteilungen (oder sinnvollen Handlungen)«. (Bateson 252) Semiotisch gesehen ist ein Frame ein Metacode. Dieser Metacode lässt eine bestimmte Anzahl von Handlungen zu und schließt alle anderen Handlungen aus. So gesehen enthält der Metacode die potentiellen Erzählungen, die sich innerhalb des Rahmens abspielen können. Wenn wir also den Rahmen kennen, kennen wir im Prinzip auch die Erzählung (Eco, Lector 100).

Das wäre aber nicht möglich, wenn diese Erzählungen nicht innerhalb der Semiosphäre bereitstehen würden und wir nicht auf sie zurückgreifen könnten. Diese Erzählungen werden zumindest auf zweierlei Arten weitergegeben und vor dem Verschwinden bewahrt. Einerseits stehen sie uns als aus dem Geist ausgelagerte kulturelle Muster zur Verfügung, andererseits entstehen sie immer wieder neu aus dem kollektiven Unbewussten.

Ein Frame stellt also eine Möglichkeit dar, eine Geschichte zu erzählen, und begrenzt die Auswahl der Elemente. Er lässt aber gleichzeitig die Transformation vieler anderer Elemente der Erzählung zu. Außerdem ist es möglich, dass innerhalb eines Rahmens mehrere Erzählungen gleichzeitig ablaufen.

Um das zu demonstrieren, bleiben wir gleich bei unserem Beispiel vom Erzbischof und der Bananenschale. Wie wir gesehen haben, können wir von der gegebenen Situation abstrahieren und den Erzbischof gegen einen beliebigen anderen Würdenträger ersetzen. Bei der Bananenschale fällt uns das schon schwerer, aber ein Teppich aus Murmeln oder eine andere rutschige Unterlage würde denselben Zweck erfüllen.

Wir haben es also bei Erzbischof und Bananenschale mit zwei Aktanten zu tun (Greimas, Semantik 157ff), zwei Handlungsfeldern innerhalb der Erzählung. Im vorliegenden Fall haben wir es mit einer sehr einfachen Konstel-lation zu tun. Sehen wir den Erzbischof als Helden und die Bananenschale (bzw. den, der sie platziert hat) als Widersacher, so ergeben sich daraus auch die anderen Aktanten und die Isotopien, die zur Herstellung einer Erzählung notwendig sind. Ein Helfer des Helden könnte auftauchen, etwa der Sekretär des Erzbischofs, der die Bananenschale entfernt, und der Helfer des Widersachers könnte eine neue Bananenschale platzieren. Vielleicht steckt hinter dem eigentlichen Widersacher ein Auftraggeber, der den Erzbischof auf diese Weise vom Leben zum Tod befördern will. Denn der Erzbischof ist der Einzige, der das Kommen des Antichristen verhindern kann.

Wir sehen, diese Vorlage bietet zumindest die Möglichkeit für einen reißerischen Thriller. Aber darauf wollte ich gar nicht hinaus. Mir geht es um die Arbitrarität der Entitäten, die die Aktanten besetzen können. Je weiter wir die Abstraktion treiben, desto mehr nähern wir uns der Beschreibung eines Aktantenmodells an. Wir brauchen für eine Geschichte jedenfalls einen Helden, einen Widersacher und einen Konflikt. Allerdings ist hier die analytische Abstraktion so weit vorangetrieben, dass das Modell sowohl auf Erzbischof und Bananenschale wie auf Frodo und den Ring passt. Tolkien kritisiert dieses wissenschaftliche Bestreben in On Fairy-stories scharf und schießt dabei meines Erachtens etwas über das Ziel hinaus (FS 38).

Die Abstraktion ist nicht nur ein analytisches Instrument, sondern ebenso ein synthetisches. Denn Abstraktion gepaart mit der Fähigkeit, Analogien herzustellen, ermöglicht es uns, eine Erzählung mit einer anderen zu vergleichen und zu sehen, inwieweit sie einander entsprechen bzw. voneinander abweichen.

Abstraktion und Analogie sind in Wahrheit zwei Funktionen des Erzählens selbst, und wenn wir in Tolkiens Bild vom Kessel voller Geschichten bleiben wollen, dann können wir sagen: Abstraktion und Analogie verrichten ihr Werk, wenn wir anständig Feuer unter dem Kessel machen und kräftig umrühren. Das führt nämlich nicht nur dazu, Geschichten auf neue Art miteinander zu verbinden, sondern auch, sie einander anzugleichen und durchlässiger zu machen. Dieser alchemistische Prozess (FS 39) ist dafür verantwortlich, dass die alten Geschichten immer wieder aktualisiert und unserer Zeit anverwandelt werden. »The ancient elements can be knocked out, or forgotten or dropped out, or replaced by other ingredients with the greatest ease…« (FS 49) beschreibt Tolkien diesen Prozess und weist damit darauf hin, dass jeder von uns am Gelingen der Suppe mitwirkt, die da seit Jahrtausenden vor sich hinköchelt.

Die Köche

Da wir alle Geschichten erzählen, tragen wir alle zur Konstruktion unserer sozialen Wirklichkeit bei. Tolkien nennt die Fähigkeit, Geschichten zu erzählen und so eine Sekundärwelt (Secondary World) zu schaffen, eine Elbenkunst (elvish craft) (FS 61). Diese Sekundärwelt stellt eine zunächst fiktive Alternative zu unserer sozialen Wirklichkeit dar, wird aber nicht nur zum Eskapismus genutzt, sondern vorrangig zum Entwurf von Lebens- und Handlungsalternativen.

Das geschieht ständig und so automatisch, dass wir uns dessen nicht bewusst sind. Aber schon die banale Entscheidung, ob ich nach diesem Vortrag einen Kaffee trinke oder doch lieber ein Glas Mineralwasser, erfordert den Entwurf von möglichen Welten. So geht jeder unserer Handlungen ein Entwurf voraus, und dieser Entwurf hat die Gestalt einer Erzählung. Alfred Schütz war wohl der erste, der diesen Umstand erkannte. Er meint, unser Denken würde beim Entwurf der Handlung *modo futurum exacti* (Schütz/Luckmann 465) funktionieren und so die Fantasie als Vehikel des Weltentwurfes einsetzen.

Dieser Modus des Denkens und Fühlens kommt aber nicht nur bei kurzfristigen und banalen Entscheidungen zum Einsatz. Er ist eine universelle Funktion menschlichen Geistes, und jeder Weltentwurf bedarf dieser geistigen Anstrengung.

Beim Entwurf unserer Handlungen sind wir an die kulturellen Muster gebunden, die unsere Semiosphäre bereithält. Das bedeutet, wir bewegen uns innerhalb einer Bandbreite von möglichen Geschichten, in die wir eintreten und in denen wir mitspielen können. Diese Geschichten, die Aktantenstruktur, die sie bestimmt, die Topoi verweisen auf die zugrunde liegenden Archetypen, die unsere Gesellschaft bestimmen.

Hier, auf der Ebene der Archetypen, endet unser Einfluss. Als Köche am Kessel voller Geschichten müssen wir uns damit abfinden, dass es einen Kessel gibt, dass in diesem Kessel Geschichten herumschwimmen und wir dafür verantwortlich sind, dass das Feuer nicht ausgeht. Die Aborigines haben die Notwendigkeit des Erzählens in ein wunderbares Bild gefasst. Die Welt wird ihrer Auffassung nach nur so lange bestehen, wie die Menschen die Traumpfade abschreiten und so die Geschichte der Welt immer und immer wieder erzählen. Die Weltschöpfung ist in ihren Augen kein abgeschlossener Prozess, sondern muss von uns immer wieder aufs Neue angestoßen und aktualisiert werden. Hier treffen sich die Überlegungen der australischen Ureinwohner und des Professors aus Oxford. Das Erzählen erschafft und erhält unsere soziale Wirklichkeit.

Wie Tolkien aber anmerkt, ist uns die Elbenkunst des Erzählens nicht in ihrer Vollkommenheit gegeben. Er führt das auf den Fall des Menschen zurück und liefert uns so ein theologisches Argument (FS 42). Ich will mich auf dieses Terrain nicht vorwagen, stimme aber Tolkien zu, wenn er meint, das Erzählen, also der Weltentwurf der Zweitschöpfer bringe nicht nur nette Dinge hervor.

Wie die Köche den Brei verderben

Ich denke, wir können uns an dieser Stelle darauf einigen, dass die Verfasstheit unserer gemeinsamen sozialen Wirklichkeit in hohem Maße davon abhängt, welche Geschichten wir erzählen. Es kommt aber auch darauf an, wie wir sie erzählen. Das möchte ich im letzten Abschnitt dieses Vortrags gerne demonstrieren.

Die Heldengeschichte ist mit Sicherheit die zentrale Erzählung unserer Kultur. Vom Sport über die Politik bis hinein in den privaten Bereich dient die Heldengeschichte als Vorlage für die Ausgestaltung unseres Lebens und unserer Gesellschaft.

Wie Vladimir Propp und Joseph Campbell so eindrücklich gezeigt haben, folgt die Heldengeschichte einem recht starren Schema. Beide teilen den Heldenmythos in sieben Abschnitte (Propp 117/Campbell, *Hero* 36ff). Wir wollen uns diese Grobteilung anhand einiger Parallelbeispiele vergegenwärtigen. Zunächst wählen wir zwei Heldengeschichten aus dem *Herrn der Ringe*, die einander auf den ersten Blick diametral entgegengesetzt sind. Frodo und Aragorn durchlaufen beide dieselben Abschnitte, die aber ganz unterschiedlich ausgestaltet sind. In der Ausgangssituation (Propp 119f) lernen wir sie beide als verborgene Helden kennen. Aragorn lebt als Streicher in den Wäldern des Nordens, und Frodo im Auenland weiß noch nicht einmal etwas von den Gefahren der Welt. Als Vergleich möchte ich hier Beispiele aus der uns gemeinsamen sozialen Wirklichkeit anführen.

Frodos Geschichte hat sehr große Ähnlichkeiten mit der Geschichte von Franz von Assisi. Auch Franziskus war von seiner Herkunft kaum dazu prädestiniert, ein Heilsbringer zu werden. Anders bei Aragorn, dessen Weg vorbestimmt ist. Wie König Artus wird er im Verborgenen darauf vorbereitet, einst die Macht zu übernehmen.

Der Einleitungsteil der Heldengeschichte offenbart den Konflikt. Von »The Shadow of the Past« bis zu »The Council of Elrond« breitet sich vor uns das Panorama der Problemlage aus. Einerseits geht es vor allem darum, den Ring zu vernichten, und dazu braucht man jemanden, der das Problem begreift und doch nicht allzu sehr vom Ring affiziert wird. Andererseits muss man verhindern, dass Sauron und seine Verbündeten das Land mit Krieg überziehen und dabei den Ringträger aufstöbern und den Ring in ihren Besitz bringen. Eine geradezu klassische Situation, die sich etwa in allen ideologischen Erzählungen wiederholt.

Gerade jetzt tobt im Nahen Osten ein Konflikt, der uns an den Ringkrieg gemahnen könnte. Wie Saurons Truppen erhebt sich dort der sogenannte Isla-mische Staat (IS) und vernichtet alles, was wir unter Zivilisation und Kultur verstehen. Dieser Feldzug des IS erscheint wie eine Wiederholung. Wir brauchen nur in die Geschichte zurückzublicken und sehen die NS-Diktatur, die Konquistadoren, die Kreuzzüge des Mittelalters und die Perserkriege der Antike, um nur ein paar besonders herausragende Beispiele zu nennen. Der von den USA unter George W. Bush initiierte »Kampf gegen den Terror« scheint von seinen Vertretern als so etwas wie die Allianz der Gefährten verstanden zu werden. Auch Bush und danach Barack Obama versuchen,

ihre Verbündeten zu sammeln und mit vereinter Kraft gegen das Böse vorzu-
gehen. Dieser Kampf hat bis jetzt durchaus Helden von der Art Aragorns
hervorgebracht. Obama mag da als prominenter Vertreter dieses Heldentyps
gelten. Auf eine Figur wie Frodo warten wir im Moment noch vergebens,
und das hat seine Gründe.

Den dritten Abschnitt der Heldengeschichte bezeichnet Propp als Schürzung
des Knotens. Wie im antiken Drama gibt es auch hier einen Moment, in dem
alle Akteure bereitstehen und das Drama beginnen kann. Der Kampf bereitet
sich vor, eine erste Katastrophe tritt ein. Als die Flugzeuge in das Word Trade
Center rasten, begann der eigentliche Konflikt im Krieg gegen den Terror.
Als 2008 die Weltwirtschaft in eine Schockstarre fiel, weil unter anderem die
amerikanische Immobilienblase platzte, konnten aufmerksame Beobachter den
nächsten Abschnitt des Dramas schon vorhersagen.

Ja, auch die weltweite Finanzkrise mag man als die Kulisse einer Heldengeschichte ansehen: Hier geriert sich die Spitze der Europäischen Union, der
IWF, der Weltbank und der Europäischen Zentralbank als die Gefährten, die
ausziehen, um Sauron in Gestalt verschwenderischer Mitgliedsstaaten mithilfe
der Austeritätspolitik den Garaus zu machen. Allerdings gab es in dieser Geschichte von Anfang an Zweifel darüber, ob die Selbstauslegung der Gefährten
denn nun der Wahrheit entspricht. Immer wieder sind Stimmen zu hören, die
meinen, die Gefährten seien eigentlich Abgesandte Saurons und würden sich
genau wie Saruman verhalten. Sie geben zwar vor, die Allianz jener zu unterstützen, die die Welt vor dem Sturz in den Abgrund der Armut bewahren
wollen, hätten sich aber heimlich mit den Finanzmärkten verbündet, um ein
besonders hinterhältiges Spiel zu spielen.

Egal, wie sich das auch immer verhält, die Helden müssen nun ausziehen, um
ihre Mission zu erfüllen. Auf diesem ersten Abschnitt erleben sie einige Abenteuer,
und sie scheitern. Der erste Anlauf gelingt nie. Im *Herrn der Ringe* zerbricht
die Gemeinschaft der Gefährten. Parzival stellt bei seinem ersten Besuch in der
Gralsburg die Mitleidsfrage nicht, und der Kampf gegen den Terror befreit weder
Afghanistan von den radikalen Gotteskriegern, noch befriedet er den arabischen
Raum. Ganz im Gegenteil, er gebiert Krieg, Not und Elend.

Die Heldengeschichte gewährt ihren Protagonisten für gewöhnlich eine
zweite Chance. Dieser zweite Kursus, wie man das in der Altgermanistik nennt,
dient dazu, die Fehler des ersten Versuchs auszumerzen und gereift und klüger
an das Problem heranzugehen. Im *Herrn der Ringe* gelingt das, und Sauron
wird am Ende besiegt.

Die Chefköche unserer Suppe sollten den *Herrn der Ringe* ganz genau lesen
und tief darüber nachdenken, denn diese Erzählung enthält möglicherweise den
mythologischen Schlüssel, um aus der derzeitigen Misere auszusteigen und es
besser zu machen. Tolkien schuf Aragorn als weisen Krieger und Herrscher.
Eine aus seiner Sicht wohl notwendige Figur in einer Welt des Kampfes.

Aber Aragorn ist nur ein Nebenheld in Tolkiens Geschichte. Nicht die Gewalt, sondern die Selbstlosigkeit und der Mut, friedlich und gewaltfrei gegen den größtmöglichen Schrecken aufzustehen, bringen den Sieg.

Tolkien präsentiert uns eine andere Art von Held. Er selbst sah in Sam den Haupthelden der Geschichte (L 161), und Sam vereint viele der Eigenschaften, die Tolkien einem Helden zusprechen möchte. Auf ihn trifft zu, was Thorin Eichenschild im *Hobbit* zu Bilbo sagt: »If more of us valued food and cheer and song above hoarded gold, it would be a merrier world« (H 271). Aber aus Sicht der strukturalistischen Erzähltheorie fällt Sam in die Kategorie des Helfers. Daran ändert auch seine maßgebliche Rolle bei der Vernichtung des Einen Rings nichts.

Der wahre Held, und daran gibt es keinen Zweifel, ist Frodo. Er bietet uns ein nur allzu seltenes Modell des Helden. Franz von Assisi wurde bereits als Vorbild genannt. Mahatma Gandhi, Martin Luther King und Nelson Mandela sind Beispiele aus dem 20. Jahrhundert. Diese Männer sind keine strahlenden Helden. Sie waren sich ihrer eigenen Verletzlichkeit und Unzulänglichkeit immer bewusst und haben ihren Kampf gerade darauf gestellt. Nicht das Großartige und die Selbstglorifizierung, vielmehr Bescheidenheit und spirituelle Selbstreflexion führen zu einer Welt, in der es sich leben lässt wie im Auenland.

Bibliographie

Bateson Gregory. *Eine Theorie des Spiels und der Phantasie. Ökologie des Geistes.* Frankfurt a.m.: Suhrkamp, 1985

Campbell Joseph. *Creative Mythology – The Mask of God.* New York: Penguin Arkana, 1991

---. *The Hero With a Thousand Faces.* London: HarperCollins, 1993

Eco, Umberto. *Lector in fabula.* München: dtv, 1998[3]

---. *Kant und das Schnabeltier.* München: dtv, 2003

Goffman Erving. *Frame Analysis.* Boston: Northeastern University Press, 1986

Greimas Algirdas Julien. *Strukturale Semantik – Methodologische Untersuchungen.* Braunschweig: Friedrich Vieweg und Sohn, 1971

---. »Les actants, les acteurs et les figures«. *Sémiotique, narrative et textuelle.* Hg. Claude Chabrol. Paris: Larousse, 1973

Horowitz Alexandra. *Inside of a dog – What dogs see, smell and know.* New York: Scribner, 2009

Jung Carl Gustav. *Persönlichkeit und Übertragung, Grundwerk C.G. Jung, Band 3.* Hg. Helmut Barz u.a., Olten/Freiburg im Breisgau: Walter Verlag, 1984

---. *Traum und Traumdeutung.* München: dtv, April 1997[8]

Müller Max. *Contribution to the Science of Mythology, Vol I.* London. Longmans, Green and Co., 1897

Peirce Charles Sanders. *Collected Papers of Charles Sanders Peirce,* 8 volumes. Cambridge MA: Harvard University Press, 1931-1958

Petzold Leander. *Kleines Lexikon der Dämonen und Elementargeister.* München: C.H. Beck, 2003[3]

Propp Vladimir. *Morphologie des Märchens.* München: Hanser, 1972

Rateliff John. *The History of the Hobbit. Part I. Mr. Baggins.* London: HarperCollins, 2007

Simrock Karl. *Handbuch der deutschen Mythologie mit Einschluss der nordischen.* Bonn: Adolf Marcus, 1855

Shippey Tom. *The Road to Middle-earth.* London: HarperCollins, London, 1992

Schütz, Alfred und Thomas Luckmann. *Strukturen der Lebenswelt.* Konstanz UTB/UVK, 2003

Tolkien, John Ronald Reuel. *On Fairy-stories.* Eds. Verlyn Flieger & Douglas A. Anderson, London: HarperCollins, London, 2014

---. »A Secret Vice«.*The Monster and the Critics.* London: HarperCollins 1997

---. *The Letters of J.R.R. Tolkien.* Eds. Humphrey Carpenter & Christopher Tolkien, London HarperCollins, 1995

---. *The Lord of the Rings.* London: HarperCollins, 2003

Tomasello Michael. *The Cultural Origin of Human Cognition.* Harvard: Harvard University Press, 2000

Chesterton's Chalk:
Creativity and the Commonplace in
J.R.R. Tolkien's *On Fairy-stories*

Jonathan Nauman (Vaughan Association—USA)

A significant portion of J.R.R. Tolkien's landmark essay *On Fairy-stories* aims to clear up common misconceptions about the nature and value of what is now called, in wake of Tolkien's popular success, the fantasy genre. I wish here to focus on one particular aspect of this defense, Tolkien's reply to those who find artistic fantasy symptomatic of an unhealthy detachment from reality, or who consider such art a distortion that might hinder the necessary disciplines and efforts of the workaday world—or, to put it more theoretically, Tolkien's negotiation of post-romantic presumptions of hostility between aesthetics and the commonplace. Most of Tolkien's arguments explicitly addressing these topics emerge in his essay's last parts, which explore the making of fairy stories and their reception (FS 49-79); but one may also sense implicit awareness of such utilitarian objections[1] in the pointed common sense with which Tolkien responds in the earlier parts of his essay to warring scholarly schools of mythologists and anthropologists, proponents of redaction theories and pursuers of source studies—in short, to any historical or linguistic analysis that would fail to take the real agencies and priorities of fairy story writers into account. Tolkien implies, in his surveys of Andrew Lang and Max Müller and others, that it is quite unscientific, impractical, unrealistic, when studying the products of storytellers, to sideline the tale-teller's most characteristic aesthetic and artistic motives. The impulse to boil the artist's savory soup of mixed history, biography, and imaginative invention down into its various historical or linguistic components effectively reverses the actual dynamic of the fairy story writer's creative process, in which all of these ingredients marinate to produce an artistic simmering stew (FS 46), an unquantifiable but desirable literary entrée. Or to borrow from another analogy through which Tolkien made a similarly practical literary argument, the provenance of the stones is not the main point when one is building a new tower from which to view the sea (MC 7f).

Tolkien's open replies to the utilitarian or (one might say) philistine critique of fantasy build on the aesthetic realism of these earlier observations. He dis-

---

1   Such objections of course can extend, and have been extended, beyond the fairy story genre to all forms of narrative fictional art.

sents from "the depreciative tone" so often used in referring to artistic fantasy's distinctive detachment from the primary world, instead characterizing fantasy's alterity as an excellence: in its sheer inventiveness, fantasy is literary art in its purest and "most potent" form (FS 60); and because it takes more liberties in its use of known images, it requires rather more labor and forethought than "realistic fiction" to attain credibility. The "slander" popularly perpetrated against the fantasy genre, viz., that it is equivalent to involuntary experiences in a dream or to "mental disorders in which there is not even control" (FS 60) is therefore precisely opposite to the truth, as achieved artistic fantasy is actually built through painstaking care and unusual skill. "Few attempt such difficult tasks," Tolkien ironically observes, probably with a glance at his own pending struggles with composing *The Lord of the Rings* (FS 61). His essay's section on "Fantasy" concludes with a summary reply clearly directed toward those who consider fairy stories unhealthy or desultory, a statement which delivers not only careful analysis of the human dynamics behind fairy story writing, but also some testimony to his own practical experience in the genre.

> Fantasy is a natural human activity. It certainly does not destroy or even insult Reason; and it does not either blunt the appetite for, nor obscure the perception of, scientific verity. On the contrary. The keener and the clearer is the reason, the better fantasy will it make. If men were ever in a state in which they did not want to know or could not perceive truth (facts or evidence), then Fantasy would languish until they were cured. If they ever get into that state (it would not seem at all impossible), Fantasy will perish, and become Morbid Delusion.
> For creative Fantasy is founded upon the hard recognition that things are so in the world as it appears under the sun; on a recognition of fact, but not a slavery to it.   (FS 65)

Good fantasy—and indeed any good literary art, Tolkien's argument would imply—emerges from unique human freedoms enabled by human language; and he would see art's usefulness not so much in its reproducing and thus reinforcing the known features and priorities of its audience's "Primary World," but rather in its devising of worthwhile new experiences, "living shapes that move from mind to mind" (FS 65). These new shapes make no pretension of replacing "Primary Reality"; in fact, they are clearly constructed out of materials borrowed from the public world of "scientific verity." When offered thus, with due recognition of their nature, fantasies cannot be said to delude or dominate their readers; rather, both writer and reader become willing partners "in making and delight" (FS 64), an activity Tolkien finds to be fully warranted in Christian theology: human beings have the right to act as "Sub-Creators" through their own status as creatures "in imaginem Dei."[2]

One should especially note the careful balance Tolkien pursues in answering the standard utilitarian objections to the fairy story genre. While he defends fantasy's "arresting strangeness" against those who "dislike any meddling with the Primary World" (FS 60), he certainly does not claim that fantasy has an ontological primacy or priority over the material world of "scientific verity."[3] In fact, as seen above, he agrees with fantasy's utilitarian critics in their concern that men might enter "a state in which they did not want to know or could not perceive truth (facts or evidence)"; and he also freely acknowledges that the Sub-Creative faculty can be used and in fact has in the past been used to propagate harmful untruths: "Men have conceived not only of elves, but they have imagined gods, and worshiped them, even worshiped those most deformed by their authors' own evil" (FS 66). But Tolkien would distinguish between the "desire for a living, realized sub-creative art," a neutral characteristic largely human, and "the greed for self-centred power which is the mark of the mere Magician" (FS 64); and he observes that aesthetic invention has certainly not been the sole source of humanity's mass delusions, as men have also made false gods out of "their notions, their banners, their monies; even their sciences and their social and economic theories have demanded human sacrifice" (FS 66). Such candid appraisal of human uses of science and art inclines Tolkien to advance a grounded, perspicacious romanticism, not a cult of the artist as such,[4] but an advocacy of legitimate human longing for free aesthetic response to the beauties of "the world as it appears under the sun," pursuing, in the words of Elrond at the Council, "not strength or domination or hoarded wealth, but understanding, making, and healing, to preserve all things unstained" (LotR I 353).[5]

Tolkien does not, then, reject the utilitarian critique of fantasy out of hand, but instead meets with it on its own ground, refuting its facile dismissals and posing in return the human right and ability to respond creatively to material experience using the tools of language, tools every bit as real as the struts, wires, and girders of the industrial engineers. And like the engineer, the artist

---

2   *Genesis* 1:12 (Vulgate).
3   In this he disagrees with the ideology of Fichte and the German Romantics, who would (in Tolkien's view) too much absolutize the powers of human consciousness. There is however considerable common ground between Tolkien's understanding of pre-Christian myth-building and that of Romantic thinkers such as Schlegel; on this, see Eilmann (p.37-56).
4   Let alone any endorsement of artists as "the unacknowledged legislators of the world"; see Shelley (p. 1087).
5   In a letter explicitly mentioning his essay *On Fairy-stories*, Tolkien stated that the Elves in his legendarium represent "the artistic, aesthetic, and purely scientific aspects of the Humane nature," adding that they "possess a 'subcreational' or artistic faculty of great excellence" (L 232-237).

is spurred into action by dissatisfaction with the unimproved prosaic realities around him, by a desire to make a new thing that he and other human beings will find helpful. Tolkien would in fact reverse the utilitarian disapproval of Faërie by challenging the engineers themselves toward an improved aesthetic. Quoting recent strictures against "the rawness and ugliness of modern European life" (FS 72, cf. Dawson 72), he gestures at local railway stations and states, "From the wildness of my heart I cannot exclude the question whether railway-engineers, if they had been brought up on more fantasy, might not have done better with all their abundant means than they commonly do" (FS 70). The challenge is pointed; but these gestures toward civic architecture are paired with an even stronger critique directed toward writers and scholars who ignore or oppose any concern for the virtues of "understanding, making, and healing," being over-awed and over-impressed with their post-industrial culture's "strength or domination or hoarded wealth." Those championing careful, up-to-date literary reproductions of the latest in technological innovation, characterizing all who abstain from such as fearful weaklings, would seem aesthetically "to prefer the acquiescence of the 'quisling' to the resistance of the patriot" (FS 70); and Tolkien foresees that their time-serving artistic efforts will, like the amenities they depict, be quickly dated.

But again, Tolkien's critique of the technological triumphalists does not dispute the basic human desire for improved living, in which both technology and artistry (he would say) participate as manifestations of specifically human freedom, mankind's ability to perceive and accurately analyze the objective world and also creatively rearrange it. The challenge for both the technologist and the artist is to give the world an authentic, helpful response, enacting rearrangements that truly enhance human life; and good fantasy can accomplish this by taking respectful freedoms in its borrowings from Nature. "Fantasy is made out of the Primary World," Tolkien admits,

> but a good craftsman loves his material, and has a knowledge and feeling for clay, stone and wood which only the art of making can give. By the forging of Gram[6] cold iron was revealed; by the making of Pegasus horses were ennobled; in the Trees of the Sun and Moon[7] root and stock, flower and fruit are manifested in glory.   (FS 68)

---

6   As Flieger and Anderson note, "Gram" was the Norse hero Sigmund's sword, broken when he died in battle, reforged for his son Sigurd, and then used to kill the dragon Fáfnir (FS 115). Tolkien does his own part for the aesthetic "revealing" of iron in his iconic description of the reforging of the Sword of Elendil (LotR I 362).

7   Tolkien probably refers here to an episode in the Old English *Letter of Alexander*; see Marsden 275-280.

Tolkien here not only describes but performs the felt change in human consciousness enabled by literary images related to trees, horses, and iron, conveying effectively and convincingly the real action of words as aesthetic tools. A reader might compare the prevarications of the Aesthetes, statements such as Oscar Wilde's, that "one does not see anything until one sees its beauty," and "then only does it come into existence," (Wilde 33)[8] his assertion (as once summarized by Randall Jarrell) that "before Whistler painted them there were no fogs along the Thames" (Jarrell 69). Such a reader would I think recognize that the calculated insolences of "Art for Art's Sake" were self-obstructive in compar-ison with Tolkien's incidental demonstrations of artistic effect even within the discursive confines of this essay. Outrageous aesthetic triumphalism, like blinkered technological triumphalism, founders on inaccuracy and over-statement, while Tolkien, as a maker of narrative fantasy, advances a balanced argument that also offers "beauty that is an enchantment," gems that "turn into flowers or flames" (FS 27, 68).

In short, there is a mark of exploratory authenticity in *On Fairy-stories* that in and of itself belies the generalizations of fantasy's opponents. Insisting that good fantasy must emerge from keen perception, clear reasoning, concern for truth, and "hard recognition that things are so in the world" was indeed an effective and thoughtful rejoinder against those who consider fantasy a pastime willfully out of touch with reality; but it seems also to have been a candid account of conditions Tolkien had himself found favorable for fantasy-making. Humphrey Carpenter senses rightly, I think, that this essay amounted to a personal artistic manifesto: its delivery at St. Andrews noticeably intensified Tolkien's commitment to composing the fiction of *The Lord of the Rings*, such that "he returned with a new enthusiasm to the story whose purpose he had justified" (Carpenter 191). One might add that the arguments seem truly to indicate the real circumstances of Tolkien's lifelong forays into fictional composition. As a working scholar and paterfamilias for most of his life economically vulnerable, a man who accepted with a sort of measured asceticism the conventional sur-roundings of the English middle class,[9] he was obliged to practice "recognition of fact" every day, and particularly understood the value of a sensibility that evaded "a slavery to it." The life of the imagination was a saving proviso of the highest order; and with it the constraints of less-than-ideal surroundings and situations seem to have been particularly stimulating to Tolkien's creative im-agination. One might cite as example the Tolkien family's trips to the coastal resort town of Filey in Yorkshire. "Tolkien did not like the place; he called it 'a very nasty little suburban seaside resort'" (Carpenter 105); but Carpenter notes

---

8   Read online through *Google Books* on 12 April 2015.
9   See Carpenter's musings on this subject, finally rooting Tolkien's lifestyle in a provisional acceptance of the non-ideal in view of the Fall of Man (pp. 122-126).

that poetic (and satiric) response to what he and his family experienced at Filey issued in a collection of lyrics called "Tales and Songs of Bimble Bay," evidently part of the adventurous and humorous groundwork for both *The Hobbit* and *The Lord of the Rings*. Tolkien's main animus against the tourist culture of Filey had to do with the flagrant disregard for the place, the pollution and disfigurement of streets and North Sea waterfront, by merchants and visitors alike. In these people's neglectful minds, Filey, otherwise known (in Tolkien's satire) as "Bimble Town," could also be termed "Godknowswhere" and "Theydontcare." Tolkien set about responding in a way he would later recommend in his essay—here is his "hard recognition that things are so in the world":

> sometimes late, when motor-bikes
> are not passing with a screech,
> one hears faintly (if one likes)
> the sea still at it on the beach.
> At what? At churning orange-rind,
> piling up banana-skins,
> gnawing paper, trying to grind
> a broth of bottles, packets, tins,
> before a new day comes with more,
> before next morning's charabangs,
> stopping at the old inn-door
> with reek and rumble, hoots and clangs,
> bring more folk to Godknowswhere
> and Theydontcare, to Bimble Town
> where the steep street, that once was fair,
> with many houses staggers down.   (R 106)

The Tolkiens, staying in a cottage away from and above the town center, were able to enjoy views of the sea and sky in more isolation, but during a walk on the beach young Michael lost his favorite toy, a miniature dog, which apparently became part of the tourist flotsam so graphically described in his father's later poem. Tolkien's response to the incident was to compose a fantasy, a tale that acknowledged the loss but took freedom to reimagine it: Michael's toy became a real young dog named Rover, laid under enchantment for having offended a wizard, finally returning to full biological life and to his owner under circumstances recalling some of the more remarkable and beautiful details of family time at Filey—a path of silver light on the sea leading to the moon, a memorably violent and damaging marine storm. As the editors of *Roverandom* have noted (R xvii), Tolkien's *On Fairy-stories* signaled a retreat from this tale's diminutive moon-gnomes who grew "golden apple-trees no bigger than buttercups" (R 49) and sea-fairies that ride "little green crabs with bridles of fine threads" (R 73), and the essay would also implicitly repudiate *Roverandom's* prevailing tone, much reminiscent of certain parts of *The Hobbit* in presuming an immature reader. But the tale's effective aesthetic escape from tourist-ridden Filey and its consolatory transformation of the Tolkiens' experiences there anticipated goals articulated in the essay; and it seems that this early foray into the lower folk realms of fairy story, the wry, chatty, and fantastic Edwardian realism of *Roverandom*,[10] emerged as an alternative pole in Tolkien's imagination to the developed high cosmogony and saga of the tales of the Silmarils.

These two poles of modernized folk tale and high myth would meet in *The Hobbit*, and specifically in the character of Bilbo Baggins, whose peaceable domestic practicality could not be extinguished even in the midst of heroic adventure;[11] similarly, Tolkien's contentions about the value of fairy stories would align "the deeper spirit of the romantic" (FS 76, n. 1) with other basic and intrinsically human needs, good cooking and cleaning and concern for available amenities being, along with good fantasy, part of the perfectly legitimate human desire to escape "hunger, thirst, poverty, pain, sorrow, injustice, death" (FS 73). Acceptance of one's connection with the commonplaces of human life, "das Gemeine" either neutral or negative, actually presented aesthetic opportunities, the neutral enabling artistic recovery such that one could "look at green again, and be startled anew (but not blinded) by blue and yellow and red" (FS 67), the negative providing grounds for implicit artistic protest and legitimate escape. These measured but optimistic views of the relations between art and common life also emerge in the attitudes Tolkien's leading characters take in *The Lord of the Rings* toward the sturdy (but often rather petty) conventionality of hobbit culture in the Shire. "I should like to save the Shire," Frodo Baggins says,

> if I could—though there have been times when I thought the inhabitants too stupid and dull for words, and have felt that an earthquake or an invasion of dragons might be good for them. But I don't feel like that now. I feel that as long as the Shire lies behind, safe and comfortable, I shall find wandering more bearable: I shall know that somewhere there is a firm foothold, even if my feet cannot stand there again.   (LotR I 96)

---

10 The farcical social comedy of *Mr. Bliss*, also written before *On Fairy-stories*, takes a similar tone.

11 The narrative refrain in *The Hobbit* rehearses Bilbo's wish to return to the cooking and comforts of home during rain in Rhudaur (43), after capture by goblins (68), after finding the Ring (76), amidst dreams in the eagle's eyrie (114), while alone in Mirkwood (153), on the "doorstep" at the Lonely Mountain (199), in a dream at Erebor gate (259), in the High Pass of the Misty Mountains (278), and finally in the fulfillment of actual homecoming (285).

The wizard Gandalf praises Frodo for the unexpected wisdom of this response, and later acknowledges a certain sort of "power to withstand the might of Mordor" in the ethos of the Shire (LotR I 294). Though unimaginative and thoroughly vulnerable to satirical observations such as those in the first chapter of *The Lord of the Rings*, the common respect for custom, law, and order among the hobbits and also the Men of Bree—originating in past allegiances to Arnor—reflects an accurate "recognition that things are so in the world as it appears under the sun"; and the Rangers of Arnor, initiates in elvish wisdom, help to maintain the wholesome sanity of these less-sophisticated communities by providing unilateral military protection that expects no recognizance or reward. "'Strider' I am to one fat man who lives within a day's march of foes that would freeze his heart, or lay his little town in ruin if it were not guarded ceaselessly," Aragorn says to Boromir at the Council of Elrond,

> Yet we would not have it otherwise. If simple folk are free from care and fear, simple they will be, and we must be secret to keep them so. That has been the task of my kindred, while the years have lengthened and the grass has grown.	(LotR I 96)[12]

Of course, these long efforts have in Tolkien's tale their eucatastrophe, as the good soil of the hobbit culture guarded by the Rangers has produced Frodo the Ringbearer, through whom the Kingdom of Arnor will be restored.

The Rangers, ideal retainers for whom service to the realm was a vocation not contingent on payment or prestige, bring to mind again Tolkien's own unremitting acceptance of a conventional lifestyle even as he produced his unprecedented fantasies. W.H. Auden's notorious response to Tolkien's domestic situation (as reported in the London Press)—"He lives in a hideous house—I cannot tell you how hideous, with hideous pictures"—has elicited a reasonable explanation from Humphrey Carpenter:

> As a man of sophisticated tastes [Auden] was astonished by the apparent ordinariness of Tolkien's life-style, and by the conformity of the house in the suburban road. This life-style did not specifically reflect Tolkien's own tastes; on the other hand he did not exactly object to it—indeed there was an ascetic side to him which did not even notice it.	(Carpenter 249; see also L 367)

It might be further replied, in view of the thoughts expressed in *On Fairy-stories*, that Tolkien, who willingly characterized himself as a hobbit (L 288f)—i.e., as a

---

12	Compare also the exchange between Aragorn and Halbarad at Meriadoc's departure from Helm's Deep (LotR III 61f).

typical Englishman with certain not unanticipated tastes—found the prevailing appurtenances of Oxford-suburban life, preferred by his wife Edith and reflective of their middle-class Midlands origin, to be normal human constraints and, as such, creatively energizing. The irritant of the non-ideal called forth the free reply of fantasy. Writing *The Lord of the Rings* was a response preferable to carefully surrounding oneself with decor according to taste.

Another aspect of being, as Tolkien said, a hobbit, was one's acceptance of the surrounding culture of the Shire—for Tolkien, respectable Victorian and Edwardian England, where (again) the aesthetics of fairy stories were not deemed sufficiently progressive or practical for usual adult notice. Tolkien did however find common cause for serious consideration of the fairy story genre in the person of G.K. Chesterton, an early twentieth-century author and journalist who had managed to create along with his friend Hilaire Belloc a popular aesthetic movement against the almost unanimously dominant historical narrative of the era, a simplistic progressivism championing technology, Protestantism, and elected parliaments, epitomized in the declamatory histories of Thomas Macaulay and generally propagated by the nineteenth-century English educational establishment without any effective opposition. One major component in Chesterton's critique was a revaluation of the preindustrial human imagination, and of the mythologies and Märchen that historically had vivified it.[13] It is then not surprising that Tolkien turned to Chesterton repeatedly in his advocacy of the fairy story genre[14]; indeed, the recent expanded edition of *On Fairy-stories* indicates even more explicit and extensive interactions with Chesterton in the essay's preliminary drafts (FS 109).[15] I would affirm that the theoretical component of Tolkien's essay we have here been discussing was in essence a carefully-examined re-presentation of Chesterton's aesthetic thought, and would

---

13   Auden, in his introduction to *G.K. Chesterton: A Selection from his Non-Fictional Prose*, noted Chesterton's important role in the successful removal of the nineteenth-century progressivist distortions of history, and he observed that "nobody has written more intelligently and sympathetically [than Chesterton] about mythology or polytheism" (15-17). Auden also expressed a common imaginative debt with Chesterton's to the fairy story genre (18).

14   Tolkien cites Chesterton to clarify the sense in which Faërie relates to childlike "humility and innocence" (FS 57); he mentions with approval the "limited power" of Chesterton's *"Mooreeffoc"*—i.e., Chesterton's interest in viewing commonplace surroundings "suddenly from a new angle" (FS 68); he joins with Chesterton in dismissing complacent and triumphalist attitudes toward technological innovation (FS 70); and in the earliest published version of *On Fairy-stories* (1947) he interacts with Chesterton explicitly and at length on how to avoid decadent and counter-productive efforts toward originality: see Lewis, *Essays* 73-74.

15   In manuscript A, e.g. (FS 192), Tolkien cites Chesterton's specific reaction to modern lamp-posts (a reaction rather more positive than Tolkien's own, but of course Chesterton's were gas lamps), and he also refers to Chesterton's *The Napoleon of Notting Hill*, a text whose "Introductory Remarks on the Art of Prophecy" (pp. 9-13) probably helped to inspire Tolkien's "soon-cloying game of moving at high speed" (FS 72).

further suggest that Chesterton's essay "A Piece of Chalk" (Chesterton, *Trifles* 8-16)—to this day widely considered one of his best—provided an inspirational baseline for Tolkien's distinctive answer to the presumed oppositions between the aesthetic and the commonplace.

Recapitulating Chesterton's short essay will I think show at least its relevance to Tolkien's thought. It is a (very good) specimen of a certain kind of journalistic essay popular at the turn of the twentieth century, in which serious arguments are advanced under apparently incidental contexts—episodic encounters or whimsical experiences. Chesterton presents himself at the beginning of "A Piece of Chalk" as a man on holiday who wishes to use his landlady's supply of brown packing paper to make chalk drawings while enjoying the scenery on the Sussex Downs. When his landlady offers to give him note-paper instead as a medium more conducive to drawing, Chesterton attempts to explain his initial preferences:

> I then tried to explain the rather delicate logical shade, that I not only liked brown paper, but liked the quality of brownness in paper, just as I liked the quality of brownness in October woods, or in beer, or in the peat-streams of the North. Brown paper represents the primal twilight of the first toil of creation, and with a bright-coloured chalk or two you can pick out points of fire in it, sparks of gold, and blood-red, and sea-green, like the first fierce stars that sprang out of divine darkness. All this I said (in an off-hand way) to the old woman; and I put the brown paper in my pocket along with the chalks, and possibly other things.
>
> (9f)

While Chesterton implicitly invites his reader to take his descriptions humorously, as unnecessarily overblown aesthetic enthusiasm, his self-consciousness also signals an intention to continue in similar vein this account of himself as a vacationer exploring the hills and drawing, and he creates in his audience an accurate expectation of more aesthetic unconventionalities to come. Tolkien, however, would be inclined as a philologist to consider the phenomenon of Chesterton's rhetoric more seriously. What enabled this spectacular and attractive sequence of images—brown paper, October woods, beer, "peat-streams of the North"? Quite obviously, Chesterton's explicit exercise of associating "the quality of brownness" with a series of unrelated but well-known and picturesque images from the physical world, "combining nouns and redistributing adjectives" (FS 64). Chesterton was quite agilely demonstrating the aesthetic capabilities of humanity derived from language.

After an animated and allegorical description of his walk through the Downs, Chesterton begins in his essay to describe the visionary and apocalyptic images[16] that he chooses to draw, observing that, although his "devils and seraphim, and blind old gods that men worshipped before the dawn of right, and saints in robes of angry crimson, and seas of strange green" are not realistic reproductions of the scenery around him, they are nevertheless aesthetically derived from the colors and creatures of the natural world. This observation leads him to comment on the use of the natural world by classical and medieval poets:

> They preferred writing about great men to writing about great hills; but they sat on the great hills to write it. They gave out much less about Nature, but they drank in, perhaps, much more. They painted the white robes of their holy virgins with the blinding snow, at which they had stared all day. They blazoned the shields of their paladins with the purple and gold of many heraldic sunsets. The greenness of a thousand green leaves clustered into the live green figure of Robin Hood. The blueness of a score of forgotten skies became the blue robes of the Virgin. The inspiration went in like sunbeams and came out like Apollo.   (12f)

Chesterton's arguments here in favor of "the old poets who lived before Wordsworth, and were supposed not to care very much about Nature because they did not describe it much" (12) incidentally pursue Max Müller's nature-myth theory, putting it to an affirmatively aesthetic use that Müller would not have intended. Tolkien, whose scholarship rejected Müller's theory (FS 42), was nevertheless able to advance a hypothetical argument that preserved and perhaps even consciously followed Chesterton's aesthetic observations:

> Let us assume for the moment, as this [nature-myth] theory assumes, that nothing actually exists corresponding to the "gods" of mythology: no personalities, only astronomical or meteorological objects. Then these natural objects can only be arrayed with a personal significance and glory by a gift, the gift of a person, of a man. Personality can only be derived from a person. The gods may derive their colour and beauty from the high splendours of Nature, but it was man who obtained these for them, abstracted them from sun and moon and cloud; their personality they get direct from him; the shadow or flicker of divinity that is upon them they receive through him from the invisible world, the Supernatural. There is no fundamental distinction between the

---

16 Alternatively, and more self-consciously, "silly figures" (13).

higher and lower mythologies. Their people live, if they live at all, by the same life, just as in the mortal world do kings and peasants.   (FS 42f)

While Chesterton's thoughts on "the old poets" focus exclusively on the contrast between ancient and modern artistic responses to Nature, Tolkien's version of Chesterton's argument takes a much wider view; and it is especially worth noting that, unlike Chesterton, he frames his thoughts on the delegation of human qualities and nature-observations to the gods in such a way as to allow for the possibility that the pagan gods do in fact have some objective personal existence. This particular sort of open-mindedness, quite unusual in the post-industrial academy, Tolkien also repeatedly directed toward the elves and fairies in the "lower mythologies" of folk traditions,[17] though he does quite tactfully ensure that his arguments for pursuit of fantasy and enchantment remain valid "even if the elves are, even more so in so far as they are, only a product of Fantasy itself" (FS 64).[18]

Chesterton concludes his essay with his discovery on the Downs that a color has gone missing from his drawing set: there is no white chalk. This realization deeply disappoints him and prompts remarks "on a moral significance" (13). As chalk drawings on brown paper prove, he says, white is a real color[19]:

---

17 See e.g. FS 60, 63, 64, 75. Tolkien's preparatory manuscripts for *On Fairy-stories* seem not to support Shippey's suggestion that Tolkien attempted in his address to "talk down" to "an unspecialised audience" by "pretending that fairies are real," as the pre-writing puts considerable effort into describing how the possible existence of fairies would fit into an orthodox Christian description of the cosmos (Shippey 56; FS 254-255). In pursuing such thoughts, Tolkien was following, along with his friend C.S. Lewis, a long pre-industrial tradition of speculation on the status of the "Longaevi"; see Lewis, *Image* 122-138.

18 Tolkien's stance here may owe something to Chesterton's laudatory review of *A Midsummer Night's Dream*, which essay makes gestures toward the power of the "elven" world that Tolkien's imagination was able to pursue and mature. See e.g. Chesterton's special praise for Shakespeare's final scene:

Theseus and his train retire with a crashing finale, full of humour and wisdom and things set right, and silence falls on the house. Then there comes a faint sound of little feet, and for a moment, as it were, the elves look into the house, asking which is the reality. "Suppose we are the realities and they the shadows." If that ending were acted properly any modern man would feel shaken to his marrow if he had to walk home from the theatre through a country lane.

See Chesterton, *Man* 14. Chesterton's *Midsummer Night's Dream* essay was first published in 1904.

19 Tolkien's practices in illustration may very well have been influenced by this passage. In *The Tolkien Family Album* 57-58, "Priscilla clearly recalls her father showing her how beautifully Chinese White could be used when he was painting 'Bilbo Comes to the Huts of the Raft-elves' (his favourite painting and the one chosen by the Bodleian for the poster advertising their exhibition of his work in 1987 to celebrate the fiftieth anniversary of the first publication of *The Hobbit*). He demonstrated how white could be an addition to a painting, rather than an absence of colour."

it is a shining and affirmative thing, as fierce as red, as definite
as black. When, so to speak, your pencil grows red-hot, it draws
roses; when it grows white-hot, it draws stars. And one of the
two or three defiant verities of the best religious morality, of real
Christianity, for example, is exactly this same thing; the chief
assertion of religious morality is that white is a colour. Virtue
is not the absence of vices or the avoidance of moral dangers;
virtue is a vivid and separate thing, like pain or a particular smell.
Mercy does not mean not being cruel or sparing people revenge
or punishment; it means a plain and positive thing like the sun,
which one has either seen or not seen.   (13f)

One recalls in this descant on the significance of white Gandalf's exchange
with Saruman as recounted at the Council of Elrond (LotR I 339)[20]; but the
final turn of Chesterton's observations leads back to practical aesthetics, to
Fantasy's concrete rearrangement of things as they appear "under the sun,"
as Chesterton suddenly realizes that he has his white chalk after all, for he is
sitting in the Sussex Downs.

Then I suddenly stood up and roared with laughter, again and
again, so that the cows stared at me and called a committee.
Imagine a man in the Sahara regretting that he had no sand for
his hour-glass. Imagine a gentleman in mid-ocean wishing that
he had brought some salt water with him for his chemical experiments. I was sitting on an immense warehouse of white chalk.
The landscape was made entirely out of white chalk. White chalk
was piled more miles until it met the sky. I stooped and broke
a piece off the rock I sat on: it did not mark so well as the shop
chalks do; but it gave the effect. And I stood there in a trance of
pleasure, realising that this Southern England is not only a grand
peninsula, and a tradition and a civilisation; it is something even
more admirable. It is a piece of chalk.   (15f)

White chalk emerges for Chesterton as a symbol of the unnoticed goods of free
popular democracy, and he implicitly observes vast potential for the human art
of good culture in the natural soil of England. For Tolkien's more linguistically
oriented sensibility, Chesterton's chalk meant the creation of a new myth, a

---

20 An earlier passage in Chesterton's essay, reflecting on items generally carried in one's
    pockets—"the pocket-knife, for instance, the type of all human tools, the infant of the
    sword" (10)—may also have an echo in Bilbo's exchange with Gollum in *The Hobbit* (H
    85-91).

freeing transformation of the "tone and quality" of England,[21] a revaluation of western civilization through the deep soil of the Shire (LotR III 179).

Bibliography

Auden, Wystan Hugh. *G.K. Chesterton: A Selection from his Non-Fictional Prose.* London: Faber & Faber, 1970

Carpenter, Humphrey. *Tolkien: A Biography.* Boston: Houghton Mifflin, 1977

Chesterton, Gilbert Keith. *The Common Man.* New York: Sheed and Ward, 1950

---. *The Napoleon of Notting Hill.* Harmondsworth, Middlesex: Penguin Books, 1982

---. *Tremendous Trifles.* New York: Dodd, Mead & Co., 1910

Dawson, Christopher. *Progress and Religion: An Historical Enquiry.* New York: Sheed and Ward, 1938

Eilmann, Julian T.M. "Romantic world building: J.R.R. Tolkien's concept of sub-creation and the Romantic spirit." In: *From Peterborough to Faëry: The Poetics and Mechanics of Secondary Worlds.* Eds. Thomas Honegger & Dirk Vanderbeke. Cormarë Series 31. Zurich/Jena: Walking Tree Publishers, 2014, 37-56

Jarrell, Randall. *A Sad Heart at the Supermarket: Essays and Fables.* London: Eyre & Spottiswoode, 1965

Lewis, Clive Staples (Ed.). *Essays Presented to Charles Williams.* Grand Rapids MI: Eerdmans, 1966

---. *The Discarded Image.* Cambridge: Cambridge University Press, 1964

Marsden, Richard. *The Cambridge Old English Reader.* Cambridge: Cambridge University Press, 2004

Shelley, Percey. "A Defence of Poetry". In: *English Romantic Writers.* Ed. David Perkins. New York: Harcourt Brace Jovanovich, 1967, 1087

Shippey, Tom. *The Road to Middle-earth*, revised edition. Bury St. Edmunds, Suffolk: HarperCollins, 2005

Tolkien, John and Priscilla. *The Tolkien Family Album.* Boston: Houghton Mifflin, 1992

Tolkien, John Ronald Reuel. *The Fellowship of the Ring.* New York: Ballantine Books, 1965

---. *The Hobbit.* New York: Ballantine Books, 1966

---. *The Letters of J.R.R. Tolkien.* Ed. Humphrey Carpenter. Boston: Houghton-Mifflin, 1981

---. *The Monsters and the Critics and other Essays.* Ed. Christopher Tolkien. London: HarperCollins, 2006

---. *Mr Bliss.* London: HarperCollins, 2011

---. *The Return of the King.* New York: Ballantine Books, 1965

---. *Roverandom.* Eds. Christina Scull & Wayne G. Hammond. London: HarperCollins, 1998

---. *Tolkien On Fairy-stories: Expanded Edition with Commentary and Notes.* Eds. Verlyn Flieger & Douglas A. Anderson. London: HarperCollins, 2008

Wilde, Oscar. *Intentions.* Leipzig: Heinemann and Belestier, 1891

---

21 See Tolkien's comments on his aims to provide a new mythology for England (L 144), apparently presented as a follow-up to his correspondent's reading of *On Fairy-stories*.

Elbisches Theater am Küchentisch – Pen&Paper-Rollenspiel als *fairy story*

Christian Weichmann (Braunschweig)

Als J.R.R. Tolkien seinen Artikel *On Fairy-stories* schrieb, gab es noch kein Pen&Paper-Rollenspiel und es gibt auch keinerlei Hinweise, dass dieser Essay bei der Entwicklung der Spiele irgendeinen Einfluss hatte. Aber da es sich auch beim Pen&Paper-Rollenspiel um eine Art der Erzählung handelt, sogar mit dramatischen Elementen, lohnt es sich, einmal zu untersuchen, inwiefern sie vielleicht *fairy stories* im Sinne Tolkiens sein könnten.

Pen&Paper-Rollenspiel

Zunächst ist zu klären, was Pen&Paper-Rollenspiele sind: Da sich im Laufe der Zeit eine große Bandbreite von unterschiedlichen Systemen entwickelt hat, beschränke ich mich auf die typischen Merkmale. Damit bleiben zwar einige Pen&Paper-Rollenspiele außen vor, aber um die Nähe zu oder Ferne von *fairy stories* beurteilen zu können, sollten die hier gewählten Kriterien ausreichen.

Pen&Paper-Rollenspiele sind, wie der Name schon sagt, Spiele[1], bei denen man Rollen spielt und dafür Stift und Papier benutzt. Letzteres dient zur Abgrenzung gegenüber Liverollenspielen (LARP, siehe dazu Bauer) und Computerrollenspielen, die beide nicht Thema dieses Essays sind. Der Einfachheit halber wird im Weiteren der Begriff Rollenspiel verwendet, gemeint ist aber speziell das Pen&Paper-Rollenspiel.

Beim üblichen Rollenspiel sind mehrere Spieler und ein Spielleiter[2] um einen Tisch versammelt. Jeder Spieler hat sich im Rahmen der Regeln des Spiels eine Rolle, den sogenannten Charakter, ausgedacht, die er spielen will. Diese Charaktere entstammen der Welt des jeweiligen Rollenspiels. Sehr häufig sind das typische Fantasy-Welten, sodass die Charaktere Magier, Elben, Zwerge oder auch Orks sind und Berufe wie Dieb, Krieger oder Schamane ausüben.

---

1   Zur Definition von Spiel siehe Weichmann 160 beziehungsweise Poehl 37.
2   Spielleiterlose Rollenspiele, bei denen diese Funktion auf alle Spieler verteilt wird, sind selten und unüblich. Außerdem ist dieser Unterschied für unsere Betrachtungen nicht relevant. Sogenannte Solo-Abenteuer mit nur einem Spieler, bei denen die Spielleiterrolle von einem Buch übernommen wird, in dem der Spieler abhängig von seinen Entscheidungen an unterschiedlichen Stellen weiterlesen muss, sind zwar auch von den Rollenspielen abgeleitet, bilden aber aufgrund des völligen Fehlens von Interaktion eine so spezielle Art, dass man sie schon als eigene Kategorie sehen muss.

Die Charaktere werden auf einem Blatt Papier durch eine mehr oder weniger große Menge an Werten beschrieben, die beispielsweise angeben, wie stark oder klug der Charakter ist, und mit Fähigkeiten wie *Schwimmen, Fechten* oder auch *Lesen* und *Landeskunde Auenland*. Oft kommen noch ein Hintergrund, besondere Gewohnheiten, Stärken und Schwächen sowie Ausrüstung dazu.

Der Spielleiter hat keinen eigenen Charakter[3], sondern spielt den »Rest der Welt«. Er hat normalerweise ein Abenteuer vorbereitet, das er selbst erdacht oder aber von einem Abenteuerautor übernommen hat und das die Spieler mit ihren Charakteren erleben sollen. Dazu schildert er die Situationen, in denen sich die Charaktere der Spieler befinden, und spielt alle Personen, denen sie begegnen. Die Spieler reagieren auf diese Schilderungen bzw. die Aktionen des Spielleiters, wodurch sich dann eine Geschichte entwickelt.

Da es immer wieder Situationen gibt, in denen der Ausgang einer Handlung von den Fähigkeiten des Charakters abhängt (zum Beispiel ob eine Mauer überklettert werden kann), gibt es in den Rollenspielen Regeln, um zu klären, ob in einem solchen Fall ein Erfolg eintritt. Die meisten führen dabei ein Zufallssystem ein, um die Spannung zu erhöhen. Dazu werden ein oder mehrere Würfel[4] gewürfelt.

Es handelt sich also beim Rollenspiel um das gemeinsame Erzählen einer Geschichte durch die Interaktion mehrerer Personen unter bestimmten Regeln. Wie weit dabei die Geschichte durch den Spielleiter beziehungsweise den Abenteuerautor bestimmt ist oder von den Spielern gemacht wird, hängt von der jeweiligen Gruppe ab. Denn es ist ebenso möglich, dass der Spielleiter seinen Spielern sehr wenig Raum lässt, von dem vorgesehenen Abenteuerverlauf abzuweichen (sogenanntes »Railroading«), oder dass er nur ein Szenario oder eine sogenannte »Sandbox« vorgibt, wo sich die Spieler-Charaktere beliebig bewegen können.

Das Pen&Paper-Rollenspiel findet üblicherweise in geschlossenen Räumen um einen Tisch sitzend statt[5]. Das heißt, die Darstellung der Charaktere durch die Spieler und den Spielleiter beschränkt sich auf Beschreibungen, gesprochenen Text (mit oder ohne verstellte(r) Stimme), Mimik und Gestik. Ganz selten stehen die Spieler auf, um eine Situation nachzustellen. In manchen Runden werden Karten/Spielpläne und Figuren oder Marker verwendet, um kritische Situationen für alle gleichmäßig klar abzubilden.

---

3 Auch das ist der typische Fall, von dem es Abweichungen gibt. Aber da solche Charaktere meist entweder untergehen, weil der Spielleiter zu viel anderes zu tun hat oder sich zurückhält, oder aber einen zu starken Einfluss auf das Abenteuer haben, sind sie sehr selten und meist auch nicht sehr hilfreich.

4 Meist nicht nur klassisch sechsseitige, sondern auch vier-, acht-, zehn-, zwölf- und zwanzigseitige, die fast so etwas wie ein Erkennungszeichen von Rollenspielern sind.

5 Daher wird im Deutschen manchmal auch der Begriff Tischrollenspiel verwendet.

Geschichte des Rollenspiels[6]

Rollenspiele entwickelten sich aus dem Umfeld der taktischen Spiele, Konfliktsimulationen und Tabletop-Schlacht-Simulationen. In den 1960er und 1970er Jahren gab es eine aktive Szene von Spielern, die regelmäßig Schlachten nachstellten und zeitaufwändige Konfliktsimulationen spielten. Allerdings wurden bei all diesen Spielen Armeen und Gruppen gespielt und nicht Einzelpersonen. Außerdem waren die Spielhintergründe an die reale Welt angelehnt oder dieser entnommen. Phantastische Elemente fehlten noch. Aber gleichzeitig entstand gerade auch unter diesen Spielern ein Interesse an phantastischer Literatur, wie zum Beispiel an Tolkien.

Doch das erste Element, das in die Richtung auf die Rollenspiele eingeführt wurde, war die Idee, dass Spieler einzelne Figuren spielen. Dies geschah ungefähr 1968 durch David Wesely in seinem Spiel *Braunstein*, das in einer fiktiven von Napoleon besetzten Stadt namens Braunstein spielt. Obwohl Wesely am Ende der Partie meinte, die Idee sei gescheitert, da er keinen Sieger feststellen konnte, bemerkte er doch gleich, dass seine Spieler anderer Meinung waren. Den nächsten Schritt machte Dave Arneson, der eine mittelalterliche *Braunstein*-Variante einführte namens *Blackmoor*, die noch eine weitere wichtige Neuerung aufwies: Die Spieler bekamen die Möglichkeit, ihre Charaktere über mehrere Spiele hinweg weiterzuentwickeln. Und Arneson führte die über lange Zeit im Rollenspiel so wichtigen Dungeons ein – unterirdische von Monstern bewohnte Labyrinthe, die von den Charakteren erforscht wurden.

Bei den Regeln wurde er durch ein anderes Spiel, das aus den Konfliktsimulationsspielen (Kosims) hervorgegangen ist, beeinflusst: *Chainmail*, ein von Gary Gygax adaptiertes Regelwerk für mittelalterliche Schlachten und Fantasykämpfe, die mit Miniaturen nachgestellt werden. Auch dieses weicht von den klassischen Kosims insofern ab, als dass es empfiehlt, einzelne Miniaturen für einzelne Personen (und nicht ganze Truppenteile) zu verwenden, wobei es immer noch möglich ist, dass eine Figur einen ganzen Trupp darstellt. Außerdem beschränkt *Chainmail* sich im Wesentlichen auf Kämpfe. Andere freiere Aktionen sind nicht vorgesehen. Aber es ist stärker an literarischen Vorbildern orientiert. So erlauben die Regeln zum Fantasy Supplement, »die epischen Schlachten nachzukämpfen, von denen J.R.R. Tolkien, Robert E. Howard und andere Fantasy-Autoren erzählen« (zitiert nach Hillenbrand/Lischka 184). In den Jahren 1972/1973 entwickelten Gygax und Arneson gemeinsam das Spiel *Dungeons & Dragons* (D&D), das aus den Vorgängerspielen modifiziert wurde und das erste kommerziell verkaufte Pen&Paper-Rollenspiel im heutigen Sinne ist. Das Spiel kam 1974 auf den Markt – damals noch mit Monstern wie Ents oder Balrogs, die in späteren Versionen aber aus gutem Grund umbenannt wurden.

---

6   Diese Darstellung bezieht sich hauptsächlich auf Hillenbrand/Lischka 172ff.

Wie auch *Der Herr der Ringe* hatten diese Spiele zunächst große Erfolge an den Universitäten. Und es erschienen im Laufe der Zeit weitere Spiele ähnlicher Art: in Deutschland 1984 *Das Schwarze Auge* (DSA, Schmidt Spiele-Verlag) von Ulrich Kiesow, Werner Fuchs und Hans Joachim Alpers. Allerdings ist dies nicht das erste deutsche Rollenspiel. Das war 1981 das Spiel *Midgard* (Franke) von Elsa und Jürgen Franke, das auf der schon länger als Kosim bespielten Welt „Magira" des Fantasy-Klubs Follow angesiedelt ist.

Die Vielfalt an Rollenspielen erhöhte sich im Laufe der Jahre immer mehr. Insbesondere wurden immer wieder neue Welten und Hintergründe mit neuen Rollenspielen eingeführt. Aber auch die Regeln wurden auf unterschiedlichste Art und Weise verändert, wobei es Tendenzen gab, einerseits immer detailliertere Regeln zu erfinden, die alle Möglichkeiten abdecken (wofür speziell *Rolemaster* bekannt ist (vgl. Hillenbrand/Lischka 298f)), als auch andererseits Systeme zu entwickeln, die mit so wenig Regeln wie möglich auskommen.

Wenn auch, wie oben angedeutet, schon die D&D-Erfinder durch Tolkiens Werk inspiriert waren, dauerte es doch bis 1984, bis ein explizites *Mittelerde-Rollenspiel* (MERS) (Charlton) auf den Markt kam, das auf einer vereinfachten *Rolemaster*-Variante beruhte (vgl. Hillenbrand/Lischka 301). Und auch bei diesem war es durchaus umstritten, wie gut es Tolkiens Welt darzustellen erlaubt. Aus Lizenzgründen wird dieses Spiel nicht mehr hergestellt und es hatte inzwischen schon zwei Nachfolger: *Der Herr der Ringe* (Long et al.) von Decipher, das in der Zeit der Peter-Jackson-Trilogie erschienen ist und sich sehr an den Filmen orientierte; und *Der Eine Ring* (Nepitello), das wieder mehr auf die Bücher zurückgeht, wenn es auch bei diesem Zweifel an der Darstellungsqualität gibt.

Kinder

Schon die Geschichte zeigt, dass die Rollenspiele, wie auch die fairy stories, nicht ursprünglich mit Kinderspielen zu tun haben. Im Gegensatz zu den fairy stories sind die Rollenspiele aber am Küchentisch geblieben und nicht zum Kinderzimmertisch gewandert. Es gibt zwar Rollenspiele speziell für Kinder[7], aber das sind große Ausnahmen. Und auch bei den üblichen Rollenspielrunden und -veranstaltungen sind Kinder eher selten anzutreffen.

Die typischen Rollenspieler sind älter als 20 Jahre. Warum das so ist, lässt sich schwer sagen, denn genau genommen entspricht vieles, was beim Rollenspiel gemacht wird, typischen Kinderspielen: Es werden andere Rollen angenommen und Geschichten nachgespielt, in denen man normalerweise nicht aktiv ist. Mögliche Gründe für den trotzdem fehlenden Enthusiasmus bei Kindern könnten sein: Die Geschichten sind zu weit entfernt von der eigenen Erlebnis- und

---

7   Zum Beispiel *Hero Kids* (Halliday).

Wahrnehmungswelt. Selbst wenn sie Feen spielen, spielen Kinder diese oft in ganz alltäglichen Situationen. Oder die doch immer in einem gewissen Maße vorhandene Formalisierung der Regeln der Rollenspiele schreckt die Kinder ab, deren Spiel eher frei ist. Und möglicherweise ist auch die lange Bindung an eine Geschichte, die Erwachsene oft gerade als besonders interessant ansehen, für Kinder zu langatmig oder gar langweilig.

Fantasy

Für J.R.R. Tolkien ist in *On Fairy-stories* (FS 59) der Begriff der Fantasy ein wesentlicher Bestandteil dessen, was fairy stories leisten sollen. Wenn wir also prüfen wollen, inwieweit Rollenspiele als fairy stories im Tolkien'schen Sinne angesehen werden können, ist es wichtig zu sehen, inwieweit sie Fantasy liefern. Speziell da ja Tolkien sagt, »In human art Fantasy is a thing best left to words, to true literature« (FS 61), und dann: »But Drama is naturally hostile to Fantasy« (FS 61). Denn wenn Rollenspiele auch im Wesentlichen über Worte funktionieren, sind sie doch keine »echte Literatur«. Im Gegenteil, durch die Darstellung der Charaktere haben sie einen mehr oder weniger dramatischen Einschlag.

Trotzdem gelingt es dem Rollenspiel immer wieder, das von Tolkien geforderte Kriterium des »secondary belief« (FS 52) zu erreichen. Dazu ist es natürlich notwendig, dass alle Beteiligten eine gewisse Vertiefung in ihre Rolle(n) haben und dass die vom Spielleiter dargestellte Welt eine »inner consistency of reality« (FS 60) bietet. Bei ausgearbeiteten Rollenspiel-Welten ist das oft der Fall. Sie sind so aufgebaut, dass alle relevanten Elemente bekannt und konsistent sind.

Warum wirkt sich aber die von Tolkien festgestellte »natürliche Feindschaft« des Dramas gegenüber der Fantasy beim Rollenspiel nicht negativ aus? Es ist richtig, dass das Rollenspiel gewisse dramatische Elemente hat (einzelne Personen spielen einzelne Rollen und interagieren darin; Darstellung durch Mimik, Gestik, Stimme), die es deutlich von der Literatur unterscheiden. Aber es ist eben nicht vollständig so, wie es Tolkien beim Drama erwartete: »presented… audibly and visibly acted« (FS 61). Die Spieler sitzen nicht in Kostümen, die ihre Rollen darstellen, um den Tisch[8] und sie stellen die meisten Szenen auch nicht vollständig nach, sondern nutzen einen Wechsel von Erzählung (Beschreibung der Handlungen des Charakters: »Ich klettere die Mauer hoch«) und Darstellung (Mimik, sprechen als Charakter etc.). Insbesondere ist auch alles Phantastische einer Geschichte im Wesentlichen in der Vorstellung der Spieler enthalten:

---

8   Üblicherweise. Es gibt Fälle, in denen eine Gruppe meint, dass passende Gewandung das Einfühlen ins Setting erleichtert. Und es gibt sogar Rollenspielsysteme, die einen regeltechnischen Bonus dafür vorsehen, dass Spieler passende Kleidung tragen. Aber selbst in diesen Fällen ist es normalerweise nicht so, dass die Spieler als ihre Charaktere verkleidet sind, sondern nur passend phantastische oder mittelalterliche Kleidung tragen.

Spricht ein Zauberer seinen Spruch, stellen sich die Spieler die Durchführung und den Effekt des Spruchs vor. Es ist nicht nötig, irgendwelche Spezialeffekte zu nutzen. Gleiches gilt für phantastische Wesen wie Drachen, Trolle oder auch Hobbits. Somit ist auch in den dramatischen Elementen des Rollenspiels noch die Fantasy führend. Wenn sich die Spieler den Drachen nicht vorstellen könnten, wäre er nicht da.

Hierin liegt aber auch eine Gefahr für den *secondary belief*. Wenn sich die Vorstellungen der Spieler untereinander oder von denen des Spielleiters unterscheiden, führt das leicht dazu, dass der Spielfluss und damit die Immersion und der *secondary belief* unterbrochen werden. Denn dann unterscheiden sich die von den Spielern erwarteten, beziehungsweise vorgesehenen Handlungsmöglichkeiten voneinander und es kommt zu einer Diskussion darüber, was »tatsächlich ist« und was möglich ist. Dies ist einer der Gründe, visuelle Hilfen wie Pläne und Figuren zu nutzen, um Situationen darzustellen. Dies schränkt aber die Fantasy ein. Außerdem ist es natürlich auch ein Grund dafür, dass Rollenspiele oft und gerne bekannte Klischees ausnutzen[9]. Denn diese führen zu einer starken Ähnlichkeit der Vorstellungen der Beteiligten. Wenn Zwerge klein, stark, gierig und trinkfest sind, wundert sich ein Spieler eher wenig, wenn ein Versuch, einen Zwerg unter den Tisch zu trinken, nicht gelingt. Man könnte darin auch eine Einschränkung der Fantasy sehen, aber dies ist eine Einschränkung, die in der Literatur oft genug genauso auftritt.

Bei der Erhaltung des *secondary belief* spielt auch die Freiheit der Entwicklung des Abenteuers zwischen »Railroading« und »Sandbox« eine gewisse Rolle, obwohl es individuell verschieden ist, was für den secondary belief besser ist. Das »Railroading« erleichtert es dem Spielleiter, die Welt konsistent darzustellen, da er alle Elemente der Welt, denen die Charaktere begegnen werden, schon vorher kennt. Das vermeidet Situationen, in denen der *secondary belief* durch Widersprüche (zum Beispiel unterschiedliche Entfernungs- oder Zeitangaben für denselben Ort oder dasselbe Ereignis) oder fehlende Informationen (»das muss ich erst mal nachschlagen«) gestört wird. Andererseits können sich die Spieler aber an den Einschränkungen stören (»Der Zauberer hat gesagt, wir sollen zur Burg gehen, aber ich möchte vorher noch einen Abstecher ins Dorf machen.« – »Das geht nicht.« – »Warum?«). Welches die größere Gefahr ist, hängt davon ab, wie der Spielleiter sich vorbereitet und wie er in der Lage ist, die Einschränkungen vor den Spielern zu verbergen, und umgekehrt, wie sehr die Spieler sich in ihrem Spiel leiten lassen beziehungsweise auch gerade geleitet werden wollen.

---

9   Oder auch einfach in bekannten Welten wie Tolkiens Mittelerde spielen. Ein solches Vorgehen wird eben aus diesen Gründen zum Beispiel von Laws empfohlen (Laws 15). Eine dritte Möglichkeit ist, seine Welt mehr oder weniger stark an die reale Welt anzulehnen, wobei das natürlich beim Aspekt der Flucht wieder zu Einschränkungen führt. Die unterschiedlichen Ansätze dazu diskutiert (Baur).

Wiederherstellung, Flucht, Trost

Einen Aspekt der Wiederherstellung, den Tolkien betont, erfüllt das Rollenspiel ganz offensichtlich: »We should meet the centaur and the dragon, and then perhaps suddenly behold, like the ancient shepherds, sheep, and dogs, and horses – and wolves. This recovery fairy-stories help us to make« (FS 67). Denn wenn auch nicht alle Rollenspiele Zentauren oder Drachen vorsehen, so ist zumindest eins von beiden bei den meisten Fantasy-Rollenspielen enthalten. Und es ist meist gerade der Wunsch, solche Wesen zu treffen, der die Spieler antreibt. Aber nicht nur solche Wesen. Häufig reicht schon die Vorstellung, auf einem Pferd durch einen dunklen Wald zu reiten und Wölfen zu begegnen, um das Gefühl eines neuen Blickwinkels zu bekommen. Und selbst Schafe[10] sind für viele Spieler heute so fern ihrer eigenen Lebenswirklichkeit, dass sie im Spiel zu einem Mittel werden können, die Distanz zur Realität aufzubauen und den Blick auf die Grundlagen dessen zu lenken, was unser Leben bestimmt.

Ein wesentlicher Aspekt der Wiederherstellung des klaren Blicks, die Tolkien als Aufgabe der *fairy stories* sieht (FS 67), sind aber bei den Rollenspielen weniger die phantastischen Wesen. Vielmehr bieten die Spiele eine Möglichkeit, mehr oder weniger alltägliche Situationen in einer nicht-alltäglichen Art und Weise darzustellen. Die Charaktere können beispielsweise als Fremde in ein anderes Land kommen und dort auf Ablehnung stoßen. Oder die Geschichte kann dahin geführt werden, dass ein oder mehrere Charaktere vor eine Gewissensentscheidung gestellt werden. Ein häufiger Ansatz dafür ist es, die Charaktere einen Auftrag übernehmen und später herausfinden zu lassen, dass sie eigentlich für die aus ihrer Sicht falsche Seite arbeiten. Wenn sie nun stark genug verpflichtet sind, stehen sie vor der Entscheidung, wie sie sich weiter verhalten sollen. Auch von den »36 dramatischen Situationen« (Wäsch 152ff), die Wäsch beschreibt, liegt mindestens 15 eine Gewissensentscheidung zugrunde.

Ein weiterer Aspekt der Wiederherstellung des klaren Blicks, der aber auch schon zum Aspekt der Flucht gehören kann, ist die Möglichkeit für die Spieler, Charaktere mit ganz anderen Fähigkeiten und Eigenarten zu spielen. Wenn eine eher dominante Spielerin eine schwache Person spielt, die von den anderen abhängig ist, kann das ganz klar zu einem neuen Blickwinkel und vielleicht zu einem klaren Blick auf ihr eigenes Verhalten führen. Wenn umgekehrt ein Spieler einen Charakter wählt, der viel stärker und mächtiger ist als er selbst, kann das zwar auch dazu führen, dass der Spieler sich und andere aus einem neuen Blickwinkel sieht, aber es ist oft auch ein Versuch der Flucht. Ob es sich

---

10 Auch wenn es keine Wer-Schafe sind, die aber einen bleibenden Eindruck bei Spielern hinterlassen können.

dabei um »Escape of the Prisoner« (FS 69) oder »Flight of the Deserter« (FS 69) handelt, ist individuell verschieden.

Das Rollenspiel gibt zunächst einmal die Möglichkeit, für eine gewisse Zeit die reale Welt zu verlassen und in eine andere Welt einzutauchen. Diese andere Welt hat für die Spieler im Allgemeinen mindestens einen Aspekt, der für sie besser ist als in der realen Welt. Das muss nicht heißen, dass es eine »bessere Welt« sein muss. Es gibt durchaus auch dystopische Rollenspiele. In diesen könnte der bessere Aspekt einfach darin liegen, dass die Welt im Gegensatz zur realen mehr oder interessantere Herausforderungen liefert. Sicherlich sind die Welten der Rollenspiele einfacher als die reale Welt. Selbst in einem sogenannten »gritty setting«, in dem die Charaktere sehr leicht sterben, ist das Schlimmste, was passieren kann, dass ein Spieler einen neuen Charakter entwerfen muss, bevor er weiterspielen kann. Dieser Aspekt unterstützt oft den Vorwurf, dass es sich dabei um die »Flucht des Deserteurs« handelt, der seine Verantwortung dadurch loswerden will, dass er in die einfachere Welt eintaucht. Andererseits unterstützt diese Einfachheit aber auch die Möglichkeit, unterschiedliche Blickwinkel zu erkunden und somit den klaren Blick zurückzubekommen. Gegen den Vorwurf der »Flucht des Deserteurs« spricht eben der Punkt, dass die Spieler sich nur für eine begrenzte Zeit in die Welt des Spiels begeben. Das kann zwar bei den einzelnen Spielen schon einige Stunden sein und je nachdem wie die Gruppe aufgestellt ist auch regelmäßig wöchentlich oder seltener stattfinden. Aber die Rückkehr in die reale Welt ist gegeben, insbesondere auch dadurch, dass das Spiel eine Gruppenaktivität ist, bei der die Spieler sich gegenseitig kontrollieren können. Dieser Aspekt führt auch dazu, dass zwar die Spieler beim Eintauchen in die Sekundärwelt des Rollenspiels einen Teil der Verantwortung, die sie in der realen Welt haben, ruhen lassen, aber auch eine andere Verantwortung dadurch übernehmen, dass jeder Beteiligte seinen Beitrag dazu leisten muss, dass alle zusammen den gewünschten Spaß und das erhoffte Erlebnis haben.

Hinsichtlich des Kriteriums »Consolation of the Happy Ending« (FS 75) unterscheiden sich die Rollenspiele sehr deutlich voneinander. Einige Systeme geben in den Regeln und in den angebotenen vorgefertigten Abenteuern Hinweise, was der Spielleiter in Situationen tun soll, in denen sich das Spiel negativ für die Charaktere oder sogar die Welt entwickelt, um eben doch noch ein positives Ende zu erreichen.[11] Andere Systeme gehen davon aus, dass die Charaktere nicht lange überleben werden und dass sich die Welt eher negativ verändert.[12] Prinzipiell steht es einer Spielgruppe aber immer offen, ein positives Ende zu erreichen. Und die Spiele, in denen ein solches zumindest als Standardfall vorgesehen ist, überwiegen deutlich.

---

11 Dazu gehören beispielsweise *Earthdawn* (Prosperi et al.) und *Das Schwarze Auge* (Römer/Don-Schauen).
12 Hierzu gehören unter anderen *Dark Sun* (Denning/Brown) und *Cthulhu* (Petersen et al.)

Die meisten Systeme sehen in den Charakteren der Spieler »Helden«, die ihren potentiellen Gegnern prinzipiell überlegen sind, wenn es auch möglich ist, dass sie versagen. Dieser Punkt ist insofern relevant, als dass dies eine gewisse Herausforderung an die Spieler darstellt, die viele als wesentlich für den Spielspaß ansehen. Auch wenn bei Rollenspielen der Aspekt des Wiederspielwerts, den ich bei Brettspielen als wesentlich für den offenen Ausgang feststellte (Weichmann 162), nicht gegeben ist, da dieselben Abenteuer von denselben Spielern normalerweise nicht zweimal gespielt werden. Insofern kann man davon ausgehen, dass Rollenspiele in den meisten Fällen keine Garantie für ein gutes Ende haben, aber trotzdem die überwiegende Zahl der Spielrunden ein gutes Ende erreicht.

Dieses Kriterium war natürlich für Tolkien sehr wichtig: »Almost I would venture to assert that all complete fairy-stories must have it« (FS 75). Immerhin hat er dafür speziell das Wort »eucatastrophe« gefunden und meinte: »The *eucatastrophic* tale is the true form of fairy-tale, and its highest function« (FS 75). Wenn man diese Eukatastrophe genauer als »sudden joyous *turn*« (FS 75) sieht, wird sie noch seltener in Rollenspielabenteuern erreicht, da diese häufig eine allgemeine ständige Entwicklung zum guten oder schlechten Ende aufweisen. Aber auch wenn in diesem so wichtigen Punkt nicht unbedingt Übereinstimmung erzielt wird, so ist er doch in einer so großen Menge der tatsächlichen Spiele (zumindest im Sinne eines »Happy Endings«) erreicht, dass ich von einer überwiegenden Erfüllung auch dieses Kriteriums sprechen möchte.

Fazit

Auch wenn Pen&Paper-Rollenspiele in der Durchführung dramatische Element enthalten, sind sie im Wesentlichen doch kollektiv erzählte Geschichten, die die meisten der Kriterien erfüllen, die Tolkien für *fairy stories* aufgestellt hat. Sie erreichen einen *secondary belief* in einer *secondary world*. Sie bieten Gelegenheit für die Wiederherstellung des klaren Blicks und die (temporäre) Flucht aus der realen Welt. Und auch wenn die Eukatastrophe nicht garantiert ist, so ist sie auf jeden Fall eine oft realisierte Möglichkeit.

Natürlich sind sie kein ›Faërian Drama‹ (FS 63) im Tolkien'schen Sinne, also »plays... the elves have often presented to men« (FS 63), und führen auch nicht über den *secondary belief* hinaus. Aber sie erreichen eine Mischung aus den von Tolkien als gegensätzlich angesehenen Formen des Dramas und der *fairy story* (FS 63).

Bibliographie

Bauer, Stephanie. »Leben in Mittelerde? Tolkien-Adaptionen im Liverollenspiel«. *Hither Shore* 10 (2013): 118-133

Baur, Wolfgang. »How Real is your World?«. *The Kobold Guide to Worldbuilding*. Hg. Silverstein, Janna, Kirkland: Open Design, 2012. 25-34

Charlton, S. Coleman. *Mittelerde – Das klassische Rollenspiel System*. Troisdorf: Queen Games, 1993

Denning, Troy und Timothy B. Brown. *Dark Sun – Unter der Dunklen Sonne – Regelbuch*. Cambridge: TSR Ltd, 1993

Franke, Jürgen E. *Midgard – Der Kodex*. Stelzenberg: Elsa Franke, 2013

Halliday, Justin. *Hero Kids – Fantasy RPG*. Melbourne: Hero Forge Games, 2012

Hillenbrand, Tom und Konrad Lischka. *Drachenväter*. Münster: Edition Octopus, 2014

Laws, Robin D. *Gutes Spielleiten*. Friedberg: Pegasus Spiele, 2010

Long, Steven S. *The Lord of the Rings Roleplaying Game – Core Book*. Los Angeles: Decipher, 2003

Nepitello, Francesco. *Der Eine Ring – Abenteuer am Rande der Wildnis*. Erkrath: Uhrwerk, 2011

Poehl, Henning. »Von der Evolution der Spiele«. In: *Spiele Entwickeln 2007*. Hg. Casasola Merkle, Marcel-André, Christwart Conrad et al., Berlin: Pro BUSINESS, 2007. 17-37

Römer, Thomas, und Florian Don-Schauen. *Das Schwarze Auge: Basisregelwerk*. Waldems: Ulisses Spiele, 2006

Petersen, Sandy, et al. *Cthulhu für Einsteiger*. Friedberg: Pegasus Spiele, 2011

Prosperi, Louis J., et al. *Earthdawn*. München: Games-In, 2006

Tolkien, John Ronald Reuel. *On Fairy-stories*. London: HarperCollins, 2014

Wäsch, Dominic. *Spielleiten*. Duisburg: Prometheus Games, 2009

Weichmann, Christian. »Kein Kinderspiel: Brettspiele als Adaptionen des *Herrn der Ringe*«. *Hither Shore* 10 (2013): 160-176

On Fairy Tales and Games: A Phenomenological Comparison of two Storytelling Media

Zsuzsa Gáti (Wien)

The thoughts described in this paper were inspired by J.R.R. Tolkien's text *On Fairy-stories*, as he wrote about fairy tales: "I feel that it is more interesting, and also in its way more difficult, to consider what they are, what they have become for us, and what values the long alchemic processes of time have produced in them" (FS 22). I would like to examine precisely these questions from a phenomenological point of view and compare—as well as work out the differences of—the characteristics of the (orally spread) fairy tale as a classical storytelling medium and the (digital) game as a modern one.

At this point, phenomenology will not be treated in the 'classical' sense as defined by Edmund Husserl in his works—not as a philosophical and psychological science of consciousness phenomena—but in a mere descriptive way, as a walkabout around certain phenomena in order to be able to comprehend them as holistically as possible and to adjust eventually deployed examination methods appropriately to suit the specific characteristics of the object of investigation. Dealing with different media phenomena and/or with specific genres, such considerations are very important in my opinion, because they often tend to require a modification of methods and approaches of a certain discipline. It is essential to work with the media and not against them and to respect their basic and possibly very special traits.

Fairy Tales

First of all, the question arises as to how to define fairy tales. In this paper, they will be considered as a genre-group of the oral tradition, one, which is probably most deeply and naturally enrooted in the oral form of storytelling.

As Stith Thompson points out, the German word *Märchen* is, in contrast to the English expressions, much better suited to describe this phenomenon. In the English language, terms are either too narrow or too broad in their definition: 'fairy tale' is the most popular phrase (and also the reason why this paper tends to use this word), but as a matter of fact, fairy tale is too focused on fairies. On the other hand, 'household tale' and 'folk tale' are expressions which allow far too much interpretation. Thus, Thompson gives the following definition and suggestions:

> A Märchen is a tale of some length involving succession of motifs or episodes. It moves in an unreal world without definite locality

or definite characters and is filled with the marvelous… Since Märchen deal with such a chimeratical world, the name "chimerat" has been suggested for international usage, though it has not yet received wide adoption.   (Thompson 8)

Thus, regarding the terminology, this genre stands on feet of clay. Max Lüthi also refers to the expressions being very vague and he states that researchers resort to "stopgap terms" ("Verlegenheitsbegriffe") such as "Ordinary Tales of Magic" ("Märchen im eigentlichen Sinn")—the diversity of definitions still being problematic (Lüthi 2).

Most researchers consider the group of 'Tales of Magic' to be 'Ordinary Folk Tales' as categorised in the Aarne-Thompson-Uther-Index (ATU):

The ATU files many hundred tales from around the world, classified by their motifs. Antti Aarne started the work with the first index in 1910, which was edited and expanded by Stith Thompson until 1961. The division derives from Aarne's work1, Thompson having added the last two categories. The five large classes are further subdivided, as the Folk Tale category shows in this extract:

I. Animal Tales
II. Ordinary Folk Tales
  A. Tales of Magic
  B. Religious Tales
  C. Novelle (Romantic Tales)
  D. Tales of the Stupid Ogre
III. Jokes and Anecdotes
IV. Formula Tales
V. Unclassified Tales   (Aarne/Thompson 19f)

Hans-Jörg Uther revised the Tale Type Index in 2004 and it is unavoidable in folk tale research down to the present day.[2]

Regarding the particular types, other ways of categorisation are also imaginable and sometimes even reasonable—horror stories, for example, which have a strong moral message, are not easy to fit into this scheme. Thus, Hans-Jörg Uther mentions for instance in his edition of the Brothers Grimm's collection different classes (and even their hybrid forms) to distinguish the tales.[3]

---

1   Aarne's categories are the following: I. Tiermärchen, II. Eigentliche Märchen – A. Zaubermärchen, B. Legendenartige Märchen, C. Novellenartige Märchen, D. Märchen vom dummen Teufel (Riesen), III. Schwänke (Aarne 65f)

2   Uther's arrangement is the following: Animal Tales, Tales of Magic, Religious Tales, Realistic Tales (Novelle), Tales of the Stupid Ogre (Giant, Devil), Anecdotes and Jokes, Formula Tales (Uther 284ff)

3   "Ätiologien…, Exempla…, Fabel…, Horrorgeschichten…, Kettenmärchen…, Kinderlied…, Legenden…, Legendenmärchen…, Legendenschwank…, Lügengeschichten…, [Zauber-] Märchen…, Neckerzählungen…, Parabeln…, Rätsel…, Rätselmärchen…, Rätselschwän-

The genre of fairy tales holds many possible categories, the borders of which are blurred. For this reason a rigid classification makes no sense, the organising systems mentioned should be regarded as auxiliary means in this respect, not as a defining, tight terminology.

Fairy tales can be identified as a literary genre—though as a literary genre with very specific demands reaching beyond the threshold of literature. This interesting interplay of elements leads to the constitution of a fascinating story-telling medium. But let us take a look on the details:

Fairy tale is to be understood here in the sense of 'Ordinary Tale of Magic' using Lüthi's phrase (Lüthi 2), or *Zaubermärchen* using Aarne's term (Aarne 11), as well as in the terms of Tolkien, who also distinguished 'Fairy-Stories' from other marvelous tales (FS 15-20).

The following 'fairy tale profile' was constructed along the central work of Lüthi already mentioned, in combination with the thoughts of the German folk tale scholar Heinz Rölleke and my own ideas—other notions having also left their mark, such as the Vladimir Propp's theories and Kathrin Pöge-Alder's overview.

Fairy tales are shaped in the first place by the way of narration—by oral lore. This also seems to be linked to the quite fixed, modular composition of fairy tales (modular units are after all easier to memorise, in contrast to complex, intertwined structures). The typically linear progression as well as the action-focused entity of fairy tales is connected to the way of dissemination, for a verbally told story must immediately be able to take effect and maintain the attention of the audience. Also the general schematism of 'Tales of Magic' must be mentioned in this context: the flat, black and white, stereotype characters, the frequently used set phrases, but also the use of repetition.

Nevertheless, it must be mentioned that through oral lore fairy tales tend to possess a certain grade of freedom—the narrator is allowed to change or adjust elements, this granting these stories vitality and the ability to adapt to new contexts. In the case of recorded fairy tales this aspect ceases to exist, which is why they have had to bear the overall 'flat rate' accusation of being conservative and regressive. This is unjustified, of course, since they only mirror the conventions of the times in which they were recorded. Orally circulated fairy tales are certainly far more flexible and able to adapt to the current conditions of the given historical period, even though they still carry all the previously sedimented, ancient, socio-cultural layers. Thus, becoming 'literalised' has advantages as well as disadvantages to fairy tales—they gain persistence on one hand, they lose their flexibility and some of their specific traits on the other.

---

ke..., Sagen..., Schwänke..., Schwankmärchen..., Tiermärchen..., Tierschwänke...."
(Grimm/Grimm 232f)

One characteristic typical of everyday, functional texts is also connected to the oral way of dissemination, as fairy tales have no (known) authors or creators, nor is copyright a relevant issue.

The text intention of *Zaubermärchen* is in the first place entertainment. Tolkien writes about "Recovery, Escape, Consolation" (FS 52) in this regard, which is especially interesting in anticipation of the characteristics of games. Summing up Lüthi, we can speak of light, playful fiction with intentional unreal (i.e. wondrous, magical) elements—the main criterion of Tolkien's *On Fairy-stories*, after all he writes: "Faërie itself may perhaps most nearly be translated by Magic" (FS 15). At this juncture moral or didactical aims appear marginally at the most or as mere undertones. The obligatory happy ending—with Tolkien's expression "Eucatastrophe" (FS 62)—of 'Fairy stories' should also be mentioned here.

Due to the oral way of narration and the text intention, fairy tales are highly audience-dependent, which is why they are heavily influenced by historical and social conventions. They are usually narrated over a long time period, which requires adjustments and leads to a very interesting effect: different historical and cultural layers are sedimented in these narrations—Tolkien's very colourfully depicted "Cauldron of Story" (FS 28), in which the soup of narration is boiling and new pieces keep falling (or being thrown) into the stew. This is also the reason for the great difficulties in research trying to determine the origin and age of fairy tales—which is at the most possible in a speculative way. Tolkien even compares the origin of fairy tales to the complexity of human language development (FS 23). Despite these problems the sedimented layers contribute to the longevity, or even timelessness of the genre.

As a result of the already mentioned functional text character—the lack of an author—, the narrator rises to a special position. She/He is the one who is authorised to make modifications—this is even her/his duty in order to ensure the continued existence of this kind of narration. She/He updates contents and requisites, she/he has the power to change details or if she/he is in the mood, even to shift some typical traits—for example moralising in case of Zaubermärchen (even though we stated that moral is not a central concern of these stories). The two most important traits of fairy tales which reach beyond literature are also linked to the person of the narrator: this is on the one hand a performative aspect, for the narrator is actively shaping the story through her/his style of presentation, her/his gestures and facial expressions. On the other hand a participative aspect is also very important, a good narrator is after all sensitive to her/his audience and adapts her/his narration according to the composition, mood, social class and even local affiliation of the audience. The Swedish folklorist Carl Wilhelm Sydow also emphasises the importance of these elements:

> All these questions about the bearers of tale-tradition... are naturally of the greatest weight for a scientific study of the folk-tale; and the results of such study cannot, even by the best of methods, be correct unless they are based on a right knowledge of the life of the folk-tale, and the laws by which it is governed.
>
> (Sydow 214)

Games

Regarding games, the term should be defined in the first place according to its usage in this paper: the characteristics of the so-called 'superior or complicated'—social—games will be the focus of the following description and considerations, the 'simple or primitive' game—e.g. those of children or animals—will be left aside.[4] The traits of games will be characterised based on the work of the psychologist and anthropologist Frederik Jacobus Johannes Buytendijk, the cultural historian Johan Huizinga and the sociologist Roger Caillois, complemented with the thoughts of the German scholars Hans Scheuerl und Eugen Fink.

The complicated game:

• is voluntary and requires leisure time.

The voluntariness of games is an extraordinary important aspect. As soon as any kind of compulsion or constraint appears, there can be no talk of a game any more. The satisfaction of this need for freedom is also often mentioned in the context of games, and seems to be quite plausible: game as a voluntary phenomenon takes place outside of the daily routine in our leisure time. This is valid for all kinds of games. Even if they only last for a short time period, during the game everyday life is replaced by the gaming sphere.

• occupies an own gaming sphere: gaming place, ~ time, ~ rules.

The gaming sphere is crucial for social games. It includes a particular time, which can be predetermined, if the players only have a certain amount of time for the game or for specific elements of the game. If there is no set time limit, the game time is assigned by the time span the player is willing to spend within the gaming sphere. This also contains a gaming place (a kind of 'playground') or world, which can be fictitious or virtual as well, and rules, their bandwidth reaching from very simple and flexible to extremely complex and rigid.

• is outside of the gaming sphere purposeless and unproductive.

The gaming sphere creates solid boundaries for the game. Inside, it can absolutely have certain goals, aims or purposes. It can also include very complicated

---

4   For more detailed explanations of this topic see my dissertation (Gáti 78-88).

processes and even require excessive training—but in order to keep the game character of the activity, these must not cause intended changes in the sphere of everyday life, except for the fulfillment of the basic gaming motivations. So it can be stated that games are outwardly purposeless and unproductive.

• is engaging and serves as entertainment, distraction and relaxing.

Basic gaming motivations are entertainment, distraction from everyday routine and closely linked to this, relaxing or even catharsis. Motivation of games and the validity of different points of view regarding this topic is a controversial and vast issue, which raises discussions again and again with a huge variety of opinions. Relaxing in particular is a matter of dispute, for playing to the point of total exhaustion is absolutely possible. Buytendijk distinguishes different kinds of exhaustion in everyday life: physical, sensory (cognitive) and propulsion fatigue (*Antriebsermüdung*), which arises from the monotony of repeatedly executed tasks (Buytendijk 55ff). Different types of games can serve as a distraction to all these kinds of exhaustion and therefore provide relaxation. If everyday life is physically demanding, mentally challenging games can be refreshing, just as in the case of intellectual work physical games (sports games for example) can provide compensation. But even propulsion fatigue can be relieved by certain game spheres, which lead far away and are disconnected from everyday life and thus able to lift monotony.

• is repeatable.

Repeatability is also an important aspect of games, for they cannot be absolutely unique experiences. After all, if their main purpose is to ensure our entertainment and relaxation, we want to 'use' them over and over again. Games do indeed provide such stimuli, for they are not only suitable for repetition, but are straightforwardly designed to be repeated.

• can get corrupted by reality.

Regarding games the question arises, where the threshold lies at which the game ceases to be a game. Concerning this aspect Caillois' thoughts are very revealing, who stated that games end at the point where reality flows into the gaming sphere (Caillois 52-65). This happens for example, when voluntariness is lost—as a matter of fact constrains are quite unfriendly manifestations of reality. This also happens when motivations, goals, aims and contents of a game leave the gaming sphere and reach into the outside world. Games are of course not completely cut off from their 'real' surroundings—they are influenced from the exterior and they do leave their marks on their outside environment themselves. But if an outward-reaching aspect becomes dominant, the game turns into something else, for example labour or unfair competition or addiction, even psychosis. On the positive side it can become a job or even a piece of art, if the motivations tend in this direction and if the inherent repeatability gains aspects of uniqueness.

Various cultural phenomena contain game traits, nevertheless they can only be referred to as actual games, if their main aspects and aims stay inside of the gaming sphere.
• is interactive and often builds communities.

Game as action and interaction appears more or less subtly in all of the theories mentioned. Buytendijk describes games as movement—of any kind whatsoever—, as "Back and Forth" (*Hin und Her*) (Buytendijk 118). He also points out that games always involve playing with something and this something also playing with us. So he describes nothing else than mutual action between two partners—in other words: interaction. If we play a game, we indeed always play with something or somebody (and this something or somebody is also playing with us). A game without a medium is therefore unimaginable—the term medium being taken very widely, including abstract notions such as thoughts for example.

Caillois' considerations about game as an activity with an 'uncertain' outcome also lead to interaction (Caillois 16). In his opinion the initiative of the player is necessary for the game leading to a result—which implies a definitely active deed inside of the gaming sphere, an interaction with the game world according to the game rules.

This leads to the conclusion that games are always active and interactive. Probably in different grades, but even at the very bottom of the scale they still require a certain amount of activity. In comparison, passivity can be claimed as a valid description for readers of books or viewers of films, if they completely devote themselves to their automated associations during reception (even though not even these subconscious, automated processes represent total passivity). They abandon their relatively passive stance as soon as they start to deal with the subject actively—if they 'work' or 'play' with it, if they interpret it consciously.[5]

The community-building aspect of games is also related to interaction. Huizinga (16-21) and Fink (137) both emphasise this quality which can even exist on two different planes: as a community inside of the gaming sphere and as a community in the reality of the outside world, forming around the central theme of a certain game.

Analogies and Differences

First to the differences: Even considering their contextual circumstances, fairy tales are in the first place narrations, while games are more than that. They are able to include narrations as well (alongside other facets), but primarily they are interactive tasks. As a consequence, the 'classic' communications

---

5   Even though it has to be stated that active interpretation can also not be regarded as interactivity for the premise of mutuality is missing in this process—books or films rarely react.

hierarchy between author and reader (or in the current context: producer and recipient)—which is also changed in fairy tales through the lack of an author—is extremely altered: in games, both sides hold possibilities of composition which can be regarded as (depending on the kind of a given game more or less) equal (Gáti 178-188). In orally spread fairy tales, this power of composition generally rests with the narrator.

The oral lore of fairy tales is another distinction, even though orality can appear in various forms and—with the notion and term of Jay David Bolter und Richard Grusin—remediated on different levels; apart from that it may obtain new dimensions through the changes of the concept of orality itself in electronic space: in the case of digital media it can be spoken—as a continuation of Walter Ong's terminology[6]—of Tertiary Orality (cf. Enders 58-61), one which does not appear as a by-product of a basically literate culture (a kind of archive-culture), but in which writing adopts traits of orality: the speed, the synchronicity of communication (written communication tends to be asynchronous under normal circumstances of analogue media) and also the volatility.

Nevertheless fairy tales share, especially due to their characteristic features which go beyond those of literary narrations, several commonalities with games.

The tendency to repetition is an interesting similarity, for games and fairy tales alike can be and are willingly repeated, because they change with each repetition—games through the various possibilities of composition also on the part of the recipient and through their specific design, fairy tales through the changes made by the narrator(s). But the details of repetitions are also fascinating: games contain so-called trial and error elements, for playful experiments are an inherent part of the interactive process. This is also valid for fairy tales: failed hero incarnations represent the trial and error notions and also possess didactic functions according to the psychologist Bruno Bettelheim.

> Der Tod der Gescheiterten – wie der Tod der Königssöhne, die versuchten, Dornröschen zu wecken, bevor die Zeit dazu reif war, und in den Dornen umkamen – drückt symbolisch aus, daß der Betreffende noch nicht reif genug war, die schwere Aufgabe zu meistern, die er törichterweise (vorzeitig) auf sich genommen hat. Solche Personen müssen erst noch weitere Wachstumserfahrungen sammeln, die ihnen dann die Fähigkeit geben, die Aufgabe zu lösen. Diese Vorläufer des Helden, die im Märchen sterben, sind nichts anderes als frühere, unreife Inkarnationen dieses Helden.
> (Bettelheim 207f)

---

6   For Ong, Primary Orality exists in illiterate cultures, while Secondary Orality appears in literate cultures, created by technical media, e.g. telephone (Ong 136).

Another common thing is that both phenomena serve as entertainment, distraction and relaxation—both are said to have a cathartic effect.

The performative and the participative aspects of fairy tales move them close to interactivity, which is unfolded entirely in games. Their dependence on the audience and on context cause a similar community-building power such as games have—which today certainly has traits of escapism. Escapism here is to be understood in a positive sense, in a way also emphasised by Tolkien, as an escape searching for consolation in the sometimes gloomy world of everyday life, which shackles and holds us captive with all its rules and conventions: "It is part of the essential malady of such days—producing the desire to escape, not indeed from life, but from our present time and self-made misery..." (FS 59). This thought brings the alternative worlds of fairy tales and games very close to each other, for the demarcation from everyday routine is a crucial aspect of games (even up to the possibility of becoming corrupted and ceasing to exist as such).

Thus, these two storytelling media are quite compatible and can benefit from each other. Another interesting aspect regarding fairy tales is not only Tolkien's thought, which stood at the beginning of these considerations, "... what they are, what they have become for us..." (FS 22), but also what they will (possibly) become in the future. I see them definitely in the proximity of games and find the thought enthralling that—especially through the means of electronic media—new ways of storytelling could unfold, which would combine the 'old' phenomenological elements of both forms.

Pen-and-paper-role-playing games represent a first step in this direction, since they already connect both ways and constitute a hybrid storytelling form, containing as they do the special role of the narrator (in this case she/he is called the 'Game Master'), as well as the orality (after all, the actual story develops verbally during the game) of fairy tales, and on the other hand the typical game traits of interactivity and the influence of the recipient (as the story unfolds only through the—verbally communicated—actions of the players).

Bibliography

Aarne, Antti. *Verzeichnis der Märchentypen.* (Folklore Fellows' Communications No. 3), Helsinki: Suomalainen Tiedeakatemia, 1910

Aarne, Antti, and Thompson, Stith. *The types of the folktale. A Classification and Bibliography. Antti Aarne's Verzeichnis der Märchentypen (FFC No. 3) translated and enlarged.* (Folklore Fellows' Communications No. 184, 2. revision), Helsinki: Suomalainen Tiedeakatemia, 1961

Bettelheim, Bruno. *Kinder brauchen Märchen.* München: DTV, 1991[15]

Bolter, Jay David and Grusin, Richard. *Remediation. Understanding New Media.* Cambridge MA: The MIT Press, 1999

Buytendijk, Frederik Jacobus Johannes. *Wesen und Sinn des Spiels – Das Spielen des Menschen und der Tiere als Erscheinungsform der Lebenstriebe.* Berlin: Kurt Wolff Verlag, 1933

Caillois, Roger. *Die Spiele und die Menschen – Maske und Rausch.* Stuttgart: Curt R. Schwab GmbH & Co. Verlagsgesellschaft, 1960

Enders, Angela. *Der Verlust von Schriftlichkeit.* Berlin: Lit Verlag, 2007

Fink, Eugen. *Spiel als Weltsymbol.* Stuttgart: W. Kohlhammer Verlag, 1960

Gáti, Zsuzsa. *Verspielte Erzählungen – Die Veränderung der Erzählung im digitalen Raum.* Wien: Praesens, est. 2016 (Work in Progress; also available at the Library of the University of Vienna: Gáti, Zsuzsa. *Verspielte Erzählungen – Die Veränderung der Erzählung im digitalen Raum.* (Dissertation), Wien: Universität Wien, 2013)

Grimm, Jacob, und Grimm, Wilhelm. *Kinder- und Hausmärchen.* (Hrsg. & Kommentiert von Hans-Jörg Uther), Bd. 3, Darmstadt: Wissenschaftliche Buchgesellschaft, 1996

Huizinga, Johan. *Homo ludens.* Reinbek bei Hamburg: Rohwolt Taschenbuch Verlag, 2006[20]

Lüthi, Max. *Märchen.* Stuttgart: J.B. Metzler, 2004[10]

Ong, Walter Jackson. *Oralität und Literalität.* Opladen: Westdeutscher Verlag, 1987

Pöge-Alder, Kathrin. *Märchenforschung, Theorien, Methoden, Interpretationen.* Tübingen: Narr Verlag, 2011[2]

Propp, Vladimir. *Morphologie des Märchens.* München: Carl Hanser Verlag, 1972

Rölleke, Heinz. *Die Märchen der Brüder Grimm. Eine Einführung.* Stuttgart: Philipp Reclam jun. GmbH & Co. KG, 2004[3]

Scheuerl, Hans. *Theorien des Spiels.* Weinheim/Basel: Beltz Verlag, 1975[10]

Sydow, Carl Wilhelm. "Folk-tale Studies and Philology". In: *Selected Papers on Folklore.* Copenhagen: Rosenkilde and Bagger, 1948, 189-219

Tolkien, John Ronald Reuel. "On Fairy-stories". In: *Tree and Leaf.* London [et al.]: Unwin Hyman Limited, 1988[2], 9-74.

Thompson, Stith. *The Folktale.* New York: The Dryden Press, 1951[2]

Uther, Hans-Jörg. *The Types of International Folktales: A Classification and Bibliography. Based on the system of Antti Aarne and Stith Thompson.* (Folklore Fellows' Communications no. 284-286), Helsinki: Suomalainen Tiedeakatemia, 2004

Macht und Verantwortung.
Von Magie und Wissenschaft, Kunst und Kreativität, Ethik und Moral

Friedhelm Schneidewind (Hemsbach)

›Magie‹ sollte ausschließlich die Maßnahmen eines Magiers bezeichnen. ›Kunst‹ heißt die menschliche Tätigkeit, die beiläufig
(dies ist nicht ihr einziges oder letztes Ziel) auch den sekundären
Glauben erzeugt, und einer Kunst von gleicher Art, nur feiner und
müheloser, können sich auch die Elben bedienen; dies jedenfalls
scheinen unsere Quellen zu besagen. Die stärkere und spezifisch
elbische Kunst aber will ich mangels eines weniger anfechtbaren
Wortes die Verzauberung nennen. Verzauberung erschafft eine
Sekundärwelt, in die sowohl der Schöpfer wie der Betrachter eintreten können, zur Zufriedenheit ihrer Sinne, solange sie darinnen
sind; in ihrer reinen Form aber ist Verzauberung nach Zweck
und Bestreben eine Kunst. Magie bewirkt eine Änderung in der
Primärwelt oder gibt vor, sie zu bewirken. Gleichgültig, wer es
ist, ob Geist oder Sterblicher, dem man nachsagt, daß er sie übe,
bleibt sie von Kunst wie von Verzauberung unterschieden. Magie
ist keine Kunst, sondern eine Technik; was sie will, ist Macht in
dieser Welt, Herrschaft über Dinge und Willenskräfte.

Nach dem Elbenhandwerk, nach Verzauberung trachtet die
Phantasie, und wenn sie gelingt, kommt sie ihm von allen Formen
menschlicher Kunst am nächsten… Dieses Schöpfungsverlangen
wird durch Nachahmungen nur betrogen, ob durch die harmlo-
sen, plumpen Kniffe des menschlichen Dramatikers oder durch
den böswilligen Schwindel des Magiers. In dieser Welt ist es für
den Menschen unstillbar und damit unvergänglich. Wo es nicht
verderbt ist, strebt es nicht nach Trug, Herrschaft und Behexung:
Nach gemeinsamem Reichtum sucht es, nach Gefährten beim
Schaffen und Genießen, nicht nach Sklaven.   (ÜM 108f)[1]

---

1   Im Englischen steht »magic« für Magie und »enchantment« für Verzauberung. In seiner
     Belletristik benutzt Tolkien die Begriffe aber nicht in dieser Form, sondern verwendet
     meistens die Wörter Magie und magisch: »›Magie‹ habe ich nicht in gleichbleibendem Sinne
     verwendet, und die Elbenkönigin Galadriel muß den Hobbits sogar Vorhaltungen machen,
     weil sie dies Wort mißverständlich sowohl für die Machenschaften und Maßnahmen des
     Feindes wie für die der Elben gebrauchen. Ich konnte nicht anders, weil es für die zweite
     Art kein Wort gibt (weil alle menschlichen Geschichten dem gleichen Mißverständnis

Aus dieser und anderen Passagen in *On Fairy-stories* lässt sich Manches über Tolkiens Vorstellung der moralischen Verpflichtung von Kunstschaffenden schließen, aber auch über ihre Gefährlichkeit. Nimmt man zwei fiktionale Texte hinzu, in denen sich Tolkien wenig verschlüsselt über Kreativität, ihre Chancen und Gefahren auslässt – das Gedicht *Muschelklang* (*The Sea-Bell*) und seine letzte Geschichte, *Der Schmied von Großholzingen* (*Smith of Wootton Major*)² –, ist es möglich, ein schlüssiges Bild über Tolkiens Vorstellung von der »richtigen« Anwendung der Phantasie zu gewinnen, sowohl im Hinblick auf andere Menschen und die Gesellschaft wie auf die Zweitschöpfenden selbst. Das lässt sich leicht auch auf Magie und noch allgemeiner auf Machtanwendung übertragen.

In diesem Artikel wird zunächst Tolkiens Vorstellung herausgearbeitet und dargelegt, diese dann verglichen mit modernen Ideen zur Verantwortung von Magie und Wissenschaft und schließlich gezeigt, wie Tolkiens Ideen auch unsere moderne Welt befruchten können.

I   Magie, Macht, Wissenschaft

In dem oben zitierten Text geht es Tolkien um menschliches (Zweit-)Schöpfertum, um die »richtige«, die moralisch verantwortbare Anwendung von Phantasie und Kreativität. Durch seinen Vergleich von Magie, wie er sie definiert, in der Sekundärwelt mit Kunst in unserer, der Primärwelt, vor allem aber auch mit Machtausübung und Machtstreben, lassen sich seine Gedanken über Verantwortung und Moral übertragen auf unsere Welt³, seine Vorstellungen zu Kunst und Phantasie auf den Umgang mit Magie bzw. Wissenschaft. Denn

---

unterliegen). Aber die Elben sind dazu da (in meinen Geschichten), den Unterschied zu demonstrieren. Ihre ›Magie‹ ist Kunst, aber von vielen menschlichen Beschränktheiten entbunden: müheloser, schneller, vollständiger (Ergebnis und Vorstellung in makelloser Entsprechung). Und ihr Zweck ist Kunst und nicht Macht, Zweitschöpfung und nicht Bezwingen und tyrannisches Re-Formieren der Schöpfung« (Brief Nr. 130, 1950, B 194). Und: »Ich fürchte, mit ›Magie‹ und besonders mit dem Gebrauch dieses Wortes bin ich viel zu flüchtig verfahren...« (Brief Nr. 155, 1954, B 263).

2   In meinem Essay »Zwischen Genie und Wahnsinn: Gedanken eines Künstlers über Muschelklang und Elbenstern« habe ich über diese beiden Texte unter dem Aspekt der Kreativität geschrieben.

3   Tolkien hielt zwar den Einsatz von Allegorien in der Fantasy-Literatur für nicht unproblematisch (z.B. ÜM 74 f.) und wehrte sich insbesondere für sein Werk dagegen: »Es gibt keine ›Symbolik‹ oder bewußte Allegorie in meiner Geschichte« (Brief Nr. 203, 1957, B 344) und »Ich verabscheue die Allegorie – die bewußte und beabsichtigte Allegorie« (Brief Nr. 131, 1950, B 193) sowie »Ich halte nichts von der Allegorie (wenn sie mit Recht so genannt wird: die meisten Leser scheinen sie mit Bedeutung oder Anwendbarkeit zu verwechseln)« (Brief Nr. 215, 1959, B 390). Aber er hatte nichts gegen die Anwendbarkeit seiner Texte in der Primärwelt: »Daß es keine Allegorie gibt, heißt natürlich nicht, daß es keine Anwendbarkeit gibt. Die gibt es immer. Und weil ich den Kampf nicht völlig einseitig gemacht habe ... darum nehme ich an, daß meine Geschichte auf heutige Zeiten anwendbar ist.« (Brief Nr. 203, 1957, B 344)

zumindest bei den Elben ist dies nach Tolkien aufs Engste verbunden: »Ihre ›Magie‹ ist Kunst, aber von vielen menschlichen Beschränktheiten entbunden: müheloser, schneller, vollständiger … Und ihr Zweck ist Kunst und nicht Macht, Zweitschöpfung und nicht Bezwingen und tyrannisches Re-Formieren der Schöpfung« (Brief Nr. 130, 1951, B 194).

Tolkien selbst vergleicht Magie und Wissenschaft und betont deren Ähnlichkeit wie auch den ethischen Aspekt:

> Ich gedenke nicht, mich auf eine Diskussion einzulassen, ob ›Magie‹ in irgendeinem Sinne wirklich oder in der Welt möglich ist. Aber ich denke, manche würden sagen, daß für die Zwecke dieser Erzählung eine latente Unterscheidung getroffen wird, eine, die man früher einmal die Unterscheidung zwischen *magia* und *goeteia* nannte. Galadriel spricht von den ›Betrügereien des Feindes‹. Nun gut, aber *magia* konnte für gut (per se) gelten, galt dafür, und *goeteia* für schlecht. Beides ist in dieser Erzählung (per se) weder gut noch schlecht, sondern nur wegen des Motivs, Zwecks oder Gebrauchs. Beide Seiten verwenden beides, aber aus verschiedenen Motiven. Das zutiefst schlechte Motiv ist (in dieser Erzählung, denn sie handelt speziell davon) die Herrschaft über den ›freien‹ Willen anderer.   (Brief Nr. 155, 1954, B 263f)

Im Deutschen werden im allgemeinen Sprachgebrauch die Begriffe Magie, Zauberei und Hexerei in der Regel gleichgesetzt. Im wissenschaftlichen Sinne gibt es aber Unterschiede. Als Magie (abgeleitet von Magier[4]) im weitesten Sinne werden alle Praktiken bezeichnet, die dazu dienen, den Verlauf von Ereignissen auf »übernatürliche« Weise zu beeinflussen. Seit alters her unterscheidet man zwei Hauptformen der Magie: die weiße Magie und die schwarze Magie. Die

---

4   Das Wort Magier kommt vom altiranischen *maga* (Opfergabe, Opferdienst); Herodot bezeichnete so Angehörige einer Sippe des medischen Volkes mit priesterlichen Funktionen und großem politischen Einfluss. Zu ihren Praktiken zählten Astrologie, Dämonologie und Magie, sie galten als Stern- und Traumdeuter sowie Wahrsager. Die Anhänger des persischen Propheten Zarathustra (um 630-550 v. Chr.) waren stets in den Kampf zwischen Gut und Böse verstrickt. Denn Zarathustra lehrte einen Dualismus zwischen Angra Mainju, dem bösen Gott, und Ahura Mazda (»Gott Weisheit«), dem guten Gott. Wahrheit und Lüge durchdringen als Gegenpole das ganze Universum. Alles Gute ist ein Ausfluss von Ahura Mazda und wird verkörpert durch die schöpferische Kraft Spenta Mainyu, den »Heiligen Geist« oder »Erhöhenden Geist«. Alles Böse beruht auf dem Angra Mainyu, dem »bösen Geist« auch Ahriman genannt. Die Menschen müssen sich zwischen Gut und Böse entscheiden. Diese ethisch und dualistisch geprägte Religion wirkte auf zahlreiche Philosophien und Religionen ein, bis hin zu Judentum und Christentum. Noch heute gibt es in Indien, Iran und Pakistan etwa 150.000 Anhänger dieser Religion (in Indien Parsismus genannt), ihre Priester könnten heute als die einzig »echten Magier« betrachtet werden.

weiße, die »gute«, ethisch nicht fragwürdige Magie will den Menschen nutzen, sie dient auch dazu, die Wirkungen der schwarzen Magie zu beheben und ihr entgegenzuwirken. Die schwarze, egoistische, machtorientierte Magie wird meist dazu verwendet, Lebewesen Schaden zuzufügen, zumindest aber dazu, eigene Interessen ohne Rücksicht auf andere durchzusetzen. In Antike und Mittelalter umfasste die schwarze Magie vor allem die Anrufung von Dämonen und anderen bösen Mächten, die weiße Magie beschäftigte sich eher mit Alchemie, Astrologie und Kräuterkunde.

Tolkien verwendet spezielle Termini, die im Deutschen nicht üblich sind. *Goeteia* oder *Goetia* ist ein im Mittelalter entstandenes griechisch-lateinisches Wort und bezeichnet ab dem 16. Jahrhundert die Invocation, die Anrufung von Geistern, Dämonen und Engeln, wie man sie Salomon nachsagte. Im englischen, französischen und italienischen Sprachraum wurde dieser Begriff dann in manchen Kreisen verwendet für die »schwarze Magie« im Gegensatz zu »magia«, der weißen Magie. Darauf bezieht sich Tolkien. Zu seiner Vorstellung von Magie – die hier die Verzauberung einschließt! – erläutert er:

> Ein Unterschied im Gebrauch der ›Magie‹ in dieser Geschichte ist jedenfalls, daß sie nicht durch ›Kunde‹ oder Zaubersprüche zu erlangen ist; sondern sie ist eine eingeborene Kraft, die von Menschen als solchen nicht besessen oder erworben werden kann. Aragorns ›Heilkraft‹ könnte man als ›magisch‹ betrachten, oder wenigstens als eine Mischung von Magie mit pharmazeutischen und ›hypnotischen‹ Verfahren … während A. kein bloßer ›Mensch‹ ist, sondern in entfernter Verwandtschaft eines der ›Kinder Lúthiens‹.   (Brief Nr. 155, 1954, B 264)

Was Tolkien als »Magie« beschreibt, wird in Religionswissenschaft und Ethnologie als Hexerei bezeichnet. Diese wird bei den meisten Völkern als die angeborene oder ererbte Fähigkeit angesehen, durch übernatürliche Kräfte anderen Personen Schaden oder Nutzen zufügen zu können, wobei diese Fähigkeit auch unbewusst eingesetzt werden kann. In vielen Regionen Afrikas unterscheidet man Hexen, denen ihre Fähigkeiten angeboren sind, von Zauberern, die sie durch oft blutige oder schamanistische Initiationen erwerben müssen. Zauberei ist also eher der »wissenschaftliche« oder zumindest technologische Teil der Magie.[5] Unter diesem Aspekt entspricht Tolkiens Vorstellung von Magie eher der klassischen Zauberei:

---

5   Bei Zauberei handelt es sich immer um eine bewusste Aktivität, die mit bestimmten Ritualen und/oder Worten bzw. Anrufungen (Invocationen) und/oder Substanzen verbunden ist, also magische Verfahren, in der Regel mit negativer Wertung und meist mithilfe böser (seltener guter) Mächte. Dies schließt die »Volksmagie« ein, auch »niedere Magie« genannt, und die Magie in betrügerischer Art, das Gaukelspiel. – Das Wort Zauber wird

Die Maßnahmen des Feindes sind keineswegs ausschließlich
goetische Täuschungen, sondern auch ›Magie‹, die in der physi-
schen Welt echte Wirkungen erzielt. Aber seine *magia* dient ihm
dazu, Menschen und Dinge niederzuwalzen, und seine *goeteia*,
einzuschüchtern und zu unterjochen. Die Elben und Gandalf
wenden ihre *magia* an (sparsam): eine *magia*, die echte Resultate
erzielt (z.b. Feuermachen mit einem nassen Reisigbündel), zu
bestimmten guten Zwecken… Der Feind, oder diejenigen, die wie
er geworden sind, setzen auf die ›Maschinerie‹ – mit bösartiger
und destruktiver Wirkung –, weil ›Zauberer‹, wenn ihr Interesse
einmal hauptsächlich auf den Gebrauch der *magia* zugunsten der
eigenen Macht ausgerichtet ist, dies tun würden (tatsächlich tun).
Das Grundmotiv für *magia* … ist Unmittelbarkeit: Geschwin-
digkeit, Verringerung von Mühe und auch Verringerung auf ein
Minimum (oder einen Fluchtpunkt) der Kluft zwischen der Idee
oder dem Wunsch und dem Ergebnis oder Effekt.

(Brief Nr. 155, 1954, B 264)

Hier taucht bei Tolkien die Verwandtschaft von Magie und Technik, von
Zauberei und Wissenschaft auf, wie sie nicht nur historisch gegeben[6], sondern
inzwischen allgemein anerkannt ist, bis hin zur möglichen Verwechselbarkeit.
Da Magie im weitesten Sinne alle Praktiken bezeichnet, die dazu dienen, den
Verlauf von Ereignissen auf übernatürliche Weise zu beeinflussen, kommt es
bei der Frage, ob etwas als Wissenschaft oder als Magie bezeichnet wird, da-

---

abgeleitet vom althochdeutschen *zoubar*, einer Bezeichnung der roten Farbe, mit der die
eingeritzten Runen bestrichen wurden. (Das englische Wort *spell* für Zauberspruch kommt
vom angelsächsischen *speld*, Span, Splitter, das auch das Runentäfelchen bezeichnete.)
Der Begriff Hexe stammt vom althochdeutschen *hagzissa* und bedeutet ein sich in Hecken
oder auf Zäunen aufhaltendes Wesen, er wird oft mit »Zaunreiterin« übersetzt.

6   Magie bzw. Zauberei und Alchemie kann man als legitime Vorläufer der modernen Wissenschaft betrachten. Zahlreiche moderne Wissenschaften stammen aus Vorformen, die heute
als magisch abqualifiziert werden, etwa Physik und Chemie aus der Alchemie und die
Astronomie aus der Astrologie. Astrologische Systeme wurden unabhängig voneinander in
verschiedenen frühen Zivilisationen entwickelt, so in Babylonien um 3000 v. Chr. und in
China ab etwa 2000 v. Chr.; der Ursprung der Alchemie liegt vermutlich im alten Ägypten,
wo man bereits 3000 v. Chr. Gold aus der Erde gewann. Spätestens im Mittelalter wurde
die Alchemie/Alchimie zur geheimen »Schwarzen Kunst«, die sich noch lange neben der
Naturwissenschaft behaupten konnte, ihre Hauptziele waren die Verwandlung unedler
Metalle in Gold (Transmutation) und die Suche nach der Unsterblichkeit, aber auch die
»einfache« Verjüngung oder Erschaffung eines künstlichen Menschen. Noch Paracelsus
behauptete, er könne einen Menschen künstlich erzeugen. Astrologie und Astronomie
galten in Europa bis ins 16. Jh. als ergänzende Wissenschaften, und noch heute sind viele
magische Praktiken bei uns verbreitet, wie Astrologie, Nummerologie oder Weissagung.
Auch ist die zunehmende Anerkennung nicht (natur-)wissenschaftlicher Praktiken zu
beobachten, etwa in der Esoterik- oder New-Age-Bewegung, in der alternativen Medizin,
im Glauben an Schutzengel, Dämonen oder den Teufel.

rauf an, inwieweit man die Mechanismen und Zusammenhänge der Welt als natürlich oder nicht (aner)kennt.

Der Schriftsteller und Wissenschaftler Sir Arthur C. Clarke (1917-2008) formulierte 1973 Clarkes Drittes Gesetz: »Jede weit genug entwickelte Technologie ist von Magie nicht zu unterscheiden« (Clarke 37)[7].

Claudia Knepper betont und erweitert dies 2011 in ihrem Überblick zur Magie: »In der jüngeren Forschung zur Magie besteht weitgehend Einigkeit, dass nicht so einfach zwischen Magie und Religion unterschieden werden kann, ebenso wenig, wie Magie und Wissenschaft sich klar voneinander abgrenzen lassen« (Knepper 355).

Erkenntnis können Menschen – und in der Fantasy auch andere Wesen wie Elben oder Istari – nun mal auf verschiedene Weise gewinnen. Wie man diese nennt oder wie sie gestaltet ist, hängt ab von der Kultur und der Gesellschaft, in der sie gewonnen wird, von den bereits vorhandenen Kenntnissen, aber auch von politischen Entscheidungen, ethischen Regeln und möglicherweise sogar ökonomischen oder Macht-Interessen.[8] Egal, ob Wissenschaft oder Magie, in unserer Welt wie in Mittelerde wurden und werden sie oft missbraucht und häufig bewusst manipulativ eingesetzt zum Erhalt politischer oder religiöser Macht, bei der Erschaffung von Zombies in Haiti wie bei den Herrschern der Maya.[9] Und ebenfalls egal, ob Wissenschaft oder Magie verwendet wird: Die

---

7   In der ersten Auflage von *Profiles of the Future: An Inquiry into the Limits of the Possible* (London: Gollancz 1962) gab es in dem Essay »Hazards of Prophecy: The Failure of Imagination« nur ein »Gesetz«. Eine zweite Regel – »Der einzige Weg, die Grenzen des Möglichen zu finden, ist, ein klein wenig über diese hinaus in das Unmögliche vorzustoßen.« – kam darin zwar schon vor, wurde jedoch erst zwei Jahre später in der französischen Ausgabe als »zweites Gesetz« bezeichnet (*Profil du futur. Un panorama de notre avenir.* Paris: Editions Planète, S. 17). Das veranlasste Clarke, diese Aussage in der ersten Überarbeitung seines Buches (London: Gollancz 1973) selbst als zweites Gesetz zu bezeichnen und das berühmt gewordene dritte Gesetz zu formulieren: »Any sufficiently advanced technology is indistinguishable from magic.« Je nach Ausgabe erscheint dieses Gesetz im Vorwort (MILLENIAL EDITION, London: Indigo Paperback 1999, S. 2) oder in einer Anmerkung, wie im Gollancz-eBook (London 2013, Pos. 3736) und in der deutschen Ausgabe (S. 37). Den dort abschließenden Satz »Nachdem drei Gesetze beiden Isaacs genügt haben – Newton und Asimov –, habe ich beschlossen, mich auch damit zu begnügen« (Clarke 37), findet man in den neueren englischen Ausgaben nicht mehr. In der revidierten Ausgabe von 1973 steht nur: »As three laws were good enough for Newton, I have modestly decided to stop there.« – Clarke ist Autor von *2001: Odyssee im Weltraum*, von ihm stammt u.a. die Idee, geostationäre Satelliten zur technischen Kommunikation zu nutzen. Der geostationäre Orbit wird im englischen Sprachraum auch *Clarke Belt* oder *Clarke Orbit* genannt.

8   Ich beschränke mich hier auf (Er-)Kenntnisse in eher weltlichen Bereichen. Auf der spirituellen und/oder transzendentalen Ebene, in Bereichen wie Mythos und Religion, gibt es weitere Erkenntnismöglichkeiten, die in unserem Zusammenhang nicht interessieren, wie Offenbarungen und mystische Erleuchtungen.

9   Bei den Maya wird deutlich, wieviel Magie mit Wissenschaft zu tun haben kann bzw. mit Herrschaftswissen, also Wissen, das der »gewöhnlichen Bevölkerung« vorenthalten wird: »Die Manipulation der Mayas war besonders raffiniert, weil sie nicht auf faulem Zauber oder persönlichem Charisma oder dem Appell an niedrige Instinkte beruhte,

Verantwortung der Handelnden bleibt ihnen erhalten und sie müssen sich ihr stellen.

Wie Tolkien dies in Bezug auf den Umgang mit Magie und/oder Verzauberung darstellt, wird im Folgenden an einem seiner frühen Gedichte, seiner letzten Geschichte und Mittelerde gezeigt.

II   Elbland, Faërie, Mittelerde: Handeln ohne Gebot

Das Gedicht *Muschelklang*, entstanden 1934 und veröffentlicht 1962, sowie Tolkiens letzte Geschichte, *Der Schmied von Großholzingen* (1967), schildern unterschiedliche (Extrem-)Positionen des Umgangs mit der eigenen schöpferischen Kraft, Phantasie und Kreativität: im Gedicht eine unverantwortliche, eigensinnige, ja egozentrische Haltung, in der Geschichte verantwortliches Handeln, das letztlich zum zufriedenen Leben führt.

Die beiden Protagonisten machen sehr verschiedene Erfahrungen im jeweiligen Andersland und kehren unterschiedlich »heil« zurück. Der Erzähler in »Muschelklang« fühlt sich fremd, ja abgestoßen im »Vergessenen Land«; nach seiner Rückkehr ist er, traumatisiert, auch zu Hause ein Fremder, ein Ausgestoßener. Der Schmied hingegen erlebt zwar Zurückweisungen, aber auch freundliche Aufnahme im Elbland und kann sein heimisches Leben erfolgreich fortführen, wenn auch leicht entfremdet von Gesellschaft und Familie.

Die Begegnung mit *Faërie* – Anderswelt, Elbland, vergessene Lande – habe ich in einem früheren Artikel interpretiert als Konfrontation mit der eigenen Kreativität, der eigenen Schöpfungskraft (Schneidewind, *Genie*). Noch stärker aber ist die Analogie zur Anwendung von Macht, sei es durch Magie oder Wissenschaft/Technik.

---

sondern auf wissenschaftlichen Erkenntnissen. Die Mayas waren glänzende Mathematiker und Astronomen. Und wenn du dich am Himmel auskennst, dann weißt du alles über die Jahreszeiten und das Wetter, dann kannst du den Regen voraussagen oder, was unangenehmer wäre, eine Dürreperiode – kurz, von deinen Voraussagen hängt die landwirtschaftliche Produktion und damit der Lebensstandard deines Volkes ab. Aber: Du enthältst deinen Untertanen wohlweislich die wissenschaftliche Erklärung vor und bietest ihnen statt dessen eine magische Erklärung dafür! Nicht weil du an deinem Hof die Elite der Astronomen beschäftigst, weißt du das alles – sondern weil du ein Sohn der Götter bist. Wer diese Manipulation durchschaute, war ein Störfaktor, der entweder beseitigt oder in die High-Society integriert werden mußte. Auf diese Weise bildete sich mit der Zeit ein Hof aus Intellektuellen, Künstlern und Handwerkern, die unablässig damit beschäftigt waren, den Abstand zwischen dem unwissenden Volk auf der einen und den Göttersöhnen auf der anderen Seite zu vergrößern.« (Linder 96)

Die Handelnden bei Tolkien betreten die »Anderswelt« freiwillig, lassen sich freudig, wie in »Muschelklang«, von einem Schiff davontragen in unbekannte Gefilde oder wandern gerne mit dem Elbenstern ins Elbland. Und dann müssen sie entscheiden, wie sie umgehen mit diesen fremden Einflüssen, wie sie sich verhalten in diesem fremden Land – sie stehen vor ähnlichen Entscheidungen wie Menschen in unserer Welt.

Manche versuchen, sich zum »Herrscher« aufzuschwingen und bekommen keine Antwort: »Warum bleibt ihr alle vor mir, eurem König, stumm?« (ATB 80). Das Erzwingenwollen von Erkenntnis, von Wissen, von Macht scheitert, zumindest, wenn es gegen den Rest des Landes und der Bevölkerung erfolgt, am Ende muss sich der Eindringling gebrochen davonschleichen und kann sogar in seiner Heimat nicht mehr heimisch werden – eine Metapher für den Einzelgänger; in unserer Primärwelt ist das große einsame Genie, das für sich alleine etwas (er)findet, selten geworden. Hier weist Tolkien auf die Gefahren hin, die jemandem drohen, der sich zu zügellos seinen Begierden, seiner Kreativität, seiner Neugier hingibt, andere Menschen und die Gesellschaft vernachlässigt oder gar zu beherrschen wünscht.

Mit dem Schmied zeigt Tolkien uns den richtigen Weg, den einer sich befruchtenden Ko-Existenz zwischen alltäglichem Mensch-Sein und besonderer, in diesem Fall technisch-handwerklicher Begabung und Tätigkeit – modern gesprochen: Der Schmied lebt in perfekter Work-Life-Balance, und das mit sinnvoller, ethisch positiv zu bewertender Tätigkeit.

Eine besondere Begabung, eine gewisse Genialität kann auch in unserer Primärwelt entfremden von Familie und Gesellschaft, wie die Reisen in das fremd-eigene Ich mit dem Elbenstern: wenn die eigene Familie, das persönliche Umfeld nicht verstehen, womit sich die Molekularbiologin oder der Quantenphysiker beruflich beschäftigen, welche moralischen Probleme den Kerntechniker oder die Nanotechnikerin plagen, warum sie mit ihrem Gewissen ringen oder sich Fragen über die Verantwortbarkeit ihrer Tätigkeit stellen. Wichtig ist, wie der Schmied, immer wieder zurückzufinden aus diesem fremden Land in die menschliche Welt, sich die Anbindung zu bewahren an die Gesellschaft, *für* diese und nicht nur *in* ihr zu arbeiten, etwas Sinnvolles mit dem eigenen Können, der eigenen Macht zu leisten.

In Tolkiens Hauptwerk *Der Herr der Ringe* spielt der verantwortliche Umgang mit Wissen und Macht natürlich eine ganz zentrale Rolle. Die ganze Erzählung kann gelesen werden als Parabel über die Korrumpierbarkeit durch absolute Macht.[10]

---

10 Natürlich kannte Tolkien John Lord Actons berühmtes Bonmot von 1887: »Power tends to corrupt, and absolute power corrupts absolutely« (»Macht neigt dazu, zu korrumpieren, und absolute Macht korrumpiert absolut«). Acton kommentierte so in einem Brief (5.4.1887) die 1870 vom 1. Vatikanischen Konzil verkündete Unfehlbarkeit des Papstes

In Mittelerde gilt wie in den beiden oben behandelten Texten: Es gibt keine erkennbare religiöse Grundlage für die Protagonisten. Sie handeln aus eigenem Ermessen, tun das, was sie für gut und richtig halten. Nur dadurch wird es möglich – wie in Kapitel IV –, Tolkiens Gedanken und Empfehlungen für »richtiges«, moralisches Handeln auf die Situation der in Technik und Wissenschaft Tätigen in unserer Welt zu übertragen, von denen viele aus anderen als aus religiös begründeten Moralvorstellungen heraus handeln.

Tolkien hält zur Religion der Elben in Mittelerde fest: »Die Hochelben waren Auswanderer aus dem Segensreich der Götter…, und sie hatten keine ›Religion‹ (oder besser, religiöse Bräuche), denn die hatten in den Händen der Götter gelegen« (Brief Nr. 156, 1954, B 269). Zu anderen Völkern schreibt er: »Daher gibt es keine Tempel oder ›Kirchen‹ bei den ›guten‹ Völkern in dieser ›Welt‹. Sie hatten wenig oder gar keine ›Religion‹ im Sinne eines Kultes… Ich glaube nicht, daß die Hobbits irgendeine Form von Kult oder Anbetung praktizierten« (Brief Nr. 153, 1954, B 256).

Zur religiösen Verfasstheit in Mittelerde haben wir 2005 in unserem Buch *Eine Grammatik der Ethik* ausführlich dargelegt, »dass in Mittelerde weltanschaulich weitestgehend neutrale und damit sehr moderne ethische Überzeugungen vertreten werden…, dass ›Gut‹ und ›Böse‹ hier auch aus areligiöser Sicht charakterisiert werden können…« (Honegger 8). Einige zentrale Thesen von Frank Weinreich seien zur Verdeutlichung hier zitiert:

…ein wichtiger Unterschied zwischen christlicher (oder jeder religiös begründeten) Moral und der in Mittelerde [ist] nicht zu übersehen: Den wichtigsten der ›guten Charaktere‹ fehlt das religiöse Motiv dafür, moralisch zu handeln. Religiös begründete Moral ›funktioniert‹ nur dann, wenn das zugrundeliegende Weltbild geglaubt wird.   (Weinreich 128)
Christliche Moral lässt sich aus der Mythologie Mittelerdes ableiten. Bestand hat jedoch auch in diesem Fall der Einwand, dass einige der wichtigsten Protagonisten moralisch richtig – und sicherlich auch ›christlich richtig‹, aber ohne die spezifische Motivation dazu – handelten, ohne sich des besonderen metaphysischen Hintergrunds von Mittelerde bewusst zu sein, was heißt, dass sie einer universellen, aber areligiösen Moral folgen.   (Weinreich 129f)

Besonders wichtig sind die Hauptprotagonisten, die Hobbits, die freiwillig viel auf sich nehmen. Was ist ihre moralische Grundlage?

---

in Glaubensfragen (»Letter to Archbishop Mandell Creighton«, http://history.hanover.edu/courses/excerpts/165acton.html (eingesehen 31.7.2015)).

…die Hobbits? Die sind nahezu völlig ungebildet in Bezug auf die
Geschichte und Mythologie Mittelerdes… Ohne Kenntnis aber
kann die Anerkenntnis religiös fundierter Ethik nicht erfolgen, und
die von den vier Hobbits so mannigfach demonstrierte Moralität
kann sich nicht darauf beziehen! Wir wissen nicht, woher genau
die moralischen Einstellungen der Hobbits stammen. Überliefert
ist nur, dass… die sichtbaren Handlungen den moralischen Wert
einer Person bestimmen. Das aber ist eine Abwandlung des schon
durch den gesunden Menschenverstand begründbaren Grund-
satzes der Goldenen Regel: ›Was Du nicht willst, das man dir tu,
das füg auch keinem and'ren zu‹, und dieser ist als solcher durch
eine moderne universalisierbare Ethik erklär- und begründbar.
(Weinreich 130)

Weil dies so ist, lassen sich Tolkiens Vorstellungen gut auf unsere Welt übertragen. Deshalb folgt nun eine kurze Darlegung moderner ethischer Positionen
zur Verantwortung der Wissenschaft.

III   Die Weisheit der Vielen

In unserer Primärwelt gibt es viele Grundlagen für ethisches Verhalten, in
diesem Kapitel betrachte ich Haltungen, die von einer prinzipiellen Verantwortung der Einzelnen in einer demokratischen Gesellschaft ausgehen, und lasse
religiöse Motivationen und Einstellungen außer Acht – es genügen die Allgemeine Erklärung der Menschenrechte und der gesunde Menschenverstand.[11]

»Wissenschaft« ist – wie die Magie in Tolkiens Sekundär- und heute in
unserer Primärwelt – ein Teilbereich unseres Lebens, der seine Berechtigung
hat, aber weder Allmacht noch Allzuständigkeit oder Unfehlbarkeit beanspru-
chen kann. »Wissenschaft« ist ein Werkzeug – ein Werkzeug des Erkennens,
das der Mensch geschaffen hat[12] und dessen er sich bedient, um besser (über-)
leben zu können, so wie das Werkzeug »Technologie«. Wissenschaft ist nicht
mehr – aber auch nicht weniger.

Der Vorwurf der »Unwissenschaftlichkeit« hat dann seine Berechtigung,
wenn er erhoben wird gegen Leute, die versuchen, Erkenntnisse als wissen-

---

11 Vgl. Schneidewind, *Wissen.* »Historisch muss betont werden, dass die Menschenrechte nicht
mit, sondern gegen die Kirchen erkämpft wurden… Religionen können die Menschenrechte
also sowohl unterstützen als auch behindern. Zur Begründung der Menschenrechte sind
sie nicht erforderlich« (Tiedemann, *Menschenrechte*).
12 Wenn in diesem Kapitel von Menschen die Rede ist, kann für Mittelerde und andere
phantastische Welten immer auch Elben, Zauberer etc. gedacht werden, so wie »Wissenschaft«, »Technik« und »Technologie« stets auch für Magie stehen.

schaftlich zu »verkaufen« und damit an Reputation zu gewinnen, obwohl sie
es nicht sind. Er hat nichts damit zu tun, dass auf »unwissenschaftliche« Weise
gewonnene Erkenntnisse prinzipiell schlechter oder weniger wert wären, wie
der Wissenschaftstheoretiker Paul Feyerabend 1975 in seinem legendären Werk
»Wider den Methodenzwang« ausführt:

> Wenn man Regentänzen eine Wirkung auf die Natur abspricht, so
> gibt es dafür... weder unmittelbare noch mittelbare Gründe. Das
> Urteil beruht vielmehr auf einer Ideologie, die nie im einzelnen
> formuliert wird, für die man aber das gleiche Gewicht wie für
> wissenschaftliche Theorien beansprucht. Viele ›wissenschaftliche‹
> Argumente‹ gegen Gedanken und Erscheinungen, die die Wissen-
> schaftler nicht mögen, haben diesen ideologischen Charakter...
> (Feyerabend 79)

Erkenntnisse der Physik und der Philosophie, z.B. der evolutionären Erkenntnistheorie, zeigen deutlich, wie unsicher unsere Wahrnehmung der Welt ist
und dass man schon gar nicht von so etwas wie einer »Kausalität« oder auch
nur der Allgemeingültigkeit von Raum und Zeit ausgehen kann... Selbst der
Solipsismus (»Gibt es mich, oder werde ich nur gedacht?«) ist allein durch Logik
nicht widerlegbar.

Die (Natur-)Wissenschaft mit ihrer – mehr oder weniger festgelegten – Metho-
dik, mit ihren Dogmen der Überprüfbarkeit und Wiederholbarkeit kann nur
Aussagen über bestimmte Bereiche unserer Welt machen – dies allerdings mit
großer Wirksamkeit. Gerade in ihrer Beschränkung liegt denn auch ihre Stärke.
Die Aussagen sind innerhalb ihrer Grenzen hinterfrag- und überprüfbar – mit allen Fehlern und Risiken, die menschliches Sein und menschliche Fehlerhaftigkeit
mit sich bringen. »Vernünftige« Wissenschaftler/innen werden nicht versuchen,
mit ihren wissenschaftlichen Methoden an Bereiche heranzugehen, die ihnen
versagt, die einer wissenschaftlichen Betrachtungsweise nicht zugänglich sind.

Aber: Methoden und Techniken, die auf modernen wissenschaftlichen
Erkenntnissen beruhen, sind oft weitaus gefährlicher oder können das Leben
der Menschen, vielleicht der Menschheit, stärker beeinflussen als andere, als
Beispiele mögen die Atomkraft, die Nanotechnologie und die Gentechnologie
genügen. Die Risiken etwa für uns und die Umwelt durch die gentechnische
Veränderung von Pflanzen und Mikroorganismen, die bei deren Freisetzung
und/oder unkontrollierten Mutationen im schlimmsten Fall zur Zerstörung
unserer Biosphäre oder der Vernichtung der Menschheit führen kann, sind
enorm und werden in der Öffentlichkeit gewaltig unterschätzt; die Gefahren der
Nanotechnologie sind noch gar nicht absehbar. Doch umso höher die Risiken
sind, desto größer ist die Verantwortung der daran Beteiligten!

»Durchschnittliche« Naturwissenschaftler/innen sind gar nicht in der Lage, auch nur alle Auswirkungen auf ihrem eigenen Fachgebiet zu überblicken, geschweige denn die soziologischen und ökonomischen Implikationen – und das wäre auch eine absolute Überforderung! Sie können sich nur darauf verlassen, dass ihnen bei der Entscheidung, wie ihre Entdeckungen anzuwenden sind, geholfen wird. Schließlich sind sie ganz normale Menschen mit Schwächen, Vorurteilen, eigensüchtigen Interessen und politischen Überzeugungen.

Man kann natürlich von den in der Wissenschaft Tätigen verlangen, sie sollten, um ethisch verantwortlich entscheiden zu können, über ihren Tellerrand blicken, den Elfenbeinturm verlassen, sich die notwendigen Kenntnisse aneignen etwa in Soziologie und Gesellschaftswissenschaften, wie Helmut Schmidt 2008: »Von der Verantwortung, von der gesellschaftlichen Moral eines Wissenschaftlers her, bleibt die Anstrengung zum umgreifenden Überblick unausweichlich geboten!« Doch damit macht Schmidt es sich zu einfach, und weil er dies weiß, reduziert er seine Forderung am Ende darauf, »sich auch der Anstrengung um einen einordnenden Überblick des eigenen Feldes zum Zweck einer geistigen Ordnung insgesamt nicht zu entziehen« (Schmidt).

Natürlich sollten Wissenschaftler/innen und Forscher/innen sich um gesellschaftliche Kenntnis und Einordnung bemühen, aber dies in der nötigen Tiefe zu tun, ist zu viel verlangt, ist sogar eine Zumutung; ein Naturwissenschaftler weiß wahrscheinlich von Gesellschaftswissenschaften so viel wie ein Germanist von der Quantenphysik! Es tut not, von jener Wissenschaftsgläubigkeit wegzukommen, die meint, weil ein Mensch einen weißen Kittel trüge, sei er kompetent auf allen oder auch nur besonders vielen Gebieten und könne auf diesen sachgerecht und verantwortlich entscheiden.

> Die theoretische Autorität der Wissenschaft ist viel geringer, als angenommen wird. Ihre gesellschaftliche Autorität dagegen ist inzwischen so übermächtig geworden, dass politische Eingriffe notwendig sind, um eine ausgewogene Entwicklung wiederherzustellen… Die Wissenschaft ist nur eines der vielen Mittel, die der Mensch erfunden hat, um mit seiner Umwelt fertig zu werden. Sie ist nicht das einzige, sie ist nicht unfehlbar, und sie ist zu mächtig, zu aufdringlich und zu gefährlich geworden, als dass man sie sich selbst überlassen könnte.   (Feyerabend 304)

Wir müssen uns verabschieden vom Bild des einzelkämpferischen (verantwortlichen) Wissenschaftlers, wie ihn Dürrenmatt 1962 mit seinem »Physiker« Möbius entwirft. Dass die Entscheidungen über die Anwendung von Forschungsergebnissen von der gesamten Gesellschaft getroffen werden müssen, hat schon Dürrenmatt in seinen 21 Anmerkungen zu den *Physikern* gefordert:

16 Der Inhalt der Physik geht die Physiker an, die Auswirkung
alle Menschen.

17 Was alle angeht, können nur alle lösen.

18 Jeder Versuch eines einzelnen, für sich zu lösen, was alle angeht,
muss scheitern.   (Dürrenmatt 79)

Einzelkämpfer können in der heutigen komplexen Gemengelage nur scheitern
– wie Tolkiens »Held« in *Muschelklang*. Die Gesellschaft muss Wege finden,
insgesamt über die Anwendung von Forschungsergebnissen zu entscheiden, sei
es durch gewählte Vertreter/innen, durch Volksabstimmung oder in Gremien.
Doch was können Laien, was können Nichtwissenschaftler/innen beitragen? Viel:

> Vertreter der nicht unmittelbar interessengebundenen Bevölke-
> rung können und sollen keine eigenen wissenschaftlichen oder
> wirtschaftlichen Gesichtspunkte zu diesem Entscheidungsver-
> fahren beisteuern ... Aber sie können und sollen allgemeiner
> Fragen formulieren und andere Interessen berücksichtigen als
> die Gruppen, die diese Entscheidungen der Technikpolitik bisher
> dominiert haben.   (Herbig 233)

Wichtiger als Wissen sind bei allen Entscheidungen immer Menschlichkeit
und Reife – man könnte es auch Weisheit nennen –, so zumindest Feyerabend:

> Eine Demokratie ist eine Versammlung reifer Menschen und nicht
> eine Versammlung von Schafen, geleitet von einer kleinen Gruppe
> von Besserwissern. Reife fällt nicht vom Himmel, Reife muss er-
> worben werden ... Reife ist wichtiger als Spezialwissen, denn sie
> entscheidet über die Anwendung und Tragweite solchen Wissens.
> Ein Wissenschaftler nimmt natürlich an, dass nichts besser ist als
> die Wissenschaft. Die Bürger einer Demokratie können bei einem
> solchen Glauben nicht stehenbleiben. Die Teilnahme von Laien an
> grundlegenden Beschlüssen ist daher selbst dann geboten, wenn sie
> die Erfolgsrate solcher Beschlüsse herabsetzt. Gerade ein solcher
> Effekt ist aber nicht sehr wahrscheinlich...   (Feyerabend 17f)[13]

Und damit hätten wir auch die notwendige Entlastung für die einzelnen in
der Wissenschaft Tätigen. Diese müssen nicht alles wissen und berücksichti-
gen, wenn sie sich darauf verlassen können, dass die demokratische Kontrolle

---

13 Man verwechsle diese Weisheit der Vielen nicht mit der sogenannten Schwarmintelligenz,
    die auf ganz anderen Regeln basiert und nicht selten bedenkliche Ergebnisse zeigt.

funktioniert. Sie können sich konzentrieren auf ihre eigentliche Aufgabe: zu forschen und Erkenntnisse zu sammeln. Denn zunächst, so Carl Friedrich von Weizsäcker, ist »der Wissenschaftler der glückliche Mensch, den die menschliche Gesellschaft dafür bezahlt, dass er sein Leben lang seiner kindlichen Neugier folgt« (Weizsäcker). Ist er damit nicht vergleichbar dem Schmied, der seiner Neugier und seinem Wissensdurst ins Elbland folgt?

Aber da »Macht eine unausweichliche Folge der Erkenntnis ist« (Weizsäcker), gibt es auch Menschen, die der Versuchung erliegen, wie Saruman – und deshalb darf man nicht diesen allein die Entscheidungen überlassen, denn: »Wissenschaftler und Techniker werden ihre Tabus immer so gestalten, dass sie das, was sie machen wollen, auch machen können« (Altner).

IV   Eine Ethik für die Primärwelt

Was den Hobbits (und anderen Charakteren in Tolkiens Büchern) zugemutet wird, unterscheidet sich im Prinzip nicht wesentlich von dem, was manchen Menschen in unserer Welt widerfährt.

Frodos und Sams Weg durch Mordor hat epischen Charakter. Doch wie es zu der Entscheidung, ihn überhaupt erst zu beschreiten, kam, ist wenig übermenschlich. Sich anfangs ängstlich und zweifelnd zu einer Aufgabe zu bekennen, von der man weiß, dass sie schwer zu bewältigen, aber richtig und wichtig ist – obwohl man den Weg nicht weiß –, diese Anforderung kann jedem Menschen begegnen. Und zu all diesen Kämpfen und Entscheidungen, die in viel kleinerem Maßstab auch Bestandteil des realen Lebens sind, hat Tolkien etwas zu sagen. Zu den Problemen von Versuchungen, dem Kampf zwischen Pflicht und Neigung, der Reaktion auf drohende Verzweiflung und Selbstaufgabe und vielem anderen bietet Tolkien überzeugende Lösungen mit und ohne Gottes unterstellten Beistand an (Weinreich 133f).

Damit bewegen sich die Hobbits (und mit ihnen Tolkien) ganz im Bereich der westlichen Tradition: So »funktioniert die Tugendlehre des Aristoteles sehr gut ohne Gott« (Tiedemann, *Moral*) und »die kantische Philosophie ist ein weiterer Beleg dafür, dass ethische Systeme ganz ohne Religion entwickelt werden können« (Tiedemann, *Pflicht*).

Was kann man als moderner Mensch von ihnen, dem Schmied und damit Tolkien lernen? Ethisch modern eingestellt– ob religiös oder areligiös – kämpfen für die eigene Freiheit und die aller Anderen, sich ohne Dominanzgelüste einsetzen für das Wohl der Gesellschaft, Sinnvolles tun unter Einsatz der eigenen besonderen Fähigkeiten, durchhalten und die Hoffnung nicht aufgeben, kurz: »einfach das moralisch Richtige tun und nach getaner Arbeit nach Hause gehen« (Weinreich 125).

Bibliographie

Altner, Günter. »Mit Homunkulus auf Du«. *Kirche in der Zeit* 11/1984

Carpenter, Humphrey, (Hg.) unter Mitwirkung von Christopher Tolkien. *J.R.R. Tolkien. Briefe.* Stuttgart: Klett-Cotta, 22002

Clarke, Arthur C. *Profile der Zukunft. Über die Grenzen des Möglichen.* München: Heyne, 1984

Dürrenmatt, Friedrich. *Die Physiker. Eine Komödie in 2 Akten.* Zürich: Verlag der Arche, 1962

Feyerabend, Paul. *Wider den Methodenzwang. Skizze einer anarchistischen Erkenntnistheorie.* Frankfurt am Main: Suhrkamp, 1976

Herbig, Jost: *Die Gen-Ingenieure. Durch Revolutionierung der Natur zum neuen Menschen?* München/Wien: Hanser, 1978

Honegger, Thomas; Johnston, Andrew James; Schneidewind, Friedhelm; Weinreich, Frank. *Eine Grammatik der Ethik. Die Aktualität der moralischen Dimension in J.R.R. Tolkiens literarischem Werk.* Saarbrücken: Verlag der Villa Fledermaus, 2005

Knepper, Claudia. »Magie«. *EZW-Materialdienst* 9/11. Berlin: Evangelische Zentralstelle für Weltanschauungsfragen, 2011, 354-358

Linder, Leo G. *Unter der Jaguarsonne. Begegnungen mit der Geschichte der Maya.* Düsseldorf: ECON, 1995

Schmidt, Helmut: »Gesellschaftliche Moral des Wissenschaftlers. Sind Wissenschaftler verantwortlich für die gesellschaftlichen Folgen ihres Handelns?«. *DIE ZEIT*, 28.02.2008

Schneidewind, Friedhelm: »Zwischen Genie und Wahnsinn. Gedanken eines Künstlers über Muschelklang und Elbenstern«. *Hither Shore 4* (2007): 199-201

---. »Wissen und Verantwortung. Mögliche Positionen zur Wissenschaft zwischen Freiheit und Verantwortung«. *Lern-Bögen Deutsch 2011.* Abi-Boxen für das Zentralabitur: Wissensspeicher. Hannover: Brinkmann.Meyhöfer, 2011, 40-54

Tiedemann, Markus. »Kann es eine Moral ohne Gott geben?« *Brief 20.* Frankfurter Rundschau, 25.06.2015

---. »Wie wäre es mit der Pflicht der Vernunft?« *Brief 22.* Frankfurter Rundschau, 10.07.2015

---. »Gibt es Menschenrechte ohne Religionen?« *Brief 23.* Frankfurter Rundschau, 16.07.2015 (Alle Briefe: www.fr-online.de/fanatiker (eingesehen am 31.07.2015))

Tolkien, John Ronald Reuel. »Über Märchen«. *Gute Drachen sind rar. Drei Aufsätze.* Stuttgart: Klett-Cotta, 1983, 51-141

---. »Muschelklang«. *Die Abenteuer des Tom Bombadil und andere Gedichte aus dem Roten Buch.* Stuttgart: Klett-Cotta, 1984, 78-83

---. »Der Schmied von Großholzingen«. *Fabelhafte Geschichten.* Stuttgart: Klett-Cotta, 1975, 85-126

Weinreich, Frank. »Ethos in Arda. Charakteristika der Ethik in Mittelerde«. *Eine Grammatik der Ethik. Die Aktualität der moralischen Dimension in J.R.R. Tolkiens literarischem Werk.* Saarbrücken: Verlag der Villa Fledermaus, 2005, 111-134

Weizsäcker, Carl Friedrich von. »Fortschritt ohne Bewußtseinserweiterung wäre eine Katastrophe. Gespräch mit Dieter Mersch anläßlich Weizsäckers 80. Geburtstags«. *Frankfurter Rundschau*, 25.06.1992

Gems all turn into Flowers: *On Fairy-stories* und die romantische Poetologie

Julian Tim Morton Eilmann (Jülich)

W ill man wie im vorliegenden Artikel romantische Aspekte in Tolkiens Werk untersuchen, dann ist es als erster Schritt unerlässlich, zwischen der Romantik als historischer Epoche (ca. 1795-1848) und einer daraus resultierenden romantischen Geisteshaltung zu unterscheiden. Dass Tolkien aufgrund seiner Lebensdaten (1892-1973) nicht der romantischen Ära angehören kann, versteht sich von selbst. Stattdessen kann es nur darum gehen, Aspekte der romantischen Geisteshaltung bei ihm nachzuweisen. Der Begriff Geisteshaltung soll deutlich machen, dass es sich hierbei um bestimmte philosophisch-poetologische Positionen handelt, die für die Epoche der Romantik charakteristisch sind, sich aber auch bei späteren Dichtern finden lassen, beispielsweise bei Tolkien. Diese Definition der romantischen Geisteshaltung verwendet auch Rüdiger Safranski:

> Die Romantik ist eine Epoche. Das Romantische eine Geistes-
> haltung, die nicht auf eine Epoche beschränkt ist. Sie hat in der
> Epoche der Romantik ihren vollkommenen Ausdruck gefunden,
> ist aber nicht darauf beschränkt; das Romantische gibt es bis
> heute.   (Safranski 12)

Der Kern des Romantischen

D as wesentliche Charakteristikum der romantischen Geisteshaltung ist die Hinwendung zum Wunderbaren, Unendlichen und Transzendenten und so bezeichnet Safranski diese Hinwendung zum Transzendenten auch zutreffend als die »romantische Metaphysik des Unendlichen« (ebd. 179). In zahlreichen Texten diskutieren die Romantiker diese Transzendenzsehnsucht des modernen Menschen. Hierbei konstruieren Autoren wie August Wilhelm Schlegel, Heinrich Heine oder Jean Paul einen Gegensatz zwischen einem harmonischen, diesseitsbezogenem Altertum und einer in Folge des Christentums entstandenen neueren Zeit, die sich dem Unendlichen zuwendet, weil die innere Einheit verloren gegangen sei. So argumentiert Schlegel:

> Das griechische Ideal der Menschheit war vollkommene Eintracht
> und Ebenmaß aller Kräfte, natürliche Harmonie. Die Neueren
> hingegen sind zum Bewußtsein der inneren Entzweiung gekom-
> men, welche ein solches Ideal unmöglich macht; daher ist das
> Streben ihrer Poesie, diese beiden Welten, zwischen denen wir
> uns geteilt fühlen, die geistige und die sinnliche, miteinander

auszusöhnen und unauflöslich zu verschmelzen. Die sinnlichen
Eindrücke sollen durch ihr geheimnisvolles Bündnis mit höheren
Gefühlen gleichsam geheiligt werden, der Geist hingegen will seine
Ahnung oder unnennbare Anschauungen vom Unendlichen in
der sinnlichen Erscheinung sinnbildlich niederlegen.

(Schlegel 26)

In diesen Worten finden wir bereits den Kern des Romantischen: Die An-
schauung des Unendlichen in den sinnlichen Erscheinung. Der Romantiker
empfindet eine Trennung zwischen sich und der Welt, die ihm zwar als schön
und geheimnisvoll erscheint, aber auch als Gegenüber und demnach fremd
empfunden wird. Zu einem beglückenden Einheitsgefühl kommt es nicht.
Dies ist Schlegels »Bewußtsein der inneren Entzweiung«. Hieraus resultiert
der romantische Wunsch, den transzendenten Gehalt der Dinge – eben das
Unendliche – wieder erfahrbar zu machen. Diese romantische Sehnsucht drückt
beispielsweise Ludwig Uhland aus:

Das Unendliche umgibt den Menschen, das Geheimnis der Gott-
heit und der Welt. Was er selbst war, ist und sein wird, ist ihm
verhüllt. Süß und fruchtbar sind diese Geheimnisse… Der Geist
des Menschen aber, wohl fühlend, daß er nie das Unendliche in
voller Klarheit in sich auffassen wird und müde des unbestimm-
ten Verlangens, knüpft bald seine Sehnsucht an irdische Bilder,
in denen ihm doch ein Blick des Überirdischen aufzudämmern
scheint… Dies Ahnen des Unendlichen in den Anschauungen ist
das Romantische.   (Uhland 8)

Uhlands letzter Satz entspricht nahezu wortgleich Schlegels Formulierung:
Der Romantiker spürt, dass ihn etwas umgibt, das sein rein materielles Dasein
übersteigt, und er richtet seinen Blick auf die ihn umgebende Welt und findet
dort Reflexionen des Transzendenten. Die bekannteste Formulierung dieser
romantischen Perspektive hat der Dichter Joseph v. Eichendorff in seinem Gedicht »Wünschelrute« gefunden. Dort spricht er von einem schlafenden Lied,
das mithilfe der Poesie, also durch das magische Zauberwort des Poeten, zum
Klingen gebracht werden solle:

Schläft ein Lied in allen Dingen
Die da träumen fort und fort
Und die Welt hebt an zu singen
Triffst du nur das Zauberwort.   (Eichendorff 112)

In diesem Worten kristallisiert sich die Sehnsucht des Romantikers, das ihn
umgebende Geheimnis der Welt zu enträtseln, hinter den Schleier der vermeint-

lich prosaischen Wirklichkeit zu schauen und den Zauber, der den Menschen umgibt, freizusetzen. Die einflussreichste Definition der romantischen Poetologie hat Novalis mit seinem Prinzip der Romantisierung gefunden:

> Die Welt muss romantisiert werden. So findet man den ursprüng-
> lichen Sinn wieder. Romantisieren ist nichts als eine qualitative
> Potenzierung. Das niedere Selbst wird mit einem bessern Selbst
> in dieser Operation identifiziert... Indem ich dem Gemeinen einen
> hohen Sinn, dem Gewöhnlichen ein geheimnisvolles Ansehen,
> dem Bekannten die Würde des Unbekannten, dem Endlichen
> einen unendlichen Schein gebe, so romantisiere ich es.
> (Novalis, *Schriften* 545)

Romantisieren bedeutet demnach, die Welt neu und eben romantisch zu sehen. All dem, was der Mensch im Alltag als gegeben und bekannt vorausgesetzt hat, soll »die Würde des Unbekannten« zurückgegeben werden. Das Bekannte wird wieder geheimnisvoll und kann für den Romantiker zum Mittel der Offenbarung werden. Entscheidend ist demnach eine Veränderung des Betrachterblicks und wir werden sehen, dass es genau dies ist, was Tolkien in *On Fairy-stories* als eine der zentralen Qualitäten des Märchens definiert. Aus dem bisher Gesagten wird auch ersichtlich, weshalb das Phantastische in der Literatur der Romantik eine solch große Rolle spielt, denn das Phantastische kann dem Romantiker ideal als Vehikel dazu dienen, dem Leser die Augen für das Wunderbare zu öffnen. Dies ist auch der Grund, weshalb den Romantikern das Märchen als die romantischste Gattung überhaupt erschien. Richten wir nach dieser Erörterung der romantischen Poetologie unseren Blick auf Tolkien Vorlesung und überprüfen, welche romantischen Spuren wir darin wiederfinden können.

Romantische Aspekte in *On Fairy-stories*

Die Schlüsselstellung von Tolkiens Märchenvorlesung für das Verständnis seines literarischen Schaffens ist ein Konsens der Tolkien-Forschung, wie nicht zuletzt Flieger und Anderson in der Einleitung zur erweiterten Neuausgabe von *On Fairy-stories* betonen. Dort bezeichnen sie die Vorlesung als »landmark in its field«, als »definitive discussion of fairy-stories and their relationship to myth and fantasy« sowie als »the most explicit analysis of his [Tolkien's] own art«. Auch heißt es: »Tolkiens defining study of and the centrepoint in his thinking about the genre, as well as being the theoretical basis for his fiction« (alle FS 9). Nimmt man diese Aussagen ernst, dann müssen wir auch die romantischen Elemente in *On Fairy-stories* ernst nehmen und können diese berechtigterweise als wichtigen Schlüssel für Tolkiens Werk verstehen.

In seiner Vorlesung diskutiert Tolkien den Ursprung und den Zweck des Märchens und leistet damit, wie wir sehen werden, in letzter Konsequenz eine selbstbewusste und starke Verteidigung der romantischen Phantasie gegenüber dem Vorwurf des Eskapismus, Infantilismus und der literarischen Irrelevanz. Wenn Tolkien zu Beginn seiner Vorlesung behauptet, dass die Phantasie eine natürliche menschliche Aktivität darstelle (»Fantasy is a natural human activity«, FS 55), und seine Ausführung mit der fundamentalen Behauptung beschließt, dass die Phantasie ein regelrechtes Menschenrecht darstelle (»Fantasy remains a human right«, FS 56), dann klingt dies wie ein Echo der romantischen Vorstellung der Phantasie als einer essentiellen *conditio humana*. Im Einklang mit der romantischen Weltanschauung empört sich Tolkien denn auch gegen die Abwertung der Phantasie. Viel zu oft werde diese mit geistiger Umnachtung in Verbindung gebracht. Tolkien behauptet, dass vielmehr das Gegenteil der Fall ist:

> That the images [of imagination] are of things not in the primary world (if that indeed is possible) is a virtue, not a vice. Fantasy (in this sense) is, I think, not a lower but a higher form of Art, indeed the most nearly pure form, and so (when achieved) the most potent. (FS 48)

Wir haben es hier also mit einem Autor zu tun, der selbstbewusst behauptet, dass die Phantastik die reinste Kunstform mit dem größten schöpferischen Potential darstellt. Tolkiens Versuch einer Verteidigung der Phantasie und literarischen Phantastik reiht sich so ein in den Kampf der romantischen Bewegung bei ihrer Propagierung von romantischer – und dies bedeutet phantastischer – Kunst gegenüber dem prosaischen Geist des Philisters. Folgerichtig beginnt Tolkien seine Vorlesung mit einer näheren Bestimmung der Phantasie. So betont er, dass zwischen der Imagination und der künstlerischen Realisierung kein grundsätzlicher Unterschied bestehe, sondern nur ein gradueller:

> The perception of the image, the grasp of its implications, and the control, which are necessary to a successful expression, may vary in vividness and strength: but this is a difference of degree in Imagination, not a difference in kind. (FS 47)

Deutlicher wird Tolkien in seinem Manuskript zur Vorlesung, wo er den Weg von der geistigen Vorstellung zu deren tatsächlicher Realisierung genauer erläutert:

> The achievement of that expression which gives, or seems to give, the inner consistency of reality… is indeed another thing: the gift of Art, the link between Imagination and the final marvel of

> Sub-creation: Fantasy, the showing forth, that power which the
> Elves have to the highest degree.   (FS 111)

Die Kunst bildet so das Verbindungsstück zwischen Vorstellung und Realität,
wobei Tolkien die Kunst hier durch Großschrift besonders hervorhebt und sie
als Gabe bezeichnet, die das Wunder der Zweitschöpfung hervorbringe. Im
romantischen Diskurs verwundert uns die bedeutsame Rolle der Kunst bei
der Zweitschöpfung selbstverständlich nicht. Interessant ist, dass Tolkien das
menschliche Kunstschaffen mit der elbischen Bezauberung gleichsetzt. Die
Kunst unterscheidet sich von dieser quasi-magischen Begabung demnach nur
dem Grade nach, nicht jedoch grundsätzlich. Hier klingt bereits an, dass den
Elben von Tolkien jene Attribute zugesprochen werden, die auch den romantischen Dichtermagier mit seiner (zweit)schöpferischen Allmacht auszeichnen.

So erhoben die Romantiker die Phantasie zum höchsten Maßstab ihres
künstlerischen Schaffens und verstanden diese als eine wesentliche Form der
menschlichen Wahrnehmung. Die Phantasie ist das Mittel zur beabsichtigten
Romantisierung der Welt. Auch Tolkien versteht die Phantastik nicht als etwas,
was der reinen Unterhaltung dient oder was primär für Kinder gedacht sei. Im
Gegenteil, die Phantasie wird von Tolkien – philosophisch und poetologisch
– als eine sehr ernste Form der geistigen Betätigung verstanden, die es dem
Menschen ermöglicht, die Dinge mit neuen Augen zu sehen und einen frischen
Blick auf die oftmals übersehenen Wunder der Wirklichkeit zu erlangen. Dies
ist es, was Tolkien als *Recovery* bezeichnet:

> We should look at green again, and be startled anew (but not
> blinded) by blue and yellow and red. We should meet the cen-
> taur and the dragon, and then perhaps suddenly behold, like the
> ancient shepherds, sheep, and dogs, and horses—and wolves. This
> recovery fairy-stories help us to make. In that sense only a taste
> for them may make us, or keep us, childish. Recovery (which
> includes return and renewal of health) is a re-gaining—regaining
> of a clear view.   (FS 67)

Tolkien erklärt weiterhin, dass, obwohl wir durch diese neue Sichtweise die
Dinge nicht so sehen, wie sie eigentlich sind (»as they are«, FS 58), der Mensch
seine Sichtweise dennoch radikal verändern müsse, um die selbstverschuldete
Trübheit seiner Wahrnehmung zu überwinden: »We need, in any case, to clean
our windows; so that the things seen clearly may be freed from the drab blur
of triteness or familiarity—from possessiveness« (ebd.). Die Phantastik verhilft
dem Menschen also bei der Überwindung des getrübten Alltagsblicks, der ein
trügerisches Gefühl der Vertrautheit vermittelt. Es ist in diesem Zusammenhang kein Zufall, dass Tolkien den Begriff der Besitzgier (»possessiveness«) für

diese menschliche Hybris verwendet, von den Dingen verbal Besitz zu ergreifen. Raffsüchtige Habgier ist in Tolkiens Mythologie eine stark negativ konnotierte Sünde, die von Figuren wie Smaug, Gollum und Sauron verkörpert wird:

> Of all faces those of our *familiares* are the... most difficult really to see with fresh attention, perceiving their likeness and unlikeness: that they are faces, and yet unique faces. This triteness is really the penalty of ›appropriation‹: the things that are trite, or (in a bad sense) familiar, are the things that we have appropriated, legally or mentally. We say we know them. They have become like the things which once attracted us by their glitter, or their colour, or their shape, and we laid hands on them, and then locked them in our hoard, acquired them, and acquiring ceased to look at them.   (FS 67)

Dinge oder Lebewesen, die möglicherweise ehemals als schön oder wundervoll wahrgenommen wurden, werden durch den Fluch der Aneignung alltäglich und verlieren so die Kraft zu bezaubern. Die Analogie zwischen Tolkiens Phantastik-Theorie und der romantischen Poetologie ist offenkundig: Wenn Novalis das wesentliche romantische Anliegen darin sieht, den Dingen »die Würde des Unbekannten« zurückzugeben und so den Zauber des Unbekannten zurückzugewinnen (s.o.), dann stimmt dies mit Tolkiens Forderung überein, die fatale Vertrautheit in der Begegnung mit der Welt zu überwinden.

Auch Tolkiens Freund C.S. Lewis betont in seiner Rezension des *Herrn der Ringe*, dass die eigentliche Qualität der Phantastik in eben dieser romantischen Blicköffnung für das Wunder im Alltäglichen bestehe:

> The value of the myth is that it takes all the things we know and restores to them the rich significance which has been hidden by ›the veil of familiarity‹... If you are tired of the real landscape look at it in a mirror. By putting bread, gold, horse, apple, or the very roads into a myth, we do not retreat from reality: *we rediscover it.*   (Lewis, *Dethronement* 14f)

Die Begegnung mit dem Wunderbaren entwerte auch nicht das Alltägliche, im Gegenteil: »He [the reader] does not despise real woods because he has read of enchanted woods; the reading makes all real woods a little enchanted« (zit. n. Duriez 266). Tolkiens und Lewis' Forderung, die Alltagswelt durch die Phantastik aus der Tristesse des Alltäglichen zu erlösen, stimmen nicht nur mit Novalis überein, sondern auch mit Gedanken des englischen Romantikers Percy Bysshe Shelly aus seinem einflussreichem poetologischen Essay »Defence of Poetry« (1821):

> It [poetry] transmutes all that it touches, and… it strips the
> veil of familiarity from the world, and lays bare the naked and
> sleeping beauty, which is the spirit of its forms… It reproduces
> the common universe of which we are portions and percipients,
> and it purges from our inward sight the film of familiarity which
> obscures from us the wonder of our being.   (Shelly 372)

Wenn es bei Shelly heißt, dass die Poesie die Dinge verwandelt und so den
Schleier der Vertrautheit von den Dingen nimmt, dann sind dies Aussagen, die
Tolkien in gleicher Weise auch in *On Fairy-stories* formuliert haben könnte.
Hinzu kommt, dass sich in den erst 2008 publizierten Vorlesungsmanuskripten
eine für unsere Fragestellung höchst interessante Passage findet, in der Tolkien
einen Versuch unternimmt, Faërie[1] zu definieren, und dabei Formulierungen
wählt, die deutlich mit der romantischen Weltanschauung übereinstimmen:

> What is this <u>faierie</u>? It reposes in a view that the normal world,
> tangible visible audible, is only an appearance. Behind it is *a
> reservoir of power* which is manifested in these forms. If we can
> drive a well down to this reservoir we shall tap a power that can
> not only change the visible forms of things already existent, but
> spout up with a boundless wealth forms of things never before
> known—potential but unrealized.   (FS 270)

Faërie beruht demnach auf der Annahme, dass die Sinnenwelt lediglich eine
Erscheinung darstellt, hinter der eine machtvolle Kraft verborgen ist, die in den
Dingen manifest ist. Tolkien stimmt hier mit der romantischen Grundauffassung
überein, dass in der sichtbaren Welt eine poetische Energie verborgen ist, die
nur darauf wartet, vom romantischen Individuum geweckt zu werden (*Schläft
ein Lied in allen Dingen*). Tolkien benutzt dafür die Metapher eines Brunnens,
den man graben müsse, um an das ersehnte »reservoir of power« zu gelangen.
Das romantische Bild der Urkraft als Quelle, aus der geschöpft werden soll,
um den Fluss der Poesie freizusetzen, klingt hier an. Und übereinstimmend
damit heißt es auch an anderer Stelle im Manuskript zur Vorlesung: »As such
it [Faërie] draws from the well of creative energy that a man feels to lie behind
the visible world« (FS 260). Wenn man diese verborgene Kraft freisetze, dann
wird jener romantisch-alchemistische Verwandlungsprozess freigesetzt, bei
dem die bekannten Dinge ihre Form verändern und noch dazu ungeahnte neue
Schöpfungen hervortreten.

---

1   Tolkien benutzt für den Begriff Faery/Faërie in seinen Schriften unterschiedliche Schreib-
weisen. Im Folgenden soll die Schreibweise Faërie verwendet werden.

Neben dem Bild der Quelle, die zum Sprudeln gebracht werden soll, benutzt Tolkien eine besonders schöne Metapher für die transzendierende Wirkung, die die phantastische – oder eben romantische – Kunst auf die menschliche Wahrnehmung hat:

> Creative fantasy… may open your hoard and let all the locked things fly away like cage-birds. The gems all turn into flowers or flames, and you will be warned that all you had (or knew) was dangerous and potent, not really effectively chained, free and wild; no more yours than they were you. (FS 68)

Juwelen, die sich in Blumen und Flammen verwandeln: Die Phantastik öffnet die geistige Schatztruhe, in der all jene Dinge gefangen waren, die der Mensch sich untertan gemacht hat. Shellys Metapher des gelüfteten Schleiers kommt uns hier nicht ohne Grund in den Sinn. Wird die Schatztruhe geöffnet bzw. der Schleier gehoben, dann wird die Welt wieder wundersam – und gleichsam gefährlich. Die literarische Gattung, die für Tolkien diese Wirkung beim Leser am besten erreicht, ist eine dezidiert romantische Gattung, das Märchen: »It was in fairy-stories that I first divined the potency of the words, and the wonder of the things, such as stone, and wood, and iron; tree and grass; house and fire; bread and wine« (FS 60). Im Märchen können demnach die Wunder der Welt erfahren werden und Dinge, die uns ansonsten wohl vertraut erscheinen, sind wieder schillernd, reizvoll – eben magisch.

Angesichts der bisherigen Ergebnisse überrascht es uns nicht, dass Tolkiens immense Wertschätzung des Märchens und seiner bezaubernden Wirkung ebenfalls auf die Epoche der Romantik zurückgeht, waren es doch die Romantiker Ende des 18. und zu Beginn des frühen 19. Jahrhunderts, die sich für die Etablierung des Märchens als einer eigenständigen literarischen Gattung in der Moderne einsetzten. So preisen die Romantiker das Märchen als das ideale Vehikel zum Transport ihrer Ideen: »Das Märchen ist gleichsam der Kanon der Poesie, alles Poetische muß märchenhaft sein« (Novalis zit. n. Korff 278). Mit anderen Worten: Märchen und das Romantische sind regelrecht identisch, wie Hermann Korff zutreffend feststellt: »[Novalis] sagt damit nichts anderes, als daß alle wahre Dichtung romantisch sein muß. Denn märchenhaft und romantisch sind dasselbe« (ebd.). Das Märchen konnte in der Romantik solche Popularität erlangen, weil das Märchen den Leser besser als andere literarische Gattungen dazu befähigt, das Wunder zu erkennen. So heißt es bei Novalis:

> Es liegt nur an der Schwäche unsrer Organe, und der Selbstberührung, daß wir uns nicht in einer Feenwelt erblicken. Alle Mährchen sind nur Träume von jener heymathlichen Welt, die überall und nirgends ist. (Novalis 353)

Es ist in letzter Konsequenz demnach das Ziel des romantischen Künstlers, die alltägliche Welt in ihren Urzustand zu verwandeln – eben ein Märchen. Hierzu erneut Korff:

> Was erstrebt sie [die romantische Kunst] anders, als die natürliche Welt in das Märchen zu verwandeln, das sie nach ihrem letzten Wesen ist – mag der Verstand ihren technischen Zusammenhang auch noch so sehr im einzelnen erklären? Sie *ist* ein Märchen! Und eine Dichtung ist umso wahrer je unabhängiger sie sich von den Schranken des »natürlichen Weltbildes« macht.   (Korff 279)

Während also das Märchen als die romantische Gattung par excellence gelten kann, ist es das Reich der Faërie, das im Märchen zum Leben erwacht und das einen bezaubernden Effekt auf den Leser haben kann. Für Tolkien ist die Natur der Faërie das wesentliche Element des Märchens:

> Faërie contains many things besides elves and fays, and besides dwarfs, witches, trolls, giants, or dragons; it holds the seas, the sun, the moon, the sky; and the earth, and all things that are in it: tree and bird, water and stone, wine and bread, and ourselves, mortal men, when we are enchanted.   (FS 9)

Auch hier wird die romantische Perspektive deutlich: Nicht allein Phantasiegestalten wie Elben, Zwerge oder Drachen tragen dazu bei, dass der Leser in Faërie verzaubert wird. Auch das vermeintlich Alltägliche – See, Himmel, Erde – erscheint im Feenland als Mittel der übernatürlichen Offenbarung. Im fiktionalen Kontext des Märchens wird die Macht zur Bezauberung oftmals mit phantastischen nichtmenschlichen Wesen wie Feen und Elben assoziiert. Tolkien hat in seinem Werk viele Szenen gestaltet, in denen sterbliche Charaktere durch die Präsenz von Elben oder anderen übernatürlichen Geschöpfen bezaubert werden. Die Fähigkeit von Figuren wie Tom Bombadil, Goldbeere oder den Elben lebhafte Vorstellungen im Geistes des Rezipienten hervorzurufen, stellt so eine literarische Manifestation von Tolkiens poetologischem Konzept der Zweitschöpfung dar.

Insbesondere eine Szene innerhalb von Tolkiens Werk sticht als Beispiel der elbischen Verzauberung heraus: Im *Herrn der Ringe* erfährt Frodo während seines Aufenthalts in Bruchtal die Macht Bezauberung, indem er vollständig von Musik und Gesang verzaubert wird und dabei eine visionäre Schau erlebt und eine den Alltag transzendierende Erfahrung macht.

> At first the beauty of the melodies and the interwoven words in elven-tongues, even though he understood them little, held him in

a spell, as soon as he began to attend to them. Almost it seemed
that the words took shape, and visions of far lands and bright
things that he had never yet imagined opened out before him;
and the firelit hall became like a golden mist above seas of foam
that sighed upon the margins of the world. Then the enchantment
became more dreamlike, until he felt that an endless river of
swelling gold and silver was flowing over him, too multitudinous
for its pattern to be comprehended; it became part of the throb-
ing air about him, and it drenched and drowned him. Swiftly he
sank under its shining weight into a deep realm of sleep. There
he wandered long in a dream of music that turned into running
water.   (LotR 227)

Im romantischen Sinne macht Frodo hier eine Erfahrung, die das Alltäglich
übersteigt und damit im wahrsten Sinne als transzendent bezeichnet werden
kann. Letztendlich verwandelt die elbische Bezauberung sein Dasein in diesem
Moment in ein poetisch-romantisches Märchen. Tolkien würde sagen: Solange
die Bezauberung andauert, wandelt Frodo in Faërie. Und eben dieses Reich
der Faërie ist es auch, das uns in Bezug auf die romantische Weltanschauung
besonders interessiert, handelt es sich hierbei doch in letzter Konsequenz um
den in der literarischen Fiktion wahrgewonnen romantischen Traum: Faërie
ist die Welt im romantisierten Zustand. Dies bedeutet, dass in diesem Zustand
die – vom modernen Individuum als schmerzlich empfundenen – Grenzen
zwischen Subjekt und Objekt aufgehoben werden und die Welt wieder in
einem Zauberzustand erstrahlt. In einem solchen romantisierten Kosmos ist
das Unbelebte belebte und ein Tier, Baum oder etwas anderes kann sich dem
Menschen mitteilen und ihn bezaubern:

Essentially Faierie is the land of Wonder. There all things are
strange, or else seen in a strange light which reveal them (even
when their shape is unchanged) as things ominous and significant.
In that land a tree is a Tree, and its roots may run throughout the
earth, and its fall affects the stars. It is enchanted… It means, …
that when we cross the borders of Faerie we believe… that scientific, measureable, facts and 'laws' of the relationships of things are
only one aspect of the world. There is a world where things are
not so: where will[,] imagination and desire are directly effective.
                                                 (FS 256f)

Der Baum, der in der alltäglichen Wahrnehmung nur eine einfache Pflanze ist,
wird plötzlich wieder wundersam und als bedeutsames Einzelwesen von Tolkien
entsprechend durch Großschrift sprachlich ›geadelt‹. Tolkien lässt hier einen

urromantischen Gedanken anklingen: Der moderne naturwissenschaftliche Blick auf die Dinge schöpft das Potential der Wirklichkeit nicht aus. Es gibt noch andere Schichten der Realität, die durch eine rein rationalistische Lesart verborgen bleiben, und diese verborgene Welt ist eine romantisierte Welt, »where will, imagination and desire are directy effective«. Diese romantisierte Welt ist gleichsam wieder zu demjenigen poetischen Märchen geworden, das sie in romantischer Lesart immer schon gewesen ist, wird die Grenze zwischen Phantasie und deren Realisierung im Reich der Faërie doch mühelos überwunden. Hier muss der Künstler keinerlei Abstriche bei der Verwirklichung seiner geistigen Visionen haben, er kann sie mithilfe seines Willens ohne Abstriche ins Sein treten lassen. Eben dies ist es, was Tolkien als Faërie bezeichnet und was für ihn der Kern des Märchens ist:

> [F]aierie is a state of being in which Will can directly cause things aesthetically imagined or desired to be, present and sensible; and the very immediacy of the operation enhances the quality of the product: beautiful things produced by faierie is commensurable with the desire, and therefore wholly satisfying without satiety.
>
> (ebd.)

Der Romantiker Novalis hofft darauf, dass der Dichter zuletzt ein Zauberer werden möge, der die Realität allein mit der Kraft seines Willens gestaltet. Eben dies ist in der Faërie erreicht. Demnach ist es nur folgerichtig, wenn Tolkien zusammenfassend schreibt: »Essentially Faierie is the land of Wonder« (ebd.). Wir könnten auch sagen, Faierie ist das Land des Realität gewordenen romantischen Wunders.

Im Märchen erfüllt sich dieser romantische Traum für den nach Faërie gelangten Sterblichen jedoch gewöhnlich nur zeitweise und zumeist mit wenig angenehmen Folgen, wie z.B. einem veränderten Verstreichen der Zeit in Feenland, was bei der Rückkehr in die Alltagswelt oftmals den Verlust der gealterten oder verstorbenen Geliebten bedeutet. Eben dieser Kontrast zwischen dem sich nach dem Wunder sehnenden Menschen und dem im Feenland nie dauerhaft erreichbaren Glück ist für Tolkien charakteristisch für das Märchen als Gattung. So handelt das Märchen von Sterblichen, die sich in die bezaubernde aber gefahrvolle Welt der Faërie begeben: »Most of our fairy-stories are about the men who [are] in the presence of the marvellous« (FS 266). Während der sterbliche Protagonist im Märchen als Repräsentant des Lesers fungieren kann, der stellvertretend für ihn verzaubert wird, fungieren die Elben als Personifikation der menschlichen Schöpferkraft. Als Wesen, die mit magischen Kräften ausgestattet sind, ist es ihnen vergönnt, mühelos schöpferisch tätig zu werden. Ihre Kunst ist für den Menschen demnach Zauberei:

> Elves are in the main… an effort of human creative impulse: they
> are made by man in his own image and likeness, but freed from
> those limitations which he feels most to press upon him. They are
> immortal, and their will is directly effective for the achievements
> of their imagination and desire.   (FS 258f)

Als Wesen, die von den schöpferischen Einschränkungen des Menschen befreit
sind, verkörpern die Elben den romantischen Dichtermagier, der in Analogie
zum göttlichen Schöpfer die Produkte seiner Phantasie Realität werden lässt.
Wichtig ist weiterhin: Diese romantisierte Welt in der literarischen Fiktion zu
erleben, stellt laut Tolkien ein Urbedürfnis des Menschen dar, d. h. die Befriedi-
gung dieses transzendenten Bedürfnisses durch das Märchen ist eine ethisch
›gute‹, also für den Menschen wertvolle Erfahrung:

> The magic of Faërie is not an end in itself, its virtue is in its
> operations: among these are *the satisfaction of certain primordial
> human desires*. One of these desires is to survey the depths of
> space and time. Another is (as will be seen) to hold communion
> with other living things.   (FS 34f)

Das Märchen erfüllt also eine existentielle Sehnsucht nach harmonischer Einheit
des Individuums mit den Geschöpfen bzw. der Schöpfung allgemein und Faërie
erlaubt die Überwindung der menschlichen Hybris, wonach die Welt gekannt,
besessen und kontrolliert sei. Weiterhin gewinnt der Mensch eine gesteigerte
Wahrnehmung für andere Daseinssphären jenseits des Profanen. Diese Sehnsucht nach Gemeinschaft mit anderen nichtmenschlichen Lebewesen lässt sich
im Rahmen des romantischen Diskurses verorten, wie bereits angeklungen ist.
So ist der Wunsch nach »communion with other living things« Ausdruck des
romantischen Wunsches, die Grenzen der profanen Welt zu überwinden und
die Trennung zwischen Subjekt und Objekt aufzuheben. Eben dies ist es, was
im Novalis-Roman *Heinrich von Ofterdingen als* romantischer Parasieszustand
geschildert wird:

> Ich hörte einst von alten Zeiten reden; wie da die Tiere und Bäume
> und Felsen mit den Menschen gesprochen hätten. Mit ist gerade so,
> als wollten sie allaugenblicklich anfangen, und als könnte ich ihnen
> ansehen, was sie mir sagen wollten.   (Novalis, *Heinrich* 231)

Auch dies ist eine Beschreibung der Welt im romantisierten Zustand, in der eben
jenes menschliche Bedürfnis befriedigt ist, was Tolkien als charakteristisch für
das Märchen ansieht: der harmonische Austausch zwischen allen Lebewesen.

Dass Tolkien bei diesem menschlichen Bedürfnis den Begriff »communion« verwendet, der durch das christliche Abendmahl stark religiös konnotiert ist, ist im romantischen Kontext nicht verwunderlich. Die romantische Sehnsucht nach Transzendenzerfahrungen spiegelt sich auch in dieser Gemeinschaft zwischen Mensch und natürlicher Umwelt wieder. Auch diese »communion« stellt eine im Vergleich zum Alltag gesteigerte Erfahrungsform dar, der man demnach durchaus transzendierende Qualitäten zusprechen kann.

Poetische Bezauberung in Lothlórien

N eben Frodos transzendierendem Musiktraum in Bruchtal (s.o.) soll eine weitere Szene aus dem *Herrn der Ringe* herangezogen werden, die verdeutlicht, wie tief Tolkiens Konzept der poetischen Bezauberung in der romantischen Poetologie verwurzelt ist und in seinen Roman Eingang gefunden hat. Gemeint ist jene kurze Passage, in der Frodos Reaktion auf die ihn umgebende Natur in Lothlórien geschildert wird. Es wird deutlich, dass es sich hierbei nicht allein um die Wahrnehmung einer ästhetischen Landschaft handelt:

> Frodo stood awhile still lost in wonder. It seemed to him that he had stepped through a high window that looked on a vanished world. A light was upon it for which his language had no name. All that he saw was shapely, but the shapes seemed at once clear cut, as if they had been first conceived and drawn at the uncovering of his eyes, and ancient as if they had endured for ever. He saw no colour but those he knew, gold and white and blue and green, but they were fresh and poignant, as if he had at that moment first perceived them and made for them names new and wonderful.
>
> (LotR 341)

In dieser Passage schildert Tolkien höchst anschaulich die transzendente Erfahrung eines Sterblichen beim Eintritt ins Land der Faërie. Vor dem Hintergrund der romantischen Poetologie wird ersichtlich, dass hier der Effekt einer romantischen Wahrnehmung geschildert wird: Frodo erfährt am eigenen Leib die Wirkung der Romantisierung. Zuallererst erfahren wir, dass Frodo eine Erfahrung macht, die man in der Alltagssprache als ›magisch‹ bezeichnen würde, verfällt Frodo doch in ein andächtiges Staunen angesichts des Wunders: »Frodo stood awhile still lost in wonder.« Der Erzähler erläutert, dass dieses Gefühl des Staunens nicht primär das Resultat einer malerischen Landschaft darstellt, sondern dass es vielmehr Frodos Wahrnehmungsweise ist, die sich in Lothlórien radikal verändert hat. In den Augen des Hobbits tritt alles klar und deutlich hervor: »All that he saw was shapely.« Die Neuheit dieser gesteigerten

Sichtweise wird dadurch unterstrichen, dass Frodos Sprache keinen Begriff für das hat, was vor ihm liegt: »A light was upon it for which his language had no name.« Dies ist paradox, da Frodo sich mit Dingen konfrontiert sieht, die ihm grundsätzlich bekannt sind und für die ihm die ›richtigen‹ Worte fehlen: »He saw no colour but those he knew, gold and white and blue and green, but they were fresh and poignant.«

Diese Beschreibung der elbischen Bezauberung stimmt mit Tolkiens Schilderung der besonderen Fähigkeit des Märchens überein, das dazu befähige, die alltägliche Welt mit neuen Augen zu sehen: »We should look at green again, and be startled anew (but not blinded) by blue and yellow and red... Recovery... is a re-gaining—regaining of a clear view« (FS 67). Wir sehen, dass Tolkien in dieser Szene eines seiner höchsten poetologischen Ziele verwirklicht hat (»regaining of a clear view«). Gleichzeitig erlebt der im sprachlosen Staunen versunkene Frodo die Welt im romantisierten Zustand, in der die Dinge die Würde des Unbekannten zurückerlangt haben und das Individuum verzaubern. Frodos erwachtes Bewusstsein für den Zauber der Sinnenwelt äußert sich u.a. daran, dass er bei der Berührung eines Baumes nicht nur dessen äußere Rindenstruktur – d.h. dessen ästhetische Qualität – mit großer Klarheit erfasst, sondern dass er das Leben des Baumes selbst unmittelbar zu fühlen glaubt:

> [Frodo] laid his hand upon the tree...: never before had he been so suddenly and so keenly aware of the feel and texture of a tree's skin and of the life within it. He felt a delight in wood and the touch of it, neither as forester nor as carpenter; it was the delight of the living tree itself.   (LotR 342)

Frodo erscheint in Lothlórien wie ein Romantiker im Feenland, der mit den Lebewesen auf eine unmittelbare Weise in Kontakt tritt. Ihn interessiert die ästhetisch-metaphysischen Qualitäten eines Dings (Gestalt, Charakter, Lebendigkeit): »it was the delight of the living tree itself«. Interessanterweise ist es ein Baum, an dem Frodo seine tiefsichtigen Einsichten in die Sinnenwelt gewinnt. Tolkiens Metapher, das Grün neu sehen, wird hier zur literarischen Szene. Stellvertretend für den Leser wird Frodo also »Recovery« zuteil, die Wiedergewinnung des klaren Blicks. Darüber hinaus wird ein weiteres Grundbedürfnis des Menschen befriedigt: Die »communion with other living things«. Im romantisierten Zustand der »magic of Faërie« wird auch dies möglich und das Individuum erfährt das Wunder anderer Lebewesen.

Auch Sam kann sich dem Wunder Lothlóriens von Beginn an nicht entziehen, was angesichts seiner ausgeprägten Elbensehnsucht nicht verwundert. So sieht Frodo sein eigenes Staunen in Sams Augen gespiegelt:

Sam was now standing beside him, looking round with a puzzled expression, and rubbing his eyes as if he was not sure that he was awake. »I feel like I was inside a song, if you take my meaning.«

(ebd.)

Das Staunen und die Unmöglichkeit zwischen Traum und Wachen unterscheiden zu können, sind typische Anhaltspunkte dafür, dass auch Sam eine romantische Transzendenzerfahrung macht. Diesem Erlebnis versucht Sam auch an anderer Stelle Ausdruck zu verleihen:

»If there's any magic about, it's right down deep, where I can't lay my hands on it, in a manner of speaking.« »You can see and feel it everywhere,« said Frodo.   (ebd. 351)

Man kann es nicht mit der Hand berühren, aber das Wunder ist überall zugegen, tief in der Sinnenwelt selbst. Ein Romantiker wie Eichendorf würde sagen, dass es das schlafende Lied ist, das sich an romantischen Orten wie Lothlórien offenbart.

Zusammenfassung

V ergegenwärtigen wir uns die Ergebnisse unserer Analyse von *On Fairy-stories* im Kontext der romantischen Poetologie, dann wird deutlich, dass sich zahlreiche Gemeinsamkeiten aufzeigen lassen, die darauf hindeuten, dass Tolkien in der Tradition der romantischen Geisteshaltung steht. Tolkien selbst scheint seine Verwurzelung in der Romantik in seinem Essay zu *Smith of Wooton Major* zusammengefasst zu haben, wenn er das Reich der Faërie folgendermaßen definiert:

Faery might be said indeed to represent Imagination…: esthetic: exploratory and receptive; and artistic; inventive, dynamic, (sub) creative. This compound—of awareness of a limitless world outside our domestic parish; a love (in ruth and admiration) for the things in it; and a desire for wonder, marvels, both perceived and conceived—this ›Faery‹ is as necessary for the health and complete functioning of the Human as is sunlight for physical life.

(SWM 144-5)

Faërie repräsentiert die Phantasie selbst, d.h. jene poetische Urkraft, auf die sich die Romantik fokussierte. Wenn Faërie demnach das Herz des Märchens ausmacht und gleichzeitig die Phantasie verkörpert, dann handelt es sich hierbei um die Realisierung des romantischen Traums einer Welt im romantisierten Zustand. Hinzu kommt jenes urromatische Bewusstsein für das Unendliche innerhalb des Endlichen, was im Märchen zur Geltung kommt. Weiterhin erweckt Faërie laut Tolkien ein bewunderndes Staunen vor den Dingen und gleichzeitig eine Liebe für die Schöpfung: Tolkiens »Recovery«, das Wiedergewinnen des klaren Blicks. Zuletzt bedingt und weckt Faërie eine allgemeine Sehnsucht nach dem Wunderbaren (»a desire for wonder, marvels, both perceived and conceived«), was wir als Kern des Romantischen kennengelernt haben. Von größter Wichtigkeit ist weiterhin die heilsame Wirkung, die Tolkien dieser romantischen Phantastik allgemein zuschreibt. So sei Faërie für den Menschen lebensnotwendig, eine Aussage, die auch von Vertretern der historischen Romantik getätigt werden könnte: Die Phantasie, die im Märchen Gestalt annimmt, ist heilsam, und ein unabdingbares Menschenrecht.

Ernst genommen – und wir können sicher sein, dass Tolkien seine poetologischen Maximen und sein literarisches Schaffen sehr ernst nahm – handelt es sich hierbei um eine entschieden romantische Konzeption und um eine vehemente Verteidigung der schöpferischen Phantasie in der ersten Hälfte des 20. Jahrhunderts. Aus diesem Grund und angesichts von Tolkiens immenser Popularität erscheint es legitim und sinnvoll, Tolkien als einen der einflussreichsten Autoren der romantischen Weltanschauung zu verstehen.

Bibliographie

Duriez, Colin. *The A-Z of C.S. Lewis: An Encyclopaedia of His Life, Thought, and Writings.* Oxford: Lion Hudson, 2013

Eichendorff, Joseph v. *Ausgewählte Werke.* Hg. Paul Stapf. Wiesbaden: Emil Vollmer o.J.

Korff, Hermann August. *Geist der Goethezeit. Versuch einer ideellen Entwicklung der klassisch-romantischen Literaturgeschichte.* Bd. 3. Leipzig: Koehler & Amelang, 1959

Lewis, C.S. »The Dethronement of Power«. *Understanding* The Lord of the Rings. *The Best of Tolkien Criticism.* Hg. Neil D. Isaacs & Rose A. Zimbardo. Boston/New York: Houghton Mifflin, 2004

Novalis. *Heinrich von Ofterdingen und andere dichterische Schriften.* Hg. Rolf Tomann. Köln: Könemann, 1996

---. *Schriften. Die Werke Friedrich von Hardenbergs.* Hg. Paul Kluckhohn & Richard Samuel. Bd. 2. Stuttgart: Kohlhammer, 1960

Safranski, Rüdiger. *Romantik. Eine deutsche Affäre.* Frankfurt a M.: Fischer, 2009

Schlegel, August Wilhelm. *Vorlesungen über dramatische Kunst und Literatur.* 1. Teil. Hg. Edgar Lohner. (*August Wilhelm Schlegel. Kritische Schriften und Briefe*) Stuttgart u. A.: Kohlhammer, 1966

Shelly, Percy Bysshe. »Defence of Poetry«. *Classic Writings on Poetry.* Hg. William Harmon. New York: Columbia University Press, 2003, 351-374

Tolkien, J.R.R. *On Fairy-stories. Expanded Edition, with Commentary and Notes.* Hg. Verlyn Flieger & Douglas A. Anderson. London: HarperCollins, 2008

---. *Smith of Wootton Major.* Extended Edition. Hg. Verlyn Flieger. London: HarperCollins, 2005

---. *The Lord of the Rings.* London: HarperCollins, 1995

Uhland, Ludwig. »Über das Romantische«. *Ludwig Uhland Werke.* Hg. Hans-Rüdiger Schwab. Bd. 2. Frankfurt, 1983

Tolkiens *On Fairy-stories*: Eine Poetik der Poetologie

Markus Gut (Zürich)

D er vorliegende Beitrag soll die in Tolkiens Vorlesung *On Fairy-stories* behandelten Kategorien der *sub-creation* und der *Secondary World* unter dem Gesichtspunkt der Poetologie betrachten. Unter dem in der Literaturwissenschaft unterschiedlich verwendeten Begriff ›Poetologie‹ verstehe ich Folgendes: 1. eine innerhalb eines literarischen Textes verhandelte, *implizite* Poetik; 2. direkt von Altgriechisch *poesis*, »Tun, Herstellung, Schöpfung« (Kluge 710) abgeleitet, die innerhalb eines Textes implizit stattfindende Thematisierung der Konstituenten eines mittels Sprachzeichen erschaffenen Textes.

Der vorliegende Aufsatz ist gegliedert in eine Einleitung, die von *On Fairy-stories* ausgehend in die These mündet, Tolkiens Vorlesung entwerfe, nebst vielem anderen, auch eine Poetik der Poetologie; in einen Hauptteil, der dieser These zuerst anhand des Anfangs des *Silmarillions* nachgeht und sie danach in Beziehung zum in *On Fairy-stories* verwendeten Begriff *true* setzt; und in einen Schlussteil, in dem die vorangegangenen Ergebnisse zusammengefasst respektive weitergedacht werden.

Sub-creation innerhalb der *Secondary World*: eine Frage der Glaubwürdigkeit

O n *Fairy-stories* lässt sich u.a. als eine Poetik lesen, welche die Erschaffung (resp. *sub-creation*) einer *Secondary World* als *das* zentrale Verfahren bei der Verfassung einer *fairy story* bezeichnet:

> But in such ›fantasy‹, as it is called, new form is made; Faërie begins; Man becomes a sub-creator.   (FS 122)

Gleichzeitig fordert Tolkien von einer solchen *Secondary World*, dass sie für den aus der *Primary World* stammenden Leser ›in sich‹ schlüssig, realistisch, ihren eigenen Gesetzen treu erscheint. Aus den vielen Textstellen in *On Fairy-stories*, die dies behandeln, sei hier der Anfang des zweiten Abschnitts des Epilogs zitiert:

> Probably every writer making a Secondary World, a fantasy, every sub-creator, wishes in some measure to be a real maker, or hopes that he is drawing on reality: hopes that the peculiar quality of

this Secondary World (if not all the details) are derived from Reality, or are flowing into it. If he indeed achieves a quality that can fairly be described by the dictionary definition: 'inner consistency of reality', it is difficult to conceive how this can be, if the work does not in some way partake of reality.   (FS 77)

Daraus lassen sich folgende zwei Punkte ableiten:

1. In einer glaubhaften, aus der ›Realität‹ abgeleiteten *Secondary World* müsste also konsequenterweise auch das Bedürfnis zur *(sub-)creation selbst* in irgendeiner Form thematisiert werden. Oder anders formuliert: Eine *fairy story*, in deren *Secondary World* kein Bedürfnis zu erschaffen und damit auch kein Bedürfnis nach *fairy stories* existiert, ist nicht glaubwürdig. Es sei denn, es gilt als spezifisches inneres Gesetz einer *Secondary World*, dass dieses Bedürfnis in ihr nicht auftritt, was aber letztlich auch nur wieder eine Thematisierung ex negativo wäre.

2. (und mit 1. verbunden) Eine *glaubhafte Secondary World* muss die zentrale Frage unserer *Primary World* reflektieren (!), nämlich die Frage nach Anfang und Ende der Welt und des Lebens darin. Anfang und Ende einer *Secondary World* sind jedoch mindestens gedoppelt: Denn neben einem z.B. mythologisch erklärten Schöpfungsakt auf der Ebene *innerhalb* der *Secondary World* sind Anfang und Ende der *Secondary World* als Text, als literarische Schöpfung (zumindest zunächst) auf der Ebene der *Primary World* zu suchen. Denn Anfang und Ende einer jeden schriftlich fixierten *Secondary World* ›liegen‹ letztlich im literarischen Schreibakt, aber ebenso in ihrer potentiell unendlich oft neu zu beginnenden Lektüre oder in der Relation zu anderen ›Welten‹, zu sekundären wie auch zur primären.[1] Jene Doppelung wiederum birgt die Möglichkeit, die beiden Ebenen des Erschaffens resp. von Anfang und Ende einer *Secondary World* in ein Ähnlichkeitsverhältnis zu setzen, was mich zu folgender These führt: Jede *Secondary World*, die Tolkiens *Poetik* in *On Fairy-stories* folgt, birgt das *Potential*, literarische Schöpfung *poetologisch* zu thematisieren.

---

1 Es tun sich also semiotisch-epistemologische Fragen auf, die in einer *Secondary World* poetologisch thematisiert werden können. Umgekehrt heißt dies, dass die in der *Primary World* stattfindende wissenschaftliche Auseinandersetzung mit solchen Fragen von einer vermehrten Auseinandersetzung mit *Secondary Worlds* nur profitieren könnte.

Sub-creation innerhalb der Secondary World am Beispiel des Anfangs des Silmarillions

A nhand des ›Anfangs‹ von Tolkiens *Silmarillion* sollen nun die oben dargelegten Überlegungen exemplarisch veranschaulicht werden:

AINULINDALË

The Music of the Ainur

> There was Eru, the One, who in Arda is called Ilúvatar; and he made first the Ainur, the Holy Ones, that were the offspring of his thought, and they were with him before aught else was made.   (S 3)

Nach den oben dargelegten Überlegungen zu *sub-creation* und zu Anfang und Ende einer *Secondary World* erstaunt es nicht, dass die Überschriften und der erste Satz des ersten ›Kapitels‹ des *Silmarillions* gleich sieben Ebenen des Erschaffens – im Folgenden nach Großbuchstaben strukturiert – umfassen:

Drei Ebenen des Erschaffens finden sich bereits im ersten Wort AINULINDALË:

A) Eine[2] Ebene ist der materiale Schreibakt selbst, das Zu-Papier-Bringen von Tinte.[3] Das dadurch Erschaffene – die Anordnung von Tinte auf Papier – ist semiologisch betrachtet nur insofern zeichenhaft, als dass es indexikalisch/metonymisch auf den Akt des Erschaffens und – in einer weiteren metonymischen Übertragungsbewegung – auf den Schöpfer dieses Papier-Tinte-Arrangements verweist. Die Materialität der Schrift ist bei Tolkien – und in der drucktechnischen Gestaltung seiner Werke – nicht unbedeutend und manifestiert sich u.a. in verschiedenen, von ihm erschaffenen Systemen von Schriftzeichen. Diese, so könnte man folgern, thematisieren als fiktive, neu-erschaffene Schriftzeichen immer auch das schöpferische Potential von Schrift und Schriftzeichen im Allgemeinen.

B) Der materiale Schöpfungsakt A) zielt in unserem Fall nicht auf eine willkürliche Verteilung von Tinte auf Papier, sondern auf das Erschaffen von Schriftzeichen. Jaques Derrida hat bereits ausführlich auf das Paradox dieser Ebene des Erschaffens von Zeichen aufmerksam gemacht: Die Möglichkeit der Iteration

---

2   Gemeint ist hier ausdrücklich nicht *die Eine*, ebenso wenig *die Erste*.
3   Nach Austin wären Ebene A-C Unterbereiche der Lokution; nämlich Ebene A der *phonetic act* (hier aber eher ›graphetic act‹; B der *phatic act*; C in gewissem Sinne der *rhetic act*.

von Zeichen im Zuge ihrer Lektüre ist zugleich Bedingung und Folge des Er-schaffens von Zeichen (vgl. Derrida). Zeichen sind einerseits also immer bereits schon Nach-Schöpfungen, in einem gewissen Sinne *sub-creations,* während sie andererseits im Zuge ihres Nach-Erschaffens, im Zuge ihres Gelesen-Werdens überhaupt erst zu Zeichen werden. Man könnte also so weit gehen und sagen, dass in semiologischer Hinsicht sprachliche *sub-creation* durch Zeichen konsti-tuiert wird, während wiederum Zeichen in einem Modus konstituiert werden, der an *sub-creation* erinnert. Hinzu kommt, dass aus erkenntnistheoretischer Sicht die begriffliche Wahrnehmung und Einordnung der Welt von eben diesen Begriffen bestimmt und geformt wird. Selbst wenn wir eine Position außerhalb des Systems der Sprache einnehmen könnten (Trance, Meditation etc. zielen darauf ab), könnten wir anschließend doch nicht begrifflich darüber nachden-ken oder das Erfahrene begrifflich ›abbilden‹. So hat denn auch mit Blick auf Tolkien bereits Verlyn Flieger festgestellt:

> To hear or to speak a strange language is to be for the moment in a new and strange world created by different perception and a different imaginative vision. This is, in effect, a Secondary World which we see refracted through the prism of language. We may say, then, that *any* world in which man lives and speaks is sub-created by him, and is thus a Secondary World…
>
> (Flieger, *Light* 86f)

C) Nun handelt es sich bei AINULINDALË zwar um Schriftzeichen des lateini-schen Alphabets, jedoch repräsentieren sie Lautfolgen, die keiner Sprache entsprechen, die dem Leser außerhalb von Tolkiens Welt bekannt ist. Damit finden wir uns auf der Ebene der Fiktion wieder: Als vermeintlicher Metatext, als bloße, nicht der ›eigentlichen‹ Fiktion angehörige Überschrift verweist das Wort AINULINDALË – und bereits der Titel *The Silmarillion* – auf den im ersten Satz folgenden ›Anfang‹ jener ›eigentlichen‹ Fiktion. Nun ist aber AINULINDALË als Wort-Schöpfung einer künstlich erschaffenen, fiktiven Elben-Sprache offensichtlich bereits *Teil* der Fiktion. Im Vergleich zu anderen Autoren – im deutschsprachigen Raum etwa Jean Paul oder E.T.A. Hoffmann – geht Tolkien (oder zumindest sein letztlich mit-erschaffender Herausgeber Christopher Tolkien) mit seiner Überschrift jedoch noch einen Schritt weiter, indem bei ihm nicht nur der Kontext der Autor- und Herausgeberschaft sowie der Buchproduktion, sondern auch bereits die *Sprache* selbst der Fiktion angehört.

Unterebene C.1) »The Music of the Ainur« stellt als Übersetzung der elbi-schen Überschrift eine Nach-Schöpfung des künstlich erschaffenen Wortes AINULINDALË dar. Auch auf dieses bei Tolkien immer wieder auftauchende Element (ein Großteil des *Silmarillions* kommt ja beispielsweise als eine Übertragung elbischer Überlieferung ins Westron daher[4]) kann hier leider nicht näher eingegangen werden.

D) Im Folgenden wird von Tolkien – und dem Leser – Kapitel für Kapitel ein *fiktives* Universum erschaffen, das in der *fiktiven* Elben-Sprache Quenya den Namen *Ea* trägt.

E) Die Beschreibung jenes fiktiven Universums reicht so weit, dass sie bereits im ersten Satz die *fiktive* Geschichte der *Erschaffung* jenes Universums entfaltet.

Es lassen sich also vorerst fünf Haupt-Ebenen des Erschaffens (A bis E) festhalten. Dabei legt insbesondere Ebene E die Grundlage für eine poetologische Thematisierung des Erschaffens *von* Worten und des Erschaffens *mittels* Worten, also für die Thematisierung der Ebenen A bis D. Innerhalb der Ebene E kommt auch zum Tragen, was Uwe Wirth als Metapher für eine »mediale Aufpfropfung« beschrieben und »als Grundlage poetologischer Programme« (Wirth 421) bezeichnet hat: *Eru* erschafft die *Ainur*. Während das für den Akt des Erschaffens gebrauchte Wort *made* noch stark physisch konnotiert ist, werden die *Ainur* im Folgenden als Nachkommen resp. der Sprössling (*offspring*) von *Erus* Gedanken (*thought*) bezeichnet. Letzteres legt die Vermutung nahe, dass *Eru* die *Ainur* aus oder mit seinen Gedanken erschaffen habe. Damit rückt *Erus* Erschaffen der *Ainur* aus oder mittels Gedanken in ein Ähnlichkeitsverhältnis zu Tolkiens literarischem Erschaffen einer fiktiven Welt mittels Worten (Ebene D). Gedanken als mediale Aufpfropfung auf die Schrift.

Noch deutlicher ist jene mediale Aufpfropfung in der nächsten Unter-Ebene E.1) zu beobachten, dieses Mal von Gesang resp. Vokal-Musik ›auf‹ Schrift: Unterebene E.1) Die *Ainur* wiederum erfüllen schöpferisch mit ihrem Gesang die *Leere* (*the Void*) eben jenes fiktiven Universums (D):

> Then Ilúvatar said to them: ›Of the theme that I have declared to you, I will now that ye make in harmony together a Great Music. And since I have kindled you with the Flame Imperishable, ye shall show forth your powers in adorning this theme, each with his own thought and devices, if he will. But I will sit and hearken, and be glad that through you great beauty has been wakened into song.‹

> Then the voices of the Ainur, like unto harps and lutes, ...and like unto countless choirs singing with words, began to fashion the theme of Ilúvatar to a great music, and a sound arose of endless interchanging melodies woven in harmony that passed beyond

---

4   Und das Westron wäre wiederum ein fiktiver ›Vorläufer‹ des heutigen Englisch etc.

hearing into the depths and into the heights, ...and the music
and the echo of the music went out into the Void, and it was not
void.   (S 3f)

Damit wird ein weiteres Ähnlichkeitsverhältnis hergestellt, nämlich eines
zwischen den *Ainur* in der fiktiven Welt, die das Thema, das *Eru* vorgegeben
hat, nach eigenen Gedanken und Kunstmitteln schmücken (!)[5] sollen, und den
Lesern (und Autoren) in der ›realen‹ Welt, die im Zuge ihrer Lektüre[6] die vom
Autor Tolkien vorgegebenen Signifikanten mit immer neuen und immer leicht
anderen Signifikaten versehen. Das Verhältnis zwischen *Eru* und den *Ainur* als
poetologische Metapher für das Verhältnis zwischen Autor und Leser.
    Was die Ainur im Folgenden tun und wie sich ihr schöpferischer Gesang
entfaltet, erinnert nicht zufällig an den vorletzten Satz in *On Fairy-stories*:

So great is the bounty with which he [Man] has been treated that
he may now, perhaps, fairly dare to guess that in Fantasy he may
actually assist [und zwar sowohl als Autor wie als Leser] in the
effoliation and multiple enrichment of creation.   (FS 79)

Die poetologische Thematisierung von literarischer Schöpfung und ihrer nach-
und miterschaffenden Lektüre lässt sich zu Beginn des *Silmarillions* anhand
weiterer poetologischer Metaphorik und ebenso auf *figuraler* Ebene beobachten.
Dazu je ein Beispiel:

1. Was die poetologische Metaphorik anbelangt, ist auf den ersten zweieinhalb
Seiten eine vierfache Verwendung des Verbs ›weben‹ (*weave*) zu beobachten, und
zwar immer im Sinne eines Ineinander-Webens von Melodien und Tönen (S 3;
5) resp. von Gedanken und Vorstellungen (S 4). Die Verwendung der Weben-
Metaphorik charakterisiert die Musik der *Ainur* als ein Gewebe, das in seiner
lateinischen Form *text-um* nichts anderes als eine habitualisierte Metapher für
das Geschriebene ist. Die Musik der *Ainur* wird damit als Text(-um) ausgestellt,
der sie im Zuge der Lektüre gewesen sein wird.

2. Dies wird, die figurale Ebene betreffend, besonders deutlich in der Beschreibung des ersten Chors der *Ainur*, bei der nicht nur mittels Schriftzeichen auf
den Klang und das Echo jenes Chors *verwiesen* wird, sondern bei der auch die

---

5   *adorning*, ›schmückend‹, hier eine Meta-Metapher (Redeschmuck), die gewissermaßen
    wörtlich wird und zwar auf mind. zwei Ebenen: 1. Die Ainur schmücken das Thema
    tatsächlich mit Worten, ihrem Sprachgesang. 2. Die Beschreibung dieses Schmückens
    wimmelt von rhetorischen Figuren, also von Redeschmuck.
6   Dazu zählen auch wissenschaftliche Lesarten, wie sie im vorliegenden Band präsentiert
    werden.

zahlreichen Klangfiguren, u.a. die an prominentester Stelle eingesetzte Wort-
wiederholung *music–music* und die figura etymologica *Void–void*, im Zuge
der Lektüre ein Echo *herstellen*: »...and the **music** and the *echo* of the **music**
went out into the **Void**, and it was not *void*«(S. 4, Hervorhebungen von M.G.).
Das *echo of the music* ist also ein Doppeltes (!): einerseits das fiktive Echo des
Gesangs der *Ainur* und andererseits das ›reale‹ Echo der Stimme des Lesers im
Zuge von dessen Lektüre.

Spätestens an dieser Stelle wird diese Doppelung auch auf den Titel des Kapitels zurückgeworfen, nicht umsonst werden auch die Worte *Ainur* und *music*
selbst auf den ersten Seiten mehrfach echohaft wiederholt. Die Übersetzung
des Titels »The Music of the Ainur« kündigt in dieser Lesart nun geradezu
eine ausführliche, das Werk eröffnende poetologische Thematisierung von Vo-
kal- resp. Wort-Musik und deren schöpferischer Kraft an; handelt das Kapitel
»Ainulindalë« doch nicht nur von der schöpferischen Musik der *Ainur*, sondern
eben auch von der schöpferischen Musik der Leser.

Im Folgenden möchte ich noch etwas genauer auf dieses Verhältnis zwischen
Eru und den *Ainur* und der poetologischen Metaphorik dieses Verhältnisses
eingehen:

Eru und die Ainur – der Autor und die Leser
Während also die Ebene E), die Schöpfung *Eas* durch *Eru*, ein Ähnlichkeitsverhältnis zwischen *Eru* und dem Autor Tolkien herstellt, tut dies die Unterebene
E.1) zwischen den *Ainur* und den Lesern. Nun ist es aber *Eru*, der die *Ainur*
erschafft. Nimmt man die soeben dargelegte poetologische Metaphorik also
ernst, so würde sie uns zu lesen geben, dass der Autor die Leser erschafft. Wenn
aber nach Derrida die Iterierbarkeit der Zeichen die Möglichkeitsbedingung für
ihren Gebrauch ist (vgl. Derrida SEK), so folgt daraus, dass auch umgekehrt
das Erschaffen eines Zeichens ohne die Möglichkeit seines Gelesen-Werdens
und ebenso die Konstitution eines Autors ohne die Konstitution eines Lesers
nicht möglich sind. Die Beziehung zwischen Autor und Leser ist also chiastisch
verschränkt.

Nicht anders verhält es sich mit *Eru* und seinen Geschöpfen. Die vermeintliche
Einheit, die *Eru*, dessen Name ›der Eine‹ bedeutet, verkörpert, ist letztlich eine
ihm wortwörtlich zu*geschriebene*: Um seinen Schöpfungsakt überhaupt erzähl-
bar zu machen, muss er begrifflich fassbar, als Zeichengebilde ›neu-erschaffen‹
werden, ein Zeichengebilde, das selbst wiederum im Zuge der Lektüre immer
aufs Neue konstituiert wird. Dies gilt sowohl für die *Secondary World*, innerhalb
derer uns das *Silmarillion* als Überlieferung präsentiert wird, als auch für die
Lektüre des *Silmarillions* in der *Primary World*.

Jener Überlieferungs-Aspekt wird gleich zu Beginn des ersten Satzes der
»Ainulindalë« reflektiert, indem auf die Nennung des Schöpfers und die Über-

setzung (!) seines Namens, *There was Eru, the One*, sogleich der Nachtrag *who in Arda is called Ilúvatar* folgt. Während die auktoriale Setzung *There was Eru* den Nennakt, der eine solche Setzung überhaupt erst möglich macht, im ersten Teil des Satzes verstellt, so wird er im zweiten Teil explizit, wobei die einschränkende lokale Angabe *in Arda* eine unbestimmte weitere Zahl potentieller, erfolgter oder noch erfolgender Benennungen impliziert. *Ilúvatar*, an dieser Stelle nicht übersetzt, bedeutet ›All-Vater‹, ›Vater des Ganzen‹. Und genau diese *Zwei*-teiligkeit des Namens unterläuft die vermeintliche *Ein*-heit, die er als *Eru*, ›der Eine‹, garantieren soll. Denn die Frage, in welcher Relation die beiden Namen-Teile von *Ilúvatar* zu lesen resp. zu übersetzen sind, setzt eine die vermeintliche Einheit sprengende Dynamik frei – eine Dynamik, so ist man versucht zu sagen, von letztlich unvorstellbarer Schöpfungskraft. Zu dieser tragen mindestens drei Faktoren bei:

Erstens lässt sich die Relation der beiden Namen-Teile sowohl als genitivus obiectivus als auch als genitivus subiectivus interpretieren. Im Falle von Ersterem ist *Eru* der Vater des 'Alls', der Vater von allen und allem. Im Falle eines 'genitivus subiectivus' sind es 'alle', die ihn beim Namen *nennen* und in Relation zu denen er überhaupt erst als 'Vater' *benannt* resp. konstituiert wird.

Sowohl *Eru* als auch *Ilúvatar* sind Namen in der Elben-Sprache Quenya, was wiederum indexikalisch auf eine *Benennung* des Schöpfers durch seine Geschöpfe verweist – Geschöpfe, die freilich bei der Erschaffung der Welt noch nicht zugegen waren.[7] Der Nenn-Akt, den *Erus* Geschöpfe vornehmen, kann also selbst wiederum als Schöpfung, als das Erschaffen eines Namens bezeichnet werden.

Daraus folgt *zweitens*, dass sich in *Ilúvatar*, im 'zweiten' – oder zumindest im *Silmarillion* zweit-genannten – Namen des Schöpfers *Eru* eine chiastische Verschränkung von Schöpfer und Geschöpfen birgt: *Ilúvatar* hat sprechende Lebewesen erschaffen, die mit Sprache überhaupt erst einen Begriff ihres Schöpfers erschaffen. Mit diesem Begriff wiederum setzen sie ihn als Vater in Relation zu ihnen und sich in Relation zu ihm.

Drittens weist bereits die Vater-Kind-Relation auf eine genealogische, also metonymische, Verschiebung resp. Übertragung des Erschaffens hin, die potentiell unendlich weiter fortgesetzt werden könnte. Oder anders ausgedrückt: Bereits der Anfang des *Silmarillions* weist mit dem Gesang der *Ainur* eine *sub-creation* in der *creation Ilúvatars* auf, die wiederum eine *sub-creation* Tolkiens resp. seiner Leser ist – ein Prinzip, das theoretisch eine unendliche Verschachtelung von *sub-creations* in *sub-creations* erlaubt. Als eine solche weitere Unterebene wären z. B. aus dem *Herrn der Ringe* Sams Freude an *fairy stories* zu nennen und die

---

7   Was eine weitere Verschiebung vom implizierten Nennakt der Ainur zum Nennakt der Elben bedeutet.

von ihm auf den Treppen von Cirith Ungol geäußerte Sehnsucht, dereinst selbst in einer solchen Geschichte vorzukommen (vgl. LotR 712).[8] Verlyn Flieger hat diese Stelle auf den Treppen nicht umsonst als „the most self-referential and post-modern moment in the entire book" (Flieger 72) beschrieben.[9]

Als *Zwischenfazit* lässt sich festhalten: Der Anfang des *Silmarillions* reflektiert die Bedingungen und die schöpferische Dynamik des Nennaktes und des Erschaffens mittels Sprache in unzähligen Facetten bis hin zu einer Thematisierung der grundlegendsten damit verbundenen Fragen zur Konstitution von Zeichen, Autor und Leser. Damit hat sich die am Ende der Einleitung aufgestellte These bezüglich des poetologischen Potentials einer *Secondary World* nach Tolkiens Poetik bestätigt. Sie soll nun jedoch in einem weiteren, darauf aufbauenden Schritt mit Blick auf den in *On Fairy-stories* verwendeten Begriff *'true'* weitergedacht werden.

Poetologie und Performativität: *Primary Truth* in einer *Secondary World*?

Zuerst noch einmal zurück zur oben zitierten Beschreibung des Gesangs der Ainur (vgl. S 3f.) und der darin enthaltenen figura etymologica *Void–void*, die aufgrund ihrer zentralen inhaltlichen, klanglichen und poetologischen Vielschichtigkeit eine äußerst genaue, in den folgenden zwei Abschnitten dargelegte Analyse erfordert:

Sie ist so gewählt, dass sie auf *klanglicher* Ebene ein ›reines‹ Echo bildet; wohingegen sich die beiden Elemente sowohl auf semantischer als auch graphischer Ebene nicht entsprechen. Was Letztere betrifft, so ist der Großbuchstabe des ersten *Void* nicht zu *hören*, sondern nur als Text, als Gewebe zu *lesen*. Damit wird die poetologische Reflexion geradezu potenziert, denn es findet sich in der zitierten Stelle nicht nur eine poetologische Metaphorik für das Herstellen eines Textes (*woven*) gepaart mit dem performativen Erschaffen dessen, wovon im Text die Rede ist (ein Echo), sondern dieses Echo verweist wiederum über die in diesem Fall allein über das *Lesen* wahrnehmbare figura etymologica (sonst wäre es eine geminatio) erneut auf das Gewebe *Text*. Ein Gewebe, das wie der Gesang der *Ainur* die Macht besitzt, zu erschaffen – sei es performativ

---

8   Allein schon diese Stelle, die, bezieht man das Schöpferische der Ainur im *Silmarillion* mit ein, selbst schon eine *sub-creation* in der *sub-creation* ist, beinhaltet eine potentiell unendliche Spiegelung. Denn die Darstellung von Sam in einer fairy story, müsste wiederum auch seine Sehnsucht, in einer solchen vorzukommen, beinhalten usw.

9   Wenngleich ich autoreferentielle und poetologische Textstellen bei Weitem nicht als dem Postmodernismus vorbehalten betrachte; vgl. Gut.

Wortklang und Echo, sei es eine fiktive Welt in der Fantasie der Leser. Ein Gewebe, das aber, kaum gelesen, sofort wieder verhallt. Dieses ›Verstummen‹ der Sprachzeichen wird nirgends so deutlich wie an Klangfiguren, deren erste Teile bereits echohaft verhallt sind, noch bevor die letzten Teile gelesen wurden.

Dass die Beschreibung des Gesangs der *Ainur*, der die Leere, *the Void*, schöpferisch ›zu füllen‹ vermag, ausgerechnet in einer derart vielschichtigen *figura etymologica* gipfelt, treibt die Reflexion von Sprache und ihres schöpferischen Potentials geradezu auf die Spitze. Denn geht man, eine weitere Reflexions-Ebene hinzufügend (oder hinzu-erschaffend...), der Etymologie von *etymologica* nach, so lässt sich Folgendes feststellen:

> Das Wort Etymologie entstammt dem Griechischen *etymolog'ia* eigentlich ›Lehre vom Wahren‹ zu gr. étymos ›wahr, wirklich‹ und *-logie*. Das Gefühl, dass das Benennungsmotiv etwas über das Wesen des Bezeichneten aussagt, führt zu der Auffassung, dass das Grundwort den wahren Kern der Bedeutung bietet – wobei auch Vorstellungen über einen Zusammenhang zwischen Wortgestalt und Bedeutung eine Rolle gespielt haben mögen.
>
> (Kluge 262)

Eine figura etymologica wäre nach ihrer eigenen Etymologie also eine rhetorische Figur mit der qualitativen Eigenschaft, vermeintlich eine »Lehre[-logie] vom Wahren« zu beinhalten. Ich möchte mich von einer Ontologisierung von Zeichen resp. von rhetorischen Figuren und/oder des Adjektivs *etymologica* klar distanzieren. Dennoch lässt sich auf sprachlich-performativer Ebene an der *Void-void*-Figur etwas beobachten, das fast schon unheimlich ›wahr‹ anmutet: Ausgerechnet die *Void-void*-Figur kann einerseits *im Zuge der Lektüre* performativ ein Echo in der ›realen Welt‹, der *Primary World*, herstellen und dadurch das Echo des Gesangs der *Ainur* in der fiktiven Welt, der *Secondary World*, ›real‹ – oder pathetischer ausgedrückt ›wahr‹ – werden lassen. Dadurch stellt andererseits die figura etymologica gleichzeitig ihre eigene Semantik performativ her![10] Auf dieser sogar gedoppelten performativen Ebene beinhaltet diese figura etymologica also in gewissem Sinne tatsächlich eine ›Lehre vom Wahren‹, nämlich die poetologische Thematisierung des Potentials performativer Schöpfungsmacht, die dem System der Sprachzeichen innewohnt. Diese ›Lehre vom Wahren‹ wiederum, so ist man versucht zu sagen, ist umso ›wahrer‹, als dass sie sich geradezu ironisch als eine Leere (*Void*) zu lesen gibt. Somit stellt sie aus, dass ihr vermeintlich ontologischer Anspruch an den in der ›Leere‹

---

10 Die *Leere-leer*-Figur kann also eine unglaubliche *Fülle* an Überlegungen zur Konstitution von Zeichen und Zeichen-Welten zu lesen geben, welche das Thema Erus und Tolkiens wahrlich ausschmückt (vgl. *adorning*, S 3).

verhallenden Klang der Lektüre gebunden ist, und entkräftet diesen Anspruch damit gleich selbst.

Von der Etymologie von *etymologica* nun zu Tolkiens Vorlesung *On Fairy-stories* und dem darin *explizit* verwendeten Wahrheits-Begriff. Dazu zunächst noch einmal zwei Zitate, in denen Tolkien den Begriff 'true' prominent verwendet:

> ...the story-maker proves a successful ›sub-creator‹. He makes a Secondary World which your mind can enter. Inside it, what he relates is ›true‹: it accords with the laws of that world.   (FS 52)

Mit Bezug auf die *eukatastrophe*, ›true‹ dieses Mal nicht als *secondary truth* gemeint und deshalb auch nicht mehr in distanzierenden einfachen Anführungszeichen gehalten:

> It is not difficult to imagine the peculiar excitement and joy that one would feel, if any specially beautiful fairy-story were found to be ›primarily‹ true...   (FS 78)

Meine These ist nun: Poetologische und insbesondere performative Textstellen spielen in Tolkiens Werk gerade deshalb eine solch prominente Rolle, weil sie es vermögen, in der *Secondary World* im Zuge der Lektüre nicht nur *secondary*, sondern sogar *primary belief* herzustellen. Poetologische Textstellen, weil sie in beiden Welten auf Sprachzeichen und deren Konstituenten verweisen; performative, weil sie während der Lektüre Neues erschaffen können, das auch den ›Wahrheitsansprüchen‹ der *Primary World* standhält.

Etwas ausformulierter heißt dies Folgendes: Der Text gibt in einer poetologischen[11] Textstelle seine eigenen Konstituenten zu lesen. Die Konstituenten von Text wiederum sind in einer mittels Zeichen erschaffenen *Secondary World*, in der wiederum mittels Zeichen kommuniziert wird, weitgehend dieselben[12] wie in der *Primary World*. Poetologische Aussagen in der *Secondary World* über die Konstituenten von Sprache und ihrer Schöpfungsmacht *verweisen* also auf etwas, das entweder für beide Welten falsch oder ›wahr‹ ist. Performative Textstellen gehen sogar noch einen Schritt weiter und suchen im Zuge ihrer Lektüre das herzustellen, worauf sie verweisen. In Tolkiens Werk ist Performativität omnipräsent, sei es in performativen Textstellen, im Stile der *Void-*

---

11 Hier ›poetologisch‹ gemäß der zweiten in der Einleitung vorgenommenen Definition.
12 Einzig in den physikalischen Konstituenten der letztlich noch nicht zeichenhaften Ebene A (s.o.) sind Varianten denkbar, etwa wenn eine *Secondary World* keine Atmosphäre besitzt und deshalb nicht mittels Schallwellen Zeichen geäußert werden können. Über solche Varianten (die bislang stärker für Science-Fiction-Literatur relevant sind als für die Fantasy-Literatur) wurde bereits im 19. Jh. spekuliert, vgl. dazu z.B. Bernstein 13-15.

void-Klangfigur, die über ein Zusammenspiel von rhetorischen Figuren mit der Inhaltsebene operieren, oder, expliziter, in performativen Sprechakten einzelner Personen.[13] Im *Silmarillion* z.b. scheinen gar performative Sprechakte in der direkten Rede der Figuren eher die Regel als die Ausnahme und es erstaunt nicht, dass *Ea*, wörtlich ›es ist‹, der Name für das All selbst, bereits schon ein zum Name gewordener Sprechakt *Erus* ist.[14] In dem oben intensiv behandelten Beispiel im *Silmarillion* wird nicht nur ein Echo als Teil einer *Secondary World* erzählt, sondern es wird u.a. über die Klangfigur *Void-void* ein Echo hergestellt, das, auf fast schon unheimlich wunderbare Weise, aus der *Secondary World* hinausreicht und in der *Primary World* zu hören ist.

Kurzum mit Tolkiens neu-erschaffenem (!) Begriff ausgedrückt: Dass poetologische und performative Textstellen eine derart prominente Rolle in Tolkiens Werk einnehmen, ist kein Zufall, denn sie geben Mal für Mal eine semiologische *Eukatastrophe* zu lesen!

Zusammenfassung und Ausblick

1. Folgt man Tolkiens Forderung nach der inneren Konsistenz einer *Secondary World*, eine Konsistenz, die letztlich aus den Maßstäben der *Primary World* abgeleitet wird, so muss eine *Secondary World* zwangsläufig das Bedürfnis zur sub-*creation* im Allgemeinen sowie ihre eigene *creation* behandeln. Dadurch bietet sich auf einer abstrakten Meta-Ebene die Möglichkeit für eine poetologische Thematisierung von Schöpfung mittels Sprachzeichen *im Allgemeinen*. Dies ist dann der Fall, wenn *innerhalb* der *Secondary World* nach den inneren Gesetzen dieser *Secondary World* eine Thematisierung von Schöpferischem stattfindet, die gleichzeitig in ein Ähnlichkeitsverhältnis zum Erschaffen der *Secondary World* in der *Primary World* gesetzt werden kann.

Zur Möglichkeit dieser poetologischen Thematisierung lässt sich Folgendes festhalten, unterteilt in zwei Punkte gemäß den beiden eingangs eingeführten, hier verwendeten Bedeutungen des Begriffs ›Poetologie‹:

2.a) betr. Poetologie im engeren Sinne als ›implizite Poetik‹. Die Untersuchung des Anfangs des *Silmarillions* hat gezeigt, dass Tolkien in seinem literarischen

---

13   Diese müssten jedoch in dieser Hinsicht noch näher betrachtet werden. Denn im Gegensatz zu performativen Textstellen im Stil der Void-void-Klangfigur erschaffen performative Sprechakte (wie z.B. Eide, Flüche, Versprechen) in einer *Secondary World* neue Tatsachen zunächst einmal innerhalb dieser *Secondary World* und ›ragen‹ damit nicht direkt in die *Primary World* hinein wie etwa das oben behandelte Echo.

14   Auch auf thematischer Ebene ist das Erschaffen, z.B. der Silmarilli, aber auch das Verhältnis von Schöpfern zum Erschaffenen zentral für das *Silmarillion* und für Tolkiens *Secondary World* im Allgemeinen.

Schaffen jene Möglichkeit zur Herstellung eines Ähnlichkeitsverhältnisses äußerst ausgeprägt nutzt: Er setzt seine in *On Fairy-stories* umrissene, explizite ›Poetik‹ in dieser Hinsicht nicht nur mit aller Konsequenz um, sondern ergänzt sie auch, indem er seine Poetik implizit, also poetologisch, reflektiert, präzisiert und in einer Weise potenziert, die den Leser an die Grenzen seiner sprachlichen Erkenntnismöglichkeiten führt.

2.b) betr. Poetologie als ›implizite Thematisierung der Bedingungen und Möglichkeiten von sprachlicher Schöpfung: Gerade die Thematisierung der Konstituenten für sprachliche Welten und damit von Sprachzeichen im Allgemeinen, wie sie zu Beginn des *Silmarillions* in poetologischen und performativen Textstellen besonders prominent auftritt, verwischt auf dieser Metaebene die Grenzen zwischen *Primary* und *Secondary World* und ist damit in gewisser Hinsicht in einer *Secondary World* auch nach Maßstäben der *Primary World* ›true‹. Anders formuliert: Die *Primary World* ragt dadurch in die *Secondary World* hinein, ohne den ›Zauber zu brechen‹, im Gegenteil, er wird dadurch nur noch größer und tiefer, potenziert, ein verzauberter Zauber.

3. Aus diesen beiden Punkten folgt wiederum: Tolkiens Vorlesung *On Fairy-stories* ist, neben vielem anderen, auch eine Poetik der Poetologie. Und auch hier im doppelten Sinne, als *genitivus subiectivus* eine explizite Poetik, die sich aus der impliziten Poetik von Tolkiens *Secondary World*(s) speist und von ihr (ihnen) ergänzt wird; und als *genitivus obiectivus* eine Poetik, deren konsequente Umsetzung eine implizite Thematisierung von sprachlicher Schöpfung zur Folge hat.

4. Diese Wechselwirkung zwischen expliziter Poetik und impliziter Poetologie macht – um eine weitere Ebene der Abstraktion resp. Reflexion hinzuzufügen – auch vor der Vorlesung *On Fairy-stories* selbst nicht halt. Hierauf kann ich in diesem Rahmen, entgegen meiner ursprünglichen Absicht, leider nicht mehr ausführlich eingehen. Beispiele dafür wären etwa: dass Tolkien, mit dem wiederholten Verweis auf die Kunst der *fairies* daran arbeitet, in einer vermeintlich einzig theoretischen Vorlesung *secondary belief* an *faires* herzustellen,[15] ja sich gar selbst als Angehöriger der *fairies* inszeniert, die nach seinen Worten selbst Meister der *sub-creation* (vgl. FS 63-66) und damit auch Meister der Poetologie sind; oder dass die Vorlesung selbst ein *happy ending* hat, das wiederum – wie nach Tolkien bei allen *fairy stories* – kein Ende hat (vgl. FS 52), sondern wortwörtlich ein *Enden* ist. In diesem Sinne:

---

15 Vgl. FS, z.B. S. 35, Abschn. 17.; S. 40, Abschn. 16.; S. 63-65.

5. All diese Punkte müssten gerade auch aufgrund der Wirkmächtigkeit von Tolkiens *On Fairy-stories* und seines literarischen Werkes unbedingt auch für *Secondary Worlds im Allgemeinen* weiter untersucht werden; birgt doch, wie oben gezeigt, jede *Secondary World* (und insbesondere, wenn sie Tolkiens Poetik folgt) die Voraussetzung dafür, Sprache und deren Schöpfungsmacht zu thematisieren. So könnte auch der Blick auf die poetologische Vielschichtigkeit und Tiefe von Tolkiens Werk dazu beitragen, dass dem großen philologischen und epistemologischen Erkenntnispotential der leider oft noch immer belächelten *Secondary Worlds* vermehrt Rechnung getragen wird.

Bibliographie

Anderson, Douglas A., und Flieger, Verlyn. *Tolkien: On Fairy-stories. Expanded edition, with commentary and notes.* London: HarperCollins, 2014

Bernstein, Aaron. *Aus dem Reiche der Naturwissenschaft. Für jedermann aus dem Volke.* Berlin: Franz Duncker, 1858

Derrida, Jaques. *Randgänge der Philosophie. Herausgegeben von Peter Engelmann. 2. überarbeitete Auflage.* Wien: Passagen, 1999, S. 325-351 [*Signatur, Ereignis, Kontext*]

Flieger, Verlyn. *Interrupted Music. The Making of Tolkien's Mythology.* Kent OH: The Kent State University Press, 2005

Flieger, Verlyn. *Splintered Light. Logos and Language in Tolkien's World.* Michigan: William B. Eedermans Publishing Co., 1983

Gut, Markus. »Zur poetologischen Dimension mittelhochdeutscher Tagelieder«. *Archiv für das Studium der neueren Sprachen und Literaturen* 251:2 (2014): 255-282

Kluge. Etymologisches Wörterbuch der Deutschen Sprache. Berlin: De Gruyter, 2002

Tolkien, Christopher (Hg.). *The Silmarillion* [1977]. London: HarperCollins, 1999

Tolkien, J.R.R. *The Lord of the Rings* [based on the 50th Anniversary Edition 2004, one volume, paperback]. London: HarperCollins, 2007

Wirth, Uwe. »Hypertextualität als Gegenstand einer ›intermedialen Literaturwissenschaft‹«. *Grenzen der Germanistik. Rephilologisierung oder Erweiterung?* Hg. Walter Erhart. Stuttgart/Weimar, 2004, 410-430

Entering Faërie.
J.R.R. Tolkien's *Smith of Wootton Major*

Marguerite Mouton (Cergy-Pontoise)

It appears difficult to me to read Tolkien's essay *On Fairy-stories* without comparing it to *Smith of Wotton Major* and the drafts and essays surrounding the story in Verlyn Flieger's edition. Tolkien's last fairy tale would seem to be, as Flieger puts it, "the imaginal realization of the theoretical concept he put forward in… *On Fairy-stories*" (SWM 68)[1]. Indeed, Tolkien's conception of fairy stories evolved through time and *Smith of Wootton Major* may represent the last stage of this evolution: developed both as a story and as an essay[2], the one fleshing out, illustrating but also contesting the other, it brings out the main questions raised by the genre.

The tale begins as an allegory intended to explain what a fairy story is. It was originally part of an introduction to *The Golden Key*, by George MacDonald, but Tolkien realised that he did not like *The Golden Key* as much as he thought. Beginning his introduction with remarks undermining the very value of an introduction, Tolkien ended up offering a fable on fairy stories, which eventually developed into a fully independent story.

Most critics think that the story retains something of this original allegoric dimension and therefore offer various allegorical readings of it, often of a biographical nature, such as those, most famously, of Clyde Kilby (37) and Tom Shippey (271-280), or even, though less clearly, those of Humphrey Carpenter (242) and Paul Kocher (204)[3]. Indeed, the melancholy of the end of *Smith* and the fact that it is the last story written and published by Tolkien have led scholars to read it as a story of renouncement and bereavement (see for example Shippey 277). Scholars have interpreted Tolkien's change of the story's title from "The Great Cake" to *Smith of Wootton Major* as an effort to shift the story's focus from Faery to the central character of a maker and creator, who must eventually renounce Faery.

I would like to offer a complementary reading of *Smith*, whose main point is fairy stories themselves, or rather the transmission of them to others[4]. Indeed, if we look back at the setting in which the story appears in Tolkien's writing, it

---

1   See also Flieger&Anderson's commentary: *Smith* "is perhaps Tolkien's most pure example of a fairy-story as described in his essay" (FS 87).
2   Tolkien started to write the story in 1964 and published it 1967. The essay on *Smith* was never published until it was issued among various documents in Flieger's 2005 extended edition.
3   See the review of these critics by Flieger in *Question* 231-235.
4   The change in the title could then be interpreted as drawing the attention to the fact that the continuity of a relationship with and access to Faery depends on some Men and on their will and ability to communicate it to others.

becomes clear that the original allegory questions precisely the way in which a fairy story, even a mediocre one, may actually introduce the reader to the Perilous Realm of Faery. At the end of his draft introduction to *The Golden Key*, Tolkien wrote:

> Fairy is very powerful. Even the bad guide cannot escape it. He probably makes up his tale out of bits of older tales, or things he half remembers, and they may be too strong for him to spoil or disenchant. Someone may meet them for the first time in his silly tale, and catch a glimpse of Fairy and go on to better things.
>
> This could be put in a "short story" like this. There was once a cook, and he thought of making a cake for a children's party. His chief notion was that it must be very sweet, and he meant to cover it all over with sugar-icing...　　　　　(SWM 96)

The story does not present itself directly as a definition of fairy stories, nor as the story of Tolkien's or of any author's renouncement and parting from Faery, but as a defence of the power of fairy stories and of the efficiency of even bad fairy stories. A similar claim is also at the core of the speech of the Queen of Faery when Smith meets her for the last time: "Better a little doll, maybe, than no memory of Faery at all. For some the only glimpse. For some the awaking" (SWM 32). This new wording of the original idea introduces the central question of memory: the story stages the fall into oblivion with which Faery is threatened; the importance of Faery is thereby enforced and more or less desperate means to keep it alive in memories are developed.

Such a danger is close to the one expressed in the first pages of *On Fairy-stories* when the author fears "lest the gates [of Faery] should be shut and the keys be lost" (SWM 27). How then to communicate to others a unique and personal experience, which Tolkien considers as essential to human life?

Part I – Faery: a Place of Enchantment and Peril Essential to Life

The vital issue of Faery is made apparent both through fictional and theoretical writings, unfolding various images and conceptions of the power of Faery but also giving some discrete signs of its limitation.

1. Images of Faery: from "The Great Cake" to the "Perilous Realm"
We find two conflicting images of Faery in *Smith* and the essays. From the start, even in the draft introduction to MacDonald's story, the Cake is associated with sweets and sugar and thus with a conception of Faery as a product of childish

longings. This association causes the condescension of adults like Nokes and emphasizes appearances that bring spontaneous delight to sensibility over the inner, genuine food that "should go *inside* the Great Cake"[5].

The second image of Faery, which is already present in the 1939 conference, is that of a three-dimensional a realm that is "wide and deep and high and filled with many things" (FS 27). Smith explores such an "imaginary geography", to use Pierre Jourde's expression, discovering first its shores, then its mountains and also its vales as his desire grows "to come to the heart of the kingdom" (SWM 24).

There is no doubt that the image of Faery favoured by Tolkien is that of a world of adventures, not that of a cake. In 1939, he stated that "[m]ost good 'fairy-stories' are about the *adventures* of men in the Perilous Realm" (FS 32). Such adventures are twofold: on the one hand, the traveller meets with irreducible otherness; and yet, on the other hand, he is able to learn through his discoveries. Meeting otherness is described as a perilous adventure. Shippey depicts the many dangers awaiting the bold trespasser who enters a world whose borders and laws are unknown, whose places and inhabitants trigger a fascination like that of mythical mermaids, and lastly whose exploration may boil down to a transgression of reality and an attempt to escape from it[6].

If this meeting with alterity is dangerous, it also changes the way the traveller looks on things and reveals a deeper meaning of things. Though some experiences remain mysterious and cannot be unravelled, Faery is a place of discovery in which the traveller is transformed. It is tempting to see the story of *Smith* as an illustration of the "recovery" process described in *On Fairy-stories*, which "frees" things "from the drab blur of triteness or familiarity—from possessiveness" (FS 67).

Indeed, this change in the way one looks at things and the recovery of colours as they are through clear windows, or through no windows at all, throws a satisfactory and helpful light on the *Smith* story. This recovery of light and colour seems to be confirmed by the star Smith bears on his brow, which shines more intensely when he has just visited Faery and from which "some… light passed into his eyes" (SWM 16). He discovered this star as he "looked out of the window" to find a light and a music unknown to him. The tale of his wanderings in Faery is full of adjectives depicting the brightness and sheen of the things surrounding him. The description of the tree of the King changes the ordinary laws of nature,

---

5   "His chief notion was that it should be very sweet and rich; and he decided that it should be entirely covered in sugar-icing… But when he began preparing the materials for the cake-making he found that he had only dim memories of what should go *inside* a Great Cake" (SWM 9).

6   For a study of these dangers, see Shippey 279. Flieger also offers a poignant analysis of the perilous encounter with absolute strangeness, represented by the birch-tree episode (*Question* 241-246).

thus renewing the experience of it, while in the Vale of Evermorn "the green surpasses the green of the meads of Outer Faery as they surpass ours in our springtime" (SWM 26). The counterpart to this new attitude towards things is a new skill and ability to forge things of exceptional beauty.

Yet in the *Smith* tale, this phenomenon of "recovery" is associated in an original manner with some kind of wisdom. This is expressed in similar sentences at the beginning and at the end of Smith's travels: first he feels gratitude for the star and the protection given to him ("For that he was grateful and he soon became wise and understood"); and eventually "he remembered with gratitude all that the star had brought to him" (SWM 20; 38).

What is this gain, this wisdom acquired in Faery that would explain the Queen's insistence on the importance of Faery for men? It seems that the teachings of the Perilous realm derive from the consistency of laws proper to that world; a logic that, on the whole, tends to make visible phenomena that are ordinarily invisible in the world of men. For example, the feeling of rejection and bereavement is made apparent by the tears of the birch-tree; in the same way, Smith's new spiritual height after the dance with the Queen makes his shadow gigantic; and the Queen's power is made visible through the extraordinary flowers that spring at her feet.

The visibility of immaterial realities that are usually hidden is sometimes twinned explicitly with pedagogical dynamics for Smith's benefit. Thus, the last meeting with the Queen of Faery is bracketed by two mentions of kneeling in courtesy: before the meeting to highlight the fact that Smith does not kneel, and afterwards to say that he does. Had the Queen been wearing a crown and seated on a throne, he might have knelt at first, and it would have been understood as part of the motif of meeting a Queen. But since this motif is absent from the scene, Smith does not kneel until the end, when his action is utterly disconnected from any mechanical gesture and finds its deeper meaning restored. Indeed, Smith kneels only when he recognises the value and sense of what stands before him, thus expressing genuine acknowledgement and esteem.

2. Definition of Faery as a Vital Need

The vital function of fairy tales appears still more clearly in the subsequent essay on *Smith*: while the story itself suggests the peril both of visiting Faery and forgetting it, the essay sets out to clarify the grounds for such urgency[7].

Why does the Queen suggest that although Faery is a perilous realm, forgetting or losing it is more perilous still? Some have read this suggestion/this passage as an allegory of religious faith. Tolkien himself develops an inter-

---

7   As Flieger remarks, the essay on *Smith* concentrates on the beneficent aspects of Faery, while the tale itself maintains a stronger equilibrium between both its positive and negative aspects (*Question* 240).

pretation close to that towards the end of his essay, but his final interpretation is not clearly religious (as usual with Tolkien); neither is it purely literary. The end of his essay on his own tale suggests that Faery is necessary for spiritual and mental health:

> Faery represents *at its weakest a breaking out* (at least in mind) from the iron ring of the familiar, still more from the adamantine ring of belief that it is known, possessed, controlled, and so (ultimately) all that is worth being considered—a constant awareness of the world beyond these rings. *More strongly it represents love*: that is, a love and respect for all things, "inanimate" and "animate", an unpossessive love of them as "other". This love will produce both "ruth" and "delight". Things seen in its light will be respected, and they will also appear delightful, beautiful, wonderful even glorious. *Faery might be said indeed to represent Imagination* (without definition because taking in all the definitions of this word): esthetic: exploratory and receptive; and artistic: inventive, dynamic and (sub)creative. This compound—of *awareness* of a limitless world outside our domestic parish; a *love* (in ruth and admiration) for the things in it; and a *desire* for wonder, marvels, both perceived and conceived—this "Faery" is as necessary for the health and complete functioning of the Human as is sunlight for physical life: sunlight as distinguished from the soil, say, though it in fact permeates and modifies even that.
>
> (SWME 144-145; emphasis mine)

Tolkien successively offers three definitions of Faery, starting from the weakest one and going to the strongest:

First, Faery is conceived as a "breaking out" from two "rings" that block our experience: habit and mastery. Freedom from the commonplace and known is achieved through the development of an "awareness" that the world goes beyond our customary sphere.

The second definition connects Faery with "love", the love of "all things". This love casts a peculiar "light" on things which makes one respect them. Faery transforms both the value of objects and the attitude of the subject viewing them so that they enter into a new relationship called "love", made up of the subject's respect and acknowledgement and the object's beauty—an exchange that eventually produces delight.

The last definition equates Faery with "Imagination". Paradoxically, Tolkien claims to define Faery as imagination, while at the same time refusing to define imagination itself, in order to maintain the word's greatest possible meaning. In this context, imagination is fleshed out as both passive and active, as aesthetical perception and artistic creation, as what is received and what is passed on to others. Not only is it a *faculty* but also a *world*, implying the existence of objects, people, environments and thereby the possibility of an exchange and not merely that of a solitary adventure for whomever possesses this faculty.

This definition of Faery is further refined in the last sentence of the essay, which first summarises the three previous senses, repeating the notions of awareness and love. But the third notion, imagination, gives way to the "desire for wonder, marvels". Imagination is not merely a faculty or even a world but a *fundamental desire*, which the essay *On Fairy-stories* called "primordial human desires" (FS 34). Generalising this notion, the comparison closing the *Smith Essay* seems to indicate that Faery is essential to human mental "health" and to the functioning of the whole human being.

The distinction between "sunlight" and "soil" in the last sentence might then mean that, like the sun, Faery is necessary for life and colours it, but is not opposed to reality, which is what the firm ground of the earth would stand for, but rather interacts with it to produce the richness of life.

3. The Limits of Faery: giving Way to Wisdom

Such a positive view of the power of imagination is tempered in Tolkien's "Suggestions of the ending of the story", published in Flieger's edition of *Smith of Wotton Major*, by the discreet acknowledgement of some limitations:

> … the visions of imagination are not enough; they are only pictures and intimations. When wisdom comes, the mind though enriched by imagination, having learned or seen distant truths only perceptible in this way, must prepare to leave the world of Men and Fayery.   (SWM 106)

Wisdom is here presented as a period or as an event that happens. Should it be understood as a euphemism for ageing and the coming of death? Or does this mention of wisdom emphasise what is to be understood as the fundamental meaning of ageing?

In any case, there appears to be some limit to imagination, a time-related one if wisdom is taken as a synonym for ageing, but also a limit touching the extent of its function since it eventually gives way to the wisdom it has nurtured. If imagination is not the end of all things, but is limited by the passing of time, the transmission of Faery is all the more urgent. The second limit, the replacement of imagination by wisdom, demonstrates the peril of the travel into Faery—the danger that imagination might be considered as an absolute and might exert a fascination that would obliterate its relationship with the firm ground of reality.

Part II – Faery in Peril: the Issue of Transmission

Tolkien thus suggests that Faery is a unique, personal experience, necessary to life, whose necessity explains the extreme importance of its transmission.

1. The Access to Faery: Degrees and Means

Tolkien's essay on his own tale describes a variety of degrees and means of access to Faery: some people can wander only in the "Outer Faery" (SWME 141); some can go further, gaining access either by way of "entrances" like the one found by Smith's grand-father, or thanks to the "passport" of the star, that enables its bearer to go "deep into the realm"; others, like Smith's son Ned, learn of this world only "secondhand", "only through the lore and companionship" of those who have gone there[8].

In *Smith*, the village of Wootton Major is in danger of losing access to Faery because a materialistic trend is growing and reaches its peak when Nokes becomes Master Cook and degrades Faery to a childish entertainment. The King of Faery does not intrude at an arbitrary time but responds to a dire need, when Wootton Major is threatened ("the village was in a danger which it did not see", SWME 127) with at least economical and artistic decline.

The apparently simple initial image of the sugary Great Cake becomes more complicated when we learn that it is the King of Faery who made the sugar icing. Indeed, Alf himself makes most of the Cake and the doll of the Fairy-Queen, "mitigating it by skill and beauty" (SWME 138). Thus the Great Cake should not be caricatured as standing for a conception of Faery that is entirely independent from the true Faery. Moreover, Tolkien points out in the essay that the King builds on a "remain" of Nokes' "virtue": the fact that he is "fond of children" and therefore admits "Fairy" as an amusement for them (SWME 138). And if Nokes' Great Cake is at first presented as mere sugar icing spread over emptiness, the point is not to condemn the traditional Cake for being superficial, but to restore its content and thereby stop it from being an empty shell. Thus, the Cake is not merely the egoistic result of a materialist and selfish Cook, but a combination of half-forgotten inheritance, mistaken notions, a measure of good will on Nokes' part, and the elven skill and grace of the King. Not even the worst misconception is entirely despised by the Fairies, or quite useless for the discovery of Faery. As Tolkien writes in his essay:

---

8   In his *Smith Essay*, Tolkien elaborates a full symbolical geography of the links between Men and Faery, depicting three villages whose relationships with Faery depend on their distances from the Forest, the privileged space for these contacts: Walton, set deep within the Forest is thus the closest to Faery; Wootton Minor, built in a clearing, maintains some links with it; and Wootton Major, which lies completely outside the Forest [?], is in danger of forgetting all about Faery (SWME 126-127).

Alf... even included the silly notion that "fairies" must have "magic wands"... It was of course an insult to the Queen, and nevertheless a "glimpse" of Faery for the receptive. As the Queens later explains.   (SWME 138)

Indeed, as we have seen, the Queen herself attributes a pedagogical value to this weak representation of Faery a little later in the story (SWM 32).

2. The Mediation of Smith: Renouncing and Transmitting

To be sure, the Great Cake offers a largely degraded image of Faery; however, it is the Smith's means of access to Faery through the star he swallows; it also becomes the road to Faery for Tim and, though second-hand, for Nell and their children, and eventually for the whole village that benefits from this connexion[9].

Yet, if such exchange is to go on, Smith must himself forsake Faery. This leads to the question of renouncement and bereavement for which this tale is famous. Indeed, Paul Kocher (204) and Verlyn Flieger (*Question* 233) both consider it a story in which one gives back what one has received. In this context, the fact that the torch should pass on to someone else is a "reassuring" element within an unavoidable process.

I would argue that the main point of this tale is not simply deprivation, but also transmission. Indeed, the King of Faery does not get involved merely to take back something but to fill the gap left by the previous Master Cook: the last of them, Smith's grand-father, is unwilling to keep the position long enough and is unable to find any good apprentice. He thus creates the danger of being replaced by someone who is incapable of properly maintaining the cooking tradition. Therefore the coming of the King aims at preserving the chain of transmission between generations and restoring it where it is most needed[10].

---

9   Tolkien and after him a number of critics have reflected on this link between Faery and the world of men, on their mutual dependence. Verlyn Flieger underlined the logical difficulties, especially the time-related ones, Tolkien faced in trying to make both worlds consistent with each other, though the geographical relationship proved easier to tackle. In any case, he forcefully rejected both the idea of their independence from one another and any artificial means of access (like a tunnel) that would assure the connexion and avoid the real questions about the nature of the link. Indeed, the articulation between Faery and the world of men is not merely a matter of space or time; it is also of a symbolical, maybe psychological and spiritual kind, which the end of the tale questions. Thus, Smith's farewell to Faery is marked by the strange vision of the two worlds and of his own position with regard to them. It seems to him that he stands at the same time within both of them, and also outside of them (SWM 33). This sense of mutual permeability receives immediate confirmation with the encounter of Alf on the roads of Outer Faery.

10 The importance of restoring tradition is evident in the fact that the King intends to make two Great Cakes, remaining in the village long enough re-establish a memory, symbolically giving back its bright colours to the Great Hall.

When the King eventually asks Smith to give back the star, there is no denying that it is because, as the Queen puts it, "the time has come"; but the message is immediately supplemented by the phrase "let him choose", a hint at the transmission of the star. This balance between bereavement and transmission is also suggested when the King fulfils the message: he reclaims the star first on the grounds that "it is time for [Smith] to give this thing up" and then he adds that "someone else may need this thing". It is to this last statement that Smith yields. Surely, this could be interpreted as a means of easing the parting—and it may well be so—but the narrator remarks that Smith agrees to give up the star out of generosity and gratitude for what he has himself received.

If the end of the story is undeniably marked by a melancholy linked to old age and the inability to travel again in Faery, it also emphasizes the danger of letting the precious connexion with Faery—and its advantages for the village— fall into oblivion. In the draft entitled "Suggestions for the ending of the story", Tolkien reflects on the choices to be made for the last scenes. For instance, he would rather have Smith come back to his son alone and he seeks for a means to avoid the presence of anybody else. This could be construed as a wish to create the conditions for a transmission to the next generation.

Indeed, in his *Smith Essay*, the author describes Ned as "one precisely of the practical and plain normal men and workers whose enlightenment and vivifica- tion was one of the objects of the King's plan" (SWME 141). Such a plan and the emotional charge of this final dialogue between father and son highlight the importance of the weakened or even degraded versions of Faery, be it the Great Cake or a second-hand narrative.

One remark from the "Suggestions for the ending of the story" draws attention to the complex articulation between the two worlds. Reflecting on the pretext to be given for the absence of Nell, Smith's wife, on his return, Tolkien writes: "a commonplace very 'mortal' and domestic note should be struck, making the adventures in Fayery seem very remote, yes, even absurd" (SWM 106). Does such a contrast between ordinary life and the marvels of Faery make the second seem "absurd"? It certainly shows their limits, but it also shows that ordinary life goes on, punctuated by feasts and by the passing of experiences from one generation to the next. Indeed, Nell is away when her husband returns because she has gone to Wootton Minor to celebrate her grand-son's birthday.

There is both discontinuity and continuity between what Smith has just lived and the reality to which he comes back. Such paradox is at the centre of the experience of Faery, which is at odds with real life while, at the same time, questioning it and lending it new depth—the "remoteness" alluded to by Tolkien as the feeling provoked by the discrepancy between Faery and ordinary life.

If Faery, then, is a perilous realm, its loss is presented as more dangerous still, since it is necessary for mental and spiritual health. In *Smith of Wootton Major*, Tolkien expresses the conviction that access to Faery should be maintained at all costs, even through weak and degraded means, rather than be lost. By humorously setting the art of Cooking at the core of his fairy tale, the author himself plays with the pedagogical aspect of Faery, which makes itself accessible by means of superficial appearances hiding—and unravelling—a deeper meaning.

Bibliography

Anderson, Douglas & Verlyn Flieger (Eds.). *Tolkien, On Fairy-stories*. London: HarperCollins, 2008

Carpenter, Humphrey. *J.J.R. Tolkien: A Biography*. London: HarperCollins, 2002

Flieger, Verlyn. *A Question of Time: J.R.R. Tolkien's Road to Faërie*. Kent OH: Kent State University Press, 1997

---. (Ed.). *Smith of Wootton Major*, London: HarperCollins, 2005

Jourde, Pierre. *Géographies imaginaires de quelques inventeurs de mondes au XXᵉ siècle: Gracq, Borges, Michaux, Tolkien*. Paris: José Corti, 1991

Kilby, Clyde. *Tolkien and The Silmarillion*. Wheaton (Ill.): Harold Shaw, 1976

Kocher, Paul. *Master of Middle-earth. The Fiction of J.J.R. Tolkien*. Boston: Houghton Mifflin, 1972

Shippey, Thomas. *The Road to Middle-earth* [1982]. New York: Houghton Mifflin, 2003

Exploring Faërie: J.R.R. Tolkien's Innovative Approaches to the Fairy-tale Genre

Anca Muntean (Paris)

*T*he *Lord of the Rings* has been seducing readers, young and old, for decades by awakening their desire to find out more about Middle-earth and Faërie. The work's influence on succeeding generations of authors (fantasy or otherwise) cannot be underestimated. Maybe this is one reason why Tolkien's epic tale is often too hastily categorised as what we today call *fantasy* literature—in spite of the fact that this label can capture only one part of its complex generic pedigree. The very seduction mentioned depends on an unusual mixture and interaction of several literary genres (fairy tale, historical novel, epic, romance, and, of course, fantasy) which are at work within the text and which Tolkien uses and develops as the story unfolds.

1. Unveiling the Layers of the Text: the Generic Approach

*B*y putting the characteristics of different literary genres side by side and having them interact, Tolkien causes their inner structure to transform so that they become, within the narrative and because of it, more flexible than before, allowing them to bring into our world the atmosphere and the wind that blows from Faërie. The success of *The Lord of the Rings* can thus be explained by, among other things, the direct and immediate influence of various literary genres, which contribute in an original manner to the overall result. According to Jean-Marie Schaeffer, and in contrast to some widespread opinions, literary genres evolve continuously and redefine themselves through each new text that joins the genre.

> The generic distinctions, conceived as reading categories and far from being established once and for all, are in perpetual movement: the present state of the literature projects its shadow onto the past, here bringing up to the surface features once passive, there hiding in the shadow features once emphasised and reorganising in the same way the literary acknowledged canon.
>
> (Schaeffer 182; translation A.M.)[1]

---

[1] Conçues comme catégories de lecture, les distinctions génériques, loin d'être établies une fois pour toutes, sont en perpétuel mouvement: l'état présent de la littérature projette son ombre sur le passé, ici faisant ressortir des traits autrefois inertes, là repoussant dans l'ombre des traits autrefois marqués et réorganisant du même coup le canon littéraire reçu.

I am less interested in recording the degree of involvement of each genre within the text (as Martin Simonson has done in his original study: *The Lord of the Rings and the Western Narrative Tradition*, 2008), than in considering how each genre internally evolves when brought together in the construction of *The Lord of the Rings*, the way in which the participation of all those, seemingly antithetical, genres mentioned before favours the internal evolution of each genre present in the text and generates, in the end, the inherent coherence of the universe Tolkien created.

This question of genre has been approached on numerous occasions by the Tolkien critics. For exemple, Verlyn Flieger argues the following:

> I do not propose to assign the LOTR to a particular genre, such as fairy tale, epic, or romance. The book quite clearly derives from all three, and to see it as belonging only to one category is to miss the essential elements it shares with the others. More to the point is the way in which Tolkien used these elements.
>
> (Flieger 141)

Martin Simonson in *The Lord of the Rings and the Western Narrative Tradition* talks about the mixture of different literary genres and of their interaction at all levels of the narrative. He suggests that reducing *The Lord of the Rings* to a well-defined literary genre means ignoring the rest of the elements present in the text.

> In a narrative that constantly puts narrative traditions in dialogue, like *The Lord of the Rings*, it becomes peremptory for any critic who aims at analysing the presence of different literary genres in this work, to take into account the particular dynamics of the intertraditional dialogue. Quite obviously, given that *The Lord of the Rings* is not exclusively a novel, it would be misleading and absurd to read and judge it exclusively from a novel perspective... The challenge of analysing literary genre in Tolkien's work is further increased by the fact that the character-drawing, the descriptions of action and the treatment of different themes are not coherent from the point of view of any fixed, genre-based conventions, but seem to acquire coherence from the dialogue between traditions.   (Simonson 113)

On the French side, Vincent Ferré in *Tolkien: sur les rivages de la Terre du Milieu* (2001) also discusses the generic diversity which adds to the richness of the Tolkienian text. His approach is noteworthy since it focuses on the importance of history, very appreciated by Tolkien.

This very unusual mixture of literary genres makes J.R.R. Tolkien a "completely insular author", as Isabelle Pantin argues (*Tolkien* 8), and yet, he remains an author of his time, as Tom Shippey points out in *Author of the Century*, making more visible and successful a "major commercial genre" (XVII), which would have been otherwise less present today.

In order to exemplify the dynamic of the literary genres, I will focus on the development of the fairy tale. Even though Tolkien's texts can be integrated to the fairy tale genre, they are very different from the 'traditional' ones by Brothers Grimm or Hans Christian Andersen, for instance. *Smith of Wootton Major* is a 'traditional' tale as well and Verlyn Flieger argues that this story is an exemplification of the essay *On Fairy-stories*[2] (Flieger 165).

Taking *On Fairy-stories* as a point of reference, I will discuss how Faërie can be approached and explored, but also how the more 'traditional' fairy stories can develop into a 'fairy story for adults', such as *The Lord of the Rings* did. An analysis of the fairy story elements in *The Lord of the Rings* will show that Tolkien's text is much more than an 'unconventional fairy tale'. The multitude of genre influences to be discovered in the tale brings us face to face with an unclassifiable creation, which makes us realise that Tolkien shaped a world which is one of a kind, "a one-item category on its own", as Shippey considers (*Author* XVII).

2. The Journey Back to Hobbiton: A Long Expected Tale

The difficulty of placing *The Lord of the Rings* in a precise genre may be explained by the very distinctive genesis of the text. At the beginning, the book was meant to be a sequel to *The Hobbit*, after the success that the adventures of Bilbo Baggins encountered in 1937. Tolkien's editor, Stanley Unwin, insisted that the story should be developed, but Tolkien had no idea how to do that since, from his own point of view, that particular tale was finished. He writes to his editor on 15 October 1937: "All the same I am a little perturbed. I cannot think of anything more to say about hobbits. Mr Baggins seems to have exhibited so fully both the Took and the Baggins side of their nature" (L 24). He explains to Stanley Unwin later that year, in a letter from 16 December, why he has a hard time doing what he has been asked, both by the editor and also by his young public, who wanted to know more about hobbits:

---

2   See Flieger's academic debate on the matter with Shippey in *Green Suns and Faerie*; Flieger argues that *Smith* is a fairy tale while Shippey insists we're dealing with an allegory. "Shippey reads the first Cook as a 'philologist-figure', the crass and materialistic Nokes as a 'Critic Figure' and Smith himself as a Tolkien figure' (Flieger 165, Shippey, *Road* 242-43).

> Mr Baggins began as a comic tale among conventional and in-
> consistent Grimm's fairy tale dwarves, and got drawn into the
> edge of it [the "Silmarillion"]—so that even Sauron the terrible
> peeped over the edge. And what more can hobbits do?
>
> (L 26)

If Bilbo's adventures were part of a fairy tale addressed to children, Tolkien
realises, when struggling to go forward with the writing of *The Lord of the Rings*,
that his new story (even though conceived as a sequel to the first) is becoming
rather a fairy tale for adults, with unexpected ramifications of all sorts.

> I have begun again on the sequel to the 'Hobbit'—*The Lord of the
> Rings*. It is now flowing along, and getting quite out of hand. It
> has reached about Chapter VII and progresses towards quite un-
> foreseen goals. I must say I think it is a good deal better in places
> and some ways than the predecessor; but that does not say that I
> think it either more suitable or more adapted for its audience. For
> one thing it is, like my own children (who have the immediate
> serial rights), rather 'older'... But it is no bed-time story...
>
> (L 40-41)

To stress the fact that this particular story seems to be writing itself, if we are
to believe his *Letters*, some of the characters are a real surprise even to Tolkien
himself: "A new character has come on the scene (I am sure I did not invent
him, I did not even want him, though I like him, but there he came walking
into the woods of Ithilien): Faramir, the brother of Boromir" (L 79).

Faramir is not the only one to surprise Tolkien by his unexpected appearance, but also the Ents seem to appear at their own will as the story unfolds:

> ... though I knew for years that Frodo would run into a tree-
> adventure somewhere far down the Great River, I have no recollec-
> tion of inventing Ents. I came at last to the point, and wrote the
> 'Treebeard' chapter without any recollection of any previous
> thought: just as it now is. And then I saw that, of course, it had
> not happened to Frodo at all.   (L 231)

It is relevant that the story seems to be writing itself since that sort of inspiration channels more than the children's tale that it was supposed to be in the
beginning as a sequel to *The Hobbit*.

3. The Dynamics of the Genre: Redefining the Fairy Tale

For Tolkien, the fairy tale is a genre, which allows a truthful version of reality to be captured and transmitted, while at the same time keeping the pleasure of reading intact. The verisimilitude thus created gives substance to the Secondary World. It is therefore essential to clarify what is understood by 'fairy tale' in this precise context. Tolkien denounced in particular the false relation that is supposed to exist between children and fairy tales by developing his own view on the matter at the University of St. Andrews in 1939. He later on develops this talk into the essay *On Fairy-stories*, where he defines his very own approach to the universe he calls Faërie.

> ... fairy-stories are not... stories about fairies or elves, but stories about Fairy, that is Faërie, the realm or state in which fairies have their being. Faërie contains many things besides elves and fays, and besides dwarfs, witches, trolls, giants, or dragons: it holds the seas, the sun, the moon, the sky; and the earth, and all things that are in it: tree and bird, water and stone, wine and bread, and ourselves, mortal men, when we are enchanted.   (FS 32)

According to Tolkien, Faërie has its own laws and dynamics that cannot be explained nor entirely understood but which he tries to capture in *The Lord of the Rings*.

> The definition of a fairy-story—what it is, or what it should be— does not, then, depend on any definition or historical account of elf or fairy, but upon the nature of Faërie : the Perilous Realm itself, and the air that blows in that country. I will not attempt to define that, nor to describe it directly. It cannot be done. Faërie cannot be caught in a net of words; for it is one of its qualities to be indescribable, though not imperceptible. It has many ingredients, but analysis will not necessarily discover the secret of the whole.   (FS 32)

Indeed, *The Lord of the Rings* is not a typical fairy tale but remains also a fairy tale in the particular sense that Tolkien attributes to this notion in his essay. For example, when referring to the dwarfs Tolkien gladly invents an irregular plural form (dwarf–dwarfs; for Tolkien, dwarf–dwarves) to underline, very subtly, the fact that his dwarfs and their comrades from the German fairy tales are related but not identical:

… the dwarfs are not really Germanic 'dwarfs' (Zwerge, dweorgas, dvergar), and I call them 'dwarves' to mark that. They are not naturally evil, not necessarily hostile, and not a kind of maggot-folk bred in stone; but a variety of incarnate rational creature.

(L 207)

There is also magic, certainly, but to give just one example in *The Lord of the Rings*, animals do not simply talk; there is one exception though, that of the fox which sees the hobbits leaving the Shire. It must be noted that the fox does not talk to the hobbits as the wolf does to Little Red Riding Hood, in the two famous versions of the fairy tale, that of Perrault (1697) and the very different Brothers Grimm version, dating in its familiar form from 1857. Tolkien's fox is rather intrigued by what he sees and speaks his mind, though not apparently out loud. He does not talk clearly to any other character of the universe he inhabits:

Just over the top of the hill they came on the patch of fir-wood. Leaving the road they went into the deep resin-scented darkness of the trees, and gathered dead sticks and cones to make a fire. Soon they had a merry crackle of flame at the foot of a large fir-tree and they sat round it for a while, until they began to nod. Then, each in an angle of the great tree's roots, they curled up in their cloaks and blankets, and were soon fast asleep. They set no watch; even Frodo feared no danger yet, for they were still in the heart of the Shire. A few creatures came and looked at them when the fire had died away. A fox passing through the wood on business of his own stopped several minutes and sniffed. 'Hobbits!' he thought. 'Well, what next? I have heard of strange doings in this land, but I have seldom heard of a hobbit sleeping out of doors under a tree. Three of them! There's something mighty queer behind this.' He was quite right, but he never found out any more about it.

(LotR I 85)

It may be merely a coincidence but Lord Dunsany also gives the exemple of the fox as a fabulous creature since it can cross the border to Elfland: "The fox, which is born in our fields, also crosses the frontier, going into the border of twilight at certain seasons; it is thence that he gets the romance with which he comes back to our fields. He is also fabulous, but only in Elfland, as the unicorns are fabulous here" (Dunsany 121). It may be significant that the hobbits meet the fox closer to the borders of the Shire, not far from the edge of the Wild. Tolkien is known to have read Dunsany and was most likely familiar with this passage.

Another important aspect developed in *On Fairy-stories* concerns the happy ending that all fairy tales share as a defining trademark. It is what Tolkien calls "the consolation, the joy of the happy ending" (FS 75) and even invents a word for it, 'eucatastrophe' since there was no term fit enough to describe what he wanted to express. But is this notion also applicable to the *Lord of the Rings*? Tolkien gives several examples of eucatastrophic episodes in his letters and he himself experiences what eucatastrophe means when the eagles arrive to help for the Battle of the Five Armies: "I knew I had written a story of worth in *The Hobbit* when reading it (after it was old enough to be detached from me) I had suddenly in a fairly strong measure the 'eucatastrophic' emotion at Bilbo's exclamation: 'The Eagles ! The Eagles are coming!'" (L 101).

Concerning the characters and their relation to eucatastrophe, Aragorn is perhaps the one who most obviously never loses hope, even in the darkest hour. There are lots of examples in the text that illustrate the trust 'without guarantees' that Aragorn shows concerning the fate of men but also his own role in Middle-earth, which is revealed progressively. Flieger in *Frodo and Aragorn, the Concept of the Hero*, explains the profound connection, and important differences between Aragorn and Frodo and their major roles in the dynamics of *The Lord of the Rings*:

> In *The Lord of the Rings*, Tolkien has written a medieval story and given it both kinds of hero, the extraordinary man to give the epic sweep of great events, and the common man who has the immediate, poignant appeal of someone with whom the reader can identify. Aragorn is the traditional epic/romance hero, larger than life, a leader, fighter, lover, healer. He is an extraordinary hero who combines Northrop Frye's romance and mimetic modes. He is above the common herd. We expect him to be equal to any situation. We are not like him, and we know it. We admire him, but we do not identify with him.
>
> Frodo, on the other hand, is a fairy tale hero. He is both literally and figuratively a little man, and we recognize ourselves in him. He is utterly ordinary, and this is his great value. He has the characteristics also of Frye's low mimentic hero, the hero of realistic fiction. He has doubts, feel fear, falters, makes mistakes; he experiences, in short, the same emotions we experience. He is a low mimetic hero thrown by circumstances not of his making into high mimetic action. The ways in which he deals with that action—coping with burdens that are too great, events that move

too swiftly, trials that are too terrible—draw readers into the
narrative, so that we live it with Frodo as we never could with
Aragorn.   (Flieger 142)

I would like to bring to your attention two other writers who convey this "hope
without guarantees" and for whom eucatastrophe occurs in the end, where
both characters and readers witness the previously mentioned "consolation of
the Happy Ending". George MacDonald's *At the Back of the North Wind* (1870)
and Lord Dunsany's *The King of Elfland's Daughter* (1924), two authors whom
Tolkien knew well. He mentions their work a number of times in his *Letters*.

I will focus on chapter 28 of *At the Back of the North Wind*, called *Little
Daylight*, a fairy tale independent from the bigger story of the book that was
also published separately at one point. The main story is about a very witty and
funny little boy, Diamond, who meets this magical, at times frightening but
also protective female character, North Wind, who takes him out exploring,
mostly at night, and teaches him numerous things about life and death. The
story is interesting but becomes quite allegorical at the end, which arguably
spoils the overall effect. But *Little Daylight* is a lovely tale, reminiscent in many
ways of Tolkien, not least since princess Daylight dances and sings in the most
beautiful glade in the middle of the forest, in the moonlight, not unlike Lúthien.

> She came nearer and nearer. He crept behind a tree and watched,
> wondering. It must be some strange being of the wood—a nymph
> whom the moonlight and the warm dusky air had enticed from
> her tree. But when she came close to where he stood, he no longer
> doubted she was human—for he had caught sight of her sunny
> hair, and her clear blue eyes, and the loveliest face and form that
> he had ever seen. All at once she began singing like a nightingale,
> and dancing to her own music, with her eyes turned towards the
> moon. She passed close to where he stood, dancing on by the
> edge of the trees and away in a great circle towards the other side,
> until he could see but a spot of white in the yellowish green of
> the moonlit grass.   (MacDonald 227)

She was cursed at her baptism by a bad faery to sleep during the day and be
awake at night and to flourish and wane with the phases of the moon: "The
more beautiful she was in the full moon, the more withered and worn did
she become as the moon waned" (MacDonald 223). There were several faeries
living in the wood near the palace, "such a grand wood, that nobody yet had
ever got to the other end of it" (218), which reminds us a bit of the Old Forest.
Princess Daylight will be released from the spell, if a prince would come and

kiss her; which happens, in the end, of course. Once the prince who had to flee his own kingdom sees Daylight dancing in the glade, his fate is sealed and will do everything in his power to be near her. The curse is thus reversed and princess Daylight can finally see the sun.

In Lord Dunsany's case, the Elven Princess Lirazel, who resembles Arwen in many ways, is also in love with a noble man, the lord of Erl, whom she marries and has a son with, Orion, for whom she will return from Elfland bringing the faery creatures and the land with her, literally. The notable aspect of Dunsany's Elfland is that this magic kingdom can be moved and will be moved by his King to prevent Alveric, a very determined and hopeful Strider figure, from ever reaching his daughter.

For MacDonald and Dunsany, but also for Tolkien the eucatastrophe stands as a *sine qua non* fairy tale component.

To conclude, *The Lord of The Rings* is also a fairy tale in the perspective developed by Tolkien in his essay. Indeed, we are not dealing with a traditional fairy tale, but rather with an authentic, unique one, that enriches the genre by opening new perspectives. This innovation also included the readers, by incorporating the adults into a genre usually addressed to children only.

Tolkien's Inkling colleague and friend, C.S. Lewis, shares the same opinion about the importance of stories:

> It is usual to speak in a playfully apologetic tone about one's adult enjoyment of what are called 'children's books'. I think the convention a silly one. No book is really worth reading at the age of ten which is not equally (and often far more) worth reading at the age of fifty—except, of course, books of information. The only imaginative works we ought to grow out of are those which would have been better not to have read at all. A mature palate will probably not much care for crème de menthe: but it ought still to enjoy bread and butter and honey.   (Lewis 47-48)

The Lord of the Rings is much more than an 'unconventional fairy tale'. The multitude of genre influences to be discovered brings us face to face with an unclassifiable creation, which makes us realise that Tolkien shaped a world that is one of a kind, representing "an entire province of literature", illustrating the inherent evolution of the literary genres at work and, at the same time, excluding the restrictions supposed by an *a priori* set genre.

Bibliography

Ferré, Vincent. *Tolkien: sur les rivages de la Terre du Milieu*. Paris: Christian Bourgois Éditeur, 2001

---. *Lire J.R.R. Tolkien*. Paris: Pocket, 2014

Flieger, Verlyn. *Green Suns and Faërie. Essays on Tolkien*. Kent: Kent State University Press, 2012

La Licorne. *La dynamique des genres*. Colloque de Poitiers, 18-19 octobre 1991, sous la direction de Claudine Verley. Publications de l'UFR de langues et littératures de l'université de Poitiers, n° 22, 1992

---. *Le savoir des genres*. Études réunies par Raphaël Baroni et Marielle Macé. Presses Universitaires de Rennes, 79, 2006

Lewis, C.S. *On Stories and Other Essays On Literature*. Ed. Walter Hooper. New York: Harcourt Brace Jovanovich, 1966

Lord Dunsany. *The King of Elfland's Daughter*. New York: Random House, 1999

MacDonald, George. *At the Back of the North Wind*. London: J.M. Dent and Sons, 1959

Pantin, Isabelle. "Tolkien et l'histoire littéraire: l'aporie du contexte".In: *Tolkien aujourd'hui*. Eds. Michaël Devaux, Vincent Ferré, Charles Ridoux. Valenciennes: Presses universitaires de Valenciennes, 2011

---. *Tolkien et ses légendes: Une expérience en fiction*. Paris: CNRS Editions, 2013

Simonson, Martin. *The Lord of the Rings and the Western Narrative Tradition*. Zurich/Jena: Walking Tree Publishers, 2008

Schaeffer, Jean-Marie. *Qu'est-ce qu'un genre littéraire?* Paris: Éditions du Seuil, 1989

Shippey, Tom. *The Road to Middle-earth. How J.R.R. Tolkien created a new mythology*. London: HarperCollins, 1992

---. *Author of the Century*. Boston/New York: Houghton Mifflin, 2002

Tolkien, J.R.R. *The Letters of J.R.R. Tolkien*, London: HarperCollins, 1995

---. *On Fairy-stories*. Eds. Verlyn Flieger & Douglas A. Anderson, London: HarperCollins, 2008

---. *Smith of Wotton Major*. London: HarperCollins, 2005

---. *The Hobbit*. New York: Ballantine, 1982

---. *The Lord of the Rings, The Fellowship of the Ring*. Boston/New York: Houghton Mifflin, 1994

Faërie—Utopia?
A Theological-Philosophical Defence of Escapism

Thomas Fornet-Ponse (Hildesheim)

What is the difference between the escape of the prisoner and the flight of the deserter Tolkien emphasises in *On Fairy-stories* (cf. FS 69)? The answer seems simple enough, especially if we take into account Tolkien's own remarks that a prisoner should not be scorned for trying to get out and go home or thinking and talking about the real world outside and thus the escape of the prisoner should not be regarded as treachery. Without discussing the ethical implications of desertion, indicating that even this should not be scorned prematurely, there is a deep similarity between the two that will be the focus of this essay: in both cases, the protagonists want to get out of a specific situation they regard as negative and to enter a new situation deemed better. Although it may be a little far-fetched to claim that every escaping prisoner and flying deserter has a special utopia in mind, I assume this to be the case with fairy stories in the sense Tolkien proposes.

To support this claim, I am harking back to the distinction between utopias and heterotopias made by Michel Foucault without fully agreeing to the implied criticism of utopian thinking. With reference to Ignacio Ellacuría, it is possible to develop utopian thinking rooted in heterotopias, or more specifically, that it is possible to understand Faërie as a disturbing heterotopia that implies a concrete and realisable utopia towards which the escape of the prisoner is directed.

The Concept of Utopia

The distinction between utopias and heterotopias can already be found in the preface of Foucault's early writing *The Order of Things* (fr.: *Les mots et les choses*):[1]

> *Utopias* afford consolation: although they have no real locality there is nevertheless a fantastic, untroubled region in which they are able to unfold; they open up cities with vast avenues, superbly planted gardens, countries where life is easy, even though the road to them is chimerical. *Heterotopias* are disturbing, probably

---

1   Cf. Pittl for a concise discussion of this distinction.

because they secretly undermine language, because they make it impossible to name this *and* that, because they shatter or tangle common names, because they destroy 'syntax' in advance, and not only the syntax with which we construct sentences but also that less apparent syntax which causes words and things (next to and also opposite one another) to 'hold together'.   (*Order* xix)

Thus utopias can be the subject of fables and discourse whereas heterotopias desiccate speech and dissolve our myths. While utopias and heterotopias have in common that they can be connected to all other emplacements[2] but in a suspending, neutralising, reverting way, they can also be clearly distinguished since utopias are emplacements with no real place and maintain a general relation of direct or inverted analogy with the real space of society. "They are society perfected or the reverse of society, but in any case these utopias are spaces that are fundamentally and essentially unreal" (*Spaces* 178). On the other hand, heterotopias are real and actual places, sorts of realised utopias that represent, contest and reverse all other real emplacements. Because of their utter difference from all the emplacements they refer to, Foucault calls them heterotopias. The correlation between utopias and heterotopias is a mixed one, that of a mirror. This is a placeless place in which I see myself where I am not, in an unreal space, but it has also a return effect on the place occupied by me. While utopias allow me to see "where I am absent", heterotopias force me to "reconstitute myself there where I am" (*Spaces* 179).

They can have very diverse forms, changing from society to society. Foucault mentions two major types: first, "crisis heterotopias" in so-called 'primitive' societies, meaning "privileged or sacred or forbidden places reserved for individuals who are in a state of crisis with respect to society and the human milieu in which they live" (*Spaces* 179). In 'civilised' and/or modern societies, these heterotopias disappear and are replaced by "heterotopias of deviation", places where individuals whose behaviour is not regarded as appropriate or adequate are locked away, e.g. psychiatric hospitals, prisons, etc.

The main characteristic of heterotopias that is of interest here is their capacity to "represent, contest and invert… all the other emplacements of society" (179). The two other aspects which may be applicable to fairy stories are the principle that heterotopias are able to juxtapose several incompatible emplacements in a single real place, e.g. the succession of places in a stage play, and the last one concerning their relationship to the remaining space. On the one extreme, they create "a space of illusion that denounces all real space, all real emplacements within which human life is partitioned off, as being even more

---

2   "Emplacement" is referring to the relations between locations in space as constitutive for space perception.

illusionary" (184), e.g. brothels. Or they create as heterotopias of compensation a perfect, meticulous, well-arranged space in contrast to our disorganised, badly arranged, muddled one, e.g. the Jesuit reductions in Paraguay. But the heterotopia par excellence is the ship as,

> a piece of floating space, a placeless place, that lives by its own devices, that is self-enclosed and, at the same time, delivered over to the boundless expanse of the ocean, and that goes from port to port, from watch to watch, from brothel to brothel, all the way to the colonies in search of the most precious treasures that lie wait-ing in their gardens ... the greatest reservoir of imagination.
> (185)

In this last paragraph of his essay, Foucault links heterotopias very closely to imagination and stresses that in civilisations without ships dreams will dry up.

The main and obvious difference between utopias and heterotopias according to Foucault is the essential unreality of utopias and the essential reality of heterotopias. Thus, this approach could be used for fundamentally criticising utopias as something completely abstract and unrealistic, opposed to the real world and being prone to exclusivism and totalitarianism. But that is neither a necessary consequence of Foucault's definitions—since he emphasizes with the imagery of the mirror the interrelatedness of both—nor is it unavoidable to conceive utopias as having no foundation in a specific place.

A good example of this is the utopian thinking of Ignacio Ellacuría that is clearly rooted in the socio-economic reality of Latin America, which leads Pittl to point out "that the place of Latin America in the utopian thinking of Ellacuría resembles many of the characteristics of Foucault's heterotopias" (Pittl 218). For it is excluded from the cultural, economic and religious centres of the globalised world, but nevertheless a real place which represents, contests and inverts the hegemonic order. Ellacuría stresses the dialectical character of utopia: "Utopia is history and meta-history, but above all meta-history, although springing from history and inexorably referring to history, whether by way of escape or by way of realization" (Ellacuría 9). A Christian utopia fulfils the reign of God by both pointing out its utopian character and historicising it into the realm of the concrete.

On this basis we can address the following questions: Is Faërie as understood by Tolkien a heterotopia and if this is the case, which utopia is implied by it?

Faërie as Heterotopia

According to Foucault's definition of heterotopia summarised above, Faërie can possibly be regarded as a heterotopia if it meets the following criteria: First, it has to be a real place that represents, contests and inverts the order of things in the "normal" world by being a place or space where individuals behave in a way not regarded as appropriate in the "normal" world. Second, it should enable or force someone to reconstitute oneself where one is. Third, it juxtaposes several incompatible emplacements in one single place. Fourth, it should be opposed to the remaining space by either creating an illusionary place or by being a perfect space. Finally, it should be a reservoir of imagination.

At first glance, especially the first characteristic seems to be a problem since we normally hesitate to speak of Faërie as a real space. Flieger and Anderson summarise Tolkien's use of "Faërie" as signifying first the Otherworld, that is a parallel reality tangential to our ordinary world, second the practice of enchantment and third the "altered mental or psychological state brought about by such practice" (Flieger/Anderson 85, cf. more extensively Krüger). Interestingly, Tolkien addresses the reality of entities important for "escapists" explicitly by pointing out the permanent and fundamental things fairy stories talk about (like lightning) in contrast to "real life" as proposed by the critics (e.g. a street lamp). "The notion that motor-cars are more 'alive' than, say, centaurs or dragons is curious; that they are more 'real' than, say, horses, is pathetically absurd." (FS 71) Even more, he cannot convince himself to regard the roof of Bletchley station as more 'real' than the clouds and claims it to be a less inspiring artefact than the dome of heaven—as Bifröst is more interesting than the bridge to platform 4 and a world containing the imagination of Fáfnir richer and more powerful than one without it (cf. 55). Interestingly, when he wonders about the existence of elves independently of our tales, he does not use "real" or "unreal" but: "for if elves are true" (32) indicating a difference between existence and reality. When he later writes indicatively about elves, he makes an important modification: "even if the elves are, all the more in so far as they are, only a product of Fantasy itself" (64).[3]

Furthermore, his remarks on the supernatural character of man in contrast to the "far more natural" (28) fairies reflect not only a traditional Catholic ontology, but also challenge a simple understanding of "reality" as being essentially combined with materiality and naturalness. Similarly, by discussing

---

3   Cf. the detailed discussion in Krüger.

the several desires that are satisfied in stories, according to Tolkien using the machinery of Dream cheats on "the primal desire at the heart of Faërie: the realization, independent of the conceiving mind, of imagined wonder" (35). Obviously, the desire will not sufficiently be satisfied in the mind alone but longs for a "true" realisation. Although Tolkien does not claim that centaurs or dragons are "real" (but perhaps more 'alive' than motor-cars), his argument can be corroborated by referring to a more constructivist understanding of reality which is not primarily based on materiality or similarity but on effectiveness.

Is it plausible to say that dragons are not real if they clearly have an effect in our world?[4] The relation of fantasy to sub-creation stressed by Tolkien who claims that "[a]n essential power of Faërie is thus the power of making imme-diately effective by the will the visions of 'fantasy'" (42) can perhaps be under-stood as a hint in this direction because he points out the difference between sub-creation and mere representation or symbolic interpretation. As he writes in the epilogue, every sub-creator wants to draw on reality or truth. However, this seems not applicable to the distinction between utopias and heterotopias since utopias, too, can have an effect in our world but are specified as being unreal spaces in contrast to heterotopias. Thus, heterotopias can be visited while utopias can only be imagined.

In this regard, Faërie seems more a utopia than a heterotopia. Yet there is an important difference if we consider Faërie in literary works, e.g. *Smith of Woot-ton Major*—there it is a real space, although perhaps not easily entered, that is in relation to the "normal" world and functions as a reservoir of imagina-tion for Smith. Similarly, the tales of fairies as workers of illusion presuppose that the fairies in these stories "are not themselves illusions; behind the fantasy real wills and powers exist, independent of the minds and purposes of men" (35). It is therefore an essential trait of a fairy story to be presented as "true", as believable (in contrast to the often quoted "willing suspension of disbelief" suggested by Coleridge).[5] This is closely related to the notion of sub-creation for a successful sub-creator "makes a Secondary World which your mind can enter. Inside it, what he relates is 'true': it accords with the laws of that world... The moment disbelief arises, the spell is broken; the magic, or rather art, has failed. You are then out in the Primary World again, looking at the little abortive Secondary World from outside" (52). This secondary belief is an enchanted state which does not depend on the existence of the things mentioned or the

---

4   Cf. for epistemologies dealing explicitly with the (un)reality of the "world" the notion of "epistemologically different worlds" by Vacariu or the "New Realism" proposed by Gabriel.

5   „One who suspends disbelief does not eo ipso believe. Hence the importance of the regularity of the Secondary World's structure: suspension of disbelief allows the reader to accept flaws and inconsistencies which true secondary belief will not admit" (Shank 154). Cf. Also Sandner.

events told in "real life" because fairy stories deal more with desirability than with possibility. An important aspect of secondary worlds is their relation to the primary world as "composed of language that reflects human experience of primary reality" (Shank 152).

The very beginning of *On Fairy-stories* supports this specific "reality" of Faërie because Tolkien writes:

> Faërie is a perilous land, and in it are pitfalls for the unwary and dungeons for the overbold...
>
> The realm of fairy-story is wide and deep and high and filled with many things: all manner of beasts and birds are found there; shoreless seas and stars uncounted; beauty that is an enchantment, and an ever-present peril; both joy and sorrow as sharp as swords.   (FS 27)

Faërie is thus depicted as a deeply ambiguous space which is in itself an indication for a combination of utopia and heterotopia (like the mirror). Its strangeness and peril as well as the extremes found there are signs of its heterotopian character because they disturb and contest the order of things. They thus challenge the wanderers in Faërie to reconstitute themselves where they normally live (second criterion)—the best example being Smith who due to his contact to and acquaintance with Faërie via the star is able to produce not only good workmanship with the tools being strong and lasting and graceful, but also some things made only for delight, "and they were beautiful, for he could work iron into wonderful forms that looked as light and delicate as a spray of leaves and blossom, but kept the stern strength of iron, or seemed even stronger" (SWM 21). However, he cannot live in Faërie but has to live and work in Wotton Major. Finally, he even has to pass on the star which allows his successor to enter Faërie (cf. SWM 44ff).

As Tolkien writes in his accompanying essay, the special skill and artistic quality were primarily valid for the several crafts of Wootton only deteriorating because of their commercial success with possible negative consequences not only for the prosperity of the village but also for a good life and that which makes life worth living and transcends mere existence. "History and legend and above all any tales touching on 'faery', have become regarded as children's stuff, patronizingly tolerated for the amusement of the very young"[6] (SWM 93, cf. 100f). This evoked a reaction by Faery, namely the King of Faery com-

---

6   That this may apply for Tolkien also to contemporary England is supported by Flieger's note on his reference to a "reformed" church and the memory of "merrier" days since this "recalls the expression 'Merry England', a phrase evoking a utopian, pre-industrial way of life now ruined by the rise of commerce and the profit motive" (SWM 147).

ing and serving as an apprentice in the village, thus emphasising the serving function of Faërie for a full and proper human development by showing the importance of love—and thus indicating a utopia—, "a relationship towards all things, animate and inanimate, which includes love and respect, and removes or modifies the spirit of possession and domination" (94).

Furthermore, the plenty of Faërie mentioned in the quote above is an indication for the third criterion, the juxtaposition of incompatible things—others are these entities which in combination raise disbelief in an unsuccessful sub-creation and secondary belief in a successful one, and mark Faërie as an Other-world, e.g. a place where the well-known green sun can exist. "Fantasy, the making or glimpsing of Other-worlds, was the heart of the desire of Faërie" (FS 55). Tolkien stresses not only the connection of Faërie and imagination as the mental faculty of conceiving images but also that of Faërie and Fantasy as expressing both the sub-creative art—"the operative link between Imagination and the final result, sub-creation" (59)—and a quality of strangeness and wonder in a successful expression of the imagination.[7] Fantasy in the sense proposed by Tolkien thus combines imagination and "the derived notions of 'unreality' (that is, of unlikeness to the Primary world), of freedom from the domination of observed 'fact', in short of the fantastic" (60). Fantasy is not to be confounded with dreaming, imagining things that cannot be found in our primary world (or are seen as such) and thus implying an arresting strangeness—in measure of the unlikeness of the images and rearrangements of primary material to the primary world. This alludes clearly to the escape of the prisoner; the prison being observable facts or, more generally speaking, a primarily materialistic worldview in contrast to which Fantasy produces the 'inner consistency of reality' and thus points out the "reality" of the Fantastic.[8]

More explicitly, he deals with these two opposing worldviews in his poem *Mythopoiea*, e.g. arguing for stars being more than "some matter in a ball / compelled to courses mathematical" but "living silver made that sudden burst / to flame like flowers beneath an ancient song" (TL 85/87) and emphasising the human right to sub-creation in the likeness of their own maker in contrast to the "progressive apes" he refuses to walk with, not surrendering his golden sceptre of creativity (TL 89).[9]

---

7   Tolkien relies here heavily on the entry "Fancy" in the first edition of the OED, cf. Anderson/Flieger 110.

8   This can also be seen in a paragraph in the miscellaneous pages edited by Flieger and Anderson: Faërie "reposes (for us now) in a view that the normal world, tangible visible audible, is only an appearance. Behind it is a reservoir of power which is manifested in these forms" (FS 270).

9   In his analysis of *Mythopoeia*, Weinreich considers the critique of a materialistic worldview, the dualism implied by the proposition of a second level of existence or the notion of knowledge in light of "pure Platonism" or a poetical short version of the epistemology of *Phaidon* and *Politeia* (cf. 48).

Not speaking of an escape, but of a break-out, Tolkien summarises the several effects of Faërie in his essay on *Smith of Wootton Major*:

> Faery represents at its weakest a breaking out (at least in mind) from the iron ring of the familiar, still more from the adamantine ring of belief that it is known, possessed, controlled, and so (ultimately) all that is worth being considered—a constant awareness of a world beyond these rings. More strongly it represents love: that is, a love and respect for all things, 'inanimate' and 'animate', an unpossessive love of them as 'other'. This 'love' will produce both *truth* and *delight*. Things seen in its light will be respected, and they will also appear delightful, beautiful, wonderful even glorious.   (SWM 101)

The breaking out from familiarity combines the aspects of recovery and escape discussed below, the awareness of a world beyond, and the representation of love allude to the combination of heterotopia and utopia in Faërie. To produce the inner consistency of reality characteristic for a successful Fantasy is a very demanding task and requires labour, thought and "a special skill, a kind of elvish craft" (61) which is best accomplished in literature. Going even beyond secondary belief is possible in contact with a "Faërian Drama", a play presented to men by elves that produces a realistic and immediate Fantasy: "If you are present at a Faërian drama you yourself are, or think that you are, bodily inside its Secondary World" (63). This resembles the mirror-function of utopias and heterotopias. Tolkien calls the art necessary for producing a secondary world that can be entered by designer and spectator alike an Enchantment (in contrast to magic).[10] To this form of "realistic" sub-creative art Fantasy aspires. It is important for the ability to produce a believable secondary world that Fantasy is a natural activity for humans that does not contradict reason; on the contrary: "The keener and the clearer is the reason, the better fantasy will it make... For creative Fantasy is founded upon the hard recognition that things are so in the world as it appears under the sun; on a recognition of fact, but not a slavery to it" (65).

In addition, the otherworldliness of Faërie marks its relation to the remaining space or emplacements as an opposition (fourth criterion). When Fantasy provokes suspicion and is regarded as a childish folly, as illusionary or only suited for children or youths, it can be understood as another expression of this

---

10 'Enchantment' is both the act of enchanting and the state of being enchanted, cf. Anderson/Flieger 112. "This double meaning reflects how Faërie plays a role both in the author's production of works of Fantasy, and the reader's reception and experience of these works" (Shank 148).

relationship of opposition (as illusionary or perfect space). The otherworldliness and opposition of Faërie in comparison to the ordinary world is exemplified by the dangers and evils mentioned in *Smith* that can only be challenged with special weapons that cannot be wielded by mortals. Although Smith would have been able to forge weapons "that in his own world would have had power enough to become the matter of great tales and be worth a king's ransom, he knew that in Faery they would have been of small account" (SWM 24).

Another aspect emphasised by Tolkien is that Faërie can be perceived but not completely be described or defined, and therefore it is necessary to approach it asymptotically or circumscribe it by analysing fairy stories (cf. FS 32). That differs indeed from heterotopias that are set in a psychiatric clinic but corresponds to heterotopias undermining language by shattering or muddling common names.

Although not all of the mentioned criteria are met totally by the concepts of Faërie and Fantasy as proposed by Tolkien, the similarities should be sufficient to understand them as heterotopias in close relation to a utopia.

Which Utopia?

Having established the possibility of conceiving Faërie as heterotopia, we can now turn to the question, which utopia is hinted at and aspired to by the escape of the prisoner?

Before discussing Tolkien's account of the escape offered by fairy stories, it is important not to skip his reflections on recovery since from an epistemological perspective this is also a form of escape. Recovery—"return" in Manuscript B (FS 237) emphasises the direction towards a former state as an effect of fairy stories—is the possibility to see familiar things in a new light after having been confronted with unfamiliar ones. Tolkien uses visual metaphors of seeing clearly to describe it more specifically:

> Recovery (which includes return and renewal of health) is a re-gaining—regaining of a clear view. I do not say 'seeing things as they are' and involve myself with the philosophers, though I might venture to say 'seeing things as we are (or were) meant to see them'—as things apart from ourselves. We need, in any case, to clean our windows; so that the things seen clearly may be freed from the drab blur of triteness or familiarity—from possessiveness. (67)

Tolkien here makes the epistemological claim that familiarity hinders our ability to see things as we should see them—everything "in proper perspective and in its proper place" (Sandner 136)—but is not entering the philosophical discussion on the possibility of perceiving the noumenon (cf. Shank 155f). He illustrates the relation to possessiveness or (legal or mental) appropriation and thus the danger of familiarity narratively in *Smith of Wotton Major* where the festivals have become vulgarly self-satisfied among most of the community, with one exception being Smith and his family. They include no more dancing, singing and tale-telling but mainly eating and drinking, as he points out in his essay on *Smith* (cf. SWM 84, 93, 100). The recuperative effects of a contact with Faërie can be seen when the boy Tim swallows the star: "But soon a light began to shine in his eyes, and he laughed and became merry, and sang softly to himself. Then he got up and began to dance all alone with an odd grace that he had never shown before" (SWM 61).

Although there are several means for recovering a clear view besides fairy stories, e.g. humility or seeing things from a new angle (like in the famous *Mooreeffoc* example)[11], Fantasy does this most thoroughly and mainly concerning simple or fundamental things. While a state where we see things as we are meant to see them may be considered as an abstract or unrealistic utopia, the term "recovery" (and especially "return" in the first draft) implies it is a state which existed before and can be achieved again.

Similarly, Escape and Consolation can be achieved through various forms, one of which being fairy stories. In his defence of Escape, Tolkien underlines first the practicality of it in "real life" where it should not be blamed. He believes critics are misusing it by confusing the escape of the prisoner with the flight of the deserter (and prefer acquiescent collaborationists to resisting patriots) and thus scorn not only desertion, but also "real Escape, and what are often its companions, Disgust, Anger, Condemnation, and Revolt" (69). Tolkien gives the example of electric street-lamps that are not mentioned in stories, which illustrates that he understands Escape as a critique of things in the primary world that are often taken for granted or seen as indispensable without ruling out the possibility of reaction (e.g. pulling out the street-lamps). The accusation of escape from the so called "real life" is thus not appropriate for fairy stories in contrast to some 'serious' literature that Tolkien compares to playing "under a glass roof by the side of a municipal swimming-bath. Fairy stories may invent monsters that fly the air or dwell in the deep, but at least they do not try to escape from heaven or the sea" (71).

Tolkien seems to link Escape strongly to a critique of the modern world which does not necessarily lead to reaction but nevertheless prefers horses, castles, knights, kings and priests to factories, machine-guns and bombs. This critique is—at least in this essay—primarily aesthetical; pointing out the ugliness of modern life which seems allied with evil and thus producing the desire to

---

11 It is interesting to note the development of Tolkien's thought on *Mooreeffoc* from a rather sceptical perspective in the first drafts (cf. Manuscript B) to the given lecture and the several emendations for publication.

escape "not indeed from life, but from our present time and self-made misery" (72). But this is only a rather accidental and special 'escapist' aspect that fairy stories have in common with other stories about the past. More profound escapisms are concerned with hardships like "hunger, thirst, poverty, pain, sorrow, injustice, death" (73) or the limitations of human beings, both excusable weaknesses like the desire to visit the deep sea or flying like a bird, and more profound wishes like being able to communicate with other living things. Satisfaction or consolation of both can be found in fairy stories, e.g. talking beasts or the magical understanding of animal speech. This implies another critique of modern human life, namely human detachedness from its fellow creatures which results out of human guilt. "Other creatures are like other realms with which Man has broken off relations, and sees now only from the outside at a distance, being at war with them, or on the terms of an uneasy armistice" (74).

Thus the escape from this separation implies a utopia in which all living things not only live together in peace but also communicate with each other. But the oldest and deepest desire is the Escape from Death—at least for humans since their counterparts among the elves deal with the Escape from Deathlessness as Tolkien not only claims in this essay, but also exemplarily develops in his legendarium, discussed theoretically especially in *Athrabeth Finrod ah Andreth* (MR 301-360; cf. Fornet-Ponse). In view of this escape, Tolkien stresses the lesson taught in fairy stories of the burden of the elfish kind of immortality, meaning endless serial living. Therefore, our first assumption regarding the utopia hinted at by this escape, that it includes immortality, is challenged by this perspective establishing a utopia in which death is not seen as negative but as a necessary part not only of biological life but for human perfection.

This is a good example of how the heterotopia of Faërie forces us to reconstitute ourselves, how we are and where we are—mortal beings in a limited world. Shank emphasises that the desires are only temporarily satisfied while the individual is immersed in a secondary world and therefore offers no ultimate satisfaction. "The insatiability of desire explains why individuals may read the same story again and again, and why more and more stories continue to be told" (Shank 155, with reference to FS 75f).

This leads to the aspect of consolation provided by fairy stories which does not mean the satisfaction of the desires (which could only be temporal during the stay in the secondary world) or a successful escape but primarily the Happy Ending, especially the sudden positive turn, the Eucatastrophe which is neither escapist nor fugitive,

> a sudden and miraculous grace: never to be counted on to recur. It does not deny the existence of *dyscatastrophe*, of sorrow and failure: the possibility of these is necessary to the joy of deliverance;

it denies (in the face of much evidence, if you will) universal final defeat and in so far is *evangelium*, giving a fleeting glimpse of Joy, Joy beyond the walls of the world, poignant as grief.

(FS 75)

A good fairy story is able to produce a corresponding joyous effect in hearers or readers experiencing this turn, depending on the story and the. Tolkien explains this joy by referring to the wish of every sub-creator to make something real or draw on reality, respectively. Thus the specific quality of the joy of a successful Fantasy is a reference to the underlying reality or truth. While it is true at first only in that secondary world, it may offer a brief vision of a greater answer— "it may be a far-off gleam or echo of *evangelium* in the real world" (77).[12] His often quoted remarks on the Christian belief of human redemption in a way corresponding to their nature and thus regarding the Gospels as containing a fairy story are of interest for our question which utopia a fairy story contains, insofar as the Gospels themselves and especially the Christ-event can be re-garded as a heterotopia connected closely to the realisable utopia of the reign of God. By pointing out how according to Tolkien the joy evoked by a successful fairy story depends on its underlying reality and truth we can assume that the utopia ultimately intended by a fairy story (and Faërie) and the escape of the prisoner is this ultimate Christian utopia of the reign of God, of a living to-gether in peace and plenty not only among human beings but among the whole of creation. Although this utopia is not yet realised, it has clear consequences for Christians in their present time.

The *Evangelium* has not abrogated legends, it has hallowed them, especially the 'happy ending'. The Christian has still to work, with mind as well as body, to suffer, hope, and die; but he may now perceive that all his bents and faculties have a purpose, which can be redeemed. So great is the bounty with which he has been treated that he may now, perhaps, fairly dare to guess that in Fantasy he may actually assist in the effoliation and multiple enrichment of creation.   (78f)

These show clearly the intrinsic relatedness of this special kind of heterotopia and utopia since Faërie with Fantasy as heterotopia points to a utopia which is at present a placeless space but which can be realised and thus calls for a human contribution to realise this utopia. The necessity of Faërie as the compound of

---

12 "Eine Realitätsebene, mitsamt ihren (schrecklichen) Bedingungen, wird als nur *eine* Realitätsebene sichtbar" (Krüger 208).

awareness of a world beyond our domestic parish, love for the things in it and desire for wonder etc. is stressed by Tolkien in his essay on *Smith*: "this 'Faery' is as necessary for the health and complete functioning of the Human as is sunlight for physical life: sunlight as distinguished from the soil, say, though it in fact permeates and modifies even that" (SWM 101).

Bibliography

Anderson, Douglas, & Flieger, Verlyn. "Editors' Commentary". *On Fairy-stories. Expanded edition, with commentary and notes.* Ed. by Verlyn Flieger & Douglas A. Anderson. London: HarperCollins, 2008, 85-121

Ellacuría, Ignacio. "Utopia and Propheticism from Latin America. A Concrete Essay in Historical Soteriology". *A Grammar of Justice. The Legacy of Ignacio Ellacuría.* Eds. Matthew Ashley, Kevin Burke & Rodolfo Cardenal. Maryknoll: Orbis, 2014, 7-55

Fornet-Ponse, Thomas. "Tolkiens Theologie des Todes". *Hither Shore* 2 (2005): 157-186

Foucault, Michel. *The Order of Things. An archaeology of the human sciences.* London/New York: Routledge, 2002

---. "Different Spaces". *Aesthetics, Method, and Epistemology.* Ed. James D. Faubion. New York: The New Press, 1998, 175-185

Gabriel, Markus. *Warum es die Welt nicht gibt.* Berlin: Ullstein, 2013

---. *Die Erkenntnis der Welt. Eine Einführung in die Erkenntnistheorie.* München: Karl Alber, 2012

Krüger, Heidi. "Eine Neubewertung der theoretischen Konzeption von 'Faërie' und 'fairy-story' auf Basis der 2008 erschienenen erweiterten Ausgabe *Tolkien on Fairy-stories*". *Hither Shore* 5 (2008): 197-220

Pittl, Sebastian. "The 'crucified people' as a place of a heterotopic utopia". *Unterwegs zu einer neuen „Zivilisation geteilter Genügsamkeit". Perspektiven utopischen Denkens 25 Jahre nach dem Tod Ignacio Ellacurías.* Hg. Sebastian Pittl & Gunter Prüller-Jagenteufel. Wien: Vienna University Press, 2016, 213-225

Sandner, David. "'Joy Beyond the Walls of the World': The Secondary World-Making of J.R.R. Tolkien and C.S. Lewis". *J.R.R. Tolkien and His Literary Resonances. Views of Middle-earth.* Eds. George Clark & Daniel Timmons. Westport/London: Greenwood, 2000, 133-145

Shank, Derek. "'The Web of Story': Structuralism in Tolkien's 'On Fairy-stories'". *Tolkien Studies* X (2013): 147-165

Tolkien, John R.R. *On Fairy-stories. Expanded edition, with commentary and notes.* Ed. by Verlyn Flieger & Douglas A. Anderson. London: HarperCollins, 2008

---. *Smith of Wootton Major. Extended Edition.* Ed. by Verlyn Flieger. London: HarperCollins, 2005

---. *Morgoth's Ring. The History of Middle-earth X.* Ed. by Christopher Tolkien. London: HarperCollins, 1994

---. *Tree and Leaf.* London: HarperCollins, 2001

Vacariu, Gabriel. *Epistemologically different Worlds.* Bucharest: University of Bucharest Press, 2008

Weinreich, Frank. "Die Metaphysik der Zweitschöpfung. Zur Ontologie von *Mythopoeia*". *Hither Shore* 4 (2007) 37-50

Analogy, Sub-creation and Surrealism
Claudio Antonio Testi (Modena)

This article will show the importance of Tolkien's use of analogy in *On Fairy-stories*, a use that has often been underrated in Tolkien studies, probably because modern culture mostly ignores the theory of analogy as developed by Aquinas (the apex of this theory).

This contribution is divided in four parts: First, we will see Tolkien's use of connected pairs of nouns in *On Fairy-stories*. Then I will explain Analogy in Aquinas, trying to demonstrate that Tolkien's use of connected pairs of nouns is a language sharing the same logical structure of analogy. Third, I will deal with Tolkien's knowledge of Aquinas. Finally, I will show the role of analogy in Tolkien's conception of Art, comparing his ideas with Surrealism.

Tolkien's Use of Connected Pairs of Nouns in *On Fairy-stories*

> What really happens is that the *story-maker* proves a successful *sub-creator*. He makes a *Secondary World* which your mind can enter. Inside it, what he relates is "true": it accords with the laws of that world. You therefore believe it, while you are, as it were, inside. The moment disbelief arises, the spell is broken; the magic, or rather art, has failed. You are then out in the *Primary World* again, looking at the little abortive *Secondary World* from outside.
>
> (FS 52 par. 50, italics added)

> To make a *Secondary World* inside which the green sun will be credible, commanding *Secondary Belief*, will probably require labour and thought, and will certainly demand a special skill, a kind of elvish craft.   (FS 61 par. 69, italics added)

In the well-known texts I have emphasised nouns, or pairs of nouns, such as Primary/Secondary-world or creator/sub-creator. In those examples we can distinguish two cases:

1. There is a basic noun A to which Tolkien adds a prefix obtaining a derived noun ("creator" plus "sub-" = to "sub-creator").
2. There is a basic noun and Tolkien adds two prefixes obtaining two nouns. "World" plus "primary" or "secondary" = to "primary-world" or "secondary world".

TABLE 1

A (basic noun)	I (first prefix)	II (second prefix)	Resulting pair
Creator	/	Sub-	Creator / sub-creator
World	Primary	Secondary	Primary-world / secondary world

In both cases, there are pairs of nouns with two qualities:

1. We can predicate both the nouns in each pair: for example we can say "the secondary world is a world" and "the primary-world is a world".
2. There is an order between the nouns, because one presupposes the existence of the other: "sub-creator" presupposes "creator", "secondary world" presupposes "primary world" (the second always presupposes a first, but not vice versa).

We can make the same analysis for many pairs of nouns, as we can see in the table below.

TABLE 2

A	I-A	II-A	Occurrences I-A	Occurrences II-A
World	Primary World 12	Secondary-World 9	49, 50, 66(3), 67, 68, 71, 74, 75, 76, 77, 85, 104	50(2), 69, 72, 74(2), 75, 103(2)
Belief	Primary Belief 1	Secondary Belief 5	74	51, 66n, 69, 74, 75
Reality	Reality 12	Un reality 1	65, 66(2), 68(2), 74, 103(5), 104 (5)	66
Creation	Creation(s) 5	Sub-Creation 3	11 n.1, 65, 104(2), 106(2),	28, 66, 104
Art	Primary Art 1	Secondary (subcreative) Art 1	74	65
Creator	Creator 0	Sub-Creator 4		29, 50, 77, 103
Material	Primary material 1	Secondary material 0	68	
Truth/ True	Primar(il)y truth/true 2	Secondary truth/true 0	105(2)	

As we can see, in the left side, there are the elements of the pairs of nouns (basic noun, first derived noun, second derived noun) and under these nouns there is the number of their occurrences in FS. On the right, there is the location of those occurrences, given with the same paragraphs numbering adopted by Flieger/Anderson in their expanded edition of *On Fairy-stories*.

For example, in the first line, the composed noun "primary-world" occurs 12 times, secondary-world occurs 9 times, and Primary world occurs once in paragraph number 49 and 50, 3 times in paragraph number 66, and so on.

I asked Peter Gilliver (author of *The Ring of Words*), if some of these words could be regarded as having been invented by Tolkien. Here is the answer:

> All of the other words or phrases which you mention—primary world, secondary world, primary belief, secondary belief—are composed of such elements; and therefore it is entirely possible that other writers could have used these combinations before Tolkien. None of these four items have been included in the OED, so I cannot say for sure who first used them without doing new research. In fact I can see from doing a very little research that philosophical and theological writers were already using the expression 'primary belief' before 1870. It is possible that Tolkien may have used the words to refer to particular concepts, in a way which nobody had used them before; if the concepts he was discussing had not been discussed before, that would make these expressions similar to subcreation and subcreator. But that is not the same as 'invention'.   (e-mail 10/3/2015)

Now, returning to FS, the table below shows where the occurrences are located in the sections, and as we can see from the total and the density—that is occurrences divided by number of paragraphs—they are mainly located in the section "Fantasy" and in the "Epilogue".

TABLE 3

Occurrences of Pairs of connected Names	Total occur-rences	Fairy stories 1-22 (23)	Origins 23-41 (18)	Child-ren 42-64 (23)	Fantasy 65-80 (16)	Reco-very. 81-101(21)	Epi-logue 102-106 (5)	Notes 107-18 (12)
Primary World 12/ Secondary World 9	21			49, 50 / 50 (2)	66(3), 67, 68, 71, 74, 75, 76, 77 / 69, 72, 74(2), 75	85	104 / 103(2)	
Reality 12 / Unreality 1	13				65, 66(2), 68(2), 74 / 66		103(5), 104	
Creation(s) 5 / Sub-creation 3	8		28		11, 65 / 66		104(2), 106, / 104	
Primary Belief 1 / Secondary Belief 5	6			/ 51	74 / 66n, 69, 74, 75			
Maker 2 / Story-maker 4	6			/ 50 (2)	80 / 86, 93	103		
Creator 0 / Sub-creator 4	4		/ 29	/ 50, 77			/ 103	
Primary Art 1 / Secondary Art 1	2				74 / 65			
Primar(il)y truth-true 2 / Secondary truth 0	2						105 (2)	
Primary material 1 / Secondary material 0	1				68			
Total	63	0	2	9	36	4	14	0
Density		0	0,11	0,39	2,25	0,19	2,8	0

I have also examined at the Bodleian Library the manuscripts edited by Flieger/Anderson concerning FS. There are three of them: A, dated 1939; B, dated 1943, that also contains a *miscellanea* of texts; C (that is the basis for three typescripts that lead to the final version of the essay). Concerning A and B, I have checked the nouns mentioned earlier and the result is:

TABLE 4

Names with Prefix	MS A 1939 pp. 175-194 = 19	MS B 1943 pp. 206-251 = 45	MS B Miscellanea 1943 pp. 252-296 = 44
Sub-creator	192	223, 246	
Sub-creation		222	
Secondary World(s)		242, 246 (2)	270, 271(s), 271, 288 (2)
Primary World		246 (2)	296
Primarily true		245, 246	296
Un-real			268, 296
Primarily real			296
Primary Existence			287
Secondary Belief			288
Primary Art			295

As we can see, Tolkien developed the use of those derived nouns mainly in MS B, in 1943, hence we can say that also in FS there is an increasing presence of philosophical and theological issues[1].

At the end of this section, we can finally conclude that Tolkien makes a systematic and rigorous use of this kind of noun-pairing.

2. Analogy in Aquinas

I think it is interesting for Tolkien studies to point out that this use of pairs of nouns is the same Aquinas used to define a certain kind of analogy. Aquinas distinguishes many kinds of analogy,[2] but this is not the time and place to examine them in details (I've already done that in other philosophi-

---

1   See Fornet-Ponse.
2   For Analogy in Aquinas see: Ashwoth, "Signification"; Aswoth, "Analogy"; Basti/Perrone; Basti/Testi; Bertelè et al.; Bochenski; Boyer; Fabro, *Nozione*; Fabro, *Partecipazione*; Geiger; Lear; Schmidt; Mondin; Maurer; McInerny; Righi; Tyn.

cal articles and books[3]). The fundamental distinction in Aquinas, however, is between analogy of proportionality and analogy of attribution:

In *Analogy of proportionality* there are four nouns disposed in two pairs sharing a similar relation, so we can predicate the same relation of two different nouns. For example "night is to the day as death is to life". Here there is analogy because there is a *similar* relation ("the end of") between two *different* pairs of nouns, and we can predicate analogically this relation of different nouns saying: "night is the end of the day" and "death is the end of life".

However, this kind of analogy is not very important for Tolkien studies, because it is the basis for metaphor and allegory that Tolkien cordially dislikes. In fact, for Aristotle (*Poetics* c. 21), we obtain a metaphor when in an analogy of proportionality we attribute the third noun ("death", that is properly in relation with "life") to the first noun, saying that "night is the death of the day": so now "night" means "death". And for Quintiliano (*Istitutio Oratoria*, VIII c. 6 n. 44) "allegory" is a "continuum metaphor".

But there is also *analogy of attribution (or proportion)*, instead, that is more important for Tolkien studies. Here, there are at least three nouns A, B, C where both A and B are C ("A is C" and "B is C") but the being-C for B presupposes A. For example, we can predicate "being" of both substance and accident, but accident presupposes substance.

> ... what is predicated of some things according to priority and posteriority is certainly not predicated univocally. For the prior is included in the definition of the posterior, as substance is included in the definition of accident according as an accident is a being.
> (Aquinas, *Summa Contra Gentiles* Lib. I cap. 32 n.7)4

In fact in this classical example, we have to keep in mind that in his ontology, Aquinas defines substance as "ens per se (*being in itself*)" and accident as "ens in alio (*being in something else*)", or "ens in substantia (*being in a substance*)". This means that accident in its definition presupposes substance, so "being" is primarily predicated of "substance" and secondly of "accident". For example, the accident "white" is a colour that cannot exist for itself, but needs a substance (for example a piece of paper) in which this "white" can exist. It is paramount that Aquinas (like Tolkien) uses two prefixes ("in itself", "in something else") added to a noun ("being") to define two different beings ("substance" and "accident").

---

3 Testi, "Analogia"; Testi, "Logica"; Testi, "Formalizzazione".
4 "Quod praedicatur de aliquibus secundum prius et posterius, certum est univoce non praedicari: nam prius in definitione posterioris includitur: sicut substantia in definitione accidentis secundum quod est ens. Si igitur diceretur univoce ens de substantia et accidente".

TABLE 5

A (basic noun)	"I" (first prefix)	II (second prefix)	Resulting pair
Being	In itself	In something else	Being in itself (=substance) / Being in something else (=accident)

TABLE 6

A	I-A	II-A
Being	Substance (= being in itself)	Accident (being in something else)

In this case (as in Tolkien's cases previously examined), there is a pair of nouns with two qualities:

Firstly, we can predicate a noun ("being") of both the pair nouns: we can say "substance is a being" and "accident is a being" (as we have said that "the secondary world is a world" and "the primary-world is a world").

Secondly, there is an order between these nouns, because there is a noun that presupposes the existence of the other: an accident always presupposes the existence of a substance (as sub-creator presupposes creator, or secondary world presupposes primary world).

It is also impressive to note how Tolkien and Aquinas use the same notion of participation to connect the terms (Reality / Secondary World in Tolkien; substance / accident in Aquinas):

> In an analogical community different things *partake* of the same thing in a *primary or secondary* order, as it happens for… substance and accident.[5]   (Aquinas, In I Liber Sententiarum, Prologus, q. 1 art. 2 ad 2; italics added)

> Probably every writer making a *secondary world*, a fantasy, every *sub-creator*, wishes in some measure to be a real maker, or hopes that he is drawing on reality: hopes that the peculiar quality of this *secondary world* (if not all the details) are derived from *Reality*, or are flowing into it. If he indeed achieves a quality that can fairly be described by the dictionary definition: 'inner consistency of *reality*' it is difficult to conceive how this can be, if the work does not in some way *partake of reality*.   (FS 77 par. 103, italics added)

---

5   "Aut ex eo quod aliqua participant aliquid unum secundum prius et posterius, sicut potentia et actus rationem entis, et similiter substantia et accidens"

So, I hope to have demonstrated that Tolkien systematically uses a language that has the same logical structure of Aquinas' analogy.

3. Tolkien's Knowledge of Aquinas

I t is less important to demonstrate that Tolkien makes a conscious use of Aquinas' analogy, but now I will sum up some arguments which show that Tolkien was aware of Aquinas' ideas.[6]

1. I own an old edition of the *Summa Theologica* where each volume bears Tolkien's signature, and some Tolkien experts (like Milbank, Hostetter, Flieger, Hammond/Scull, Collier) have unofficially confirmed the authenticity of the signatures. Thanks to Carl Hostetter, I obtained from Christopher Tolkien a confirmation that this same edition of the *Summa* is mentioned in a list of books, written by Tolkien himself, which his father bought in the early 1920s. Within this *Summa* there are many notes in pencil (grey, blue, red) and in purple ink: in the books at the English Faculty Library of Oxford, I found many notes by Tolkien written in margins in pencil in the same colours. A precise examination of all the annotations has not been completed yet, but we can assert that Tolkien certainly owned and probably consulted this important theological book.[7]
2. Father Francis Morgan, Tolkien's legal guardian, had a broad theological culture and, as a catholic priest, must have received a Thomistic education, because the encyclical *Aeterni Patris* (1879) established that every priest must receive an education based on Aquinas's ideas.[8]
3. In the Birmingham Oratory the religious teaching was relevant, as Tolkien affirms in *Letter* n. 306.
4. In addition, King Edward's School was founded by Cardinal Newman who often quotes Aquinas in his writings[9] (Father Francis was also his Secretary).
5. Carpenter affirms that during the Inklings meetings a copy of *Summa Theologica* was always sat side by side with a copy of *Beowulf*[10]
6. We should remember that C.S. Lewis often quotes Aquinas in his writings.[11]

---

6   For Tolkien and Aquinas see: Birzer; Kocher; MacIntosh, *Flame*; MacIntosh, "Ainulindalë"; Testi, "Tommaso"; Milbank, "Tolkien"; Milbank, *Tolkien*; Nimmo; Testi, "Logic"; Hart.
7   For more information about this item see also: Testi, "Logic".
8   See Bru.
9   I.e. Newman 269, 272.
10 Carpenter, chapter 3.
11 I.e. Lewis *Problem* ch. II and VIII; *Allegory* 19, 21, 110.

7. Also Barfield perfectly knew Aquinas's writings, as is evident when reading his *Saving the appearances[12]*. Verlyn Flieger has suggested investigating if the notion of participation used by Barfield (he theorises an Original and a Final participation) has some connections with the notion used by Aquinas. I can briefly say that this notion has in Aquinas primarily an ontological content: as seen before, it is between substance and accident (and so on). This is different from Barfield's use of this notion: for him participation is only (and always) a relation between human consciousness and the known world.

8. The Inklings also included Father Matthews, a member of the Oxford Dominicans, where Tolkien often attended mass:[13] still now these Dominicans are very "devoted" to Aquinas's Teachings.[14]

9. Christopher Tolkien (in an e-mail quoted by Jonathan MacIntosh) affirms that Tolkien knew the books written by Jaques Maritain, one of the most important Thomists of the last century.[15]

4. Tolkien, Analogy, and Surrealism

In the final part of this article, it will be shown that Tolkien's use of an analogical language is important for a more complete understanding of his ideas concerning Art and the connection between Fantasy and Reason that share an analogical relationship: this is paramount when Tolkien analyses the surrealist conception of art. Surrealism is an artistic movement (both literary and pictorial) that affirms a radical separation between reason and Art, the reality and the production of images, and promotes a concept of Art that has to be a pure, automatic and irrational expression of man's unconscious.[16] Breton, in his Surrealist Manifesto dated 1924, defines surrealism as such:

> SURREALISM, n. Psychic automatism in its pure state, by which one proposes to express... the actual functioning of thought. Dictated by the thought, in the absence of any control exercised by reason, exempt from any aesthetic or moral concern.
>
> (Breton, *Manifestoes* 26)

In 1936, a very important surrealist exhibition was held in London and the painting *Harlequin's Carnival* by Joan Miró was also exhibited there. Concerning his paintings, Miró affirms that

---

12 Barfield, ch. XIII.
13 Carpenter 186f.; West.
14 See i.e. McCabe.
15 MacIntosh, *Flame* 29.
16 See: Bertoli; Hoffmann; Mink.

> I don't know where ideas come from. Every night I went to my bed in atelier at Paris Rue Blomet. Sometimes I ate nothing. I saw something and I took notes. On the ceiling I saw weird shape images. (Mink 43)

I have no proof that Tolkien visited this exhibition or that he read Breton's *Manifesto*. But it is worth noting that Tolkien was certainly well informed in contemporary movements like this, and the similarities between some Breton's and Tolkien's sentences (see below) is impressive. In fact, in FS he gives a very precise description of surrealism, also adding his personal evaluation, as we can see in this well-known text:[17]

> In human art Fantasy is a thing best left to words, to true litera-ture. In painting, for instance, the visible presentation of the fantastic image is technically too easy; the hand tends to outrun the mind, even to overthrow it. Silliness or morbidity are frequent results. [There is, for example, in surrealism commonly present a morbidity or un-ease very rarely found in literary fantasy. The mind that produced the depicted images may often be suspected to have been in fact already morbid; yet this is not a necessary explanation in all cases. A curious disturbance of the mind is often set up by the very act of drawing things of this kind, a state similar in quality and consciousness of morbidity to the sensations in a high fever, when the mind develops a distressing fecundity and facility in figure-making, seeing forms sinister or grotesque in all visible objects about it.]   (FS 61 and 81-82, Note E)

Comparing these two different conceptions of art, we can now sum up the most significant similarities and differences:

A) Similarities

1) Breton and Tolkien are moved in their reflections on Art by a similar pro-blem that is the relation between "reality" (observed facts) and "unreality" (the product of artistic activity):

> A special part of its [of surrealism] function is to examine with a critical eye the notions of *reality and unreality*, reason and irration-ality, reflection and impulse, knowledge and 'fatal' ignorance, usefulness and uselessness.
>   (Breton, *Manifestoes* 140, italics added)[18]

---

17 See also Hammond/Scull 10-11.
18 See also Rosemont 210f.

> For my present purpose I require a word which shall embrace both the Sub-creative art in itself and a quality of strangeness and wonder in the Expression, derived from the Image: a quality essential to fairy-story. I propose, therefore, to arrogate to myself the powers of Humpty-Dumpty, and to use Fantasy for this purpose: in a sense, that is, which combines with its older and higher use as an equivalent of Imagination the derived notions of *"unreality"* (that is, of unlikeness to the Primary World), of freedom from the domination of *observed "fact"*...
>
>   (FS 59-60, italics added)

2) The surrealists[19] and Tolkien[20] hold the activity of dreaming in high regard; both disagree with the typically modern dualism between dream and "reality" (that is considered the only true experience), as is theorised e.g. by Descartes in his first *Meditation in First Philosophy*

> And since it has not been proved in the slightest that, in doing so, the 'reality' with which I am kept busy continue to exist in the state of dream, failing to sink back down into the immemorial, why should I not grant to dream what I occasionally refuse reality, that is, this value of certainty in itself, which, in its own time, is not open to my repudiation?
>
>   (Breton, *Selections* 147, Second Manifesto, 1930)

> It is true that Dream is not unconnected with Faërie. In dreams strange powers of the mind may be unlocked.   (FS 35 n. 17)

But, concerning dreams, Tolkien's ideas differ from surrealists' in two important aspects, because Tolkien perspective is founded in an analogical conception of truth and reality.

B) Differences

1) In Western culture, there are two main conceptions of dream[21]:
   a) Dream as an effect of inner (physiological or psychological) dispositions of the subject.
   b) Dream as a "place" where supernatural revelations (also concerning the past or prophecies about the future) are grasped.

---

19 Rosemont 412 sgg.
20 See: Flieger (*Question* and "Episode"); Amendt-Raduege; Smol 44, 49; Hoffman; Triebel.
21 See Mancia.

Breton and the surrealists mainly agree with the first conception that has its origin in Aristotle and reaches its peak in modern culture with Freud that, in the conclusion of his *Interpretations of Dreams* (1900), explicitly refuses the second conception:

> And what of the value of dreams in regard to our knowledge of the future? That, of course, is quite out of the question. One would like to substitute the words: 'in regard to our knowledge of the past.' For in every sense a dream has its origin in the past. The ancient belief that dreams reveal the future is not indeed entirely devoid of truth. By representing a wish as fulfilled the dream certainly leads us into the future; but this future, which the dreamer accepts as his present, has been shaped in the likeness of the past by the indestructible wish.   (Freud 1135)

But in Tolkien's works there are a lot of true prophetical dreams, the most famous of which is probably Frodo's one in the House of Tom Bombadil concerning his departure from the Grey Havens. And dreams are also considered the "road" to the past, as in Tolkien's use of them in NCP and *The Lost Road*[22], while also the (enigmatical) conception of Faërian Drama[23] presupposes a conception of dream where it is possible to "know" truths that otherwise would be impossible to achieve. This means that also for dreams in Tolkien we have an analogical situation: dreams are different from reality (and sub-creation), but they are not simply false; instead, they possess a derived truth that presupposes the primary truth of the Primary world, which is similar to the Aquinas's conception of dreams[24], who never says dreams are simply false (see Descartes, or Freudian refutation of prophecies) but have an analogical degree of truth.

2) But the main difference between Tolkien and the surrealist is about the connection between Art and dreams. For Breton, as we have seen above, Art has to be similar to dreaming, where logic and reason are completely absent.

> We are still living under the reign of *logic* that, of course, is what I am driving at. But in this day and age, logical methods are applicable only to solving problems of secondary interest.
>   (Breton, *Selections* 145, First Manifesto, italics added)

---

22 And we must also remember Tolkien's recurrent dreams of the great wave (*Letter* n. 163). On dreams and time see Flieger, *Question*.

23 For Verlyn Flieger this is still an "enigma" (Flieger, "What"), but some scholars tried to give it an answer. See Croft and Makai.

24 *Summa Theologica* II-II.95.6; see also Kruger.

> When will we have sleeping *logicians*, sleeping *philosophers*! I
> would like to sleep, in order to surrender myself to the dreamers,
> the way I surrender myself to those who read to me with eyes
> wide open; to stop imposing, in this realm, the conscious rhythm
> of my thoughts.
>
> (Breton, *Selections* 148, First Manifesto, italics added)

Tolkien is completely at the opposite of this ideas, as is paramount in the lines
of FS he explicitly dedicated to Surrealism (see above). For Tolkien, dream is
mainly a device internal to his stories, and the activity of Fantasy is absolutely
different from dreaming because it has to be extremely "logical" and conscious.
In this version of FS, Tolkien really seems to have in mind Breton's sentences,
with which he disagrees:

> … making of fairy stories… judging by the results, it is best left
> to bankers, *logicians*, philologists, *philosophers* and theologians.
>
> (FS B 285; see also B 229, italics added)

But also in the published version of FS there can be no doubt about the ratio-
nality of Fantasy:

> Fantasy is a rational, not an irrational, activity.   (FS 60, note 1)

It is enough to read *The Magnetic Fields*, where Breton (with Soupault) mas-
terfully uses the technique of automatic writing, and compares his work with
Tolkien's, and the gulf that divides their conceptions of Art becomes obvious.
Fantasy must be fundamentally rational and conscious because it must give
its creations "the inner consistence of reality", which does not happen when a
sub-creation is constructed like a dream, as is the case for instance with *Alice
in Wonderland*. In fact, Tolkien affirms that

> … if a waking writer tells you that his tale is only a thing imagined
> in his sleep, he cheats deliberately the primal desire at the heart
> of Faërie: the realization, independent of the conceiving mind,
> of imagined wonder.   (FS 35)

But it is important to understand and emphasise that those sentences by Tolkien are "only" consequences of his analogical conception of the relationships
between Primary and Secondary World:

> Fantasy is a natural human activity. It certainly does not destroy or even insult Reason… The keener and the clearer is the reason, the better fantasy will it make. If men were ever in a state in which they did not want to know or could not perceive truth (facts or evidence), then Fantasy would languish until they were cured. If they ever get into that state (it would not seem at all impossible) Fantasy will perish, and become Morbid Delusion.   (FS 65)

For Tolkien, in conclusion, sub-creation and Fantasy presuppose for their activity a primary world that is primarily true and that must be primarily understood by human Reason [1], as—in Aquinas's analogy of attribution—accident is a being that for his existence presupposes substance that is a primarily being at the base of accident's existence [see 2-3]. It is because this analogical perspective that Tolkien's conception of Art differs from the Surrealist's one [4].

Bibliography

Amendt-Raduege, Amy M. "Dream Visions in J.R.R. Tolkien's *The Lord of the Rings*". *Tolkien Studies* 3 (2006): 45-55

Aquinas, Thomas. *Somma Teologica*. Bologna: Edizioni Studio Domenicano, 1987

---. *Summa Contra Gentiles*. 3 Vols. Torino: Marietti, 1961-1967

---. *Commento alle sentenze*. Bologna: Edizioni Studio Domenicano, 2002

Arduini Roberto et.al. (Eds.). *Tolkien e i Classici*. Torino: Effatà, 2015

--- & Claudio Testi, Eds. *The Broken Scythe: Death and Immortality in the Work of J.R.R. Tolkien*. Zurich/Jena: Walking Tree Publishers, 2012

Aristotele. Opere 4 (*Del sonno e della veglia, Dei sogni, Della divinazione nei sogni*). Bari: Laterza, 1982

---. Opere 10 (*Retorica, Poetica*). Bari: Laterza, 1992

Ashworth, Elizabeth J. "Signification and Modes of Signifying in Thirteenth-Century Logic: a Preface to Aquinas on Analogy". *Medieval Philosophy and Theology* 1 (1991): 39-67

---. "Analogy and Equivocation in the Thirteenth-Century Logic: Aquinas in context". *Medieval Studies* 54 (1992): 94-135

Barfield, Owen. *Saving the Appearences*. Middletown: Wesleyan University Press, 1988

Basti, Gianfranco & Claudio Testi (Eds.). *Analogia e Autoreferenza*. Milano: Marietti 1820, 2004

Basti, Gianfranco & Antonio Perrone (Eds.). *Le radici forti del pensiero debole, dalla metafisica alla matematica al calcolo*. Padova/Roma: Il Poligrafo ~ Pontificia Università Lateranense, 1996

Bertelè, Franco et.al. *Scienza, analogia, astrazione*. Padova: Il Poligrafo, 1999

Bertoli, Antonio (Ed.). *La rivoluzione surrealista*. Firenze: Giunti, 2007

Bochenski, Joseph. "On Analogy". *The Thomist* 11 (1948): 424-447

Boyer, Charles. "Le sens d'un texte de saint Thomas: De Veritate, q. 1, a. 9". *Doctor Communis* 1 (1978): 3-19

Breton, André. *Manifestoes of Surrealism.* The University of Michigan Press, Ann Arbor Paperbacks, 1972

---. *Nadjia.* London: Grant & Cutler, 1986

---. *Selections.* Berkeley/Los Angeles: University of California Press, 2003

--- & Philippe Soupault. *The Magnetic fields.* London: Atlas Press, 1985

Bru, Josè Manuel Fernandez. "'Wingless fluttering': Some Personal Connections in Tolkien's Formative Years". *Tolkien Studies* 8 (2011): 51-65

Carpenter, Humphrey. *The Inklings. C.S. Lewis, J.R.R. Tolkien, Charles Williams and Their Friends.* London: George Allen & Unwin, 1978

Croft, Janet Brennan. "Tolkien's Faërian Drama: Origins and Valedictions". *Mythlore* 32.2 (2014): 31-45

Descartes, René. *Meditations on First Philosophy.* Peterborough: Broadview Press, 2013

Fabro, Cornelio. *Partecipazione e causalità secondo S. Tommaso d'Aquino.* Torino: SEI, 1960

---. *La nozione metafisica di partecipazione secondo S. Tommaso d'Aquino.* Torino: SEI, 1950

Flieger, Verlyn. *A Question of Time.* Kent OH: Kent State University Press, 1997

---. *Splintered Light: logos and language in Tolkien's world.* Kent OH: The Kent State University Press, 2002

---. "But What He Did Really Mean?". *Tolkien Studies* 11 (2014): 149-166

---. "The curious episode of dream at the Barrow: Memory and Reincarnation in Middle-earth". *Tolkien Studies* 4 (2007): 99-112

Fornet-Ponse, Thomas. "Die steigende Präsenz von Philosophie und Theologie". *Hither Shore* 3 (2006): 37-50

Freud, Sigmund. *Interpretations of Dreams.* USA: Plain Label Book, 1950

Geiger, Louis-Bernard. *La participation dans la philosophie de S. Thomas d'Aquin.* Paris: Vrin, 1942

Gilliver, Peter et.al. *The Ring of Words.* Oxford: Oxford University Press, 2006

Hammond, Wayne G. & Christina Scull. *Tolkien Artist and Illustrator.* London: HarperCollins, 2004

Hart, Trevor. "Tolkien, Creation and Creativity". In: *Tree of Tales. Tolkien. Literature and Theology.* Eds. Trevor Hart & Ivan Khovacs. Waco: Baylor University Press, 2007, 39-54

Hoffman, Curtiss. *"Wings over Numenor: Lucid Dreaming in the Writing of J.R.R. Tolkien".* In: *Lucid Dreaming: New Perspectives on Consciousness in Sleep.* Eds. Ryan Hurd & Kelly Bulkeley. Santa Barbara CA: Praeger, 2014

Hoffmann, Werner. *I fondamenti dell'arte moderna.* Roma: Donizelli, 1987

Kocher, Paul. *Master of Middle-earth – The Fiction of J.R.R. Tolkien.* New York: Ballantine Books, 2002

Kruger, Stephen. *Il sogno nel Medioevo.* Milano: Vita e Pensiero, 1996

Lear, Jonathan. *Aristotle and logical theory.* Cambridge: Cambridge University Press, 1980

Lewis, Clive Staples. *The Allegory of Love.* Cambridge: Cambridge University Press, 2013

---. *The Problem of Pain.* London: HarperOne, 1996

MacIntosh, Jonathan S. *The Flame Imperishable: Tolkien, St. Thomas and the Metaphysics of Faerie.* Ann Arbor: UMI, 2009

---. "Ainulindalë: Tolkien, St. Thomas, and the Metaphysics of the Music". In: *Music in Middle-earth.* Eds. Heidi Steimel & Friedhelm Schneidewind. Zurich/Jena: Walking Tree Publishers, 2010, 53-74

Makai, Peter Kristof. "Faërian Cyberdrama: When Fantasy Becomes Virtual Reality". *Tolkien Studies* 7 (2010): 35-54

Mancia, Mauro. *Breve storia del sogno.* Padova: Marsilio, 1998

Maurer, Armand. "St. Thomas and the Analogy of Genus". *The New Scolasticism* 29 (1955), n. 2: 127-144

McCabe, Herbert. *On Aquinas*. New York: Continuum, 2010

McInerny, Ralph M. *Aquinas and Analogy*. Washington DC: The Catholic University of America Press, 1996

Milbank, Alison. "Tolkien, Chesterton, and Thomism". *Tolkien's* The Lord of the Rings. *Sources of Inspiration*. Eds. Stratford Caldecott & Thomas Honegger. Zurich/Berne: Walking Tree Publishers, 2008, 187-198

---. *Tolkien and Chesterton as Theologians*. New York: T&T Clark, 2009

Milburn, Michael. "Coleridge's definition of Imagination and Tolkien's Definition(s) of Faërie". *Tolkien Studies* 7 (2010): 55-66

Mink, Janis. *Miró*. Los Angeles: Taschen, 2003

Mondin, Battista. "Triplice analisi dell'analogia e del suo uso in teologia". *Divus Thomas* 63 (1960): 336-348

Montagnes, Bernard. *La doctrine de l'analogie de l'être d'après Saint Thomas d'Aquin*. P aris: Béatrice-Nauwelaerts, 1963

Newman, John Henry. *Apologia pro vita sua*. Milano: Jaca Book, 1982

Nimmo, Andrew. "Tolkien and Thomism, Middle-earth and the States of Nature". *Universitas* 10, 2001: http://copiosa.org/Lord_Rings/lord_ring_tolkien.htm (check: 16/2/2014)

Quintiliano. *Istituzioni Oratorie*. Torino: UTET, 1992

Righi, Giulio. *Studi sull'analogia*. Milano: Marzorati, 1981

Rosemont, Franklin. *André Breton: What is Surrealism*. Vol. 1. New York: Pathfinder, 2012

Schmidt, Robert. *The domain of logic according to S. Thomas Aquinas*. Boston/Lancaster: Martinus Nijhoff Publishers, 1966

Smol, Anna. "Frodo's Body". *The Body in Tolkien's Legendarium*. Ed. Christopher Vaccaro. Jefferson NC: McFarland, 2013, 39-63

Testi, Claudio A. "Logica formale, causalità e partecipazione". In: *I fondamenti logici e ontologici della scienza*. Ed. Alberto Strumia. Siena: Cantagalli, 2006: 168-202

---. "Formalizzazione dell'analogia di attribuzione". In: *Il problema dei fondamenti*. Ed. Alberto Strumia. Siena: Cantagalli, 2007: 169-192

---. "Analogia, Logica formale e paradossi". In: Basti/Testi, *Analogia e Autoreferenza*, Milano: Marietti 1820, 2004, 267-332

---. "Tolkien, l'analogia e la verità delle fiabe". *Endore* 10 (2007): 17-26

---. "Tolkien e Tommaso d'Aquino". In: Arduini, *Tolkien e i Classici*, Torino: Effatà, 2015, 75-84

---. "Logic and Theology in Tolkien's Thanatology". In: Arduini/Testi, *The Broken Scythe*, Zurich/Jena: WTP, 2012, 175-192

Tolkien, John R.R. *On Fairy-stories*. Expanded edition with commentary and notes by Verlyn Flieger & Douglas A. Anderson. London: HarperCollins, 2008

---. *Letters: The Letters of J.R.R. Tolkien*. Eds. Humphrey Carpenter & Christopher Tolkien. London: HarperCollins, 1999

Triebel, Doreen. "Dreams and Dream Visions in J.R.R. Tolkien's *The Hobbit*". *Hither Shore* 5 (2008): 67-82

Tyn, Thomas. *Metafisica della sostanza. Partecipazione e analogia entis*. Bologna: Edizioni Studio Domenicano, 1991

West, Richard, "Mattews, Fr. Antony Gervase". *Tolkien Encyclopedia*. Ed. Michael Drout. London: Routledge, 2007, 411f

»A Survey of the Depths of Space and Time.«
Zur Erkenntnistheorie in *On Fairy-stories*

Frank Weinreich (Bochum)

> *In manchen Fällen wirkt es Wunder.*
>
> (J.R.R. Tolkien: *Blatt von Tüftler*)

D er *Essay On Fairy-stories* erscheint in seiner ausgearbeiteten Version 1947 am Ende des kreativsten Lebensjahrzehnts von J.R.R. Tolkien und damit vielleicht in einer Lebensphase, da er sich des eigenen Werkes am sichersten war. Mit *Hobbit* und *Ringerzählung* hatte er einen Weg gefunden, der künstlerischen Seite seiner Kreativität Ausdruck zu verleihen, und so nimmt es nicht Wunder, dass er in der gleichen Zeit auch Gedanken über die Grundlagen seiner Kunst öffentlich macht. Wobei man hier wie meist, wenn es um die Werke Tolkiens geht, einen langen Zeitraum von deutlich mehr als zehn Jahren betrachten muss und mehrere Werke heranziehen sollte. Diese Spanne lässt sich begrenzen von zwei Ereignissen: der Publikation von *Mythopoeia* 1933 und der Veröffentlichung der maßgeblichen Version von FS 1947.[1] Für das Thema ebenfalls wichtig ist die Kurzgeschichte *Leaf by Niggle* aus den frühen 1940er Jahren. Das sind zudem drei von Tolkien selbst veröffentlichte Werke, was in diesem Zusammenhang zu betonen ist, da die Schriften in der vom Autor vorgesehenen und autorisierten Form erschienen sind, was bei Tolkien ja mittlerweile nur noch auf den geringeren Teil seines Gesamtwerks zutrifft.[2]

In allen drei Publikationen lässt sich das gleiche Thema identifizieren, auch wenn es nicht jeweils den einzigen behandelten Topos darstellt. *Mythopoeia* stellt in erster Linie eine sowohl kondensierte als auch poetisch verklausulierte Verteidigung des Werts der Mythen dar, die ich an anderer Stelle einmal als »the creed of Tolkienian ontology« (Weinreich, *Metaphysics* 325) beschrieben habe. FS ist eine Auseinandersetzung mit der Rolle der Phantastik in Kunst

---

1   Flieger und Anderson legen dar, dass FS seit der ersten Version, dem Vortrag 1939 an-
    lässlich der Andrew-Lang-Lectures, massiv erweitert und überarbeitet wurde, weshalb
    man bei einer Diskussion des jetzt i.d.R. zugrunde gelegten Textes aus den Essays auf den
    Entstehungszeitpunkt in den 1940er Jahren gegen Ende des Krieges rekurrieren sollte.
2   Neben einigen wissenschaftlichen Aufsätzen sind nur die *Ring*-Trilogie, der *Hobbit* und
    ein paar Kurzgeschichten zu Lebzeiten erschienen, der sehr viel größere Teil, insbesondere
    die umfangreichen Schriften des Mittelerde-Legendariums, wie die *History* und deren
    Vorgänger *Silmarillion* und *Unfinished Tales*, erschien unter der Ägide und herausgegeben
    von Christopher Tolkien, und jüngere Editionen der Geschichten über Hurin und seine
    Kinder, über Kullervo, Artur sowie Sigrid und Gudrun lassen den Berg der nicht autori-
    sierten Bücher ins kaum mehr Ermessliche anschwellen.

und Literatur und mit dem ontologischen Status von Kunst. *Leaf by Niggle* schließlich ist zuallererst eine allegorische Betrachtung des eigenen Lebens. Doch alle drei behandeln auch die spezielle Tolkien'sche Metaphysik, und um deren Rolle als erkenntnistheoretisches Mittel geht es mir in dieser Arbeit.

I

D ie metaphysischen Überzeugungen Tolkiens als solche zeigen sich am deutlichsten als eine Form eines stark christlich beeinflussten platonischen Idealismus in *Mythopoeia*, wie ich in besagtem Artikel über das Gedicht herausarbeitete. Das Folgende schließt direkt an diesen Artikel an, weshalb ich in Teilen darauf zurückkomme. Was sich aber in FS besonders herausarbeiten lässt, sind Postulate, die darauf hindeuten, dass die ontologischen Voraussetzungen des künstlerischen Schaffensprozesses für Tolkien auf einer metaphysisch fundierten Erkenntnistheorie basieren. Entscheidend dafür ist der in Mythopoeia zentrale Begriff der Wahrheit, zu dem er in FS einen Weg weisen will, denn auch dort heißt es, »Fantasy« könne erklärt werden als »a sudden glimpse of the underlying truth or reality« (FS 77).

Eine Wahrheit bezeichnet nun allerdings die Darstellung eines objektiv zutreffenden Sachverhalts. Sie erhebt damit einen hohen Anspruch und ist etwas, das seit Etablierung der modernen Wissenschaft mindestens um das Wörtchen »vorläufig« ergänzt werden muss. Die antike Metaphysik trat mit viel mehr Überzeugung auf, und deshalb muss man auf sie referenzieren, wenn man Tolkiens Behauptung einschätzen will, dass es möglich sei, absolut gültige Wahrheiten zu erkennen[3].

Grundgelegt wurde eine sich als objektiv verstehende Metaphysik in den Lehren Platons, besonders in den Dialogen *Phaidon* und *Politeia*; und alle folgenden Modifikationen bei Aristoteles und den Neoplatonisten beziehen sich darauf. Hier tritt erstmals eine kraftvolle Metaphysik auf, die sich eines rein intellektuellen, rationalen Zugangs rühmt, der das wabernd-subjektive Element des zeitgenössischen Spiritualismus zu überwinden verspricht.

Die platonische Metaphysik geht von der faktischen Existenz einer ewigen und unveränderlichen Seinsebene aus, von der Sphäre der idealen Dinge. In Opposition zu Heraklits Beobachtung des panta rhei, der ständigen Veränderung aller Bestandteile der empirischen Welt, ist es Platons Ziel, eine Metaphysik zu entwickeln, in der alle Erscheinungen der empirischen Welt als imperfekte Umsetzungen perfekter Vorbilder verstanden werden. Dabei kommt den idealen Schablonen oder Musterstücken für die Erscheinungen der empirischen Welt letztlich ein größerer Realitätsgehalt zu, weil sie ewig und unveränderlich sind,

---

3   Wie er es in *Mythopoeia*, Z. 134 (»the likeness of the True«), behauptet.

während unsere normale Welt grundsätzlich unbeständig ist. Erreicht werden kann die Sphäre der idealen Dinge auf rationale Weise durch das Begreifen der platonischen Metaphysik und die Einsicht in ihre Richtigkeit.

Das kann man schon aufgrund prinzipieller Nichtfalsifizierbarkeit heute nicht als wissenschaftliche Methode gelten lassen, doch der Gedankengang besticht in gewisser Weise: Wir werden niemals in der Lage sein, den perfekten Kreis zu zeichnen, denn wenn man nur nahe genug an den Kreis herangeht, wird man die Imperfektion der ausgeführten Linienführung wahrnehmen. Trotzdem wissen wir durch den bloßen Denkakt – und die Unterstützung der Mathematik in Gestalt der Kreisformel –, dass es den perfekten Kreis eben doch gibt ... in der Theorie. Wieso sollte es also nicht einen realen Ort geben, an dem der perfekte Kreis existiert? Als Denkort gibt es ihn auf jeden Fall.

Den Weg zu diesem Denkort hat Platon auch beschrieben. Der Apparatus, den der Mensch zur Erkenntnis braucht, ist ihm dabei sozusagen eingegeben, denn ein Stück seiner selbst hat Anteil an der Welt der Ideen und der idealen Formen, den er im Symposion als Ausdruck eines Drangs nach Wahrheit und Schönheit beschreibt (*Gastmahl* 210c-212a). Der Weg dorthin führt über ein Sich-Erinnern an diese Sphäre, was Platon als Anamnesis-Theorie[4] ausführt.

Es bleibt festzuhalten, dass es nach Platon eine Ebene gibt, auf der alle Dinge in ihrer perfekten Form existieren, und dass die Möglichkeit besteht, über die der eigenen Seele innewohnende Erinnerung Erkenntnisse aus dieser Sphäre der idealen Formen und Gedanken zu gewinnen, wenn es auch keine Möglichkeit gibt, diese selbst unversehrt in die empirische Welt herüberzutragen. Wichtig in Bezug auf Tolkien ist dabei, dass die ideale Welt auch eine ästhetische ist – wahre Schönheit und Kunst in Perfektion sind ebenfalls dieser metaphysischen Ebene vorbehalten, denn letztlich kulminieren alle Dinge in diesem metaphysischen Bereich im sogenannten »Göttlich-Schönen« (*Gastmahl* 212a). Schönheit und Kunst sind nun genau das, worüber Tolkien in FS, *Mythopoeia* und *Leaf by Niggle* spricht.

Für einen akademisch gebildeten Menschen gehörten die platonischen und aristotelischen Schriften in der ersten Hälfte des 20. Jahrhunderts zum Kanon. Tolkien studierte die antiken Autoren zudem nachgewiesenermaßen sowohl in Schule wie auch Universität[5], so dass man mit Nagy davon ausgehen kann, dass der Professor Platon und die platonische Metaphysik gut kannte: »Tolkien certainly knew Plato's works and possibly read some in the original

---

4 Was natürlich auch eine Setzung metaphyischen Charakters und als solche ebenfalls eine Glaubenssache ist.
5 Vgl. die entsprechenden Abschnitte in Carpenters Biographie (Carpenter 62-70). John Garth weist darauf hin, dass Tolkien zwar unfähig gewesen sei, sich für die klassischen Sprachen zu begeistern, dass er aber nichtsdestotrotz gute Prüfungsleistungen im Griechischen vorlegte (Garth 54).

Greek« (Nagy, _Plato_ 513).[6] Damit ist die notwendige Voraussetzung gegeben, dass Tolkien vom klassischen Idealismus unmittelbar beeinflusst sein kann.

II

Mythopoeia als im zeitlichen Verlauf erste Publikation mit deutlich idealistischen Tönen bei Tolkien drückt gleich an mehreren Stellen der platonischen Metaphysik ähnliche bis gleichartige Inhalte aus.[7] Das Gedicht kritisiert die seinerzeit von Tolkien als materialistisch und phantasiefeindlich empfundene Lebens- und vor allem Denkweise der Menschen, die sich von der Spiritualität zugunsten einer mechanisch-effektiven und technologisch-bürokratisch bestimmten Lebensführung abgewandt haben.

Hier sei auch an die tiefe Religiosität des Professors erinnert, die es nicht erlaubt, eine vom christlichen Glauben unbeeinflusste Metaphysik in seine Schriften zu interpretieren. Deshalb muss man auf den unübersehbaren Spiritualismus in _Mythopoeia_ verweisen, der mit der um Rationalität bemühten Metaphysik Platons nicht einfach in Einklang zu bringen ist. Trotzdem besteht inhaltlich eine große Näherung, ja teilweise Deckungsgleichheit zum platonischen Denken.

Das besondere von Tolkien eingebrachte Charakteristikum besteht jedoch nicht nur in der christlichen Einfärbung antiker Metaphysik, sondern vor allem in einer Art eigenem linguistic turn. Ähnlich der der allgemeinen linguistischen Wende unterliegenden Sichtweise mit ihrer Konzentration auf Sprache als Erkenntnisgegenstand hebt Tolkien besonders darauf ab, wie die Dinge benannt werden. Im Gedicht ist das beispielsweise der stellvertretend für die materielle Welt stehende Baum, dessen wahres Wesen als Baum eben nicht in seinen »endless multitude of forms« erscheint (_Mythopoeia_, Z. 15), sondern darin, dass sein Wesen als Baum von einem Beobachter erkannt wird und er diesen als Baum _benennt._

Doch es geht nicht allein darum, isolierte Einzelobjekte im richtigen Licht darzustellen, sondern vor allem darum, über die Welt und den Kosmos in seiner Gesamtheit zu informieren. Aufgabe des Künstlers ist es nicht, auf den perfekten Kreis hinzuweisen, sondern die von ihm erzählten Geschichten in den großen Zusammenhang aller Geschichten zu stellen.

---

6 In dem von Jane Chance herausgegebenen Sammelband _Tolkien and the Invention of Myth_ gibt es eine eigene Sektion, die sich mit dem Einfluss besonders der griechischen Antike auf Tolkien befasst, die in der Zusammenschau derzeit den besten Überblick über diesen Zweig der Tolkien-Forschung gibt. Dort finden sich auch vielfältige Hinweise auf Lektüren und Studien Tolkiens die Zeit und ihre Autoren betreffend.

7 Eine Interpretation, die Zeile für Zeile das Gedicht entlanggeht und diese Elemente komplett herausarbeitet, habe ich in Weinreich, _Metaphysics_ veröffentlicht; im Folgenden greife ich nur die wichtigsten Punkte heraus.

Diese Rolle der wahren Geschichtsschreibung kommt dem Mythos zu, der von ausdrücklich als gesegnet bezeichneten Erzählern (Z. 91, »blessed are the legend-makers«) vorgetragen wird. Und die berichten gerade nicht von mühsam verifizierten Ereignissen und Jahreszahlen, wie sie normalerweise von Historikern vorgetragen werden. Die legend-makers berichten von Dingen »not found within recorded time« (Z. 92). Und das kulminiert in der Schlussstrophe, wo enthüllt wird, dass es ein Paradies gibt, in dem die Schau der Wahrheit möglich ist: »In Paradise the eye may stray... to see... from mirrored truth the likeness of the True.« Hier sind alle Dinge so zu sehen, wie sie wirklich sind (Z. 131-136). Und das ist ein Bild, das sehr an Platons berühmte Höhle erinnert.

In *Leaf by Niggle* findet sich das Thema einer perfekten Welt im Bild von Niggles Land und Parishs Garten. Der kaum verhohlene Tolkien in Person Niggles hat sein Leben damit verbracht, den perfekten Baum zu malen, und ist doch nie darüber hinaus gekommen, allenfalls ein ganz gutes einzelnes Blatt auf die Leinwand zu bringen. Doch als ihm nach seinem Tod die Gnade gewährt wird, ein – vergleichsweise angenehmes – Fegefeuer mit seinem alten Gegner Parish zu teilen, erblickt er dort in Niggles Land und Parishs Garten den Baum genau so, wie er ihn sich vorgestellt hatte (BT 414f.). Tolkiens publizierte Welt Mittelerde in der Realität kann man dann als eben dieses eine schöne Blatt ermitteln, das nach Niggles Tod in dessen Nachlass gefunden wird, und es dann als Blatt am Stamm des unendlichen Baums der Mythen und Geschichten einordnen.

III

Ähnlich eindeutige und vielfältige Bilder wie in dem Gedicht und kunstvoll gesetzte Metaphern wie in *Leaf* darf man bei dem nüchterneren Aufsatz FS nicht erwarten. In *Mythopoeia* ging es noch darum, mit einem gewissen Furor einen Angriff auf die geliebte Welt der Mythen abzuwehren. In *Leaf* dient der Verweis auf das kleine Stückchen absoluter Wahrheit, das Niggle in Form eines einzelnen Blattes in die reale Welt brachte, dazu, den unverstandenen Künstler zu exkulpieren. Der Märchenaufsatz hingegen soll auf wissenschaftlichem Niveau informieren.

Tolkien sagt, er wolle mit FS drei Fragen beantworten: »What are fairy-stories? What is their origin? What is the use of them?« (FS 27). Er bleibt ein bisschen vage bei der ersten Antwort, doch es wird klar, dass fairy stories immer etwas mit Überschreitung der Realität zu tun haben. Damit ist zumindest festgelegt, dass es neben der Welt, die wir miteinander teilen, noch andere Welten gibt. Dies sind die Welten, die von Menschen in Form verschiedenster künstlerischer Aktivitäten erschaffen werden. Die Kunst als spezifisch menschlich-schöpferische Tätigkeit ist also der Ursprungsort von fairy stories, ist ihr »origin«, und damit die Antwort auf Frage zwei.

Für die Erkenntnisfähigkeit ist im Rahmen von künstlerischen Schöpfungsprozessen von Interesse, welche Bedeutung Tolkien dem künstlerischen Gebrauch von Zuschreibungen zumisst. Er zeichnet in diesem Zusammenhang die freie Nutzung von Adjektiven als machtvollstes Mittel aus: »no spell or incantation in Faërie is more potent [than the adjective]« (FS 41). Der Künstler kann diese Zuschreibungen frei verwenden, er kann Gesichter grün, den Mond blau und Blätter silbern und golden färben, um die Effekte hervorzurufen, die er zu erreichen trachtet (41). Er ist aus Gründen der Glaubhaftigkeit und Überzeugungskraft seiner Geschichten zwar nicht völlig frei, sondern muss auf Konsistenz und innere Wahrhaftigkeit seiner Erzählungen achten, und er darf sich nicht so weit von den Erfahrungen der mit dem Publikum geteilten Realität entfernen, dass dieses seinen Äußerungen und Bildern nicht mehr zu folgen vermag, doch im Prinzip sind einem Künstler keine Grenzen gesetzt.

Das wiederum bedeutet, dass er auch den Beschränkungen der Realität nicht unterliegt und eben fairy worlds erschaffen kann, deren wesentliches Merkmal die Überschreitung der Empirie und ihrer Grenzen ist. Die Erzählmacht des Künstlers ist so groß, dass sie über die empirische Welt hinausgehend sogar Götter zu erschaffen vermag, wie es beispielsweise in der Antike in den griechischen Göttermythen einen Ausdruck findet (42).[8] Die Olympier, sagt Tolkien, bekommen ihre Persönlichkeiten sowie alle Attribute von den Menschen zugesprochen, und das gilt auch für ihre Göttlichkeit selbst, die der Mensch aber als Mittler zwischen Übernatürlichem und Göttern ihnen sozusagen aushändigt:

> [T]heir personality *they get direct from [man]*; the shadow or flicker of divinity that is upon them *they receive through him* from the invisible world, the Supernatural.   (FS 43, meine Hvhbg.)

Die Götter, die eigentlich also dem über sie berichtenden Menschen alles zu verdanken haben – Schönheit, Macht, gar die Göttlichkeit selbst –, bekommen ihre metaphysischen Attribute aus der unsichtbaren Welt, aus dem Reich des Übernatürlichen, »from the Supernatural«. Da sie das aber ausdrücklich »through him«, also durch den Menschen, überreicht von Menschenhand in Form adjektivischer Zuschreibungen, bekommen, konstituiert Tolkien spätestens damit das »Supernatural« als einen eigenständigen Bereich. Das Aussehen und die erratischen Verhaltensweisen der Götter sind menschlich, doch ihre Göttlichkeit, ihre Metaphysik, weist über den Menschen hinaus.

---

8 Die griechischen Götter waren nach Tolkien zuerst sogar nicht mehr als »allegories«, denn das sei ein besseres Wort als »myths« (FS 42); was mithin eine durch und durch rationale Erklärungsweise ist.

IV

Bei der Antwort auf die Frage nach dem Nutzen von fairy stories stellt Tolkien zunächst klar, dass der Mensch die Fähigkeit besitzt, mentale Bilder zu schauen, er verfügt über »imagination« (FS 59). Ferner besitzt er die Fähigkeit, seiner Vorstellungskraft Ausdruck zu verleihen, und zwar in Form der Kunst, die als menschliche Eigenschaft das Bindeglied zwischen der Imagination und dem Kunstprodukt ist, der Zweitschöpfung. Tolkien könnte es sich deutlich einfacher machen und sagen, dass der Mensch eine bestimmte Vorstellung von Dingen hat, die er dann in die Welt setzt. Dem Musiker fällt eine Melodie ein, die schreibt er in Form von Noten auf, die er dann auf einem Instrument spielt, so dass alle Welt sie hören kann. Der Schriftsteller hat eine Idee für einen Plot und eine Idee von einer Welt, in die er diesen Plot setzt, bringt alles zu Papier und veröffentlicht es. Als bloße Abfolge ist beides eine banale Angelegenheit. Doch Tolkien teilt viel strikter in erstens »Imagination«, zweitens Kunst als »operative link« und drittens künstlerisches Produkt, die »Sub-creation« (FS 59; Großschreibungen im Original).

Diese Unterscheidung ist notwendig, weil Tolkien darauf bestehen will, dass die genannten *drei prinzipiell verschiedene Dinge* sind, und er spricht dann auch in der Tat von einer »difference in kind« (FS 59). Die »imagination« findet als »mental power of image-making« (59) statt. Da fairy stories definitionsgemäß nach Tolkien das Übernatürliche behandeln (32, 68), kann man sich das image-making als Zugriff auf »the Supernatural« vorstellen, welches die »sub-creations« dann sozusagen ›through the artist‹ erhalten, genau wie einst die Olympier ihre Göttlichkeit aus den Händen der Menschen empfingen. Die Inhalte des Katalogs der übernatürlichen Quelle werden in FS durch den mehrfachen Verweis auf eine sogenannte »elvish craft« (61, 64 u. ö.) allenfalls angedeutet. Doch in *Mythopoeia* hat Tolkien klarer gesagt, dass es diesen Katalog gibt, hat einige Beispiele gegeben und darauf verwiesen, dass jedermann sich der Bestandteile dieses Katalogs zu erinnern vermag (vgl. Weinreich, *Metaphysics* 336).

In FS geht es um Prozesse, und zwar behandelt die zweite Hälfte der Schrift vornehmlich den Prozess des Entstehens von Kunst respektive sub-creation, und die Behandlung dieses Prozesses scheint ihm genauso wichtig zu sein, wie die Beantwortung der drei den Aufsatz initiierenden Fragen. Damit ist schließlich auch der Punkt erreicht, an dem sich die erkenntnistheoretischen Ansätze in Tolkiens Kunsttheorie zeigen.

Der Prozess besteht darin, dass der Künstler außerhalb seiner selbst existierende Bilder verwendet und modifiziert – durch die Zuschreibung von adjektivischen Attributen – und so eine sub-creation ins Werk setzt. Der Künstler ist demnach mehr Mittler als Schöpfer. Niggle hatte, wie es in *Leaf* heißt, eine sehr genaue Vorstellung davon, wie sein Baum aussehen sollte, auch wenn ihm die Umsetzung fast nie so geriet, dass sie der Vorstellung, der Imagination, entsprach.[9]

Das erkenntnistheoretische Element in dieser Beziehungskette »Supernatural – artist[10] – Sub-creation« ist der Zusammenhang der Enden Übernatürliches und Zweitschöpfung. Tolkiens implizite These lautet, dass es das Reich der idealen Bilder und Formen gibt und dass es sich in den Zweitschöpfungen ausdrücken lässt. Doch dazu muss es ›übersetzt‹, besser vielleicht übermittelt werden. Das Problem mit der Sphäre des Übernatürlichen und ihrer wunder-baren Inhalte ist, dass sie sich Tolkiens Erfahrung nach in der Alltagswelt nicht zeigt, ja dass die Alltagswelt mit ihrer zunehmenden Industrialisierung, Bürokratisierung, Naturfeindlichkeit und der Abkehr vom Schönen sich der Sphäre gegenüber immer weiter verschließt. Das ist im Prinzip der gleiche Sachverhalt, den Platon schon mit seiner Höhle thematisierte: Die Menschen in ihren Fesseln starren gezwungenermaßen in die falsche Richtung und erkennen die Wahrheit nicht, sondern nur irreführende Schatten derselben. Und so wie der Philosoph nach Platon den Schlüssel in der Hand hält, um die Ketten der Höhlenbewohner aufzuschließen, so ist der Mensch als Künstler in der Lage, die Wahrheit und Schönheit aus der Sphäre des Übernatürlichen in Zweitschöpfungen abzubilden.

Was die reale Welt phantastischen künstlerischen Erzeugnissen, den »operations of [Faëry]« (FS 34), verdankt, ist eine ganz entscheidende Bereicherung in Form einer Befreiung, denn die »notions of unreality« die Bestandteil aller fairy stories und vergleichbarer Kunst sind, versteht Tolkien als »freedom from the domination of observed ›fact‹« (FS 60). Diese Befreiung wiederum führt zu den vielzitierten Funktionen von fairy stories: recovery, consolation und escape. Fairy stories beziehungsweise die Phantasie, wie Tolkien das im Fortschreiten des Essays zunehmend synonymisiert, erfüllen also grundlegende menschliche Bedürfnisse, und an anderer Stelle sagt er das auch explizit: »The magic of Faerie is not an end in itself, its virtue is in its operations: among these are the satisfaction of certain primordial human desires« (FS 34).

Allerdings führt er in diesem Zusammenhang nicht die vergleichsweise einfachen Bedürfnisse Trost und Erholung an, sondern bezieht sich auf tief- wie weitergehende Bedürfnisse, die den intellektuellen wie den spirituellen Bereich

---

9 »Alle Blätter, mit denen er sich abgemüht hatte, waren da, und eher so, wie er sie sich vorgestellt als wie er sie gemalt hatte« (BT 414).

10 Künstler und Kunst fallen in der Tat in diesem Modell ineinander und sind äquivalent; auch wenn Tolkien Unterschiede in der Qualität von Kunst und Künstlern macht, ist die Rolle des Künstlers wie auch seiner Kunst – verstanden als Prozess des Herstellens einer sub-creation! – vergleichsweise marginal, denn es kommt darauf an, dass die Bilder aus dem Reich des Übernatürlichen in der sub-creation ihren Ausdruck in der primary world finden. Wie sie das tun, ist demgegenüber nachrangig.

betreffen. Explizit nennt er die »survey of the depths of space and time« (FS 35), der die vorliegende Arbeit ihren Titel entlehnt. Es ist davon auszugehen, dass er damit nicht die normale Erforschung der physikalischen Raumzeit meint, und dass dieses spezifische Bedürfnis darüber hinaus in die Metaphysik zielt. Als FS entsteht, ist die Allgemeine Relativitätstheorie über dreißig Jahre bekannt, und auch Tolkien wusste, dass man zur Untersuchung von Raum und Zeit Bohrer Richtung Erdkern schicken und Teleskope ins All richten musste und nicht hoffen konnte, deren Geheimnisse durch die Introspektion der Bilder in der eigenen Psyche aufzufinden. Die angemahnte »survey of space and time« kann deshalb nur metaphorisch als Untersuchung aller Räume und Zeiten gemeint sein, die dem menschlichen Geist zugänglich sind, das schließt dann aber die durch Denk- und Vorstellungsprozesse betretenen metaphysischen Räume mit ein.

V

Doch etwas fehlt noch an einer Erkenntnistheorie, nämlich die Herleitung des Zugangs zu den Erkenntnissen. Verortet sind sie in einer Tolkien'schen Abwandlung der platonischen Ideenwelt. Doch wie gelangt Tolkien, wie gelangt der Künstler in die Position, Aussagen über diese Welt machen zu können? Hier ergibt sich wiederum eine besondere Nähe zu Platon, und zwar eine der analogen Methode. Wie eingangs gesagt, geht Platon davon aus, dass man sich der ewigen Wahrheiten erinnern kann, da sie als verborgenes Wissen in der Seele abgelegt sind. Platons gesamte Philosophie funktioniert über die sogenannte Anamnesis (vgl. *Phaidon* 72e-74a; *Menon* 81c-d), das Wiedererinnern, und er legt Sokrates die zentralen Worte in den Mund, dass alle Philosophie Mäeutik sei, Hebammenkunst (vgl. *Theaitet* 150b-151d). Soll heißen: Der Philosoph hilft durch seine fragende Methode den Menschen, sich an die absoluten Wahrheiten zu erinnern, denen der Weise – einer Hebamme gleich – zur Welt zu kommen hilft. Und genau dieses Erinnern gibt es auch bei Tolkien, der in *Mythopoeia* davon spricht, dass der wahre Mythos ein Ausgraben verschütteten Wissens sei.

In FS spricht Tolkien davon, dass fairy stories »a sudden glimpse of reality« ermöglichen (FS 77). Darin steckt zum einen die unzweifelhafte Aussage, dass »reality« im Übernatürlichen zu finden sei, was ganz eindeutig an eine metaphysische Ideenwelt anknüpft. Zum anderen lese ich den »glimpse« analog zum platonischen Erinnern, denn letztlich beziehen sich alle mythischen Inhalte auf Überliefertes und Vergangenes, woran der Dichter das Publikum erinnert. Doch dafür muss er sich vorher selbst erinnert haben, so dass Anamnesis der wahrscheinlichste Mechanismus zur Erkenntnis der Inhalte und des Wesens von

fairy stories ist, besonders wenn man FS mit den diesbezüglich eindeutigeren
Passagen aus *Mythopoeia* verbindet (vgl. Weinreich, *Metaphysics*).

VI

Doch wie ist Tolkiens Metaphysik im wissenschaftlichen Sinn als Erkenntnistheorie einzuschätzen? Das ist einfach zu beantworten, denn ihr wissen-
schaftlicher Ertrag ist mit ›gleich null‹ zu beziffern. Ihre wissenschaftliche
Rolle beschränkt sich auf die einer Fußnote zur platonischen Ideenlehre, die
als im wissenschaftlichen Sinn gescheitert angesehen werden muss. Spätestens
seit Etablierung der wissenschaftlichen Erkenntnis als nur dann gültig, wenn
sie falsifizierbar ist, kann die platonische Ideenlehre nur noch als Spekulation
bezeichnet werden, denn sie ist wie alle Metaphysik nicht widerlegbar.

Das heißt aber nicht, dass die Tolkien'sche Erkenntnistheorie bedeutungslos
ist. Gerade an der Ideenwelt hängen vielfältige spirituelle Modifikationen, und
die Essenz dieses Konzeptes, dass es eine faktisch existierende metaphysische
Realität vorbildhaften Charakters gibt, ist in manche Religion eingegangen,
unter anderem über den Neoplatonismus machtvoll in die christliche. Es ist
gar nicht abzusehen, wie Theologie und auch die Philosophie heute aussähen,
wenn es Platons Metaphysik nicht gegeben hätte. Kant beispielsweise hat die
grundlegende Bestimmung der Möglichkeiten und Grenzen des wissenschaftlichen Denkens in der Kritik der reinen Vernunft gerade in Opposition zum
klassischen Idealismus entwickelt.

Auch können Tolkiens in FS formulierte Überlegungen zwar nicht als
Grundlage einer wissenschaftlichen Theorie dienen, sie sind aber trotzdem von
Bedeutung für die Tolkien-Forschung. Sie sind nämlich erstens in der Lage,
die christlichen Elemente in der Mittelerde-Dichtung und anderen Schriften
des Professors weiter auf- und erklären zu helfen. Und sie werfen zweitens ein
Licht auf den Erfolg des Werks und darüber hinaus eventuell auf den Erfolg
der Fantasy als Genre insgesamt. Phantastische Kunst als Suche nach von der
Empirie unabhängigen metaphysischen Gewissheiten kann als Anker in einer
als undurchsichtig und allzu wandelbar empfundenen Welt interpretiert werden; der Erfolg phantastischer Kunst ebenfalls, denn man könnte die durchaus
testfähige Hypothese aufstellen, dass die Darstellung solcher Gewissheiten in
poetischer oder anderer künstlerischer Form einen mindestens teilweisen Grund
für den Erfolg der Phantastik darstellt.

»The primal desire at the heart of Faerie [is] the realization... of imagined
wonder«, heißt es in FS (35). Das ist ein durchaus hinreichender Grund für
das Erschaffen von phantastischer Kunst und Literatur. Es kann ebenso hin-
reichend als Motiv für den Genuss dieser Dinge sein, und selbst wenn es das

allein nicht ist, so trägt es meiner Überzeugung nach doch dazu bei, dass man sich der Phantastik zuwendet, selbst wenn man die reiche Ideenwelt, die dem Genre unterliegt, nur unterschwellig ahnt. Ich habe die Motivation für die Zuwendung zum Genre Fantasy einmal dergestalt erklärt, dass sie von einem metaphysischen Bedürfnis des Menschen ausgelöst werde (vgl. Weinreich, *Fantasy* 38f.). Das ist ein Bedürfnis, das er in einer zunehmend sinnentleerten Welt längst nicht mehr überall stillen kann, zumal vielen Menschen auch die etablierten Religionen diesbezüglich nicht mehr auszureichen scheinen. Was ich in den in FS beschriebenen Prozessen finde, bestärkt mich darin, dass da etwas dran sein muss, auch wenn Tolkien in fairy stories zuvörderst eine Art von christlichem Gottesdienst sah.

Bibliographie

Aristoteles, *Metaphysik*. Bücher VII(Z) - XIV(N), griech.-dt., 3. Auflage, übers. v. H. Bonitz, hrsg. v. H. Seidl, Hamburg: Meiner, 1991

Carpenter, Humphrey, *J.R.R. Tolkien. Eine Biographie*, Stuttgart: Klett-Cotta, 1979

Chance, Jane. *Tolkien and the Invention of Myth. A Reader*. Lexington: University Press of Kentucky, 2004

Cox, John, »Tolkien's Platonic Fantasy«. In: *Seven: An Anglo-American Literary Review* 5 (1984): 53-69

Flieger, Verlyn, »Naming the Unnamable: The Neoplatonic ›One‹ in Tolkien's *Silmarillion*«. In: *Diakonia: Studies in the Honor of Robert T. Meyer*. Eds. Thomas Halton & Joseph P. Williman. Washington: Catholic University of America Press, 1986, 127-133

---. *Interrupted Music. The Making of Tolkien's Mythology*. Kent: Kent State University Press, 2005

Garth, John. *Tolkien und der Erste Weltkrieg. Das Tor zu Mittelerde*. Stuttgart: Klett-Cotta, 2014

Nagy, Gergely. »Saving the Myths: the Recreation of Mythology in Plato and Tolkien«. In: *J.R.R. Tolkien and the Invention of Myth: A Reader*. Ed. Jane Chance. Lexington: University Press of Kentucky, 2004, 81-100

---. »Plato«. In: *J.R.R. Tolkien Encyclopedia: Scholarship and Critical Assessment*. Ed. Michael C. Drout. New York: Routledge, 2007, 513f

Platon: *Sämtliche Dialoge*. Hrsg. v. O. Apelt. Hamburg: Meiner, 1993

Rose, Mary Carman. »The Christian Platonism of C.S. Lewis, J.R.R. Tolkien, and Charles Williams«. In: *Neoplatonism & Christian Thought*. Ed. Dominic J. O'Meara. New York: State University of New York Press, 1981. 203-212

Tolkien, John Ronald Reuel. *The Monster & the Critics and Other Essays*. Ed. Christopher Tolkien. London: HarperCollins, 1997

---. *Tolkien On Fairy-stories. Expanded Edition, with Commentary and Notes*. Eds. Verlyn Flieger & Douglas A. Anderson. London: HarperCollins, 2008

---. „Blatt von Tüftler". In: *Das Tolkien Lesebuch*. Hg. Ulrike Killer. Stuttgart: Klett-Cotta, 1991. 401-421

Weinreich, Frank. *Fantasy. Einführung*. Essen: Oldib, 2007

---. »Metaphysics of Myth. The Platonic Ontology of ›Mythopoeia‹«. In: *Tolkien's Shorter Works*. Eds. Margaret Hiley & Frank Weinreich. Zurich/Jena: Walking Tree Publishers, 2008. 329-352. [Deutsch: *Hither Shore* 4 (2007): 37-50]

Heidegger and Tolkien:
Thankful Thinking and "the Love of Love"

Danko Kamčevski (Kragujevac)

Folk wisdom teaches us that *in every joke there is a grain of truth*, and I would like to begin this paper with a joke, hoping that it will prove to be serious enough for the discussion. It is—fittingly for a meditation on Tolkien—a philological joke, and goes like this: "Philosophy = love of wisdom. Philology = love of words. Phenomenology = love of love." The punch-line, of course, rests in the last part; and it is this element that will be the crux of the following discussion, namely the connections between Tolkien and phenomenology, that is, what Tolkien himself has to say about this 'love of love'.

Phenomenology appears both in philosophy and philology. In philosophy, it appears most prominently within the philosophy of Edmund Husserl. Husserl made an argument for the 'phenomenological reduction', that is, the method by which we approach phenomena by peeling off ideological, sociological, cultural, psychological and other layers, until we get to the pure phenomenon and hence to a certain knowledge of it. Husserl was a trained mathematician and the purity he was seeking for was analogous to the clarity of geometrical concepts. However, his greatest student, Martin Heidegger, although trained in phenomenology by Husserl himself, was not truly a phenomenologist. Heidegger argued that searching for a pure phenomenon is essentially a fruitless and perhaps even vain effort. Man is always already within a world—thrown into it. Perfect object observed by an external, unrelated subject is a continuation of the Cartesian thinking, which Heidegger viewed as a fundamentally flawed stance. Subject is actually always somehow related to the object, *in or into it* in one way or the other. The phenomenon of chair is given within the context of sitting, dining, lying down, standing, resting, listening to, and so forth. This means that the context of understanding is pre-given, and guides understanding of phenomena in all cases. Basically, there is no way to get outside the world, to look at it from above. The world is full of things which we use, or even more generally things about which we care, and which thus appear to us as useful, needed, beloved, meaningful. Some such view is to be found in the more visibly philosophic of the Inklings, C.S. Lewis. In his cosmic romance, *Out of the Silent Planet*, Ransom (a philologist modeled partly on Tolkien himself) ventures high into the mountains of the planet Malacandra (Mars)—so high, in fact, that he somehow loses the existential relationship with the world. From the distance, things disappear or are blurred or merge into an unrecognisable mass, and Ransom muses:

> It was no longer 'the world', scarcely even 'a world': it was a planet,
> a star, a waste place in the universe, millions of miles from the
> world of men. It is impossible to recall what he had felt about
> Hyoi, or Whin, or the *eldila*, or Oyarsa. It seemed fantastic to
> have thought he had duties to such hobgoblins—if they were not
> hallucinations—met in the wilds of space. He had nothing to do
> with them: he was a man.   (Lewis 81)

We should especially note—besides the obvious mention of 'world'—the words
such as 'felt', and 'duties', and a symptomatic phrase 'nothing to do with them'.
Ransom is a man: things belonging to Malacandra no longer show themselves
as meaningful phenomena to him. He lost closeness to them; he no longer cares
about them. For a moment they are suspended from his *human context*. I do
not, of course, argue that Lewis read or was influenced by Heidegger, but the
similarity is all too striking not to point out. And at least it is quite certain
that Tolkien was familiar with the idea, for he read and recommended *Out of
the Silent Planet* for publication.

The other intrusion of phenomenology of interest to us is in the field of philology. It did not pass long before the phenomenological method was adopted in
approaches to understanding and interpreting literary works. Polish phenomenologist Roman Ingarden articulated an understanding of literary works that
would aim at a similar reduction leading to the *works themselves*, composed
of the following layers: sound, sense, schematised aspects, and represented
objectivities. Since a literary work is not a logical statement, it necessarily
produces many indeterminations in sense, and that is its virtue. In its lack of
complete logical determination, it "opalizes". However, Ingarden's focus remains
linguistic in essence. We need not go outside the work too much and search
for historical or cultural discrepancies or political messages: the *language itself*
is sufficient to provide for endless possibilities of recovering meaning. In
American literary studies there was a very similar trend called New Criticism.
It also called for not going beyond the text itself, and introduced the 'heresy
of paraphrase'. However, it was soon realised that text-immanent criticism of
this sort was actually much better suited for poetry than for complex works
such as novels, in which we find ideological, cultural, historical, political and
other layers and aspects that were *intentionally* placed there.

At this point the reader will most probably recall Tolkien's forceful argument
laid out in "Beowulf: the Monsters and the Critics"—the argument against
reducing a literary work to something else: at worst an historical document,
an anthropological evidence, or somewhat better, a typical genre or a kind of
story. *Beowulf* is not forgotten even in *On Fairy-stories*. Anti-reductionism is
very important to Tolkien, as we can see not only in its implications for under-

standing literary works but in a more, we dare say, metaphysical sense: "We read that *Beowulf* 'is only a version of *Dat Erdmänneken*'; that 'the *Black Bull of Norroway* is *Beauty and the Beast*', or 'is the same story as Eros and Psyche...'" (FS 38). Just how much Tolkien stresses the importance of a work to speak for itself, and not through mediating phenomena such as genres, styles, historical periods, is highly visible when he pronounces: "It is precisely the colouring, the atmosphere, the unclassifiable individual details of a story, and above all the general purport that informs with life the undissected bones of the plot, that really count" (FS 39). *De individuo nulla scientia.* This indeed sounds like 'story and nothing but the story'.

Still, how does it compare with relying only on the actual layers of the text? From Tolkien's lecture "A Secret Vice", it would seem that there is indeed some correspondence between his fascination with euphony and phenomenological reliance on the layer of sound as one of the sources of proper interpretation. However, in the much later lecture "English and Welsh" there is a difference between *mother tongue* and *cradle tongue* that presupposes that even taste in languages and the way they sound could be inborn, or at least not universal. Even the layer of sound, seemingly the most "objective" one, could in Tolkien's view also very much depend upon personal tastes, and then these personal tastes could be projected on the literary text. Not much is different in terms of the layer of meaning. Individual words for Tolkien were not merely signs, understood in contradistinction from other words in some linguistic system (as in De Saussure). Much has been written about Tolkien's fascinations with single words, and indeed he himself has written articles—such as "The Sigelwara Land" and "Middle English 'Losenger': Sketch of an etymological and semantic enquiry"—devoted to single words revealing the enormous potential of meaning behind them. To utter a single word means to (consciously or unconsciously, depending on one's knowledge) bring up a whole mythology, a whole world giving rise and sustaining the meaning of that single word. Hence, no pure phenomenological approach of remaining solely within the confines of the text is possible. Every single word we read is able to transport us out of the text into the world of its origin. This necessarily means that every text is full of various kinds of cultural and historical imports.

In this manner, Tolkien was able to locate cultural condemnation of over-zealousness or 'ofermod' in "The Battle of Maldon", or to identify a Germanic mythological matrix with its 'northern theory of courage' in *Beowulf.* Paying attention to the texts themselves for Tolkien did not mean divorcing the text from its context, but realising its proper context. The difference may sound subtle, but it is in fact very important. In her paper "Contextualizing the Writings of J.R.R. Tolkien on Literary Criticism", Sherrylyn Branchaw makes a similar argument. According to Branchaw, the critical trends in Tolkien's time were such that he had to argue more forcefully to counteract such approaches as psycho-analytical or anthropological criticisms (both of which elicited two refuting essays by C.S. Lewis as well). In the words of another Inkling, Owen Barfield,

> when the psychologists join hands with the anthropologists, he sees a whole cloud of these projectiles flying off in the same direction and landing on the same target—namely, the mind of that luckless repository, primitive man. One thing at least is made very clear from what all these informative people are fond of telling us about primitive man and that is that, whatever else he was doing, he was always projecting his insides onto something or other. It was his principal occupation.   (Barfield 85)

Therefore, it is reasonable to conclude that Tolkien's approach to understanding literature is not to view a work as some perfect, self-sufficient object of investigation that does not necessitate other works for its explanations; nor is he making a case for immersing works into a network of sciences and arts, thus leveling a work down to a cultural product or an historical document. Clearly then, there is in Tolkien something of a phenomenology, but also something of a hermeneutics of Hans-Georg Gadamer who maintained that the real goal of understanding literary works is not knowing them in totality (which is not possible), but in bringing closer two horizons: the horizon of the reader, and the horizon of the literary work that is interpreted. These two horizons can never be completely fused, but the more successful the fusion, the richer the understanding. What is aimed at is not completeness or perfection of knowing all and everything about the work investigated, but the Platonic dictum that all knowledge is self-knowledge. Every fusion of horizons spreads the reader's horizons. After reading a work, he is no longer the same reader. This is also one of the points made in Barfield's *Poetic Diction* which so influenced Tolkien—reading poetry, says Barfield, leads to an expansion of reader's consciousness.

In Heidegger, Gadamer's teacher and friend, this meeting between the reader and the work would amount to a meeting of two worlds. That is why Heidegger insisted so much on minute philological and etymological analyses of words appearing in ancient philosophical treatises: he wanted to encounter the ancient thinkers as authentically as possible. For the very same reason Tolkien thought so highly of editing as the first important step towards a more genuine understanding of works. As Tom Shippey writes in his contribution for the *Blackwell Companion to J.R.R. Tolkien*, "Editing is the foundation, the most important part of bringing ancient works and forgotten authors back to life. All the rest is merely superstructure" (Shippey 41).

Philosopher William J. Richardson wrote an influential book on Heidegger called *Heidegger: Through Phenomenology to Thought*. The title itself implies that Heidegger went beyond phenomenology into a new area of thought. In a similar manner, Tolkien too went beyond mere textual criticism relating, like Barfield did, consciousness and language and through the latter what he thought the highest function of language: literature. He approaches works integrally, organically; not analytically by separation into categories that have nothing to do with each other. And there is, as Verlyn Flieger noticed, a linguistic relationship between Heidegger's *phenomenon* and Tolkien's *fantasy*: "Both terms––*phenomenon* and *fantasy*––derive from Greek, *phenomenon* from *phainesthai*, "to appear," and *fantasy* from *phantazein*, "to make visible" (Flieger 45). And as Laurence Paul Hemming notes, there is a further relation between language and phenomena: "The verbs φαίνω, to bring to light, to allow to be seen, and φάσκω, to say or deem, have the same root and are really the same word" (Hemming 10).

Heidegger was most probably aware of most of these connections, if not all, for he says in his relatively early (yet seminal) work, *Being and Time*, that phenomena "are thus the totality of what lies in the light of the day or can be brought to light" (Heidegger, *Being* 27). There seems to be a thread connecting phenomena, fantasy, and language. The same thread also connects Tolkien and Heidegger on a more different level: that of deep thought and fascination with these issues. It is for this reason that I now turn to the examination of this level of agreement between these two, the most philological of philosophers and the most philosophical of philologists.

Heidegger and Tolkien start from similar premises—works themselves, phenomena—and then work out wider and more significant implications that are, as we shall see, congruous with each other. Where do we find points of intersection between Martin Heidegger and J.R.R. Tolkien? One could begin with biographical facts. Both were born at the very end of the nineteenth century, and lived for the most part of the twentieth century. Tolkien was a devout Catholic, and so was Heidegger, who in his beginnings was even about to become a Thomist philosopher before he renounced his Catholicism. Both, Tolkien and Heidegger spent their childhoods in rural areas and kept strong affinities with the country-side and nature. Also, both were esteemed academics: Tolkien was a professor at Oxford University, while Heidegger lectured at the University of Freiburg.

An anecdote about Heidegger goes that he once said at the beginning of a lecture on Aristotle, "He was born, lived, and died, and now let us see what he thought". Essential correspondences are of primary interest in this paper, and these too have not passed unnoticed in Tolkien scholarship. Michael C. Drout's *Encyclopedia*, in its entry on "Existentialism", written by Robert Eaglestone, singles out three possible connections between Tolkien and Heidegger: authenticity, technology, and language (Eaglestone 179-180). Eaglestone, however, makes a mistake in too easily calling Heidegger an 'existentialist'. Heidegger refuted this stance several times in his writings, and insisted that he was dealing with ontology, not existentialism. The error is visible in the encyclopedia which, due to this, is unable to make a parallel between Tolkien and Heidegger in terms of existentialism, but is able to do so in the case of comparing Tolkien and Sartre. The two other parallels do indeed prove that true similarities lie in ontology, in viewing the world at large, not simply from the perspective of human authenticity, living meaningfully, achieving happiness, and so on. Eaglestone is completely right to relate Tolkien and Heidegger via issues of technology and language, the former being a very serious problem for both Tolkien and Heidegger, and the latter being a life-long fascination and mystery for both. Since both Heidegger's *thinking* and Tolkien's *fantasy* partly stem from confrontation with modernity and its spirit of technology, we shall here turn towards this aspect first.

For Heidegger, the essence of technology is the very summation of metaphysical thinking pursued by the Western philosophers and scientists for centuries. That kind of consciousness is technological consciousness that comes before technology. For Heidegger, western philosophy has for a very long time confused beings with being. More obvious attempts to equate all being with a particular being can be found in such systems which claim that all is fire, all is water, all is air, all is spirit, or 'all is matter' which is the current materialistic view of things. If all is fire, what is fire? If all is matter, what is matter? Hence God is absolute being in the theology of Thomas Aquinas—but the understanding of this being is based on human, not God's perception of what being is. This God is ultimately God according to human measure. And we now live in the age in which what exists is what is calculable—a stance formulated by physicist Max Planck. Everything is seen as a resource. "The essence of modern technology starts man upon the way of that revealing through which the real everywhere, more or less distinctly, becomes standing-reserve" (Heidegger, *Question* 24). On the Tolkien side of the analogy, it can be remarked that it is a Sauronian mindset, him being the one who wants 'order and coordination' above all.

Another aspect of the technological mindset is its connection with magic. For what is metaphysical thinking (as seen by Heidegger) if not a kind of magical thinking present even in pre-scientific epochs? We have magic objects, and they fit in an understanding of interconnectedness. One thing stands for another. If you eat a fruit in the shape of a heart, it could be good for your heart. If you eat red beet it is good for the blood, since red beet is red as blood. So there is some sort of law of similarity—*similis simili gaudet*. In the world of folklore it is quite normal that power can reside in part of the body—like hair for example.

Cutting one's hair or beard could lead to losing vital strength. It is therefore small wonder that Koschei the Immortal has his power residing in some object, and when this object is destroyed, so is Koschei. In *The Lord of the Rings*, there is a technology of rings. Saruman, who is the most industrially-minded of all characters ('mind of wheels' as Treebeard calls him) is researching into this technology. At the same time the Ring is Sauron's life-force, an example and a symbol of technology. But it is not a mere substitute for technology. There is enough symbolism in the Ring to understand that it is not only Sauron's heart that went there, but also his *mind*, his specific kind of consciousness—the kind of consciousness that makes something like the Ring possible.

This kind of consciousness cares only about efficiency and results, and will not admit as real something that cannot be put into an equation. Heidegger makes an interesting remark on how sciences view a thing such as a tree:

> For we shall forfeit everything before we know it, once the sciences of physics, physiology, and psychology, not to forget scientific philosophy, display the panoply of their documents and proofs, to explain to us that what we see and accept is properly not a tree but in reality a void, thinly sprinkled with electric charges here and there that race hither and yon at enormous speeds.
>
> (Heidegger, *Thinking* 43)

Distressed by this kind of seeing that does not see the tree but virtually nothing[1], Heidegger pronounces that "...the thing that matters first and foremost, and finally, is not to drop the tree in bloom, but for once to let it stand where it stands. Why do we say 'finally'? ...to this day, thought has never let the tree stand where it stands" (Heidegger, *Thinking* 44). And thus we are reminded by Tolkien that trees *are* real, *are living beings*, and are worth all the respect we can give them. Tolkien achieves this by giving us a cognitive shock of a sort. Because trees and other plants, being unable to move, usually do not qualify as beings in their own right, he confronts us with talking and walking trees having their own interests and rights to live and prosper.

The materialistic worldview haunting Middle-earth was noticed by Dodds in a very similar way. This is no wonder, for in Dodds' paper, in the bibliography section, we find Heidegger's study on Nietzsche. Dodds writes: "All that is not will comes to be seen as raw material for will to act upon. Not only in the external world but in oneself. And the human nature which becomes raw material for one's 'creative' making is not only in oneself, but other people"

---

1   Much like Descartes and mechanistic philosophers following him who did not think animals felt pain because they could not think ("Cogito, ergo sum") and hence were not beings such as humans.

(Dodds 170). This is not merely Sauron's invention, but is an option available to other characters as well, for Dodds remarks that

> 'God' is proclaimed, but not a god to limit the will to power of the Númenórean tendency to represent reality in terms of power and indeed 'technology' appears in the way Sauron tempts them to destruction. The Númenóreans, in their preoccupation with Death and fear of it, tend to perceive Mortality as a 'problem' which could be 'solved' by the right 'technology', by possession and use of the appropriate tool. It is a practical limit to their work which they would overcome.   (Dodds 178)

Campbell notes that Sauron is a representative of the technological worldview, stating: "Sauron, who was once referred to by Tolkien as the 'Lord of magic and machines' (L 146) is the architect of the assault on both the people and the landscapes of Middle-earth: he is the bringer of destructive machines and technology" (Campbell 439).

Let us remind ourselves once more that no such violent approach to nature (and humanity by implication) would be possible without a prior understanding of nature as resource. To make a slight return to the beginning of this paper, this approach is not at all different from critical methods that too approached literary works as gold-mines of history or anthropology. The devaluing that it brings is universal. That is why Tolkien could grieve both about the many trees cut by the diabolical chainsaw and about *Beowulf* being misused and abused as a silly tale, good only for teaching some history.

Why does this happen? Heidegger believes that we have become careless about things, that there is not enough admiration of single beings. They no longer shine forth and we no longer notice them. There is *oblivion of being*. Heidegger notices a symptom of it in language, giving a slightly comic example: "Presumably no one here has ever given serious thought to what has already come to pass when you, instead of *University*, simply say 'U.' 'U'--that is like 'movie.' True, the moving picture theater continues to be different from the academy of the sciences. Still, the designation 'U' is not accidental, let alone harmless" (Heidegger, *Thinking* 34). Language is becoming banal, a mere tool, something to be used and the significance of which is overlooked in the speed of effective conversation and passing of information. "It therefore might be helpful to us to rid ourselves of the habit of always hearing only what we already understand" (Heidegger, *Way* 58). And since words relate to things, the carelessness too easily spreads to the rest of the world we inhabit. It is from this perspective that Tolkien muses on how too ordinary the things have become for us: "We say we know them. They have become like the things which once attracted us by their glitter, or their colour, or their shape, and we laid hands on them and then locked them in our hoard, acquired them, and acquiring ceased to look at them" (FS 67). Basically, because we are not looking at them, they cease to exist meaningfully. They no longer belong to a story, and as Treebeard points out, real names "tell you the story of the things they belong to" (LotR II 468). But let us observe now the same thing happening in Middle-earth as with University and "U". Treebeard gives us quite a phenomenological description while seeking for the appropriate word: "I do not know what the word is in the outside languages: you know, the thing we are on, where I stand and look out on fine mornings, and think about the Sun, and the grass beyond the wood, and the horses, and the clouds, and the unfolding of the world" (LotR II 468). When finally, the hobbits suggest to him the correct word, he is not very satisfied with it—and there is an echo of Heidegger's dissatisfaction in it:

> 'Hill?' suggested Pippin. 'Shelf? Step' suggested Merry. Treebeard repeated the words thoughtfully. *'Hill.* Yes, that was it. But it is a hasty word for a thing that has stood here ever since this part of the world was shaped.   (LotR II 469)

Entish "a-lalla-lalla-rumba-kamanda-lind-or-burúmë" is, as Treebeard points out, only "a part of my name for it" (LotR II 468), even though it sounds like a full sentence. But 'hill' is simply opaque: it conceals the essence and lived experience of the hill, so important for Treebeard—and which should be important for us, lest the words become just useful signs instead of wells of significance. The wonder is gone—and it is exactly the wonder and joy that are necessary to appreciate beings. How do we recover it? In *What is Called Thinking*, Heidegger makes one of his recognizable etymological illustrations—also curious for us because it refers to Old English, Tolkien's special interest:

> The Old English *thencan*, to think, and *thancian*, to thank, are closely related; the Old English noun for thought is *thanc* or *thonc*--a thought, a grateful thought, and the expression of such a thought; today it survives in the plural *thanks*. The "thanc," that which is thought, the thought, implies the thanks.
> (Heidegger, *Thinking* 139)

Hence, in thinking he have something quite opposite to calculating, scientific approach. Seeing things as belonging to a category, type, or reducing them to more basic elements, is exactly *not* what we should do. We should appreciate things, leave them standing as with the mentioned trees, and allow them to show themselves to us. Beings are not finished objects to be manipulated and taken for granted, but sources of possibility. For Heidegger, possibility ranks higher than actuality, for actuality is another way for accepting things "as they are" (but in fact only as they appear to be in the present moment) and at the same time forgetting everything they *could be or become*. Being for Heidegger is not some 'highest being' or sum total of all available beings in the world. Being is that by which we are able to experience beings. Only by having some sense of Being are we able to meet individual beings. It is a hotly debated issue in Heideggerian studies how to define the exact meaning of Being, but there is a strong resemblance to Tolkien's view on *Faërie*. Unlike many who tried to equate *Faërie* with specific beings, like elves, Tolkien takes another anti-reductionist stance declaring:

> Fairy-stories are not in normal English usage stories *about* fairies or elves, but stories about Fairy, that is *Faërie*, the realm or state in which fairies have their being. *Faërie* contains many things besides elves and fays, and besides dwarfs, witches, trolls, giants, or dragons: it holds the seas, the moon, the sky; and the earth, and all things that are in it: tree and bird, water and stone, wine and bread, and ourselves, mortal men, when we are enchanted.
> (FS 32)

Through Being things become meaningful for us and we are able to perceive them; fantasy or *Faërie* is that which enables us to perceive the wonderful side to each thing by viewing it from a different angle or with different eyes. Peter Kreeft discusses this philosophy of wonder in Tolkien—the philosophy according to which the world is bigger than we can imagine—and says:

> For if you believe the first philosophy, as Shakespeare did, as Tolkien did, and as most pre-modern peoples did, then your fundamental attitude towards all reality is wonder and humility. You are like a small child in a large house. As Tolkien said in one of his letters, "You are inside a very great story." You expect mysteries, you expect moreness: terrors to stop your heart and joys to break it. Reality is big.   (Kreeft 33)

Tolkien's well-known views on fantasy provide one solution to the destructive reduction of the world undertaken by modern science and technology. Is there a parallel in Heidegger? In his *Contributions to Philosophy*, he says cryptically: "The paths and modes of sheltering: *beings*" (Heidegger, *Contributions* 25). Beings in profusion are ways of sheltering Being and retaining relationship with it and escaping its oblivion. But how can we reveal things once again, how can we again become aware of them so that we may glorify and celebrate them? One hint was already given in *Being and Time*: "The elaboration of the domain in its fundamental structures is in a way already accomplished by pre-scientific experience and interpretation of the region of being to which the domain of knowledge is itself confined" (Heidegger, *Being* 8). What Heidegger is saying is actually quite similar to what Tolkien states in *Mythopoeia*—that is, before any scientific investigation of phenomena can begin, the phenomena themselves have to be revealed as such by pre-scientific thinking, such as poetry or mythology:

> There is no firmament,
> only a void, unless a jewelled tent
> myth-woven and elf-patterned; and no earth,
> unless the mother's womb whence all have birth.   (TL 98)

Poetry is that region in which beings are discovered and in which they are appreciated for the first time—as 'jewelled tent' or as 'mother's womb'—before they turn into 'gaseous spheres' and 'tectonic plates'. That is why Heidegger asks (but in fact states) perceptively: "Could it be that the fine arts are called to poetic revealing? Could it be that revealing lays claim to the arts most primally, so that they for their part may expressly foster the growth of the saving power, may awaken and found anew our look into that which grants and our trust in it?" (Heidegger, *Question* 35). In another essay he is in a more affirmative mood, saying: "Open which poetry lets happen, and indeed in such a way that only now, in the midst of beings, the Open brings beings to shine and ring out" (Heidegger, "Origin" 70). In lectures on Parmenides, Heidegger is more specific about mythology opening up worlds: "Muthos is the Greek for the word that expresses what is to be said before all else. The essence of muthos is thus determined on the basis of aletheia. It is muthos that reveals, discloses and lets be seen; specifically, it lets be seen what shows itself in advance and in everything as that which presences in all 'presence'" (Heidegger, *Parmenides* 60).

Although Heidegger does not specifically address fantasy like Tolkien does, there still is the element of the uncanny, of foreignness prompting man to restoration of the relationship with Being. Capobianco writes of both forgetfulness of Being and its remembrance in his study *Engaging Heidegger*:

> Because of this 'forgetting' of Being, human beings are lost among beings and founder among beings, 'the foreign land,' and for this reason, they are intrinsically 'unsettled' and 'unhomely' among beings. Nonetheless, some, like Antigone, take up this unsettledness and unhomeliness resolutely; they choose a 'bold forgetting' as they journey through the 'foreign land.' Such passing through the foreign land is necessary for human beings if they are to come to re-cognize Being *as* Home and to dwell at the Source in 'thoughtful remembrance' (Andenken).   (Capobianco 63)

In this fragment one can discern space in which not only tragedy, but Tolkien's Faërian drama can find its place. The story of adventure, like *The Lord of the Rings*, begins in an all too familiar world, but shortly afterwards the characters are thrown into the wide world full of unimaginable things. The subtitle of *The Hobbit*, "there and back again" sums up this dialectic. The point of the adventure is going back home—but neither that home nor yourself are the same when you return. All that is clearly stated by Tolkien in *On Fairy-stories*, and the argument is repeated in his essay on *Smith of Wootton Major* (published in the expanded edition by Verlyn Flieger): "Faery represents at its weakest a breaking out (at least in mind) from the iron ring of the familiar, still more from the adamantine ring of belief that it is known, possessed, controlled, and so (ultimately) all that is worth being considered—a constant awareness of a world beyond these rings" (SWM 145). Colin Duriez states that Inklings as a group of friends had this common goal and interest in literature: "They looked beyond what they saw as the intellectual wasteland of the merely modern to glimpses of a larger world" (Duriez 130). *Merely modern* is the context that prompted both Heidegger and Tolkien into reaching for ways of thinking and imagination that would rescue us and the world from such a situation.

In view of these similarities between Tolkien and Heidegger, the question arises about the differences between them. One is particularly interesting. While Heidegger's *thinking* is associated with awe and thankfulness, Tolkien's *Faërie* is associated with love, which encompasses wonder and the glory of beings:

> More strongly it represents love: that is, a love and respect for all things, 'inanimate' and 'animate', an unpossessive love of them as 'other'. This 'love' will produce both ruth and delight. Things seen in its light will be respected, and they will also appear delightful, beautiful, wonderful even glorious… This compound— of awareness of limitless world outside our domestic parish; a love (in ruth and admiration) for the things in it; and a desire for wonder, marvels, both perceived and conceived—this 'Faery' is as necessary for the health and complete functioning of the Human as is sunlight for physical life: sunlight as distinguished from the soil, say, though it in fact permeates and modifies even that.
>
> (SWM 145)

Love is the impulse that is able to individuate beings, to be the source of awe and respect before them, to let them be what they are. Heidegger famously remarked that *Sein ist lassen*, Being is letting be. The feeling of love makes it possible to let things be whatever they are, instead of putting them in boxes and drawers and claiming we already know them. In *Charles Dickens*, Chesterton writes:

> It is a great mistake to suppose that love unites and unifies men.
> Love diversifies them, because love is directed towards individual-
> ity... Thus, for instance, the more we love Germany the more
> pleased we shall be that Germany should be something different
> from ourselves, should keep her own ritual and conviviality and
> we ours.   (Chesterton 253-254)

This love motivates even the adventure, the quest itself. As Linda Greenwood says: "Love defines the ultimate use of deconstruction, and love allows myth to invade the reality of this world and become fact. In Tolkien's work, love motivates faith to reach beyond the boundaries of the known, to rekindle hope in the midst of the uncertain" (Greenwood 171).

At the very end of this discussion, we are arriving at the place from where we started. For in his essay on *Smith of Wootton Major* Tolkien has something more to say about *Faërie* that will remind us of the joke at the beginning—and it is also connected to the instrumentalism and utilitarianism of the modern civilisation. According to him, even these cannot prosper without the contents of that humorous definition of phenomenology:

> The love of Faery is the love of love: a relationship towards all
> things, animate and inanimate, which includes love and respect,
> and removes or modifies the spirit of possession and domination.
> Without it even plain 'Utility' will in fact become less useful; or
> will turn to ruthlessness and lead only to mere power, ultimately
> destructive.   (SWM 131)

Perhaps Tolkien, who was not a phenomenologist, unwittingly glimpsed what phenomenology should really be like—not merely an analytical tool, nor just a road to self-knowledge, but an affective relationship with this world and things in it. In a similar way, Husserl saw in phenomenology a new, scientific, mathematical philosophy, whereas Heidegger went beyond perceived scientism and maintained that we must be motivated by admiration.

Tolkien's analyses of *Beowulf* and fairy stories would not be so deep and would not remain influential even now, had they also not been *loving* analyses. Tolkien cared about what a hasty analyst would call 'mere sounds' or 'mere words'. He cared enough about Germanic legends to see not only 'primitivism' but also heroism and bravery, and was not afraid to write a very long story about a pre-Christian world. Motivated by love, he was able to *let it be*, and in its being show its worthiness and individuality. Heidegger incisively saw that the essence of being human lies in care. Tolkien saw the fullness of care in love. Phenomenology is hallowed in Heidegger's thankful thinking and Tolkien's *Faërie*, "the love of love".

Bibliography

Barfield. Owen. *The Rediscovery of Meaning*. San Rafael: The Barfield Press, 1977

Branchaw, Sherrylyn. "Contextualizing the Writings of J.R.R. Tolkien on Literary Criticism". *Journal of Tolkien Research* 1 (2014): 1-36

Campbell, Liam. "Nature". *A Companion to J.R.R. Tolkien*. Ed. Stuart D. Lee. Oxford: Wiley Blackwell, 2014. 431-445

Capobianco, Richard. *Engaging Heidegger*. Toronto: University of Toronto Press, 2011

Chesterton, Gilbert Keith. *Charles Dickens*. New York: Dodd Mead & Company, 1906

Dodds, David Lllewellyn. "Technology and Sub-creation: Tolkien's Alternative to the Dominant Worldview". *Scholarship and Fantasy: Proceedings of the Tolkien Phenomenon*. Ed. K.J. Battarbee. Turku: University of Turku, 1993, 165-186

Duriez, Colin. *The Oxford Inklings: Lewis, Tolkien and their Circle*. Oxford: Lion Hudson, 2015

Eaglestone, Robert. "Existentialism". *J.R.R. Tolkien Encyclopedia: Scholarship and Critical Assessment*. Ed. Michael C. Drout. New York: Routledge, 2007, 179-180

Flieger, Verlyn. *Splintered Light: Logos and Language in Tolkien's World (revised edition)*. Kent/London: The Kent State University Press, 2002

Greenwood, Linda. "Love: 'The Gift of Death'". *Tolkien Studies* 2 (2005): 171-195

Heidegger, Martin. "Origin of the Work of Art". *Poetry, Language, Thought*. New York: HarperPerennial, 2001

---. *Being and Time*. Translated by Joan Stambaugh. Albany: State University of New York Press, 2010

---. *Contributions to Philosophy (of the Event)*. Translated by Richard Rojcewicz and Daniela Vallega-Neu. Bloomington and Indianapolis: Indiana University Press, 2012

---. *On the Way to Language*. Translated by Peter D. Hertz. New York: HarperOne, 1982

---. *Parmenides*. Bloomington and Indianapolis: Indiana University Press, 1998

---. *The Question Concerning Technology and Other Essays*. New York/London: Garland Publishing Inc., 1977

---. *What is Called Thinking*. Translated by J. Glenn Gray. New York: HarperPerennial, 2004

Kreeft, Peter J. *The Philosophy of Tolkien*. San Francisco: Ignatius Press, 2005

Lewis, Clive Staples. *The Space Trilogy*. London: HarperCollins, 2013

Shippey, Tom. "Tolkien as Editor". *A Companion to J.R.R. Tolkien*. Ed. Stuart D. Lee. Oxford: Wiley Blackwell, 2014, 42-55

Tolkien, John Ronald Reuel. *Smith of Wootton Major* (edited by Verlyn Flieger and illustrated by Pauline Baynes). London: HarperCollins, 2015

---. *The Two Towers*. London: HarperCollins, 2002

---. *Tree and Leaf*. London: Unwin Hyman, 1964

---. *Tolkien On Fairy-stories* (edited by Verlyn Flieger and Douglas Anderson). London: HarperCollins, 2008

---. *The Monsters and the Critics and Other Essays*. London: HarperCollins, 2006

"Children are meant to grow up, and not to become Peter Pans."

Guglielmo Spirito (Assisi)

I am almost inclined to set it up as a canon or rule that a children's story which is enjoyed only by children is a bad children's story. The good ones last. What, if any, are the values and functions of fairy stories now? So we come to a rather important question.

> Among those who still have enough wisdom not to think fairy-stories pernicious [I find that there really are human beings who think fairy tales bad for children, wrote Chesterton], the common opinion seems to be that there is a natural connexion between the minds of children and fairy-stories, of the same order as the connexion between children's bodies and milk.
> Actually, the association of children and fairy-stories is an accident of our domestic history. Fairy-stories have in the modern lettered world been relegated to the "nursery," as shabby or old-fashioned furniture is relegated to the play-room, primarily because the adults do not want it, and do not mind if it is misused. It is not the choice of the children which decides this. Children as a class— except in a common lack of experience they are not one—neither like fairy-stories more, nor understand them better than adults do; and no more than they like many other things. They are young and growing, and normally have keen appetites, so the fairy-stories as a rule go down well enough. But in fact only some children, and some adults, have any special taste for them; and when they have it, it is not exclusive, nor even necessarily dominant. It is a taste, too, that would not appear, I think, very early in childhood without artificial stimulus; it is certainly one that does not decrease but increases with age, if it is innate.   (FS 42-44)

> Critics who treat adult as a term of approval, instead of as a merely descriptive term, cannot be adult themselves. To be concerned about being grown up, to admire the grown up because it is grown up, to blush at the suspicion of being childish; these things are the marks of childhood and adolescence. And in childhood and adolescence they are, in moderation, healthy symptoms. Young things ought to want to grow. But to carry on into middle life or even into early manhood this concern about being adult is a mark of really arrested development. When I was ten, I read fairy tales

in secret and would have been ashamed if I had been found doing
so. Now that I am fifty I read them openly. When I became a man
I put away childish things, including the fear of childishness and
the desire to be very grown up.   (Lewis 34)

Lewis equates the "very grown up" desire to label fairy stories as nothing more
than "childish," with childishness itself, and consequently makes a strong case
for stories as an intrinsic part of the journey to a kind of true adulthood where
childish things—including the desire to be "very grown up"—have successfully
been put aside.

This tension can be recognised in a couple of significative dialogues on the very
first pages of the *Lord of the Rings*, which set the most important—and maybe
secret—thematic lines of all that will follow:

> "I can hear fireside-tales and children's stories at home, if I want
> to", said Ted.
> "No doubt you can," retorted Sam, "and I daresay there's more
> truth in some of them than you reckon. Who invented the stories
> anyway? Take dragons now."
> "No thank 'ee," said Ted, "I won't. I heard tell of them when I was
> a youngster, but there's no call to believe in them now. There's
> only one Dragon in Bywater, and that's Green," he said, getting
> a general laugh.   (LotR 44f)

> It is far easier to believe in a million fairy tales than to believe in
> one man who does not like fairy tales. Look at these plain, homely,
> practical words. 'The Dragon's Grandmother,' that is all right; that
> is rational almost to the verge of rationalism. If there was a dragon,
> he had a grandmother. But you—you had no grandmother! If you
> had known one, she would have taught you to love fairy tales. You
> had no father, you had no mother; no natural causes can explain
> you. You cannot be. I believe many things which I have not seen;
> but of such things as you it may be said, 'Blessed is he that has
> seen and yet has disbelieved'.   (Chesterton 34)

> But Ted laughed.
> "Well, that isn't anything new, if you believe the old tales. And I
> don't see what it matters to me or you."
> "Well I don't know," said Sam thoughtfully... Of all the legends
> that he had heard in his early years such fragments of tales and
> half-remembered stories about the Elves as the hobbits knew, had
> always moved him most deeply.   (LotR 44f)

> "Halflings!" laughed the Rider [Éothain] that stood beside
> Éomer. "Halflings! But they are only a little people in old songs
> and children's tales out of the North. Do we walk in legends or
> on the green earth in the daylight?"
> "A man may do both," said Aragorn. "For not we but those who
> come after will make the legends of our time".   (LotR 434)

Grownups have a tendency to remember the land of make-believe as a heavenly,
sun-kissed bunny land. But the land of make-believe is less heaven and more
like hell. Children play is not escapist. It confronts the problems of the human
condition head-on. Chesterton reminds us in *The Red Angel* that fear does not
come from fairy tales; the fear comes from the universe of the soul.

> Fairy tales, then, are not responsible for producing in children fear,
> or any of the shapes of fear; fairy tales do not give the child the
> idea of the evil or the ugly; that is in the child already, because it
> is in the world already. Fairy tales do not give the child his first
> idea of bogey. What fairy tales give the child is his first clear idea
> of the possible defeat of bogey. The baby has known the dragon
> intimately ever since he had an imagination. What the fairy tale
> provides for him is a St. George to kill the dragon. Exactly what
> the fairy tale does is this: it accustoms him for a series of clear
> pictures to the idea that these limitless terrors had a limit, that
> these shapeless enemies have enemies in the knights of God, that
> there is something in the universe more mystical than darkness,
> and stronger than strong fear. At the four corners of a child's bed
> stand Perseus and Roland, Sigurd and St. George. If you withdraw
> the guard of heroes you are not making him rational; you are
> only leaving him to fight the devils alone. For the devils, alas, we
> have always believed in. The hopeful element in the universe has
> in modern times continually been denied and reasserted; but the
> hopeless element has never for a moment been denied.
> (Chesterton 36)

Every day, children enter a world where they must confront dark forces, fleeing
and fighting for their lives.

Worst of all, when the boys played pirates or robbers, they needed what all
hard men need most: victims. And what better victims than the girls? Priscilla
Tolkien told in Assisi in 2007—and telling the story with stunning mimicry—
that once during their childhood, her brother Christopher, using one of the
teddy bears as pilot, bombed her dolls, gathered for a wedding party, smashing
and ruining everything.

If we use *child* in a good sense (it has also legitimately a bad one) we must not allow that to push us into the sentimentality of only using *adult* or *grown-up* in a bad sense (it has also legitimately a good one). The process of growing older is not necessarily allied to growing wickeder, though the two do often happen together. **Children are meant to grow up, and not to become Peter Pans. Not to lose innocence and wonder, but to proceed on the appointed journey**: that journey upon which it is certainly not better to travel hopefully than to arrive, though we must travel hopefully if we are to arrive. **But it is one of the lessons of fairy-stories (if we can speak of the lessons of things that do not lecture) that on callow, lumpish, and selfish youth peril, sorrow, and the shadow of death can bestow dignity, and even sometimes wisdom.**   (FS 62, emphasis added)

Tolkien's initial drafts of the lecture have a few differences:

Manuscript A (190):
Children are meant to grow up **and to die**, and not become Peter Pans (**a dreadful fate**)

Manuscript B (237):
Children are meant to grow up **and to die**, and not **to** become Peter Pans

Essay (58):
Children are meant to grow up, and not to become Peter Pans

The mention of *death* and of *dreadful fate* disappeard, but Peter Pan remained.

Now the modern critical world uses 'adult' as a term of approval. It is hostile to what it calls 'nostalgia' and contemptuous of what it calls 'Peter Pantheism'. Hence a man who admits that dwarfs and giants and talking beasts and witches are still dear to him in his fifty-third year is now less likely to be praised for his perennial youth than scorned and pitied for arrested development.

The modern view seems to me to involve a false conception of growth. They accuse us of arrested development because we have not lost a taste we had in childhood. But surely arrested development consists not in refusing to lose old things but in failing to add new things?

The word 'adult' derives from the Latin *adultus*, the past participle of *adolescere* 'to grow to maturity'. To be adult is the culmination of a process of maturation. It implies that one is in a story, with various stages, which gives a unity and shape to one's life. Adult identity is the fruit of the past, and open to a future.

In James Barrie's play *Peter Pan* (1904), the Darling children adventure in Neverland, but eventually they get homesick and return to the real world. The play suggests that kids have to grow up, and growing up means leaving the pretend space called Neverland behind. But Peter Pan stays in Neverland. He will not grow up. Is it not *this* the dreadful fate of becoming Peter Pans that Tolkien says children need to avoid?

There is a type of eternal adolescent which spends his life daydreaming outlandish dreams that never amount to anything. He wants to be loved unconditionally for his potential, and he refuses to be assessed on the basis of his accomplishments. For him the tree is to be judged not for its fruit, but for its seeds and the promise they contain. By so doing he castrates himself and cuts off his real creative potential. Living in an unreal world, he loses his grasp on reality, and this can have tragic consequences.

Marie-Louise von Franz, the talented disciple of Jung, devoted a book to the problem of the eternal adolescent, entitled *Puer Aeternus*. In her book, von Franz includes a lengthy study of *The Little Prince* by Antoine de Saint-Exupéry. But we see a good difference between the two: unlike Peter Pan, who forgets Wendy, the Little Prince knows that he must be responsible for his rose.

Can't we see a glimpse of overcoming this dreadful fate in Pippin's progressive—but rather fast—growth?

> "What's that?" cried Gandalf. He was relieved when Pippin confessed what he had done—he groped for a loose stone, and let it drop over the edge into the well—; but he was angry, and Pippin could see his eye glinting. "Fool of a Took!" he growled. "This is a serious journey, not a hobbit walking-party. Throw yourself in next time, and then you will be no further nuisance. Now be quiet!"   (LotR 313)

It is through the dialogue between Pippin and Beregond—and then with Bergil—, that we see his growing:

> "No, my heart will not yet despair", said Pippin. Gandalf fell and has returned and is with us. We may stand, if only on one leg, or at least be left still upon our knees."
> "Rightly said!" cried Beregond, rising and striding to and fro. "Nay, though all things must come utterly to an end in time, Gondor shall not perish yet... There are still other fastnesses, and secret ways of escape into the mountains. Hope and memory shall live still in some hidden valley where the grass is green." …

"Farewell for this time!" said Beregond. "Maybe you would like
a merry guide about the City. My son would go with you gladly.
A good lad, I may say."
… The boy drew himself up proudly. "I am Bergil son of Beregond
of the Guards," he said. "So I thought," said Pippin, "for you look
like your father. I know him and he sent me to find you… He says
that you might show me round the City for a while. I can tell you
some tales of far countries in return."   (LotR 766-769)

If fairy-story as a kind is worth reading at all it is worthy to be
written for and read by adults. They will, of course, put more in
and get more out than children can. Then, as a branch of a genuine
art, children may hope to get fairy-stories fit for them to read and
yet within their measure; as they may hope to get suitable intro-
ductions to poetry, history, and the sciences. **Though it may be
better for them to read some things, especially fairy-stories that
are beyond their measure rather than short of it. Their books
like their clothes should allow for growth, and their books at
any rate should encourage it**.   (FS 63, emphasis added)

"You never know what is enough unless you know what is more than enough"
(Blake 15). Folk-lore means that the soul is sane, but that the universe is wild
and full of marvels. Realism means that the world is dull and full of routine,
but that the soul is sick and screaming. Therefore, these wise old tales made
the hero ordinary and the tale extraordinary.

For Caspian the stories of Old Narnia are a source of delight: "he liked best
the hour of the day when the toys had all been put back in their cupboards and
the Nurse would tell him stories" (Lewis, *Prince* 42). Lewis subtly distinguishes
between a child's toys, which are tidied away—*or put aside*—and the stories:
Caspian will outgrow his childhood's playthings, exchanging them for swords
and learning, but his love of stories will not be set aside (cf. Slack 108-118).

"Train a child in the way he should go, and when he is old he will not depart
from it" (Prov 22,6). Perhaps the greatest lesson Proverbs offers to every reader,
both young and old, is its claim that what pertains to the child's growth in
wisdom also applies to the adult (Prov1,5), namely, instruction and joy.

Begining with… consistency: During their years at Northmoor Road,
Ronald would invite John, Michael and Christopher to sit on the study floor
and there he would read chapters of *The Hobbit* to them. Each chapter was an
evening's entertainment: this period took the story up to 'Riddles in the Dark'.
Christopher was always much concerned with the consistency of the story

and on one occasion (as he recounted in his foreword to the 50th anniversary edition) interrupted:

> 'Last time, *you* said Bilbo's front door was blue, and *you* said Thorin had a golden tassel on his hood, but you've just said that Bilbo's front door was green, and the tassel on Thorin's hood was silver'; at which Ronald exclaimed 'Damn the boy!' and strode across the room to make a note.   (H 50, 2)

> "But my lad Sam will know more about that. He's in and out of Bag End. Crazy about stories of the old days he is, and he listens to all Mr. Bilbo's tales. Mr. Bilbo has learned him his letters— meaning no harm, mark you, and I hope no harm will come of it"…"*Elves and Dragons*" I says to him. "*Cabbages and potatoes are better for me and you. Don't go getting mixed up in the business of your betters, or you'll land in trouble too big for you,*" I say to him.
>   (LotR 24)
> "All the big important plans are not for my sort. Still, I wonder if we shall ever be put into songs or tales. We're in one, or course".
>   (LotR 712)

"Tell me a story" is a request we might associete with children, but narrativity is pivotal for all human development.

The stories we tell about ourselves—including fairy tales—, through which we construct our sense of self, are woven out of the threads and into the cloth of the stories present to us in our social world and communal traditions. The story we accept sets the terms of what we take to be true, normal, and good. It shake our patterns of thinking, feeling, and acting and serves as a conceptual scheme that is at once *conceptual* (a way of seeing things), *conative* (a set of beliefs and values to which a group and its members are deeply attached), and *action-guiding* (we seek to live according to its terms).

Anna Foeret refers to humans as *"Homo Narrans Narrandus*—the storytelling person whose story has to be told", who tells stories to make sense of the world and to form personal identity and community (cf. Green 220f).

Accordingly, it is crucial to inquire, what stories are shaping the worlds we indwell. What stories are we embodying? What sorts of identity, formation, and performance are the consequence of inhabiting this narrative?

We have seen a few significative dialogues among Tolkien's characters; the deepest (and longest), is among Frodo and Sam, and it is the one more clearly pertinent to our topic:

"I wonder what sort of a tale we've fallen into?"

"I wonder," said Frodo. "But I don't know. And that's the way of a real tale. Take any one that you're fond of. You may know, or guess, what kind of a tale it is, happy-ending or sad-ending, but the people in it don't know. And you don't want them to."

"No, sir, of course not. Beren now, he never thought he was going to get that Silmaril from the Iron Crown in Thangorodrim, and yet he did, and that was a worse place and a blacker danger than ours. But that's a long tale, of course, and goes on past the happiness and into grief and beyond it… And why, sir, I never thought of that before! We've got—you've got some of the light of it in that star-glass that the Lady gave you! Why, to think of it, we're in the same tale still! It's going on. Don't the great tales never end?"

"No, they never end as tales," said Frodo. "But the people in them come, and go when their parts ended. Our part will end later—or sooner."

"All the big important plans are not for my sort. Still, I wonder if we shall ever be put into songs or tales. We're in one, or course; but I mean: **put into words, you know, told by the fireside, or read out of a great big book with red and black letters**, years and years afterwards. And people will say: **"Let's hear about Frodo and the Ring!"** And they'll say: **"Yes, that's one of my favourite stories. Frodo was very brave, wasn't he, dad?"** "Yes, my boy, **the famousest of the hobbits, and that's saying a lot."**

"It's saying a lot too much," said Frodo, and he laughed, a long clear laugh from his heart. Such a sound had not been heard in those places since Sauron came to Middle-earth. To Sam suddenly it seemed as if all the stones were listening and the tall rocks leaning over them. But Frodo did not heed them; he laughed again. "Why, Sam," he said, **"to hear you somehow makes me as merry as if the story was already written.** But you've left out one of the chief characters: Samwise the stouthearted. **"I want to hear more about Sam, dad. Why didn't they put in more of his talk, dad? That's what I like, it makes me laugh. And Frodo wouldn't have got far without Sam, would he, dad?"** "

"Now, Mr. Frodo," said Sam, "you shouldn't make fun. I was serious."

"So was I," said Frodo, "and so I am. We're going on a bit too fast. You and I, Sam, are still stuck in the worst places of the story, and it is all too likely that some will say at this point: **"Shut the book now, dad; we don't want to read any more."**

> **"Maybe,"** said Sam, **"but I wouldn't be one to say that**. Things
> done and over and made into part of the great tales are different.
> (LotR 712f, emphasis added)

We need to recall the special importance of parents, in both childhood and
adulthood. A father plays a pivotal role in his son's life. He is above all a pro-
genitor who gives life to a tiny being whom he loves as his own flesh and who,
with his wife and from a profound sense of love, does everything possible to
guide this little person through life and help him become fully human. In the
beginning, with the mother, he protects the child; he nourishes him and watches
over him. Little by little he must allow the child to make choices, help him to
express his independence and build his self-confidence, so that the child can
strike out on his own, become fully himself, and bear the weight—including
the crosses—of life.

Again this is plain enough in Beregond's relation with his son:

> "My son would go with you gladly. A good lad, I may say".
> The boy drew himself up proudly. "I am Bergil son of Beregond
> of the Guards," he said.
> "So I thought," said Pippin, "for you look like your father."
> "Come, Master Perian!" said the lad. "You are still in pain, I see. I
> will help you back to the Healers. But do not fear! They will come
> back. The Men of Minas Tirith will never be overcome. And now
> they have the Lord Elfstone, and Beregond of the Guard too."
> (LotR 884)

The father is the first significant *other* that the child meets outside his mother's
womb and arms. He embodies, then, the outside reality, the world with its
riches, its challenges and its limitations. Without adequate fathering, sons are
often faced with confusion about their sexual identity, their sense of self-esteem
is unsteady, their need for self-affirmation unmet. Their insufficient internal
structure results in a certain inability to organize their lives effectively; the
inability of recognising limits and boundaries; trouble in accepting responsabil-
ities, how to deal with their aggressivity; their clinging to strong hierarchical
gangs; abuse of drugs and alcohol; emptiness and insecurity; self-hatred and
scapegoating; wildness violence and suicide, etc.

Many try to find escape in a morbid dream of lack of boundaries, and
regression, the refusal to grow and become adults in a healthy way. Men who
remain unable to suffer frustrations remain puerile, exiled from the reality
of human life. The presence and the words of a father, that share, reveal, and
confirm, are an essential part of an initiatory experience to adult life. As in
The Road, by Cormac McCarthy:

I want to be with you.
You can't.
Please.
You can't. You have to carry the fire.
I don't know how to.
Yes you do.
It is real? The fire?
Yes it is.
Where is it? I don't know where it is.
Yes you do. It's inside you. It is always there. I can see it.   (298)

It is true, we need "to be born again" (cf. Jn 3:3-5) to let the new life develop in us, keeping us *childlike* but *not* childish: full of *trust, playfullness* and *wonder*. Beside acceptance, affection, protection, comfort and security, the child needs guidance, advice and discipline, and the provision of a role model. The same children who are ennobled or made endurable by fairy stories grow in time into ennobled and endurable adults themselves. Somehow, this was Gandalf's role:

> "They are the shepherds of the trees," answered Gandalf to Théo-den. "**Is it so long since you listened to tales by the fireside? There are children in your land who, out of the twisted threads of story, could pick the answer to your question.** You have seen Ents, O King, Ents out of Fangorn Forest, which in your tongue you call the Entwood"…The king was silent. "Ents!" he said at length. "Out of the shadows of legend I begin a little to understand the marvel of the trees, I think. I have lived to see strange days… **Songs we have that tell of these things, but we are forgetting them, teaching them only to children, as a careless custom. And now the songs have come down among us out of strange places**, and walk visible under the Sun".   (LotR 549)

> "I am with you at present," said Gandalf, "but soon I shall not be. I am not coming to the Shire. **You must settle its affairs yourselves; that is what you have been trained for.** Do you not yet understand? My time is over: it is no longer my task to set things to rights, nor to help folk to do so. And as for you, my dear friends, you will need no help. **You are grown up now. Grown indeed very high; among the great you are, and I have no longer any fear at all for any of you.**   (LotR 996, emphasis added)

This is exactly what the fairy tale does: it accustoms us from childhood for a series of clear pictures to the idea that limitless terrors had a limit, that shapeless enemies have enemies in the knights of Light, that there is something in the universe more mystical than darkness, and stronger than strong fear.

Indeed sorrow, and the shadow of death can bestow dignity, and even sometimes wisdom to proceed on the appointed journey…

> *As you leave the blurred wood*
> *You entererd while still a boy,*
> *And light clarifies around*
> *Your emerging, manly form,*
> *May you discover gradually*
> *A natural confidence in your body.*
>
> *Always have the courage*
> *To change, welcoming those voices*
> *That call you beyond yourself.*
>
> *Beyond your work and action,*
> *Remain faithful to your heart,*
> *For you to deepen and grow*
> *Into a man of dignity and nobility.*   (O'Donohue 81-83)

We try to teach children *emotional literacy*—the ability to read and under-stand our emotions and those of others. Lacking an emotional education, a boy meets the pressures of adolescence and that singularly cruel peer culture with the only responses he has learned and practiced—and that he knows are socially acceptable—the tipically "manly" responses of anger, aggression, and emotional withdrawal.

Boys need an emotional vocabulary that expands their ability to express themselves. Parents can help in simple but meaningful ways: a bedtime story makes a difference. It gives him access to powerful experiences that speak to his inner life and let him know that he is entitled to have the full range of human experience.

Why is language given so much power? In essence, language imposes order and makes distinctions from the undifferentiated swirl of primal, unconscius impulse, feeling and thought.

When adults fail to take on this important task, children lose the opportun-ity to be transported by a parent's voice into realms of imagination and learn-ing. When parents read to their children, they tend to do so by holding them in their lap or sitting with them in bed just before bedtime. The physical close-ness, the time together, and the enjoyable experience of reading a good book all combine to create an enviroment conducive to relationship growth. Joint book reading provides fathers with an opportunity to interact with their children

across multiple domains of development: physical, intellectual, social, and emotional. A father—or mother—and a child who spend days together reading an
adventurous book (such as *Smith of Wootton Major*) have, in a sense, traveled
on a journey together. And this has a life long effect.

There is still a lot to be discovered about the extent and magnitude of a story's
sculpting power. We humans are constantly "marinating" ourselves in fiction,
and all the while it is shaping us, changing us. We do not retreat from reality,
we rediscover it. As long as the story lingers in our mind, the real things are
more themselves... by dipping them in myth we see them more clearly.

"Well, there you are—wrote Tolkien to Christopher on 6 May 1944—: a
hobbit amongst the Urukhai. Keep up your hobbitry in heart, and think that all
stories feel like that when you are in them. You are inside a very great story!"
(L 78). Truly growing up is discovering that you are in a larger story of which
you are not the centre.

Is something more needed *now*, in our own days? What are *our own challenges*
in helping our children to grow up?

I think the literary scholar Brian Boyd is right to wonder if overconsum-
ing in a world awash with junk stories could lead to something like a "mental
diabetes epidemic", one of the symptoms that may suggest an even worse
desease, a sort of cultural *implosion*. Maybe we can avoid this fate. Maybe, like
disciplined dieters, we can make nutritious choices and avoid gorging on story
(cf. Gottschall 198).

To educate in discernment and taste (plain good hobbit-sense and taste) is
even *more urgent nowadays that 50 years ago*, both for children *and* for grownups. Remember that we are, by nature, suckers for a story. When emotionallly
absorbed in character and plot, we are easy to mold into the *real healthy virtous
life* of men which is of that mythical and heroic quality.

For that reason it is so important to offer a solid healthy *ecosystem* while
educating our children, the type of environment that we may assume was Farmer
Maggot's: "There's earth under his old feet, and clay on his fingers; wisdom in
his bones, and both his eyes are open", said Tom Bombadil (LotR 132). Or the
Gaffer's proverbs, which accompany Sam, helping him to shape his thoughts
and actions: "*It's the job that's never started as takes longest to finish*', as my
old Gaffer used to say." (LotR 361)

Helping others—and ourselves—to grow, and to mature (cf. 1 Cor 14:20) is a
huge, delicate challenge, a rather risky one, unavoidable but possibly rewarding:
Denethor was deceived in his despair: the Shadow *can* be defeated.

> Saruman rose to his feet, and stared at Frodo. There was a strange
> look in his eyes of mingled wonder and respect and hatred. "**You**

have grown, Halfling," he said. "**Yes, you have grown very much**. You are wise, and cruel. You have robbed my revenge of sweetness, and now I must go hence in bitterness, in debt to your mercy.

(LotR 1019, emphasis added)

Very well, then. If adults are to read fairy-stories as a natural branch of literature—neither playing at being children, nor pretending to be choosing for children, nor being boys who would not grow up—what are the values and functions of this kind? That is, I think, the last and most important question. I have already hinted at some of my answers. First of all: if written with art, the prime value of fairy-stories will simply be that value which, as literature, they share with other literary forms. But fairy-stories offer also, in a peculiar degree or mode, these things: Fantasy, Recovery, Escape, Consolation, all things of which children have, as a rule, less need than older people. Most of them are nowadays very commonly considered to be bad for anybody.

(FS 64)

What we have seen over the last years is the corrosive effect of a new and flat model of society, for we have all found ourselves members of the global market, buying and selling, being bought and sold. The basic institutions of civil society that sustained the professions and vocations, have lost much of their authority and independence. Like everything else, they must submit to market forces. Helpless, like little orphans. Worse than in Sharkey's time.

The ecosystems have weakened and crumbled, like the fragile habitats of rare toads or snails. Society is becoming homogenised. All one is left with is the individual and the state, or even the consumer and the market. Much simpler but more lonely and vulnerable. *Kingdom Come*, by J.G. Ballard is rather suggestive.

The hopeful element in the universe has in modern times continually been denied and reasserted; but the hopeless element has never for a moment been denied. We can deal strongly with gloomy mystery, but not with happy mystery; we are not rationalists, but diabolists. We may become easely—and dreadfully—"denethorians".

The image that comes more readily to my mind is of a mini *ecosystem* which sustains a unique form of life. To flourish as a butterfly you need more than a nice definition; you need an ecological context that will get you from egg to caterpillar, and from cocoon to butterfly. They need to be helped in growing up, as young Aragorn in Rivendell, otherwise they cannot make it.

To be an adult is to be able to make significant decisions about one's life, but these somehow must hang together, make a story. To have an identity is for the choices that one makes throughout one's life to have a direction, a narrative unity. What I do today must make sense in the light of what I did before. My life has a pattern, like a good story.

To be a healthy *grown up* implies the paradox of becoming *childlike* (cf. Mt 18:3; 1 Pt 1:3.23): to become a real "halfling", in wisdom and mercy.

We are not alone, we are not merely *individuals*, we are *persons*, we are truly alive when we live in relationship and communion (cf. Eph 4:16): "the whole body, joined and held together by every supporting ligament, grows and builds itself up in love". Each family, community and *network* of true friends, alive or dead, may offer the necessary inter personal environment to sustain us on the way And if we are not to be seduced by the sad consumer society, if we are to offer islands of a counter culture—a happy mystery, the possible defeat of whatever dragon—, then we must work very hard to build and nourish that environment in which our children and our brothers and sisters can flourish as we journey together.

Reading and sharing stories and fairy tales can really help in the task. Building a house—a *home*—woven in words and gestures of tenderness, strength and care:

> The consolation of fairy-stories, the joy of the happy ending: or more correctly of the good catastrophe, the sudden joyous "turn" **(for there is no true end to any fairy tale** [*"Don't the great tales never end?" asked Sam… "no, they never end as tales," said Frodo*]): this joy, which is one of the things which fairy-stories can produce supremely well, is not essentially "escapist," nor "fugitive." In its fairy tale—or otherworld—setting, it is a sudden and miraculous grace: never to be counted on to recur. It does not deny the existence of *dyscatastrophe*, of sorrow and failure: the possibility of these is necessary to the joy of deliverance; it denies (in the face of much evidence, if you will) universal final defeat and in so far is *evangelium*, giving a fleeting glimpse of Joy, Joy beyond the walls of the world, poignant as grief.
>
> It is the mark of a good fairy-story, of the higher or more complete kind, that however wild its events, however fantastic or terrible the adventures, it can give to **child** or **man** that hears it, when the "turn" comes, a catch of the breath, a beat and lifting of the heart, near to (or indeed accompanied by) tears, as keen as that given by any form of literary art, and having a peculiar quality.
>
> (FS 99f, emphasis added)

And when Sam [in the field of Cormallen] heard that ["I will sing to you of Frodo of the Nine Fingers and the Ring of Doom"] he laughed aloud for sheer delight, and he stood up and cried: "O

great glory and splendour! And all my wishes have come true!"
And then he wept.
And all the host laughed and wept, and in the midst of their
merriment and tears the clear voice of the minstrel rose like silver
and gold, and all men were hushed. And he sang to them, until
their hearts, wounded with sweet words, overflowed, and their
joy was like swords, and they passed in thought out to regions
where pain and delight flow together and tears are the very wine
of blessedness.   (LotR 954)

If there is no true end to any fairy tale, why, to think of it, we're in the same
tale still! It's going on… even in our own days, when the gathering shadows
weigh heavy on man's hearts, and a great dread is widespread. Yet it is not our
part to master all the tides of the world, but to do what is in us for the suc-
cour of those years wherein we are set, uprooting the evil in the fields that we
know—*for one, our own children who are growing into manhood*—, so that they
who will live after us may have clean earth *in their hearts* to till.

As Bilbo was *meant* to find the Ring, and Frodo was *meant* to bear it, well,
we too were *meant* to be in the same tale, and to share with those who grow a
fleeting glimpse of Joy. For "the *eucatastrophic* tale is the true form of fairy-tale,
and its highest function" (FS 98; 104): so we are *meant* to share nothing less
than *this*, as Beregond did with Bargil… and the Professor with us.

And *that*—as Gandalf would say—, "that may be an encouraging
thought"…   (LotR 56)

Bibliography

Chesterton, G.K, *Tremendous Trifles*. digireads.com. New York, 2011

Corneau, Guy. *Absent Fathers, Lost Sons. The Search for Masculine Identity*. Boston/London: Shambala, 1991

Flieger, Verlyn & Douglas A. Anderson (Eds.). *Tolkien On Fairy-stories. Expanded Edition with Commentary and Notes*. London: HarperCollins, 2008

Gottschall, Jonathan. *The Storytelling Animal. How stories make us human*. Boston/New York: Mariner Books Houghton Mifflin Harcourt, 2012

Green, Joel B., "'Tell Me a Story': Perspectives on Children from the Acts of the Apostles". *The Child in the Bible*. Ed. Marcia Bunge. Grand Rapids/Cambridge: William B. Eermans, 2008, 215-232

Green, Stephan D. "Exploring New Worlds Together: Reading, Relationships, and Father Involvement". *Why Fathers Count. The Importance of Fathers and Their Involvement with Children*. Eds. Sean E. Brotherson & Joseph M. White. Harriman: Men's Studies Press, 2007, 131-143

Kindlon, Dan & Michael Thompson. *Raising Cain. Protecting the Emotional Life of Boys*. New York: Ballantine, 2000

Lewis, C.S. *On Stories and Other Essays on Literature*. Orlando et al.: Harvest, 1982

McCarthy, Cormac. *The Road*. London: Picador, 2007

McGee, Robert S. *Father Hunger*. Ann Arbor: Servant, 1993

O'Donohue, John. *Benedictus. A Book of Blessings*. London et al.: Bantam, 2007

Slack, Anna (Ed.). *Doors in the Air. C.S. Lewis and the Imaginative World*. Vitoria: Portal Editions, 2010

Tolkien, J.R.R. *Tree and Leaf*. London: HarperCollins, 1988

---. *The Hobbit. 50th Anniversary Edition*, Hougthon Mifflin Harcourt, Boston, 1987

---. *The Letters of J.R.R. Tolkien*, HarperCollins, London 2012

---. *The Lord of the Rings. 50th Anniversay Edition*. London: HarperCollins, 2004

'The Eagles are coming!'

Tolkien's Eucatastrophic Reinterpretation of
the 'Beasts of Battle' Motif in
The Hobbit and in *The Lord of The Rings*

Łukasz Neubauer (Koszalin)

The spectacular and, on the whole, unanticipated appearances of the Great Eagles in the heat of decisive military confrontations in both *The Hobbit* and *The Lord of the Rings* are regularly (and justifiably) examined in view of *eucatastrophe*, Tolkien's Christian counterpart to the Classical plot device nowadays usually referred to under the Latin term of *deus ex machina*[1]. In fact, they are hardly ever mentioned in a context which would not entail some unforeseen intervention leading, directly or not, to the ultimate resolution of the ordeal, and thus bringing the narrative to a happy (or at least happier) ending. Hence, whether it be the battle of the Five Armies (*The Hobbit*) or the final confrontation between the anti-Sauron league and the forces of the East (*The Lord of the Rings*), the Eagles are always where they are meant to be, initiating or merely portending the long-awaited time of joy and deliverance to all the good souls of Middle-earth.

Before we take a closer look at their employment as a narrative tool, though, it may be worthwhile to have a glimpse into the Great Eagles' general appearance and nature. This would, of course, later serve as a useful platform of reference for their further assessment as a literary device with, perhaps most importantly, a vital theological import. The strong, majestic birds of Tolkien's Middle-earth novels are not only greater in size than their ordinary aquiline cousins (although not as big as the Eagles of Manwë, their primordial ancestors), they are indeed the supreme rulers of the skies, dedicated to their allies and merciless to their foes. It is significant, though, that notwithstanding their intimidating physique, Gwaihir's kindred are depicted as "noble-hearted" (H 150), which seems a perfect combination of features in a world where clear-cut forces of good and evil are constantly at war with one another. What is most intriguing, however, to the unwearying seekers of Tolkien's medieval stimuli is the fact that particularly in these two novels the Eagles appear solely in the broad context of various military operations, thus inevitably calling to mind the 'beasts of battle' trope repeatedly found in early medieval poems of principally Germanic provenance.

---

[1]   *Deus ex machina* is obviously a Latin loan translation of the Greek term ἀπὸ μηχανῆς θεός, meaning 'god out of the machine'. The original Hellenic expression is, however, not normally used in modern literary criticism.

The term itself was coined and discussed at length by the American scholar Francis P. Magoun Jr. in his pioneering article published in 1955 in the fifty-sixth issue of *Neuphilologische Mitteilungen*, although the very idea appears to have been first explored, albeit not so extensively, three years earlier by C.M. Bowra in his excellent (though now understandably a little bit dated) book on heroic poetry (467). As a general rule, the 'beasts of battle' trope pertains to three carnivorous animals—the raven, the eagle and the wolf—whose ominous presence prior to, during and, particularly, in the aftermath of military activities must have been a recurrent sight on the corpse-strewn battlefields of Finnesburg (5-7), Brunanburh (60-65), Maldon (96f, 106f) as well as other theatres of early medieval warfare, not necessarily on the fringes of north-western Europe.

Notwithstanding the fact that there are actually numerous and sometimes disturbingly graphic references to the aforesaid carrion-eaters (acting in varying combinations, in unison as well as in isolation) to be found in the immense corpus of early European literature,[2] it is customary today to examine them in a broad context of particularly Old Germanic culture where their depictions appear to be most conventionalised. The main focus of modern scholarship has been, by and large, on their intriguing poetic potential and its diverse implications—from the more emblematic threat of imminent death, which the fear-provoking triad unavoidably evokes, through the distinctive spiritual relationship that two of them (the wolf and the raven) have with the principal Norse deity Odin, to the more naturalistic approach where the three become a crucial element in the poet's ghastly depiction of the post-combat reality. Needless to say, all these uses find their potent verbal representation in especially skaldic poetry where various references to the 'beasts of battle' are made by way of numerous figurative (and sometimes highly elaborate) synonyms that enabled the Norse poets to meet the strict requirements of the alliterative line. This is obviously less the case with early English poetry, where the metrical pattern is not as regular, and thus the semiotic potential may be more fully realised, as in the afore-alluded battle poems where, as Magoun argued, the three creatures often appear to be "ornamental rather than... essential" (83).

Although *The Hobbit* and *The Lord of the Rings* first came out in, respectively, 1937 and 1954/55 (i.e. before the publication of Magoun's article in *Neuphilologische Mitteilungen*), it seems improbable that during the writing of his two most famous novels Tolkien was not aware of the persistent presence of ravens, eagles and wolves in especially Old Germanic literature. In fact, the very three carrion-eaters are explicitly referred to in some of his recently published allitera-

---

2   Some of the most compelling images of the 'beasts of battle' trope (albeit not necessarily depicted as a triad) may be identified in numerous texts of, for instance, early Germanic (e.g. *Beowulf*), Celtic (e.g. *Breuddwyd Rhonabwy*) as well as Slavic (e.g. *The Tale of Igor's Campaign*) provenance.

tive poems, namely *The Lay of Gudrún*[3] and *The Fall of Arthur*[4] which are both thought to have been written at some point in the mid- or late 1930s, i.e. about two decades before Magoun's clear-cut identification of the 'beasts of battle' trope. Several more analogies, both essential and ornamental, of primary as well as secondary importance to the plot, might also be identified in some of his other works, as is for instance the case with the portentous ravens that appear in an early version of the poem *Bombadil Goes Boating*[5] or the troublesome, though in all likelihood imagined, wolf in *Farmer Giles of Ham*[6].

Tolkien would not have been himself of course, if the countless themes, tropes and motifs borrowed from numerous, chiefly early medieval, sources and then superimposed on top of the colourful world of his imagination had not been subject to some fundamental alterations and/or additions whose ultimate purpose would be to make them fit in the complex ethical principles of his sub-created universe. Not surprisingly, the Great Eagles are no exception, appearing infrequently, but always spectacularly in his two most famous novels: *The Hobbit* and *The Lord of the Rings*.

Seen at face value, Gwaihir's kin might seem to have much to do with the traditional Germanic 'beasts of battle'. They are of course full-fledged members of the original cast list, which in the Middle-earth novels sometimes becomes reduced in number due to the absence of their usual companions, both corvine and lupine.[7] Just like their medieval prototypes, Tolkien's Great Eagles usually come into sight when there is a significant military confrontation under way and almost exclusively in connection with the One Ring, although the latter may not always be fully acknowledged by the birds themselves and/or the readers. In *The Hobbit* they first appear at the time when Thorin Oakenshield and his companions are assailed by the vengeful goblins on the eastern slopes of the Misty Mountains and then at the great battle of the Five Armies. In the first case, they are incited by some "uproar in the forest" and "wolves' voices... in the woods" (122), which fills them "with curiosity to know what [is] afoot" (123). In the second, they are reported to have "long had suspicion of the goblins' mustering...; and at length smelling battle from afar they... come speeding

---

3   "The hungry eagle, / the hoary wolf, / the ravens are ready / to rend your [i.e. Högni's men's] flesh" (stanza 66); "There is crying of ravens, / cold howls the wolf, / shields are shimmer-ing, / shafts uplifted" (stanza 97).

4   "Among ruinous rocks ravens croaking / eagles answered in the air wheeling; / wolves were howling on the woods border" (lines 76-78).

5   "Dwarves going to and fro, Grey-elves from the Havens / on strange journeys in the Shire, gathering of ravens, / rumours in whispering trees, shadows on the borders" (quoted in 2014 edition of *The Adventures of Tom Bombadil*).

6   "He [i.e. Giles] had his hands full (he said) keeping the wolf from the door" (10).

7   There are, of course, numerous references to wolves in both *The Hobbit* and *The Lord of the Rings* (e.g. the wargs or the battling ram Grond). Their ultimate impact on the narrative, however, does not seem to be as significant as that of the Great Eagles.

down the gale in the nick of time" (349). In *The Lord of the Rings* a mysterious eagle is spotted far in the sky by members of the Fellowship (Aragorn and Legolas) around the time of the orcs' surprise attack on Amon Hen (385, 413, 423). After that the Eagles are not to be seen until the very final moments of the War of the Ring, in their memorable last-minute appearance at the battle of the Morannon (893, 948). They are then instrumental in rescuing Frodo and Sam from the slopes of Mount Doom (949-951) and bringing the good news of Sauron's downfall to the apprehensive people of Minas Tirith (963).

The Eagles are also mentioned (usually indirectly) in the context of Gandalf's numerous endeavours, such as his dramatic escapes from the pinacle of Orthanc (495) and the peak of Zirakzigil (502). It is also the by-then-white-coated wizard who pleads their great lord Gwaihir to "spe[e]d away south" (950) and save the heroic hobbits. His special relationship with the Eagles may therefore be seen as Tolkien's creative reinterpretation of a similar bond said to exist between the Norse god Odin (who, in fact, resembles Gandalf in more than just general appearance and attire) and his two message-carrying ravens Huginn and Muninn.

However, when it comes to the most elementary aspects of their character and demeanour, the Great Eagles turn out to be poles apart from the original 'beasts of battle'. They are not only far more human in their interaction with the folks of the anti-Sauron league, but, perhaps most significantly, seem to possess certain distinctive Christian features which are obviously not to be found in their Old Germanic counterparts and whose roots evidently lie in the enormous liveliness of Tolkien's Catholic imagination. They may not always have direct parallels in the Scripture, of course, but the Judeo-Christian 'muse' is indisputably there, clearly reinterpreting the ancient heathen trope and putting it on the right track of Christian thought. Worth observing is also the fact that, regardless of Tolkien's genuine intentions, in terms of their outward appearance (mainly colouristic, but not only) and widespread cultural associations, the eagle is naturally far more likely to be associated with the Divine than the somewhat demonic black-plumed raven and the grey-coated wolf.

As far as their martial aspects are concerned, the Great Eagles do not gather above the battlefields of Middle-earth *slít[a] nái* (*Vǫluspá* 50) "to tear the corpses", and thus *æses brucan* (*The Battle of Brunanburh* 63) "partake of carrion". They are not in the least *æses georn* (*The Battle of Maldon* 107) "eager for food" that would certainly be there in abundance and ready for pecking. Their last-ditch appearances near the Lonely Mountain or at the Morannon are brought about by an entirely different set of circumstances that have far less to do with the birds' instinctive impulse and more with their conscious judgment of what is morally right and wrong. In this way one may easily observe that Tolkien's animistic eagles are in effect endowed with what in Christian theology constitutes the most fundamental ingredients of human nature, that is to say their ability to reason and the power of independent choice. Indeed, with the exceptions of Beorn's numerous companions of fang and feather as well as the message-carrying thrush and the old raven Roäc (*The Hobbit*), the Great Eagles are indeed the only animals in the Middle-earth bestiary that can truly communicate with one another and, most importantly for the course of the events, with the peoples of the West. What is more, regardless of their dealings with Gandalf, they seem to do it entirely on their own voluntary initiative, without any contract or command on behalf of those who are in sometimes desperate need of their assistance.

All this appears to be intriguingly consistent with the words of Hugh of Fouilloy, the twelfth-century French cleric for whom these magnificent creatures were a true paragon of dignity and intelligence, creatures that embodied the *subtilis sanctorum intelligentia* (*Aviarium* LX) "subtle intelligence of saints". Despite their selfless dedication to the good cause, many times reflected in their last-minute interventions, the Great Eagles are, of course, only a distant resonance of the Christian concept of sainthood or, as a matter of fact, any other form of transcendental existence, such as the angels. Nonetheless, their somewhat imprecise connection with the Divine may seem to be of particular notice here. After all, their primordial ancestors, the legendary birds of Manwë, are initially referred to as "spirits in the shape of hawks and eagles" (S 27). It must be observed, however, that, over the years, Tolkien's idea of the Eagles appears to have evolved quite significantly, the author himself appearing not to know precisely whether they ought in fact to be interpreted as bird-shaped spirits of the Maiar (MR 138) or as self-conscious and intelligent beasts, albeit with no soul of their own (411).

Endowed with the responsibility of bringing "word to him of well nigh all that passed in Arda" (S 27), Manwë's eagles may once again bring to mind Odin's corvine companions (also members of the original 'beasts of battle' cast) that, according to the Icelandic mythographer Snorri Sturluson, *sitja á ǫxlum honum ok segja í eyru honum ǫll tíðendi, þau er þeir sjá eða heyra* (*Gylfaginning* 38) "sit upon his shoulders and whisper into his ears all the tidings which they see or hear". The Great Eagles of the Misty Mountains are perhaps not as talkative as Huginn and Muninn, their possible legendary predecessors, but they do regularly communicate with Gandalf who, at least to some extent, appears to be Tolkien's Christian alternative to the Norse god of war and poetry. Much as the covertly consecrated wizard, the birds are thus assigned with alternative, if evidently analogous duties, providing immediate assistance in the matters of greatest concern. Seen in this light, the Eagles may thus to some extent resemble the Lord's angels or certain Catholic saints, patrons of difficult or even apparently impossible causes (such as, for instance, St. Rita or St. Jude Thaddeus). Gwaihir's kin are therefore there when the already faint hopes are getting even fainter and the only means of survival could be provided by some indefinite *deus ex machina*.

This brings us to the oft-discussed concept of *eucatastrophe* in which the Eagles partake as many as five times (twice in *The Hobbit* and at least three times in *The Lord of the Rings*[8]). According to Tolkien, the term he himself coined for the purpose of the essay *On Fairy-stories* (first published in 1947) should be understood as an unanticipated "happy turn [at the end of] a story which pierces [one] with a joy that brings tears" (L 89). It is "a sudden and miraculous grace: never to be counted on to recur [which] denies... universal final defeat and in so far is evangelium" (FS 99), it is indeed a "sudden glimpse of Truth" (L 89). In the Gospels, Tolkien maintains, it is obviously the two crucial moments of the Birth of Christ (as the *eucatastrophe* of Man's history) and the Resurrection (as the *eucatastrophe* of the story of the Incarnation). Seen in a military context, however, the *Evangelium* in question turns out to be the critical factor which brings about a hitherto unanticipated victory, when the odds seem to be insurmountable and there is little or no hope for the victory. Even though the Great Eagles are not quite the sole critical and decisive factors in either the battle of the Five Armies and that of the Morannon,[9] their sudden appearances have all the symptoms—emblematic as well as essential—of being eucatastrophic. At any rate, though, the dramatic comings of the Eagles in both *The Hobbit* and *The Lord of the Rings* are obviously in stark contrast with the much less promising appearance of the eagles (and/or ravens and wolves) in early Germanic literature where the carrion-eaters are far more likely to be associated with the apprehensive sense of impending misfortune, the ill-fated climax of the conflict in which they play no small part.

It cannot be denied, then, that in the two Middle-earth novels the coming of the Eagles is always an easily detectable augury of triumph, even when up to that point the course of events seems to be suggesting a diametrically differ-ent outcome. In *The Hobbit* it is the great slaughter of both men and elves at the battle of the Five Armies, in *The Lord of the Rings* it is the engulfing "sea of enemies" (891) which swarms out of the Black Gate of Mordor and from the neighbouring hills. The near-apocalyptic catastrophe in the latter scene is further strengthened by the reader's awareness that the ensuing battle is to be

---

8   The actual calculation of their eucatastrophic appearances would naturally have to depend on our assessment of whether the particular situation (say, Gandalf's imprisonment atop the tower of Orthanc) was already beyond hope, as clearly seems to be the case with the entrapment of Aragorn's army in front of the Black Gate (LotR 893, 948), Frodo and Sam's engulfment by the "rivers of fire" on the slopes of Mount Doom (950) and the growing apprehension of the people of Minas Tirith (963).

9   The real turning point obviously takes places elsewhere, in the Chambers of Fire on Mount Doom where the Ring is eventually destroyed.

the ultimate confrontation between the apparently uneven forces of good and evil, a confrontation after which nothing is ever going to be the same again. The ordeal is even worsened by the fortunately inaccurate supposition that both Frodo and Sam have been captured by the Enemy,[10] and so their quest to save the world is over.

Suddenly, amidst the sounds of trumpets and whines of arrows (891), amidst the "voices roaring like a tide" (948), the air is pierced with frenzied cries of the up till then more and more desperate peoples of the West, "The eagles are coming!" (893, 948). At this point, it is difficult not to think of the great cacophony of sounds depicted by the anonymous poets of *The Finnesburg Fragment* (5-7), *The Battle of Maldon* (106-11) or *Exodus* (162-169) in which the voracious 'beasts of battle' have their significant share. Tolkien's idea for the Eagles was of course altogether different. It looks like his intention was rather to exclude them from this sonoric dissonance and, instead, make them the actual harbingers of a new world order brought about by the concurrent destruction of the One Ring. Their assumption of an entirely new role, so much different from that of the original 'beasts of battle', appears to be ingeniously accentuated by the last thoughts of swooning Pippin who subliminally connects the last-minute coming of the Great Eagles with Bilbo's tale of long ago and, perhaps, somewhat trans-textually, with the eagles, the ravens and the wolves of the ancient poetic tradition: "But no! That came in [Bilbo's] tale long long ago" (LotR 893).

As has been observed, the foremost objective of their sudden appearances in the Middle-earth novels is the more or less explicit announcement, or perhaps even proclamation, of the eucatastrophic conclusion of the battle of the Five Armies (*The Hobbit*) and the War of the Ring (*The Lord of the Rings*). However, while the role they play in the former combat could be interpreted as militarily justified,[11] their unanticipated arrival in the last battle against Sauron is not known to have any quantifiable effect on the ultimate conclusion of the conflict. Hence, the coming of the Eagles merely coincides (provided, of course, that this expression can ever be used in what is, after all, carefully planned writing) with the destruction of the One Ring and the subsequent fall of the Dark Lord. It would be inaccurate, however, to perceive them merely as some sort of a symbol or emblem of the *Evangelium*. Seen in the light of their remote but undisputed connection with Manwë, they are indeed no less than the actual essence of revelation (as well as its outward manifestation), which in

---

10 The thought that the Ring-bearer may have been caught by the servants of Sauron appears to be less of a concern for Gandalf who evidently suspects that the actual fate of Frodo and Sam does not necessarily have to be synonymous with the dramatic workings of Pippin's imagination.

11 It was the Eagles "who dislodged the goblins from the mountain-slopes, casting them over the precipices, or driving them down shrieking and bewildered among their foes" (H 349).

Christian theology is the very act of being in communication with God, often through vision, miracle or epiphany.

The ultimate appearance of the Eagles in the context of their biblical associations is even more striking when we take into consideration the fact that the two most significant dates in the Fellowship's quest to destroy the Ring, that is to say their leaving Rivendell (25 December) and the ultimate passing of Sauron (25 March), generally coincide with those of the two most important Christian holidays, namely Christmas and, somewhat less precisely, Easter, which obviously mark the celebrations of, respectively, the Nativity and the Resurrection.[12] It would evidently be a far-fetched claim to say that the aforesaid time frame actually settles, once and for all, the dispute over the purely Christian interpretation of Tolkien's Eagles. After all, as has been observed, at least in terms of their conceptual and structural dimensions the initial inspiration probably came from elsewhere, i.e. the 'beasts of battle' trope in especially Old Germanic literature. Nonetheless, given the overall amount of almost certainly Christian associations, it would be really hard to uphold the view that the concurrence of the dates should be of purely accidental nature. It is much more likely that Tolkien's intention was rather to make sure that the ultimate destruction of the Ring (seen as the foremost catalyst of evil in Middle-earth) should fill the same matrix, and so occur at the same (or roughly the same) time of the year as the Passion and Resurrection, which are, of course, the innermost focus of all Christian thought and constitute its dogmatic backbone.

Just as eucatastrophic, although slightly less apparent in terms of its military applicability, is also the unanticipated coming of the Eagle that brings "tidings beyond hope" (LotR 963) to the apprehensive people of Minas Tirith who, much as the convalescent Éowyn and Faramir, have been living in continuous dread of the "Darkness Unescapable" (962) since the departure of Aragorn and the Host of the West. Despite the fact that the impulsive joy of the citizens actually "well[s] up in their hearts" (963) prior to the appearance of any provable sign or verbal message from the not-too-distant frontline,[13] it can hardly

---

12 Easter is obviously a movable feast which in the Western Church falls on a Sunday between 22 March and 25 April. Additionally, 25 March is also celebrated as the Annunciation Day, i.e. the day when the archangel Gabriel announced to the Virgin Mary that she would conceive the Son of God. In the early days of Western Christianity, it was believed that the date of the Annunciation coincided with that of either the Passion or the Resurrection.

13 The only signs of what the people of Minas Tirith could hitherto only have hoped for are the sudden "hope and joy" (LotR 962f) that come to Faramir, the "great wind" (962) that blows his and Éowyn's hair and the unveiling of the Sun, so that "light leap[s] forth; and the waters of Anduin sh[i]ne like silver" (962). All these super-sensual phenomena may easily come unnoticed to the readers with little or no knowledge of the Scripture, but to those of a better acquaintance with the *Acts of the Apostles* the signs that directly precede the coming of the Eagle should call to mind the descent of the Holy Spirit (*Acts* 2:1-6), whose traditional avian (dove-like) form nicely corresponds with the overall image of Tolkien's majestic birds.

be denied that this mystifying communication of the *Evangelium* should be directly associated with the subsequent coming of the Eagle, whose uplifting words clearly reverberate those of *Psalms* 24 ("The Lord's is the Earth and its fullness") and 33 ("Sing gladly, O righteous, of the Lord"), both of which accentuate the need to find the happiness in God and aim at strengthening the promise of the Parousia (i.e. the second coming of Christ):

> Sing now, ye people of the Tower of Anor,
> for the Realm of Sauron is ended forever,
> and the Dark Tower is thrown down.
>
> Sing and rejoice, ye people of the Tower of Guard,
> for your watch hath not been in vain,
> and the Black Gate is broken,
> and your King hath passed through,
> and he is victorious.
>
> Sing and be glad, all ye children of the West,
> for your King shall come again,
> and he shall dwell among you
> all the days of your life.   (LotR 963)

The irresistible joy invoked by the words of the Eagle is of course in stark contrast with the doom-laden passages in which the 'beasts of battle' typically appear in Old Germanic literature, as is evidently the case with the following section from *Beowulf,* informing the apprehensive audience (already in grief after the death of the poem's protagonist) how *se wonna hrefn / fus ofer fægum fela reordian, / earne secgan hu him æt æte speow, / þenden he wið wulf wæl reafode* (3024-3027) "the dark raven, eager for the fallen ones, shall tell many tales, say to the eagle how he fared at the feast, when he plundered the slain in the company of the wolf".

The sudden (and often apparently unexpected) consolation or "the joy of the happy ending" (FS 99), Tolkien argues in his essay, is in fact an indispensable constituent of a "true fairy-story (or romance)" (103). It must be observed, however, that this joyous turn in *The Hobbit* and particularly in *The Lord of the Rings* was not meant to be in any greater degree 'escapist' or 'fugitive'. It is, as observed by the author himself, a thoroughly unique and "miraculous grace [which] does not deny the existence of *dyscatastrophe*" (99), i.e. a disastrous (or, at any rate, unpleasant) finale, as is often the case in many a battle poem or elegy of Germanic or other provenance where eagles might sometimes be spotted in a company of wolves and ravens. It is only then that this "joy of deliverance" (99) could truly deny "universal final defeat" (99), thus becoming evangelium or the 'Good News', which in Christian theology is the fulfilment of earlier scriptural prophecies. Such is perhaps also the spectacular coming of the Eagles in *The Lord of the Rings*, in some way 'prophesised' in Bilbo's tale, "long long ago" (LotR 893).

According to Saint Paul, "ever since the creation of the world, [God's] invisible attributes of eternal power and divinity have been able to be understood and perceived in what he has made" (Rom. 1:20). Truly potent and unequivocal revelations of the Lord's glory (miracles as well as other wondrous acts and signs), however, appear to be quite rare and cannot always be so easily acknowledged by the more 'rational' people, both Christians and non-believers. Tolkien himself admits in his letter to Forrest J. Ackerman that in terms of their literary impact the Eagles are indeed a "dangerous machine" which he decided to use rather "sparingly", so as not to outstretch "the absolute limit of their credibility or usefulness" (L 210). In other words, they are an enormously potent but at the same time hazardous plot device which he sensibly chooses to employ as a eucatastrophic effect only on a handful of occasions, twice in *The Hobbit* and three times in *The Lord of the Rings*.

There are, of course, many more potential associations that may be identified in connection with the Great Eagles of Tolkien's Middle-earth novels. Being sometimes interpreted as a figurative representation of man's rescue (Deut. 32:11), his spiritual rebirth (Isa. 40:31, *Psalm* 103) and, more generally, as an emblem of resurrection, the eagle clearly ranks amongst the most intriguing beasts in the scriptural canon. Sure enough, these majestic birds were depicted in numerous ways by the biblical narrators, not at all times utterly favourable (Lev. 11:13), sometimes instructive (Prov. 23:5), sometimes portending dramatic events (Rev. 8:13), yet the overall picture appears to be distinctly affirmative, and such is today their universal cognition, conscious as well as intuitive. By placing them in the context of ruthless warfare, Tolkien appears to be superimposing the traditional pre-Christian trope onto the world of his own vivid imagination. It is, however, a world where, somewhat implicitly, the Christian ethics constitutes the most fundamental component, the moral backbone of his sub-created reality. In this way, the æses *georn[e]* (107) 'food-greedy' eagles of *The Battle of Maldon* or the *hilde grædige* (162) 'battle-greedy' birds of *Exodus* are figuratively cleansed and absolved of their previous 'sins', so that they may blend in the world of Tolkienian ethics where they could stand side by side with hallowed wizards, morally superior, if still ambiguous, elves and other imaginary creatures from the world of pre-Christian beliefs.

Bibliography

Alexander, Michael (Ed.). *Beowulf: A Glossed Text*. London: Penguin Books, 2000

Bowra, Cecil Maurice. *Heroic Poetry*. London: Macmillan, 1952

Catholic Bible. San Francisco: Ignatius Press, 2006

Kobielus, Stanisław (Ed.). *Fizjologi i Aviarium*. Tyniec Wydawnictwo Benedyktynów, 2005

Lucas, Peter (Ed.). *Exodus*. Exeter: University of Exeter Press, 1994

Magoun, Francis Peabody Jr. "The Theme of Beasts of Battle". In: *Neuphilologische Mitteilungen* 56 (1955): 81-90

Scragg, Donald (Ed.). *The Battle of Maldon*. Manchester: Manchester University Press, 1981

Snorri Sturluson. *Edda. Prologue and Gylfaginning*. London: Viking Society for Northern Research, 2005

Tolkien, John Ronald Reuel. *Farmer Giles of Ham*. Boston/New York: Houghton Mifflin, 1999

---. *Finn and Hengest. The Fragment and the Episode*. London: HarperCollins, 1998

---. *Morgoth's Ring*. London: HarperCollins, 2002

---. *On Fairy-stories*. London: HarperCollins, 2008

---. *The Adventures of Tom Bombadil*. London: HarperCollins, 2014

---. *The Fall of Arthur*. London: HarperCollins, 2013

---. *The Hobbit*. London: HarperCollins, 2013

---. *The Legend of Sigurd and Gudrún*. London: HarperCollins, 2009

---. *The Letters of J.R.R. Tolkien*. London: HarperCollins, 2006

---. *The Lord of the Rings*. London: HarperCollins, 2005

---. *The Silmarillion*. London: HarperCollins, 2006

Wyatt, Alfred John (Ed.). "The Battle of Brunanburh". *Anglo-Saxon Reader*. Cambridge: Cambridge University Press, 1965

Transformations of Fairy Stories: From *Sellic/Sælig Spell* to *Beowulf* or from Folk Tale to Epic

Thomas Honegger (Jena)

Fairy Stories

Apaper published in *Tolkien Studies* 7 (2010) opens with a very short fairy-tale summary of a story highly relevant for Tolkien:

> A king in exile, having spent years in the wilderness, asks for the hand of his beloved lady from the king of Fairy, is finally re-united with her and, after testing the loyalty of his steward, re-claims his throne and lives ever happily with his queen to the end of his days.
>
> (Honegger, "Fantasy" 117)

The ambiguity of the summary is, of course, intentional. It can be applied equally well to "The Tale of Aragorn and Arwen", with some unavoidable and intended echoes of the story of Beren and Lúthien, and to the Middle English lay *Sir Orfeo*. Its fairy-story characteristics formed part of my paper's argument for seeing the 14th century Middle English poem (lay) *Sir Orfeo* as the likely fairy-story prototype that was in the back of Tolkien's mind when he worked on his Andrew Lang Lecture for 1939.[1] His dissatisfaction with the frequently very disparate fairy stories, as found in Andrew Lang's colour-coded *Fairy Books*,[2] and the Professor's own attempt at a re-definition of the term *fairy story* is reflected in his often meandering argument of the essay.[3] As I argued in my 2010 article, it is likely that *Sir Orfeo*[4] (unconsciously) informed Tol-kien's in-ception of the new key-characteristics of his ideal fairy story. Tolkien, as many

---

1   See the edition by Verlyn Flieger and Douglas Anderson (Tolkien FS) for a competent discussion of the lecture-essay's origin and its different versions.

2   Andrew Lang published twelve colour-coded *Fairy Books* between 1889 and 1910, starting with *The Blue Fairy Book* (1889), followed by *The Red Fairy Book* (1890), containing "The Story of Sigurd", which became for Tolkien an important inspiration for his own literary endeavours. *The Lilac Fairy Book* (1910) concludes the series.

3   See Heidi Krüger's paper for an in-depth analysis of the essay's genesis and transformations.

4   Tolkien knew the text intimately since it was part of Kenneth Sisam's anthology *Fourteenth Century Verse & Prose* (1921) from which he assembled his *A Middle English Vocabulary* (1922). Later he produced an edition for teaching the naval cadets' course in English (1943-1944; see Tolkien, "Sir Orfeo") and a modern English translation in verse (see Tolkien, GPO).

other scholars since then, was intrigued to find the classical myth of Orpheus and Eurydice transformed into a genuine English (or better: British) fairy story containing not only the elements of Enchantment, Escape, Recovery, and Eucatastrophe, but also a Happy Ending.[5]

Yet while we can indeed summarise the basic plot of *Sir Orfeo* in form of the quoted fairy-tale abstract,[6] we would probably all agree that the same procedure cannot do justice to *The Lord of the Rings* as a whole—not least since Tolkien decided to lay the stress on things that are not (primarily) part of the story of Aragorn and Arwen. The adoption of a hobbit-centric point of view, for example, is responsible for a considerable shift of focus away from the main historical plot around Aragorn's rise to the throne of Gondor and Arnor.

The lesson taught by *Sir Orfeo* is, among other things, that it is possible to transfer and re-cast narrative elements in another literary form or genre. In this context, it must be stressed that *Sir Orfeo*, whatever the adaptations and changes, is not an instance of dwindling[7] but rather an example of a successful transfer from one cultural tradition into another. The original myth of Orpheus and Eurydice, already extant in different and sometimes rather varied forms in antiquity, is adopted and adapted into the British framework of the lays. This is done with ease since the new genre of the lay is a short narrative that retains a certain closeness to the assumed original genre of the folk or fairy tale, which is believed to be at the origin of or co-existing with the mythic rendering of the narrative. The poet of *Sir Orfeo* did not have to transfer the narrative elements from one hierarchical level to another, but he had merely to adapt them to the new cultural context. Hades/Pluto, the Greek/Roman god of the underworld, is simply replaced by the King of Faëry, and Thracia somewhat surprisingly equated with Winchester. This cultural translation can be seen as part of the *translatio studii et imperii*, i.e. the cultural and political continuum created by transferring and adapting key-elements from antiquity into the Middle Ages, and it is this process that is largely responsible for the attractiveness of the Middle English poem.

---

5   The happy ending was already known in earlier versions (see Friedman for an in-depth study of the matter) and "is only one manifestation of an all-pervasive difference in quality. In spirit, the story of Orpheus and the story of Orfeo have very little in common, and between them lies a belief in which death itself loses its bitterness and finality, and is swallowed up in enchantment" (Allen 111).

6   Lays are short (typically 600-1000 lines), rhymed tales that deal with matters of love or chivalry, often involving elements of the supernatural. The plot is usually limited to a single strand of action, in contrast to romances, which typically comprise multiple (parallel) sub-narratives.

7   See Tolkien (FS 42-44) on "dwindling".

Epics

M atters are different with epic narratives such as *Beowulf* and *The Lord of the Rings*—or the Homeric epics, to mention some of the oldest extant European long narratives. Here, we can no longer assume a single unified narrative core that has simply been recast and transformed. Rather we have to posit a genesis from different independent sources. Whether they were welded into a new whole with more or less equal rights or whether they began to cluster around a central element is a moot point. Fact is that the first scholars inquiring into the origin(s) and the resulting structure of the epic assumed a composition of the text from different elements. The fathers of this theory were the classical philologist Friedrich A. Wolf (1759-1824), who had researched the origin of the Homeric epics, and his near-contemporary, Karl Lachmann (1793-1851),[8] who coined the term *Liedertheorie*—a theory that was applied with great zeal to *Beowulf* by such eminent scholars as Ludwig Ettmüller or Karl Müllenhoff.[9]

The *Liedertheorie* argues that the extant epic text is the product of an amalgamation or assembly of shorter texts (lays or *Lieder*) that are (more or less skilfully) linked with each other. Many of the *Liedertheorie*-scholars were primarily interested in determining the assumed source-elements and establishing the different narrative strands and points of origin. The danger of such an approach is that scholars using this method tend to perceive the text no longer as an artistic-aesthetic or organic whole but as a kind of 'Frankenstein's monster', assembled from various parts. It was as a reaction to and also against such an approach that Tolkien wrote his seminal lecture *"Beowulf*: The Monsters and the Critics" in 1936.[10]

Yet while Tolkien, on the one hand, made a very convincing (and lasting) case for the artistic unity of the poem, he also, on the other hand, used the concept of different layers. Thus he clearly distinguishes between the original poet (Heorrenda)[11] who is responsible for giving the poem its present form (though, of course, using older material), and later editors (one of whom he

---

8   Lachmann is famous for his editorial work on the Nibelungenlied (cf. his 1816 Habilitation *Über die ursprüngliche Gestalt des Gedichts von der Nibelungen Noth*) and his posthumously published edition of medieval Minnelieder in *Minnesangs Frühling*.

9   For a concise summary of the main approaches to the poem's structure, see Kisor (230-232).

10 The genesis and development of Tolkien's landmark-lecture has been studied in depth by M. Drout in his magisterial monograph *Beowulf and the Critics by J.R.R. Tolkien* (2002).

11 See Christopher Tolkien's comment in BLT 2 (323): "… and when lecturing on *Beowulf* at Oxford he [J.R.R. Tolkien] sometimes gave the unknown poet a name, calling him *Heorrenda*." On the importance of Heorrenda as a link between Tolkien's invented mythology and Anglo-Saxon culture, see Drout, "Mythology" 233.

identifies as Cynewulf).[12] And Tolkien also feels free to experiment with the idea of an original folk tale (his *Sellic Spell*) and lays (*Lieder*) providing the source for the first part of *Beowulf*. This experiment in practical criticism is very useful for helping us to appreciate the poet's craft.

Sellic Spell

The folk or fairy tale about the exploits of the young hero Beewolf[13] is an attempt to reconstruct one possible version of the folk tale[14] that provided the inspiration and source for the first part of *Beowulf*. Tolkien was, of course, not the first scholar to try his hand at this task. Friedrich Panzer had published a comprehensive study of the international folk tale "The Bear's Son" (*Das Märchen vom Bärensohn*, 1910) which he believed to be the original folk-tale inspiration for the first part of *Beowulf*.[15] Tolkien seems to have been aware of Panzer's publication and fashions his folk-tale re-telling of the first part of the Old English poem on the pattern of the tale of "The Bear's Son".

The title *Sellic Spell*[16] derives from line 2109 in *Beowulf* where *syllic spell* (the manuscript spelling) is one of the types of entertainment offered at the feast after the defeat of Grendel. Christopher and J.R.R. Tolkien translate it as "strange/wondrous tale",[17] though the echo of Old English *sælig*, originally meaning "happy, blessed" and only later deteriorating into "silly", may be intended and welcome[18] since the tale is indeed both wondrous and happy. At the centre is Beewolf, an orphan raised at the court of a nameless king in the North. Hunters had found him in a bear-cave and taken him along to the court where he was given into the foster-care of the king. Beewolf was little appreciated and grew into a very strong but surly young man who loves swimming in the sea. He enters into a swimming-contest with Breaker (*Beowulf's* Breca) and during his swim he has to fight off numerous sea-monsters. Later, when he hears about the trouble of the neighbouring King of the Golden Hall, he

---

12 See Tolkien, *Beowulf. A Translation* 311, where he argues that Cynewulf had a hand in rendering the text as we have it today (and blames him for messing things up).
13 Tolkien's translation of *beo = bee* and *wulf = wolf*, which is a kenning for *bear*.
14 Dimitra Fimi (27) correctly points out that Tolkien seems to use the terms "folk-lore/ folk-legend/folk-tale/fairy-tale/fairy-story... more or less interchangeably."
15 See also Dimitra Fimi's article for a short but concise discussion of *Sellic Spell* and its connections to the folk tale.
16 See Christopher Tolkien's comments and quotes from his father's notes in Tolkien, *Beowulf. A Translation* 358-359.
17 *The Anglo-Saxon Dictionary* by Bosworth and Toller translates it as "wondrous, strange" (see *seld-lich*, which contains the element *seld-* that is found in words such as German *selten* "rare" or *seltsam* "strange").
18 There is yet another likely allusion to *god-spell* (> *gospel*), i.e. the joyful tidings of the New Testament.

decides to go and offer his help. On his way he meets Handshoe,[19] a typical helper/companion figure who got his name from the fact that he owns a pair of gloves that enable him to tear apart rocks or move any boulder whatever its weight. Hearing about Beewolf's intentions, he offers to join him and together they cross the sea. After their arrival on the other side they meet Ashwood, named after his magical spear that can put a host of men to flight. He, too, joins Beewolf and together they arrive at the Golden Hall where they are welcomed, and they ask for permission to await the monster Grinder (*Beowulf's* Grendel) who has been terrorising the Golden Hall for some time. Ashwood and Handshoe are given precedence over Beewolf but one after another they fail in their attempts to kill Grinder because each of them falls asleep while waiting for the monster to arrive—and are thus not able to use their magical weapons when attacked by Grinder. Beewolf, in the third night, succeeds because he does not rely on external props but on his innate strength and Grinder is only able to break free from Beewolf's grip and escape because he leaves behind one of his arms. The next day Beewolf is led by Unfriend (*Beowulf's* Unferth) to the pond where Grinder hides, dives in and has to fight off some water-monsters and face Grinder's dam (mother), against whom Ashwood's magical spear (inherited by Beewolf) has no power. Beewolf is able to kill her with the help of a great sword he finds on the wall of the cave[20] and, after also cutting off the head from Grinder's corpse, returns triumphantly to the Golden Hall. Unfriend, who had led Beewolf to the monsters' dwelling, yet later abandoned him, is disgraced and given a sound beating, and Beewolf lives for a while as an honoured guest with the King of the Golden Hall. He then returns home and later marries the only daughter of the king of the North and, after the demise of his father-in-law, he inherits the kingdom.

It is of interest to see which elements and parts from the original *Beowulf* Tolkien retained and which elements he discarded. First, the most obvious structural difference: we have only the first part of the *Beowulf* plot included in the folk/fairy tale. The dragon-killing episode, which constitutes the second part of the Old English epic, is completely missing. This makes sense since folk tales are usually mono-episodic, i.e. they focus on events taking place during one episode of the hero's life[21]—typically the time leading up to and including a

---

19 The name *Hondscioh* actually occurs in *Beowulf* where he is one of Beowulf's Geatish companions. The origin of this strange name is one of the puzzles Tolkien wanted to solve with his version of the tale.

20 The fortunate and timely finding of the magical sword is part of the original *Beowulf* and has always puzzled me a bit. It makes, however, perfect sense in the folk-/fairy-tale version and can be seen as the eucatastrophic moment in Beewolf's early career. See also Tolkien's less-than-serious take on magical swords in the form of the sword Caudimordax in his *Farmer Giles of Ham*.

21 The limitation to an episode does not mean that we cannot have multiple events within this one episode, though.

transformative experience, such as marriage or the coming of age. This limitation helps to establish a certain structural unity of the tale and ends, typically, with the return of the hero and, possibly, his marriage.[22]

Various scholars have commented on the structural autonomy of Beowulf's youthful exploits at the court of the Spear-Danes and the linking of this first part with the dragon-killing episode some five or six decades after the events at Heorot. But it was Tolkien who stressed its aesthetic-structural importance as the second part of a heroic life, balancing young Beowulf's heroic deeds in the first half of the poem.[23] By giving us a folk-tale version of the first part with a suitable conclusion (marriage to the princess and inheritance of the kingdom), Tolkien shows how the poet of the Old English epic transforms its original folk-tale theme and, by balancing it with the second part, develops the entire poem into the direction of complex tragedy.

Se wyrm onwoc

The true dragon is usually associated with the epic, and though you can find fairy/folk-tale dragons, they have always struck me as rather unconvincing creations and I think it was a wise move on Tolkien's part to keep the dragon out of his fairy story.[24] The dangers of keeping a true dragon (i.e. a typically epic element) in a folk or fairy story without proper adaptation to its new literary environment are illustrated by Andrew Lang's inclusion of "The Story of Sigurd" in his *The Red Fairy Book*. To some extent, Lang had tried to do what Tolkien did with *Sellic Spell*—to give us the folk- or fairy-tale version behind the *Volsunga saga*. However, in Lang's case the result is, in my opinion, rather disappointing and illustrates the danger of transferring the elements and plots from one category into another—and highlights the need for paying careful attention to adapting them accordingly. Thus, Lang's retention of the rather complex structure of the *Volsunga saga* with its pre-history, its intrigues and

---

22 Marriage usually signals the re-integration into society by means of a change in status from independent-irresponsible bachelor to that of a responsible member of society—which explains why protagonists who go out on adventure are usually not married (nor engaged, see Sam and Rosie).

23 See his lecture "Beowulf: The Monsters and the Critics" and Yvette Kisor's concise discussion of the scholarly debate around the structure of the poem (cf. especially 227-233).

24 See, for example, the comic (green) dragon in Tolkien's 1937 poem "The Dragon's Visit" and, to some extent, also the dragon Chrysophylax in *Farmer Giles of Ham*. Yet Tolkien is careful to avoid rendering his dragons completely ridiculous and has them retain some of their dignity and, especially, ferocity. Thus the green dragon smashes Bimble town to smithereens and kills his attackers, and Chrysophylax, upon returning to his cave after his release, fights and devours a young dragon that has usurped his place. On dragons in literature, see Honegger "A good dragon".

acts of revenge, etc.[25] makes for too complex a narrative to fit in comfortably into a folk-tale framework.

Tolkien was probably aware of the problems and dangers involved in taking over epic material into a collection of folk and fairy tales without properly adapting it and may have wanted to contrast his own re-telling of another great Northern poem, *Beowulf,* with Lang's rendering of the *Volsunga saga.* His use of the very same words from Lang's "The Story of Sigurd" for the opening sentence of his *Sellic Spell* could be interpreted in this way. Both Lang (357) and Tolkien (*Beowulf. A Translation* 360) begin with "Once upon a time there was a King in the North…" The standard opening "Once upon a time", believed to be the typical fairy-tale opening, is of no great use for proving any connection beyond a very general one. The reference to "a King in the North", however, is rather specific and Tolkien, in my opinion, deliberately points towards Lang's "The Story of Sigurd". Yet while Lang continues with "who had won many wars, but now he was old", Tolkien has "who had an only daughter". Tolkien's deviation is important, because the introduction of "an only daughter" paves the way for the final happy ending in form of the hero's marriage and succession to the throne.

The most striking difference between the two tales is, of course, the omission of the dragon-killing episode in *Sellic Spell.* Both the *Volsunga saga* and *Beowulf* feature dragon-killers as their main protagonists, and Lang kept this important element in his retelling. Yet though the killing of the dragon Fafnir by Sigurd may be seen as the high point of the heroic action, it is not used as a suitable conclusion to an (admittedly rather free-style) happy ending such as: "And Sigurd took the treasure, presented half of it to the king who in turn gave him his only daughter in marriage. After the old king died, Sigurd took over the kingdom and ruled as a wise and just king to the end of his days." Tolkien might have considered changing and adapting the *Volsunga saga* plot in such a way if he had wanted to produce a folk/fairy-tale version of the saga. Lang, however, sticks to the plotline of the entire saga and makes the killing of the dragon the starting point for the tragic events that lead to the murder of Sigurd and the death of Brynhild (not to mention the death of Grani, Sigurd's faithful horse). In the end, we have no happy ending but a triple funeral—which is fine

---

25 "The Story of Sigurd", as found in Lang's *The Red Fairy Book* (357-367), runs as follows: Sigurd kills the dragon Fafnir (originally Regin's brother) and gains the treasure together with its curse. He then kills the treacherous Regin, frees Brynhild who has been kept inside a ring of fire and enters into an engagement with her—but is somehow made to forget all about it later on by means of a magic potion and marries Gudrun. He then helps Gunnar, his new brother-in-law, to win and marry Brynhild. Things go really wrong when the two women find out about the whole affair and we have Sigurd killed by Gunnar's younger brother, who is in turn killed by the mortally wounded Sigurd. Sigurd's horse Grani passes away, too, and Brynhild, in the end, dies of a broken heart and is put on the pyre on the funeral ship next to Sigurd and Grani.

for a saga or an epic, but it is problematic for a fairy story (or even a folk tale) for which Tolkien (FS 75) rightly recognised the "Consolation of the Happy Ending" as a vital feature.

So, to leave out the killing of the dragon is crucial and Tolkien repeated in *Sellic Spell* what he had already practised some years before in his 'fairy story' of *The Hobbit*. There, we also have a dragon and the encounter between Bilbo and Smaug is undoubtedly a high point of the tale. However, it is not Bilbo who in the end slays the worm, though Tolkien briefly toyed with the idea of having Smaug killed by Bilbo sticking his sword Sigurd-fashioned into the dragon's soft belly.[26] Yet killing Smaug would have lifted Bilbo out of the fairy-tale mode into a mock epic one[27]—to the detriment of both dragon and hobbit-hero.[28] We can see best what Tolkien thought about dragons in *The Children of Húrin* where we have the truly magnificent dragon Glaurung and a deeply tragic-heroic Túrin, and the pair could be interpreted as Tolkien's Middle-earth answer to Fafnir and Sigurd.[29]

Tolkien knew that true dragons are simply too perilous to be used as props in the adventure-career of the folk- or fairy-tale hero—if you want a happy ending.[30] The *Beowulf* poet was therefore right in using the dragon-fight episode as the second part of the epic and as the final and most perilous (and in the end fatal) challenge for the hero. Indeed, as Tolkien (BMC 28-32) points out in his lecture, the poem presents two stages of a heroic life. First come the youthful exploits—some of them rash and foolhardy such as the swimming contest with Breca, but the later ones, namely the fights against Grendel and his mother, in the service of a worthy cause, aiming at restoring the peace and stability of society. Second, we have the mature (not to say old) hero-king saving his own people from the depredations of and potential annihilation by the dragon. And though the poem ends with the hero's death, it is an end worthy of a long and distinguished heroic life.

---

26 See Plot Notes C in Rateliff (496): "Bilbo [takes >] plunges his little magic knife and it disappears. he cannot wield the swords or spears. Throes of dragon. Smashes walls and entrance to tunnel. Bilbo floats <away> in a golden bowl on D's blood, till it comes to rest in a deep dark hole." See also Sullivan III (66-70) for some general observations on this aspect.

27 On the function of dragons as challenges to the heroes and their narrative functions, see Honegger "A good dragon".

28 This is not to deny that there is a development of Bilbo's heroic qualities, yet it is gradual and remains within a low mimetic framework; to put it bluntly: killing spiders is ok, but killing a dragon would be out of character.

29 The *Quenya Dictionary* (Fauskanger 102) translates *Túrin* as "victory-mood" with the element *túrë* (Fauskanger 101), meaning "mastery, victory". This corresponds, at least in its first element, to Sigurd, which consists of *sigr* "victory" and *varðr* "guard".

30 Even the rather incongruous green dragon singing in the cherry-tree in "The Dragon's Visit" is not to be trifled with.

Sellic Spell, by providing us with the raw material for the first part of the Old English poem, indirectly illustrates the *Beowulf* poet's skill in creating a balanced and aesthetically pleasing work of art from two independent episodes (fight against ogre and ogress; fight against the dragon)—and Tolkien's deep understanding of this achievement as a deliberately and skilfully composed work of art. It took the *Beowulf* poet's genius (and Tolkien's empathic understanding)[31] to combine the two elements in a way that creates a poetic whole exceeding the sum of its parts. The anonymous poet of the *Volsunga saga* achieved something comparable yet Andrew Lang, in his endeavour to make the saga fit the format of his fairy books, tried to transform it backwards into a more folk-tale-like text. The result illustrates the dangers of trying to (at least partially) revert the alchemical process of marrying baser ingredients to each other in order to create poetic gold: instead of recovering at least the silver and mercury of the original ingredients, you are more likely to end up with base copper and lead.

Poetic Alchemy

How, then, does the *Beowulf* poet transform the base material of the folk tale into the alchemical gold of his poem? And how does *Sellic Spell* help us to understand this process and its implications for Tolkien's creation of his own works (notably *The Hobbit* and *The Lord of the Rings*)? There are, in my mind, three points to consider.

First: proportion and structure. As argued before, the appeal of a poem exceeds the sum of its parts—if they are combined with the necessary skill and set in meaningful relation with each other. This is certainly true for *Beowulf* and, arguably, also for *The Lord of the Rings* with its various parallel plots and sub-plots carefully connected and balanced by Tolkien.[32]

Second: depth. *Beowulf* is famous for its digressions[33] and references to other texts or events outside the primary plot. These digressions either fore-shadow future events or provide a commentary on the main action by means of (indirect) contrasts or parallels.[34] Tom Shippey (*Road* 229) has rightly praised Tolkien for creating in his work a similar "Beowulfian 'impression of depth'".[35]

---

31 See Tolkien's identification of the *Beowulf* poet with Heorrenda (who is mentioned in *Deor*) and his statements about the poem (as found in Tolkien *Beowulf. A Translation*) that are often based mainly on a sympathetic understanding of the original poet's intentions.
32 And it is this aspect that caused Tolkien great difficulties in the creation of his legendarium and may be (partially) responsible for his inability to bring his work on the legendarium project to a successful and, for him, satisfying conclusion during his own lifetime.
33 See Adrien Bonjour's essays on the digressions and their functions.
34 See, for example, the "Finnsburg Episode" (*Beowulf* lines 1068-1159) or the reference to the dragon-slayer Siegemund (*Beowulf* lines 874-897).
35 See also Shippey, *Road* 308-317.

Third: Enchantment, which is the product of a skilful blending of fairy-tale elements, such as the monsters, with historical protagonists (e.g. Hygelac) and a basically realistic cultural and geographical setting. Heorot, the kingdom of the Spear-Danes and the neighbouring territory ruled by the Geats with their historically attested king Hygelac, as well as all the other tribes and kingdoms mentioned, can be situated within the historic-cultural framework of the late 5th to early 6th centuries of northern Europe. But within this basically realistic setting the monsters (or to use a more general term: the fairy-tale elements) constitute a vital part of the poem and are neither mistakes nor flaws, as Tolkien pointed out in "Beowulf: The Monsters and the Critics". He may have over-stated his point a bit in order to counteract the back-then prevalent scholarly concentration on the historical elements and we, standing on Tolkien's shoulders, can now re-phrase the argument in a more balanced way: it is the skilful placement and embedding of the monsters within a realistic historical setting and the interaction of the Secondary World and the Perilous Realm that creates the Enchantment of the poem.

Beowulf would lose much of its appeal if the action took place exclusively in either of the two realms. Strip away the historical framework and we are left with a fairy or folk tale that, like see *Sellic Spell*, may delight us with a naïve charm yet would lack the deep resonances and the impact of the original poem. On the other side, if you did away with the monsters you would end up with a saga that would not differ much from most other extant Old Norse sagas. And this is exactly the lesson Tolkien had learnt from *Beowulf* and *Sellic Spell*, and which he applied to the crafting of his own literary masterpiece, *The Lord of the Rings*. It was going to be a fairy story in the Tolkienian sense, i.e. a tale "about the *aventures* of men in the Perilous Realm or upon its shadowy marches" (FS 32)—and as such it had to be placed securely within the realistic setting of his Secondary World to ensure that men (or hobbits) on their forays into the Perilous Realm have a solid base to return to. This is one reason why, in contrast to the Elvish-centric view of most of the legendarium, he adopts a hobbit-centric view for both *The Hobbit* and *The Lord of the Rings* and makes sure that the reader is firmly rooted in the very down-to-earth soil of the Shire[36] before he allows him to encounter emissaries from the Perilous Realm[37] or has him venture forth into the areas bordering or even inside Faëry (such as Rivendell or Lothlórien).

---

36 This is probably one of the reasons why Tolkien, in *The Lord of the Rings*, makes the reader plod through some fourscore pages of Hobbit-lore and adventures before the action picks up and they leave the Shire proper.
37 Both the Black Riders and the Elves Frodo encounters in the Woody End count as such.

Conclusion

I t would be wrong to call *The Hobbit*, in its published form, the folk-tale pre-cursor to the epic *The Lord of the Rings*, although it retains a closer affinity to the traditional folk- and fairy-tale genre than the later work. Thus, while it is virtually impossible to reduce the multi-layered plot of *The Lord of the Rings*[38] to a single unified folk tale, we could successfully attempt to do so for *The Hobbit*, which has something of a fairy-tale centre around which the other elements have been grouped. You can take them away and strip the story to its very core, yet it remains recognisably *The Hobbit*. The same is, however, hardly possible with *The Lord of the Rings*, where different narrative strands and elements have been welded inextricably together to form an epic tale.

Yet even *The Hobbit* is already removed a considerable distance from its hypothetical folk-tale prototype, which we may call *ðæs Holbytlan sælig spell*. It may use phrases that, to 20th-century readers, sound like belonging to the fairy-tale tradition, such as "… one morning long ago in the quiet of the world, when there was less noise and more green…" (H 15),[39] and stock-elements such as the dwarves or the trolls, but it also contains allusions to and incorporates epic and historical matter (the Necromancer, the Siege of Gondolin …). Had *The Hobbit* been more of a folk tale in the manner of *Sellic Spell*,[40] it would probably not have inspired Tolkien to his *The Lord of the Rings*. In its present form it illustrates Tolkien's early attempts at flexing his narrative muscles and the published text looks as much forward towards the epic-to-come as backwards to its alleged folk- and fairy-tale origins.

Ironically, it is the oldest and the most recent *Hobbit* movies that illustrate this double tendency in perfection. On the one hand, Peter Jackson has turned the children's book into the epic precursor of his supremely epic film-trilogy of *The Lord of the Rings*. On the other, Gene Deitch, almost half a century ago (1966), created an animated version of *The Hobbit* that manages to tell a much-reduced (and garbled) fairy-tale version of the story within eleven minutes—and concludes with Bilbo's marriage to the princess. While Peter Jackson's version is indeed a *sellic spell*, i.e. a wondrous tale, Gene Deitch's take on *The Hobbit* is a *sælig spell* in every sense of the word: a tale with a happy ending as well as a silly tale.

---

38   The multiplicity of its potential sources is alluded to by the inclusion or mention of some of the 'tales' and lays that could be seen as having been welded into the larger epic (cf. "The Tale of Arwen and Aragorn" and The "Lay of Frodo of the Nine Fingers and the Ring of Doom").

39   As Allan Turner rightly pointed out to me, such a sentence makes sense only for an audience living in an era suffering from the negative effects of industrialisation and thus longing for a past Golden Age. My thanks to him for this and other points of criticism and comments.

40   The creators of the 1966 short animated *The Hobbit* movie (Gene Deitch for William Snyder of Rembrandt Films; see: https://www.youtube.com/watch?v=UBnVL1Y2src) actually hit the right tone for a fairy tale—and had the wisdom to include a princess and have Bilbo marry her at the end of the tale.

Bibliography

Allen, Dorena. "Orpheus and Orfeo: The Dead and the Taken". *Medium Aevum* 33 (1964): 102-111

Anderson, Douglas A. (Ed.). *The Annotated Hobbit*. Boston: Houghton Mifflin, 2002

Beowulf – see *Klaeber's Beowulf*

Bonjour, Adrien. *The Digressions in Beowulf*. Oxford: Basil Blackwell, 1970

Drout, Michael D.C. *Beowulf and the Critics by J.R.R. Tolkien*. (Medieval and Renaissance Texts and Studies 248). Tempe AZ: The Arizona Center for Medieval and Renaissance Studies, 2002

---. "A Mythology for Anglo-Saxon England". *Tolkien and the Invention of Myth. A Reader*. Ed. Jane Chance. Lexington KY: The University Press of Kentucky, 2004, 229-247

Fauskanger, Helge C. *Quenya–English / English–Quenya Dictionary*. http://folk.uib.no/hnohf/Quettaparma.pdf (2008)

Fimi, Dimitra. "Tolkien and Folklore: *Sellic Spell* and *The Lay of Beowulf*". *Mythlore* 55 (Winter 2014): 27-28

Friedman, J.B. *Orpheus in the Middle Ages*. Cambridge MA: Harvard University Press, 1970

Honegger, Thomas. "A good dragon is hard to find, or from *draconitas* to *draco*". *Good Dragons are Rare. An Inquiry into Literary Dragons East and West*. Eds. Fanfan Chen & Thomas Honegger. (ALPH 5). Frankfurt am Main etc.: Peter Lang, 2009, 27-59

---. "Fantasy, Escape, Recovery, and Consolation in *Sir Orfeo*: The Medieval Foundations of Tolkienian Fantasy". *Tolkien Studies* 7 (2010): 117-136

Kisor, Yvette. "The Aesthetics of *Beowulf*: Structure, Perception, and Desire". *On the Aesthetics of Beowulf and Other Old English Poems*. Ed. John M. Hill. Toronto: University of Toronto Press, 2010, 227-246

Klaeber's Beowulf. 4th edition. Eds. R.D. Fulk, Robert E. Bjork, John D. Niles. Toronto: University of Toronto Press, 2008

Krüger, Heidi. "Eine Neubewertung der theoretischen Konzeption von 'Faëry' und 'fairy-story' auf Basis der 2008 erschienenen erweiterten Ausgabe *Tolkien On Fairy-stories*". *Hither Shore* 5 (2008): 197-222

Lang, Andrew (Ed.). *The Red Fairy Book*. (4th edition). London: Longmans, Green & Co, 1893

Panzer, Friedrich. *Studien zur germanischen Sagengeschichte. I. Beowulf*. Munich: C.H. Beck'sche Verlagsbuchhandlung, 1910

Rateliff, John D. *The History of* The Hobbit. *Part Two: Return to Bag-End*. London: HarperCollins, 2007

Severs, J. Burke. "The Antecedents of *Sir Orfeo*". *Studies in Medieval Literature in Honor of Professor Albert Croll Baugh*. Ed. M. Leach. Philadelphia: University of Pennsylvania Press, 1961, 187-207

Shippey, Tom A. *The Road to Middle-earth*. 3rd edition. 1st edition 1982. Boston: Houghton Mifflin, 2003

---. "Tolkien and the *Beowulf*-poet". *Roots and Branches: Selected Papers on Tolkien by Tom Shippey*. Cormarë Series 11. Zurich/Berne: Walking Tree Publishers, 2007, 1-18

Sullivan III, C.W. "Tolkien and the Traditional Dragon Tale: An Examination of *The Hobbit*". *J.R.R. Tolkien*. Ed. Peter Hunt. (New Casebooks). Houndmills, Basingstoke: Palgrave Macmillan, 2013, 62-73

Tolkien, John Ronald Reuel (Trans.). *Sir Gawain and the Green Knight, Pearl, and Sir Orfeo.* Ed. Christopher Tolkien. London: George Allen & Unwin, 1975

---. *The Hobbit.* 1st edition 1937. 4th edition. London: HarperCollins, 1991

---. "Beowulf: The Monsters and the Critics". Sir Israel Gollancz Memorial Lecture, read 25 Nov. 1936. First published in *Proceedings of the British Academy XXII. The Monster and the Critics and Other Essays.* Ed. Christopher Tolkien. London: HarperCollins, 1997, 5-48

---. "*Sir Orfeo*: A Middle English Version by J.R.R. Tolkien". Ed. Carl F. Hostetter. *Tolkien Studies* 1 (2004): 85-123

---. *Tolkien On Fairy-stories.* Expanded edition, with commentary and notes; 1st edition 1947. Eds. Verlyn Flieger & Douglas A. Anderson. London: HarperCollins, 2008

---. *Beowulf. A Translation and Commentary together with Sellic Spell.* Ed. Christopher Tolkien. London: HarperCollins, 2014

Zusammenfassungen der englischen Essays

Über Märchen und Spiele: ein phänomenologischer Vergleich zweier Erzählmedien

Zsuzsa Gáti

Dieser Beitrag ist von J.R.R. Tolkiens Text *On Fairy-stories* inspiriert, in dem er darüber nachdachte, was Märchen eigentlich sind und was sie in unseren Augen für Bedeutungen tragen. In diesem Artikel führen genau diese Fragen zu phänomenologischen Überlegungen und zu einem Vergleich der Charakteristika zwischen dem (oral verbreiteten) Märchen als klassischem und dem (digitalen) Spiel als modernem Erzählmedium.

Zunächst werden terminologische Schwierigkeiten angeschnitten und die Begriffe definiert, um dann unter Zuhilfenahme einiger Theorien die Charakteristika der beiden Erzählmedien darstellen zu können.

Märchen werden dabei in erster Linie im Sinne von ›Zaubermärchen‹ untersucht und als mündlich tradierte, modular aufgebaute, lineare, handlungsfokussierte, schematische Erzählungen definiert – mit einem Hang zur Wiederholung und einem gewissen Gebrauchstextcharakter –, die als verspielte Fiktionen mit bewusst magischen Elementen der Unterhaltung dienen und mit ihrer eher im Hintergrund durchscheinenden moralischen Aussage und ihrem Happy End mitunter eine tröstende, ja kathartische Funktion übernehmen können. Das Fehlen eines Autors hebt den Erzähler in eine besondere Position, über den auch zwei spezielle Aspekte zum Tragen kommen, die diese Art der Erzählungen über die Grenzen der Literatur führen: der performative und der partizipative Aspekt.

Spiele werden als ›kompliziertes‹ Spiel beschrieben, wobei sie freien Willen und Freizeit voraussetzen und eine eigene, spezielle Spielsphäre besitzen. Sie dienen der Unterhaltung, Ablenkung und der Entspannung und sind außerhalb der Spielsphäre zweckfrei und unproduktiv – reichen Ziele und Absichten über diese hinaus, so sind Spiele korrumpierbar. Wesentliche Eigenschaften sind daneben die Wiederholbarkeit, die Interaktivität und die gemeinschaftsbildende Kraft von Spielen.

In einer Schlussfolgerung werden die Ähnlichkeiten bzw. Verschiedenheiten der Erzählmedien dargestellt. Dabei wird ein weiterer, von Tolkien nicht erwähnter Aspekt interessant: die Frage, was Märchen in Zukunft für uns bedeuten bzw. zu was sie werden können. Eventuell werden sie zu einer neuartigen Erzählform, als Kreuzung der Erzählwege von Märchen und Spiel, in der jedoch die ›alten‹ phänomenologischen Elemente beider Medien intakt bleiben und weiterleben.

Transformationen von Märchen:
Von *Sellic/Sælig Spell* zu *Beowulf* oder
von Volksmärchen zum Epos

Thomas Honegger

Sellic Spell ist Tolkiens Versuch, das dem altenglischen epischen Gedicht *Beowulf* zugrundeliegende Volksmärchen zu rekonstruieren. Die Art und Weise, wie er dies macht, hilft einerseits, die poetologische Leistung des *Beowulf*-Dichters besser zu schätzen, der das einfache Volksmärchen in ein komplexes episches Gedicht umwandelte. Andererseits lässt sie auch Rückschlüsse über das Verhältnis zwischen dem eher ›volksmärchenhaften‹ *The Hobbit* und dem epischen *The Lord of the Rings* zu.

Der Aufsatz argumentiert für eine Verortung des *Hobbit* auf einer Stufe zwischen Volksmärchen und Epos, da dieser Roman Elemente aus beiden Kategorien vereinigt.

Theorien der Zweitschöpfung vor
On Fairy-stories

Gerard Hynes

Zu den von Tolkien in *On Fairy-stories* entwickelten Schlüsselkonzepten gehört die »Zweitschöpfung«: die künstlerische Produktion fiktionaler Umgebungen, die Leser- und Hörerschaften imaginär bewohnen können. Obwohl dies oft synonym zu dem verwandten Begriff »world-building« verwendet wird, enthält Tolkiens Begriff eine bestimmte Metaphysik der menschlichen Kreativität, die eng mit dem göttlichen Schöpfungsakt verbunden ist und von ihm abhängt. Während die Abhängigkeit Tolkiens von Personen wie Samuel Taylor Coleridge und George MacDonald anerkannt ist, wurde die Geschichte dieses Konzeptes noch nicht detailliert untersucht.

Dieser Beitrag geht kurz Tolkiens ausgewiesener Verwendung der Überlegungen und der Terminologie Coleridges und MacDonalds nach, bevor die ausführlichere Geschichte der Metapher des »Künstlers als Schöpfer« untersucht wird. Er analysiert die in den Etymologien der Wörter *create* und *shape* enthaltenen philologischen Beziehungen zwischen menschlicher und göttlicher Kreativität. Die Metapher des »Künstlers als Schöpfer« wird anschließend von biblischen und klassischen Anfängen über mittelalterliche Scholastik bis zum Humanismus der Renaissance verfolgt. Der folgende Abschnitt diskutiert Künstler und Autoren wie Cristoforo Landino, Albrecht Dürer, Leonardo da

Vinci und Federico Zuccari, der die Metapher entwickelte und unterschiedliche Implikationen aus ihr folgerte.

Die Metapher fand Eingang in die englische Kritik durch die Werke Sir Philip Sidneys und wird zu einem akzeptierten Teil der englischen Literaturkritik im 17. und 18. Jahrhundert. Ihre Entwicklung in englischen Briefen kann durch eine vergleichende Untersuchung der Schriften von Joseph Addison und des Earl von Shaftesbury beurteilt werden. Diese Autoren unterscheiden sich oft voneinander und von Tolkien über die Fragen, wie weit Künstler von den Gesetzmäßigkeiten der Primärwelt abweichen können, wie viel Respekt der natürlichen Welt entgegenzubringen ist und wo die Quellen der künstlerischen Kreativität liegen.

Indem Tolkien mit seinen Vorgängern verglichen wird, kann, ohne eine direkte Übernahme zu behaupten, seine Originalität und Bedeutung als Theoretiker der menschlichen Kreativität beurteilt werden.

Dieser Beitrag ist keine Übung in Quellenstudie oder die Skizze einer kontinuierlichen literarischen oder philosophischen Tradition, sondern ein Versuch, Tolkien in einem geschichtlichen und intellektuellen Kontext zu verorten, was es erlaubt, seinen originalen Beitrag zur Kunsttheorie klarer zu sehen.

Heidegger und Tolkien: Dankbares Denken und »Die Liebe der Liebe«

Danko Kamčevski

Tolkiens Ansichten über die Schaffung und das Verstehen literarischer Werke können am ehesten in seinem Essay *On Fairy-stories* ausgemacht werden. Jedoch sind sie auch implizit oder explizit in seinen anderen (akademischen wie fiktionalen) Werken präsent.

Dieser Beitrag möchte diese Ansichten in den Kontext der Phänomenologie des 20. Jahrhunderts stellen, die sowohl in der Philosophie (Edmund Husserl) als auch in der Philologie (Roman Ingarden, New Criticism oder Amerikanische Phänomenologie) wichtig ist.

In der Philosophie eröffnete Martin Heidegger neue Potenziale und Heidegger selbst gelangte durch die Phänomenologie zu dem, was er Denken nannte. Es bestehen Ähnlichkeiten zwischen Tolkien und dem New Criticism wie beispielsweise sich den »Texten selbst« zu nähern anstatt Methoden anderer Disziplinen wie der Psychoanalyse oder der Anthropologie zu verwenden, um sie zu interpretieren.

Wie Heidegger in der Philosophie bleibt Tolkien auch nicht beim textuellen Formalismus beim Verständnis und der Interpretation stehen. Tolkiens Ansichten sind, auch wenn sie dem Text in seiner ursprünglichen Sprache und seinem Kontext Respekt zollen, breiter und philosophischer und implizieren metaphysische Konsequenzen. Heidegger sucht die Antwort auf die Frage, was es bedeutet zu sein, während Tolkien über das Wesen der Geschichte und ihre Korrelation zum Geist sinniert.

Darüber hinaus sind Heidegger und Tolkien als Zeitgenossen mit den gleichen Problemen der Moderne wie Technologie, Szientismus oder Entzauberung konfrontiert. Technologische und instrumentelle Denkweisen der modernen Zeit beschränken die Welt und ihre Dinge auf das, was kalkulierbar und nützlich ist. Die Heidegger'sche Essenz der Technologie verwandelt alles in eine ständige Reserve an Ressourcen. Bei Tolkien haben wir Sauron, den Herrn der Magie und Maschinen, der Ordnung und Koordination über alles stellt.

Heidegger plädiert für Denken, d.h. zum selbstlosen Sorgen und Bewundern von Seiendem zurückzukehren. Sein Denken ist dankbar und voller Ehrfurcht für Seiendes. Tolkien schlägt ein Verständnis der Phantasie vor, die in der Lage ist, Dinge aus der Vertrautheit zu lösen und zu retten. Phantasie ist reine Möglichkeit und Freiheit und als solche ermöglicht sie Liebe und Respekt für die Dinge. Sobald wir die Ehrfurcht vor der gesamten Schöpfung wiedergewonnen haben, sind wir nicht länger in der Lage, sie zu benutzen oder sogar zu missbrauchen. Tolkiens Phantasie ist eine »Liebe der Liebe«, eine nichtbesitzergreifende Beziehung mit allen Dingen.

Die Meditationen und Folgerungen von Heidegger und Tolkien sind sich ähnlich, sehr einsichtsvoll und bedeutend. Als solche verdienen sie weitere Beachtung, wozu dieser einführende Vergleich beitragen will.

Aus der Realität, in die Realität: Faërie als eine konzeptuelle Rahmenstruktur für das Blending von Erzählräumen

Timo Lothmann & Janek Scholz

Dieser Beitrag postuliert *Faërie* als mentalen und kulturellen Überbau für die Konstruktion und das Verständnis von Fairy Stories im Sinne Tolkiens. Durch Zugänge aus der Kognitionswissenschaft (*blending theory*) und der Kulturtheorie (Spieltheorie, *spatial turn*) wird festgestellt, dass Tolkiens Annäherung an *Faërie* im Einklang mit Theorien zur Komplexität der Denkprozesse bei Autor und Leser steht. Die Bedeutung von Tolkiens *On Fairy-stories* liegt darin, einen abstrakten *Faërie*-Raum zu konzeptualisieren, der durch den Geschichtenerzähler in seiner Funktion als Schöpfer konstitutiv für die erzählte »Sekundärwelt« wird. Diese Realität enthält nicht nur Elemente aus *Faërie*, sondern ist auch notwendigerweise mit der »Primärwelt« verknüpft. Es ist gewissermaßen ein Spielfeld für Realitätsverhandlung – mit weiterreichender Bedeutung für beide Welten.

Beim Betreten dieses multidimensionalen und dynamischen Erzählraums halten wir die Erzählung für glaubwürdig. Je kohärenter sie ist, d.h. je stabiler der entstandene *Blend*, desto tiefer können die Leser eintauchen und desto mehr Möglichkeiten für *Enchantment* (gemäß Tolkien) bieten sich. Unglaube oder inkonsistente *Blends* führen unweigerlich zum Einsturz der zweiten Realitätswelt. Zusammen mit dem Autor einer Fairy Story reisen wir demnach, der Erzählung folgend, von Raum zu Raum innerhalb eines großen konzeptuellen Rahmens. Dieser bietet jedoch auch Räume, die (noch) nicht enthüllt wurden und die mit unserem eigenen, individuellen *Blend*-Potenzial geschaffen werden können, unabhängig vom Erstautor einer Geschichte. Solche individuellen Räume bieten Möglichkeiten für Erzählungen, die über das Original hinausgehen (z.B. Fan-Fiction). Unter den vielen Pfaden durch die narrativen Optionen ist eine Fairy Story also nur *ein* möglicher Weg mit offenem Ende. Es sind metaphorische Reisen von einem Raum zum nächsten, die, obwohl sie auch nicht-reale Elemente enthalten, das Verlangen nach unserer Lebenswelt selbst zum Ausdruck bringen.

Tolkiens *On Fairy-stories* ist ein Appell an das Sich-bewusst-Machen der Realitätswelt(en). Er verdeutlicht sein Verständnis von *sub-creation* als eine essentielle kulturelle Aktivität, die das Phantastische und das Nicht-Phantastische in ein rechtes Verhältnis zueinander setzt. Gemäß der Argumentation im vorliegenden Essay ist *Faërie* selbst ein Appell, sich geistige Räume offen zu halten, in denen Geschichten stattfinden und fortgesetzt werden können.

Auf dieser Basis bietet der Beitrag ein Modell für die Konzeptualisierung von *Faërie* an, das Text, Autor und Leser wie auch Tolkiens Haltung zu Kunst und Schöpfung im Allgemeinen berücksichtigt. Beispiele aus Tolkiens Hauptwerken werden dafür zur Verdeutlichung herangezogen.

Faërie betreten.
J.R.R. Tolkiens *Smith of Wootton Major*

Marguerite Mouton

D ie Melancholie am Ende von *Smith of Wootton Major* und die Tatsache, dass es die letzte von Tolkien geschriebene und publizierte Geschichte ist, haben Forscher dazu geführt, diesen Text als Geschichte der Entsagung und des Verlustes zu lesen.

Dieser Beitrag bietet eine komplementäre Lektüre von *Smith of Wootton Major* an, dessen Hauptanliegen die Märchen selbst sind bzw. ihre Überlieferung an andere. Wenn Faërie ein gefährliches Reich ist, wird sein Verlust von Tolkien als noch gefährlicher dargestellt, da dieses Reich für die geistige wie geistliche Gesundheit notwendig ist. In *Smith of Wootton Major* drückt der Autor die Überzeugung aus, dass der Zugang zu Faërie unter allen Umständen beibehalten und nicht verloren werden sollte.

Faërie erforschen: J.R.R. Tolkiens innovative Zugänge zum Märchengenre

Anca Muntean

*D*er *Herr der Ringe* verführt junge und alte Leser, indem ihr Begehren geweckt wird, mehr über Mittelerde und Faërie herauszufinden. Der Einfluss dieses Werks auf folgende Autorengenerationen (Fantasy und andere) ist nicht zu unterschätzen. Dies ist vielleicht ein Grund, weshalb Tolkiens epische Geschichte oft vorschnell als das kategorisiert wird, was wir Fantasy-Literatur nennen – entgegen der Tatsache, dass diese Bezeichnung nur einen Teil der komplexen generischen Herkunft abdecken kann. Die genannte verführende Wirkung verdankt sich einer ungewöhnlichen Mischung und Interaktion verschiedener literarischer Genres (Märchen, historischer Roman, Epos, Romanze und, selbstverständlich, Fantasy), die innerhalb des Textes wirken und die Tolkien verwendete und im Fortgang der Geschichte entwickelte.

Indem er die Charakteristika aller dieser literarischen Genres miteinander interagieren lässt, lässt Tolkien ihre innere Struktur sich verändern, sodass sie innerhalb der Narrative und wegen ihr flexibler werden als vorher. Dies erlaubt ihnen, die Atmosphäre und den Wind, der aus Faërie bläst, in unsere Welt zu bringen.

Mit *On Fairy-stories* als Referenzpunkt argumentiert dieser Artikel, wie man Faërie näherkommen und erforschen kann, aber auch, wie sich die stärker »traditionellen« Märchen zu »Märchen für Erwachsene« entwickeln können. Die Schwierigkeit, den *Herrn der Ringe* in ein präzises Genre zu verorten, kann durch die spezifische Textgenese erklärt werden. Zunächst war er nach dem Erfolg der Abenteuer von Bilbo Baggins als Nachfolger zum *Hobbit* geplant. Tolkiens Herausgeber bestand darauf, dass die Geschichte entwickelt werden sollte, allerdings wusste Tolkien nicht wie, da nach seiner Ansicht diese bestimmte Geschichte beendet war. Ein kurzer Vergleich mit Lord Dunsany und George MacDonald zeigt einige Ähnlichkeiten zwischen Tolkiens Werk und diesen beiden Autoren, die er bewunderte und deren Schriften ihn inspirierten.

Tolkien formte eine einmalige Welt, die eine gesamte »Provinz der Literatur« repräsentiert, indem er die inhärente Evolution literarischer Genres illustriert und zugleich die durch ein a priori gesetztes Genre angenommenen Beschränkungen ausschließt.

Chestertons Kreide: Kreativität und Gemeinplätze in J.R.R. Tolkiens *On Fairy-stories*

Jonathan Nauman

In seinem Essay *On Fairy-stories* verteidigt J.R.R. Tolkien implizit und explizit das Märchen-Genre vor denen, die solche Geschichten als minderwertig, unpraktisch und einer erwachsenen Leserschaft unwürdig ansehen. Seine Bemühungen, die spezifischen Vorzüge von Märchen als Artefakte zu erläutern und die für ihre Produktion benötigten ernsthaften ästhetischen Fertigkeiten zu loben, spiegeln seine andauernden Anstrengungen um eine künstlerische und atmosphärische Verbindung von Volksmärchen und kosmogonischem Mythos.

Die anthropologischen Annahmen und ästhetischen Ideale des Essays folgen denjenigen G.K. Chestertons, vielleicht in einer besonderen Abhängigkeit zu Chestertons ästhetischem Essay *A Piece of Chalk*.

»Die Adler kommen«: Tolkiens eukatastrophische Reinterpretation des »Tiere der Schlacht«-Motivs im *Hobbit* und im *Herrn der Ringe*

Łukasz Neubauer

Das dramatische Auftreten der großen Adler des Nebelgebirges in der Hitze entscheidender militärischer Konfrontationen sowohl im *Hobbit* als auch besonders im *Herrn der Ringe* konstituiert vielleicht die vollständigste Verwirklichung des Konzepts der Eukatastrophe in allen Werken J.R.R. Tolkiens. Diese »plötzliche glückliche Wendung« von bis dahin auf ein Desaster zusteuernden Ereignissen, die ursprünglich in seinem Essay *On Fairy-stories* vorgestellt wurde, wird umso faszinierender, wenn das gewöhnliche Bild dieser geflügelten Kreaturen aus frühen germanischen Texten in Betracht gezogen wird. Häufig begleitet von ihren rabenartigen und wölfischen Partnern, sind die Adler zunächst vollständige Mitglieder der entsetzlichen »Tiere der Schlacht«, die einst die mit Leichen übersäten Schlachtfelder von Brunanburh, Finnesburg oder Maldon in der Hoffnung auf ein blutiges Fest heimsuchten. In den beiden Mittelerde-Romanen erscheinen die großen Adler jedoch in direktem konzeptuellem Gegensatz zu ihren stärker böse wirkenden Gefährten. Somit dienen sie offensichtlich als mächtige christliche Alternative zum bis dahin etablierten Trope der »Tiere der Schlacht«.

Der Beitrag versucht, ihre eukatastrophischen Qualitäten im Licht der katholischen Imagination Tolkiens und des literarischen Mystizismus seiner literarischen Werke zu untersuchen.

Menschengeschichten oder menschliche Geschichten

Renée Vink

In seinem Essay *On Fairy-stories* stellt Tolkien fest: Während die Märchen (fairy stories) sterblicher Menschen voll der Flucht vor dem Tod seien, seien die »Menschengeschichten« der Elben zweifellos voll der Flucht vor der Todlosigkeit. Hinter dieser Überlegung steht vermutlich der Standardsatz, mit dem Märchen im Englischen üblicherweise enden: »They lived happily ever after«. Dieser Satz legt eine nachhaltigere Flucht vor dem Tod nahe als seine Entsprechungen in anderen (germanischen) Sprachen. Darüber hinaus wirkt der Satz über die Menschengeschichten der Elben wie ein linguistischer Trick, da in diesen anderen Sprachen das Wort für *fairy stories* nicht das Element *fairy* enthält. Tolkien erweitert die gewöhnliche Definition von *fairy* auch, indem er dazu (unter der Schreibweise Faërie) auch das Reich zählt, in dem die Geschichten spielen. Dieses Reich enthält auch uns Menschen, wenn wir verzaubert sind. Meint dies, dass »Menschengeschichten« in einem sterblichen Reich spielen und Fairies oder Elben enthalten, wenn diese entzaubert sind? Oder ist dies nur ein anderer Fall von Wortspiel?

Um dieser Frage nachzugehen, lohnt sich ein Blick auf Tolkiens Legendarium: Können wir irgendwelche »Menschengeschichten« finden, in denen ein Elb versucht, der Todlosigkeit zu entfliehen? Und wenn, ist dies ein erfolgreicher Versuch?

Fünf Fälle sind hier zu betrachten: Míriel, Feänor (mehr oder weniger), Aegnor, Lúthien und Arwen. Ein genauerer Blick zeigt jedoch, dass die meisten aus verschiedenen Gründen die Kriterien nicht erfüllen: Das menschliche Element ist abwesend, Todlosigkeit ist nicht das Ziel des Fluchtversuchs, die Flucht kommt nicht eigentlich vor, der narrative Gesichtspunkt ist unsicher – oder menschlich. Die beste Kandidatin ist Lúthien, deren Geschichte die ultimative Fluchtgeschichte ist. Diese wurde einige Jahre vor *On Fairy-stories* geschrieben und Tolkien hatte sie vielleicht noch im Hinterkopf, als er sein Essay verfasste.

Aber auch diese Geschichte ist eine Art Hybrid, da sie ebenfalls recht gut als Märchen für sterbliche Menschen funktioniert.

Ein übliches Element in allen diesen Geschichten ist Entzauberung, aber keiner der elbischen Protagonisten leidet unter Weltmüdigkeit, die laut *Silmarillion* todlose Elben und unsterbliche Valar gleichermaßen erwartet. Dagegen bietet etwa die *Star-Trek-Voyager*-Episode »Death Wish« ein besseres Beispiel eines weltmüden Unsterblichen, der sich nach Tod sehnt, als irgendeine der Geschichten Tolkiens. Der klarste Fall der Entzauberung in seinem Legendarium ist Arwens – aber ihre Geschichte wurde von einem Menschen geschrieben und es stellt sich heraus, dass sie von der Sterblichkeit entzaubert ist.

Tolkien lag wahrscheinlich richtig, wenn er entschied, alles im Legendarium gehe durch sterbliche Hände: Trotz der Bemerkung in seinem Essay mag er zu der Überzeugung gekommen sein, dass Sterbliche nicht adäquat die Menschengeschichten der Elben erzählen können.

Summaries of the German Essays

Gems all turn into Flowers: *On Fairy-stories* and the Romantic Poetology
Julian Tim Morton Eilmann

In his paper Julian Eilmann explores the connections between Tolkien's *On Fairy-stories* and the romantic poetology. To call aspects of Tolkien's work "romantic" can only make sense if one distinguishes between the historical era of Romanticism (ca. 1795-1848) and a romantic worldview. The term "romantic worldview" or "Weltanschauung" used by Romanticism scholars like Rüdiger Safranski implies a specific philosophic and poetologic position with the main characteristic of a longing towards the wonderful and the transcendent. The romantic notion is that a sensitive individual, especially the poet, can awaken the poetic mystery present in the cosmos with the help of the poetic "magic word" (Eichendorff). The result is what the Romantic poet Novalis calls "Romanticisation": a radical transformation of the human perception that enables to see the transcendent quality of ordinary things. This romantic fascination with the transcendent explains why the fantastic genre became the ideal vehicle for the Romantics to sensitize readers for the wonder of the physical world.

We do find echoes of this romantic worldview in *On Fairy-stories*. Tolkien shares the romantic praise of the human imagination as an essential *conditio humana* when he speaks of "Fantasy [a]s a natural human activity" (FS 55) and even claims: "Fantasy remains a human right" (FS 56). The principle of Romanticisation finds its equivalent in Tolkien's concept of Recovery:

> We should look at green again, and be startled anew (but not blinded) by blue and yellow and red. We should meet the centaur and the dragon, and then perhaps suddenly behold, like the ancient shepherds, sheep, and dogs, and horses—and wolves. This recovery fairy-stories help us to make. In that sense only a taste for them may make us, or keep us, childish. Recovery (which includes return and renewal of health) is a re-gaining—regaining of a clear view.   (FS 67)

Fantasy thus enables to see the ordinary world with a clear view and to value once again its inherent wonders. This key element of Tolkien's definition of the benefits of the fairy-story is as we see a genuine romantic conception. In

272 Hither Shore 12 (2015) Summaries

line with the romantic worldview Tolkien speaks of a "reservoir of power" that underpins the prosaic world and which can be set free in the world of Faerie: "As such it [Faërie] draws from the well of creative energy that a man feels to lie behind the visible world" (FS 260). Once this creative well flows again freely the world wonderfully transforms:

> Creative fantasy... may open your hoard and let all the locked things fly away like cage-birds. The gems all turn into flowers or flames, and you will be warned that all you had (or knew) was dangerous and potent, not really effectively chained, free and wild; no more yours than they were you. (FS 68)

In *The Lord of the Rings* we do find this romantic concept exemplified in Frodo's enchantment in Lothlórien. In this magical retreat he is "lost in wonder" (LotR 341) and sees all things that were known to him with a clear view. In Lothlórien Frodo walks in a romanticised world where the wonder of the things enchants the mortal visitor. Tolkien understands this Recovery as a basic human need: "'Faery' is as necessary for the health and complete functioning of the Human as is sunlight for physical life" (SWM 144-5).

Tolkien's *On Fairy-stories*: The Poetics of Poetology

Markus Gut

If you follow Tolkien's demand, expressed in *On Fairy-stories*, for the inner consistency of a secondary world—a consistency which is ultimately derived from primary world standards—then a secondary world inevitably has to deal with the need for sub-creation in general as well as its own creation. This results in the possibility to tackle creation poetologically, by means of signs of language *in general*, on an abstract meta-level. This is the case whenever the topic of creation is broached *inside* the secondary world by adhering to the intrinsic laws of this secondary world, which can at the same time be put in a correspondent relationship to the creation of the secondary world within the primary world.

An analysis of the beginning of *The Silmarillion* shows that Tolkien definitely used the possibility to create such a correspondent relationship in his literary work: He does not only implement the 'poetics' explicitly outlined in

On Fairy-stories with all its consequences, he also adds to it by implicitly, that means poetologically, reflecting, defining and exponentiating on his poetics in a way that leaves the reader at the limits of his cognitive linguistic potential. Particularly the topic of constituents for linguistic worlds and thus of signs of language in general, as is especially prominent at the beginning of the *Silmarillion* in poetological and performative passages, obliterates the boundaries between the primary and the secondary world on this meta-level.

The article in hand thus proposes the following thesis: Poetological and performative passages are playing such an important role in Tolkien's work because they are able to create through immersion in the secondary world not only secondary but primary belief. Poetological passages, because they refer to signs of language and constituents in both worlds; performative ones, because they are able to create new things during reading which hold up against 'claims to truth' in the primary world.

These findings should be analysed further for secondary worlds *in general*, in view of the influence of Tolkien's *On Fairy-stories* and his literary works. Each secondary world (and especially those following Tolkien's poetics) holds the prerequisite to broach the issue of language and its power of creation after all.

A Cauldron of Stories and a Banana Skin
Wilhelm Kuehs

Myth is the matrix of our comprehension of the world and of ourselves. J.R.R. Tolkien illustrated this in *On Fairy-stories* with the picture of the „Cauldron of Story". Everybody is thrown into this cauldron and becomes part and sub-creator of a matrix of fables. This essay tries to connect Tolkien's ideas with a major strain of western thinking of the 20th century.

While scholars like C.G. Jung choose to approach the problem through psychology, Tolkien knows that myth always shows itself through language. In both theories we see the influence of myth on historical and social developments, but we lack a connection. The fundamental bond between myth, narration and everyday life can only be described and understood, if we get Jung and Tolkien together. The link between these accesses has to be a new form of socio-semiotics, which this essay tries to establish.

Power and Stewardship: On Magic and Science, Arts and Creativity, Ethics and Morals

Friedhelm Schneidewind

Tolkien's notion on the responsible use of power, for example magic or imagination, can be derived from several passages in *On Fairy-stories* but also from two very different fictional texts: the poem *The Sea Bell* and his last story, *Smith of Wotton Major*. Tolkien compares imagination and creativity with magic in the secondary world, with arts and sciences in our primary world, underlines their similarity and their ethical aspect. His thoughts on the use and pursuit of power, stewardship and morality can be transferred to our world. If they are compared to modern notions on responsibility and moral conduct without the religious background, they can be fruitful to modern world discussions.

Faërian Drama at the Kitchen Table

Pen&Paper Role-Playing Games as Fairy Stories

Christian Weichmann

Pen&paper role-playing games are a special kind of collectively told tales. In these games, a group of players and one 'game master' play an adventure. Each player develops a role according to the rules of the game. These roles are called 'characters' and are determined by the world on which the game is based. These worlds are often but not always typical fantasy worlds and thus, the characters are dwarves, elves or orcs and are thieves, wizards or shamans in their profession. These characters are described by some values determining their abilities. The game master plays 'the world' in describing situations in which the characters find themselves and plays all persons they meet.

Role-playing games were developed in the 1970s from conflict simulation and table top battle games. The main changes from these sources to the role-playing games were the introduction of the idea that one person plays only one role (except the game master), the addition of fantastic elements, and the extension of the possibility for actions of the characters from only fighting to almost complete freedom of action. A main reason for this development was the game authors' interest in fantasy and especially in Tolkien. This let to the wish to simulate adventures as they are found in these books in games.

There is no indication, that Tolkien's *On Fairy-stories* influenced these games. And of course these games were not in existence when Tolkien wrote his essay. The games have some dramatic elements, as the characters are represented by the players using a reduced set of dramatic expression in facial expressions, gesture, and voice. As Tolkien found: "Drama is naturally hostile to Fantasy" (FS 61), there is legitimate doubt whether role-playing games are fairy stories as defined by Tolkien.

But the article shows, that they comply with almost all the criteria given by Tolkien in his essay. Only the eucatastrophe is not guaranteed, as some role-playing games are dystopic and even the other ones, for reasons of suspense, have at least the possibility of a negative ending. But the predominant part of role-playing games find positive solutions for each adventure. So pen&paper role-playing games (maybe most other kinds of role-playing games) can be mostly seen as fairy stories as described by Tolkien.

Epistemology in *On Fairy-stories*
Frank Weinreich

There are more than mere traces of Platonism and classical Idealism to be found in *Mythopoeia* and *Leaf by Niggle*. This article argues that the same is true for *On Fairy-stories*, and shows that the creation of art according to Tolkien is a process of translating ideal pictures and forms from a supernatural source (i.e. the metaphysical world of Idealism) into the real (secondary) world via the same maieutic method Socrates is supposed to have used to elicite knowledge in his fellow men.

To whom it may concern—a Reviewer's Complaint

Readers of my reviews may have noticed an increasing frustration on my part with what I'd call 'carelessness' ('sloppiness' would be another term that comes to mind) in matters of basic scholarly craftsmanship. Authors seem no longer to care about bibliographical research on the topic they are going to write about—and I'm not talking about chapters hidden away in books, nor even about MLA listed and also otherwise present but possibly not-so-easily available books by smaller publishers (well, Amazon does have them ....), but about publications by big names (HarperCollins) or leading journals in the field (*Tolkien Studies*). The fact that bona-fide academics writing about e.g. Fate and Free Will in Tolkien without knowing Tolkien's text with exactly this title (published in *Tolkien Studies* VI in 2009) or the paper on exactly this topic by no-one else but Verlyn Flieger (also published in *Tolkien Studies* VI in 2009), not to mention the informed response by Thomas Fornet-Ponse in *Tolkien Studies* VII, and that they still make it into volumes edited by acknowledged Tolkien-scholars and published by university presses, drives me sometimes to despair.

How are we going to advance Tolkien studies if scholars in the field are ignorant of each others research? It may be fun (and is undoubtedly important) to think things through on your own, but before publishing the fruits of these ruminations, it is a scholar's duty to make him- or herself conversant with the current scholarly discourse on the topic and to position his or her own contribution vis-à-vis the existing scholarship.

In second place the editor(s) of a volume or a journal also have the responsibility to guarantee a certain minimal level of professional quality. This does not mean that they themselves have to be experts in the field of the papers submitted (which is why most journals have a board of advisors), but they must ensure that the authors are at least aware of the 'basic standard procedures' of academic research and writing.

Finally, in the Golden Age (long gone, alas), there would have been a copy-editor at the publishers who would give the text a thorough proofing and would even check some of the dates (I am always astonished how often authors get simple basic facts wrong). A print publication should possess, in theory, all these in-built 'safety nets' and could be, ideally, superior to a simple blog entry. Yet this is only true if the steps described are taken seriously and the people involved actually do their work. As author, editor and series-editor, I am painfully aware that this is often no longer the case.

It does not lack a certain irony that, on the one hand, we have more and better research-instruments available (online bibliographies, online text-databases etc.) but they seem either ignored or not known. On the other hand, we notice that the traditional print publications are threatened by open access publications (cf. *Journal of Tolkien Research*) or by academic platforms such as *reasearchgate.org* or *academia.edu*. The latter may not offer peer-review *per se*, but it features a tool by means of which an author can invite his or her colleagues to comment on a paper and to get thus a qualified feedback before submitting it to a journal or a publisher.

However, as with the other instruments, it has to be known to the authors and has to be used—only then will we see a progress and I can, hopefully, stop ranting at mistakes expected in 'Introduction to Literary Studies 1.0' but no longer acceptable in academic print publications.

Thomas Honegger

Reviews / Rezensionen

Theresa Freda Nicolay:
Tolkien and the Modernists: Literary Responses to the Dark New Days of the 20th Century
Jefferson NC: McFarland, 2014, 196 pp.

The days when philologists and medievalists dominated Tolkien criticism are long past, and we have seen the publication of several important studies that try and locate the Professor's work within the literary and cultural discourse of the first half of the 20th century. Patrick Curry's *Defending Middle-earth: Tolkien: Myth and Modernity* (1997) and Tom Shippey's *J.R.R. Tolkien: Author of the Century* (2000) are the two seminal studies that kick-started the discussion about Tolkien's relationship with modern times and modernity. Others have continued the exploration of these themes and the last decade saw, next to individual papers, the publication of two volumes with essays on *Tolkien and Modernity 1 & 2* (2006, ed. by Frank Weinreich/Thomas Honegger), and more recently the monograph *The Loss and the Silence: Aspects of Modernism in the Works of C.S. Lewis, J.R.R. Tolkien and Charles Williams* (2011) by Margaret Hiley.

We would therefore expect Theresa Nicolay to build on this scholarly foundation and continue developing the critical discourse—which is, unfortunately, not the case. Only Shippey's ideas made it into her study, and Curry's book gets an entry in the bibliography, but none of the other publications on the topic are taken into account or even mentioned. As a consequence, Nicolay develops her arguments in splendid isolation—which does not detract from the readability of her book, but definitively lessens her impact on and connection with the current discourse in Tolkien studies at large.

A second point of criticism is Nicolay's rather vague use of 'the modernists' and 'modernism'—something that has already been criticised by Robert T. Tally Jr. in his review of her book in *Mythlore* (33.2 (2015): 171-175). As Tally correctly notes, the authors whose works Nicolay uses to illustrate her arguments are mostly modernists, yet the rather limited selection fails to cover all aspects of this multi-faceted literary and artistic movement. Thus important representatives of modernism such as James Joyce, William Faulkner or Ernest Hemingway are missing.

Yet while this is a justified point of criticism, it does not detract much from the value of her study and the reader is well advised to ignore the generalising tendency of the study's title (chosen, most likely, by the publisher's marketing department). What you actually get is a well-argued discussion of selected topics from 19th and 20th century literary texts and their respective occurrence and function in Tolkien's work. You will not learn many new things about modernism, but due to the contrastive analysis you will come away with a deeper and broader understanding of Tolkien's fiction.

As mentioned, not all texts covered by Nicolay belong to the modernist movement. We also find works that pre- and postdate modernism, but which have been included since they focus on the problems caused by industrialisation and mechanisation. The selection ranges from Herman Melville's *Bartleby, the Scrivener* (1853) to William Morris' *News from Nowhere* (1890), E.M. Forster's *Howards End* (1910), T.S. Eliot's 'The Lovesong of J. Alfred Prufrock' (1915), F. Scott Fitzgerald's *The Great Gatsby* (1925), Virginia Woolf's *Mrs Dalloway* (1925) and *To the Lighthouse* (1927), D.H. Lawrence's *Lady Chatterley's Lover* (1928) to John Gardner's post-modernist novel *Grendel* (1971). These are the works that constitute the framework of reference within which Nicolay develops her argumentation.

She prefaces her analysis proper with a necessarily brief and generalising sketch on modernity and modernism, whose nature is, according to Nicolay, dominated by a general and widespread loss of meaning and a crisis of identity caused by industrialisation, mechanisation and the atrocities of World War I.

She then proceeds to explore these aspects in the individual chapters, focussing on the themes of the isolation of the individual, the fragmentation of human existence and the loss of the traditional sources of meaning and security (religion, custom, ideology). The wasteland emerges as one of the most prominent objective correlatives symbolising this new view of life—as encountered, for example, in T.S. Eliot's eponymous poem. It also appears in form of the deforested hill in Wragby Wood in *Lady Chatterley's Lover* or as the 'Valley of Ashes' in *The Great Gatsby*. These wastelands mirror the devastations of the protagonists' inner landscape of mind and soul—often direct consequences of WW I which drive them into isolation and, in the case of Virginia Woolf's Septimus Smith, into suicide.

There are wastelands in Tolkien's works, too—be this Mordor under Sauron or Saruman's 'industrialised' Isengard. Yet in contrast to the desolate landscapes in the texts of modernist authors, Tolkien's wastelands do not represent the entirety of Middle-earth but are merely concrete manifestations of evil in a fallen world and are counterbalanced by flowering gardens, cultivated fields and forests. Furthermore, there is justified hope for the healing of the devastated earth, as seen in Isengard after the removal of Saruman and after the scouring of the Shire. Tolkien thus differs in his response to the challenges of his times.

Instead of isolation and despair we find in his works a world threatened by evil, yet ultimately governed by divine providence and holding out the hope of final salvation. Overcoming the very concrete evil is only possible by means of hope, pity, courage, solidarity, and trust—which are not always easy to accomplish, as the fate of some of Tolkien's protagonists (e.g. Denethor) illustrates. Thus both modernists and Tolkien start from similar initial situations, yet their "Literary Responses to the Dark New Days of the 20th Century" differ greatly due to their different religious and cultural backgrounds.

To sum up, Nicolay's study makes good reading. The text has been carefully proofread and edited (*pace* 'Northrop Frye', who is spelt consistently as 'Northrup Frye'), and the structure as well as the argument is easy to follow. The added value of the study is small for all those who are conversant with the current discourse on the topic in Tolkien studies. For newcomers, however, it makes good introductory reading.   Thomas Honegger

Deke Parsons:
J.R.R. Tolkien, Robert E. Howard and the Birth of Modern Fantasy.
Critical Explorations in Science Fiction and Fantasy, Vol. 47

Jefferson NC: McFarland, 2014, 188 pp.

Titles of publications seem to become more and more noncommittal labels to attract the unwary reader and, to prove this point, the rather slim volume under discussion treats Tolkien and Howard, but not the 'Birth of Modern Fantasy'. A more accurate title to Parsons's study would thus be *J.R.R. Tolkien, Robert E. Howard and Jerry Siegel & Joe Shuster—Parallel Lives*. However, in contrast to Plutrach's *Parallel Lives*, there is no connecting juxtaposition between the lives and works of the architect of Middle-earth, the father of Conan and the creators of Superman. All they seem to share is a temporal space, located vaguely somewhere in the 1930s, and the reader finishes the eleven-line 'Conclusion' with a sense of puzzlement and irritation. It is not that Parsons's book is badly written—it just is not finished.

The structure of the three main parts is identical. Parsons provides a potted biographical sketch of the author/artist, laying much of the groundwork for the following presentation and discussion of the central work(s). He bases his information on the usual biographies and summarises the work of earlier scholars. This need not be a bad thing and I, having only limited knowledge of the lives of Howard, Siegel and Shuster, found them quite informative. The interpretation of the selected texts follows the arguments found in canonical scholarship. In the case of Tolkien, it is mostly Carpenter, Garth and Shippey (no bad choice). However, central publications on the topic of Tolkien's reaction to modernity (Curry, Hiley), on the problem of the spiteful reactions of numerous literary critics to *The Lord of the Rings* (Curry again) or on the topic of Free Will (Dickerson, Flieger, Fornet-Ponse) are missing. I don't expect bibliographical completeness for completeness' sake, but Parsons's gap in the coverage of Free Will, for example, leads him into making such statements as "They [i.e. orcs] are automatons... they are organic robots whose only capacity is for cruelty" (20f). Such an impression may be caused by the interference of Jackson's movies in which orcs are indeed often portrayed as having no wills of their own. A close reading of Tolkien's text or the consultation of the relevant secondary literature would have made clear that orcs do have a Free Will!

What then is the use of this study? As said, it simply provides information on three important artistic creations of the first half of the 20th century, their respective backgrounds and a brief chapter on their 'afterlife'. Yet I have found no argument that would explain why they have been yoked together and presented as the origins of Modern Fantasy. I am sure that such an argument could be made (at least for the work of Tolkien and Howard), but Parsons simply did not bother to write this part of the book. So when John Rateliff wondered: "Have no idea why he threw Superman into the mix. No doubt all will become clear when I have a chance to actually read this." (http://sacnoths.blogspot.de/2015/02/the-new-arrivals-nine-books.html)—I have to disappoint John: it won't become clear. Thomas Honegger

Tolkien Studies: An Annual Scholarly Review, Vol. XI

Morgantown: West Virginia Univ. Press, 2014, 342 pp.

The summer break gave me the time to catch up with the most recent publications on Tolkien—and to re-adjust my inner critical benchmark. Coming back to *Tolkien Studies* after ploughing through half a dozen monographs and collections of essays of varied quality makes you realise again why *Tolkien Studies* is still the undisputed flagship in the field. Its contents, having gone through a demanding peer-reviewing process and some thorough proof-reading, are simply setting the gold standard. No misspellings or formatting mistakes (well, almost none), no plain factual errors or contradictory arguments or plain nonsense here! But enough eulogising—let us take a look at what the eleventh volume offers.

The issue opens with John Garth's fine piece investigating the nature of Tolkien's very early writings and their relevance to his legendarium. His essay will be discussed at some length since Garth does not make a single argument but presents several pieces of new evidence that potentially call for a re-assessment of what we thought about Tolkien's early writings. Garth starts by looking at 'The Voyage of Éarendel the Evening Star' in particular and detects parallels to Shelley's 'Arethusa' especially, but not only, in the metre and rhyme scheme Tolkien used. This is an interesting observation and its implications are far-reaching for the evaluation of young Tolkien's poetry. However, I was wondering whether the metre and rhyme scheme of 'Arethusa' is an original and uniquely 'Shelleyan' feature—a question that remains to be answered.

Garth then proceeds with an analysis of young Tolkien's (mostly philological) humour, investigates Tolkien's propensity for punning and discusses the 1911 parody 'The Battle of the Eastern Field'. He also considers the Stapledon Society minutes of 1913 and Tolkien's frequently humorous roles in different plays. Unfortunately, only a fraction of the early poems and plays have been made available to the public, and since we know only the titles of the great majority, we have to guess at their actual nature. Thus any conclusions must be provisional, but the evidence available suggests that the early parodic writings provided Tolkien with the opportunity to try out the rhetorical devices he later uses for more serious purposes, and the style he employed publicly for humorous effect may have been used privately more earnestly. Returning to Éarendel, Garth points out that Tolkien may not be primarily indebted to Grimm's *Teutonic Mythology* (as Shippey argued), but rather to Paul's *Grundriss der germanischen Philologie*, where Barend Symons links *Orendel* to Old Norse *aurr* = moisture, wetness and OE *eár* = sea, ocean, wave. "Thus the ur-hero behind these divergent later traditions is revealed, Symons argues, as a wanderer upon the waters, a seafarer, the central figure in a Germanic mariner myth, now lost..." (p. 14).

For the next 'source-of-inspiration' discovery Garth asks his readers to abandon their Old Norse and other Germanic source-predilections and argues for a close resemblance in some plot elements and exotic names between 'The Voyage of Éarendel the Evening Star' and Longfellow's *The Song of Hiawatha*. Longfellow's poem is also believed to be one of the sources of inspiration for Tolkien's *The Story of Kullervo* (which Garth dates to late 1914). More importantly, the names in the latter are proof for an early (1914) link between his work on Qenya and his storytelling since many of the names in *Kullervo* have a Qenya connection. "What can be stated with greater confidence is that in *The Story of Kullervo* Tolkien was combining his two parallel creative instincts—the desire to invent languages and to write stories—for the first time. His language had found a purpose beyond itself..." (p. 31) Garth thus corrects Dimitra Fimi's argument (as he points out in endnote 42, p. 41f.) which she had put forth in her fine monograph *Tolkien, Race and Cultural History* (2008), namely that Tolkien's poetic-literary creativity arose independently and parallel to his linguistic-philological impulse. Lastly, Garth argues that 'The Voyage of Éarendel the Evening Star' "pointed a way forward for creating a potentially endless stream of future stories: by inference and invention he could 'reconstruct' lost narratives that might have given rise to our surviving stock of myth, legend, folk-tale, or fairy-tale" (p. 31). All in all this is a substantial and well-argued essay and gives us food for thought since it forces us to revise some dear convictions, raises several interesting questions and shows clearly the importance of a more detailed investigation of Tolkien's early writings.

Sister Maria Frassati Jakupcak O.P. undertakes yet another 'revision' of a dear piece of 'lore'—if we take Garth's essay as a revision of a revision. Jakupcak starts by revisiting Carpenter's account of the famed evening walk by Tolkien, Lewis and Dyson and argues that the traditional focus on the theological dimension is misguided. The rift between Tolkien and Lewis, she contends, was not so much theological but rather of a literary nature. To underscore her point, Jakupcak takes Joseph Addison's (1672-1719) essays on 'The Pleasures of Imagination' in *The Spectator* (nos. 411-421) in order to compare Tolkien's and Lewis' views of literature. Her analysis uncovers numerous parallels between Addison's definition of the 'fairy way of writing' and Tolkien's concept of fairy stories as outlined in his Andrew Lang lecture in 1939. Developing her argument further, she argues that Tolkien is more on the side of *techne* (i.e. craft), and thus 18th century classicism à la Pope, whereas Lewis is on the side of brilliant inspiration and hence in line with Romanticism à la Wordsworth. Changing track, she then compares Tolkien's work to the temple of the Parthenon, whereas Lewis's work presumably resembles a Gothic cathedral. Jakupcak's architectural-stylistic argument rests on the two authors' respective ways of writing: Tolkien carefully honing his lines and phrases, whereas Lewis is known to jot down his texts more or less without revisions. Furthermore, the 19th century links fantastic literature with childhood (cf. George MacDonald), as does Lewis, whereas the 18th century and Tolkien link it with the past (cf. Macpherson). Although such a dichotomy has its charm and (limited) use in a contrastive discussion of the two authors, it seems to me a bit too exaggerated to label Lewis as a 'romanticist' and Tolkien as a 'classicist'—not least since Julian Eilmann's numerous publications on the 'romantic elements' in Tolkien's work point in the opposite direction. Jakupcak's essay works fine as a thought-experiment to highlight some peculiar features of either author, but the conclusions should not be generalised into an overall assessment.

The third contribution is a linguistic paper by Nelson Goering. It is somewhat technical but provides a sound framework for further explorations of the relationship between Sindarin and Quenya. Tolkien himself compared the two languages to the Celtic languages spoken in Britain at the time of the Roman invasion (43 AD) and Latin, respectively. Goering contends that it would thus be wrong to take contemporary Welsh, for example, as a model for Sindarin since their cultural status differs considerably. Sindarin must, on the one hand, be seen as a living, colloquial language to the learned Quenya. It is thus similar to the vernacular languages of medieval Europe that existed alongside Medieval Latin during the Middle Ages. On the other hand, Sindarin and Quenya are, typologically speaking, representatives of certain types of languages—with Quenya representing an 'archaic' stage of linguistic development, whereas Sindarin could be best characterised as 'middle' (Goering makes here use of Roger Lass' typology—which should have been briefly introduced for the non-linguist reader's sake). Goering's main point—and a valid one—is thus that we must be more careful and considerate when comparing the relationship between the Elvish languages such as Quenya and Sindarin to that between real-world languages. Simple shortcuts such as Sindarin = Welsh do not lead to mushrooms, but to linguistic error.

Bernhard Hirsch focuses on the homeward journey in *The Lord of the Rings*—a text that has not been analysed in depth by Tolkien scholars so far (though Antoine Paris, University Sorbonne, presented a paper on this topic in September 2015 at the 5th Hungarian Tolkien Conference in Budapest—obviously unaware of Hirsch's publication). Hirsch argues that both Frodo's and Bilbo's journeys are not linear but circular respectively helical and that the final part of *The Lord of the Rings* functions as a 'ritardando e diminuendo' after the dramatic climax at Mount Doom and the Field of Cormallen. He then gives a close reading of the return journey and scouring of the Shire. The former, according to Hirsch, signals the gradual transition from enchantment and mythic resonances of the Third Age toward the disenchanted realism of the Fourth Age and the re-entering into the little world of the Shire contrasts the readers' view of things with that of the inhabitants of Bree and the Shire, and thus reconnects with the mentality of the normal everyday lives—which puts events into a certain ironic contrast. 'The Scouring of the Shire' may be best seen as a coda to the War of the Ring. Structurally speaking, the coda does not necessarily provide closure, but has a retarding effect during which the hobbit protagonists experience an ascent. They who had been formerly ironic protagonists (in Frye's terminology) now become (almost?) high mimetic when confronted with their rather silly enemies. Furthermore, the 'Scouring', from the Hobbits' point of view, necessarily complements on a local level what the destruction of the Ring signalled on a universal level and also remedies some of the earlier flaws and reintegrates hobbit-society in greater harmony. Thus the return-chapters provide re-integration on several levels and complete the seasonal cycle, the stylistic arc of the text, and clean up unfinished plotlines. All in all a well-argued paper!

Richard Gallant's 'Original Sin in Heorot and Valinor' explores Tolkien's investigation of Germanic heroic elements (Northern courage, kin-slaying, oathswearing, overmastering pride, *Sippe*, feuding) in his legendarium. Gallant carefully and knowledgeably develops his argument on the basis of a plethora of medieval parallels and analogues (*Beowulf*, *The Battle of Maldon*, *Heliand*, Old Norse sagas, etc.) and draws from a wide variety of sources. The accumulated evidence leads him to identify the figure of Fëanor as the pivotal character for the tragic-heroic development of Elvish history, as the archetypical Germanic hero who is responsible for the introduction of these elements into Tolkien's Middle-earth (the Oath of Fëanor, the Kinslaying at Alqualondë and the ensuing feud)—and for urging the narrative onwards. It is Fëanor's overmastering pride, his often rash and wilful yet mostly heroic deeds that set in motion the events that, eventually, lead to the War of the Ring.

Michael Wodzak and Victoria Holtz Wodzak discuss in their contribution the nature and role of optical phenomena such as invisibility, the nature of seeing, the origin of rainbows, the workings of the convex mirror, and the nature of 'Unlight'. They start with a discussion of the phenomenon of invisibility, analyse it within the framework of modern science but also within (mostly) medieval theories of sight and perception. The latter proves a very fruitful approach since the theory of extramission seems to apply to many of the phenomena described by Tolkien. This theory, dating back to antiquity, argues that the eyes send out rays of light that touch upon the object and are thus able to produce an image. Although most of the instances discussed in the paper deal with evil protagonists and the exertion of power (Sauron, Glaurung, Smaug, Gollum, Shelob, etc.), we find also symptoms of extramission mentioned with positive characters (e.g. elves)—which would need an equally detailed analysis. The authors are also able to give the discussion of Saruman's 'multi-coloured' robe a new twist. Next to the well-known interpretation of the bands of the rainbow representing broken light, Wodzak and Wodzak adduce the medieval theory of the meteorological dome that reflects the rainbow light—making Saruman thus into a concave mirror which distorts things and people that come under his sway. Lastly, they look at the nature of Darkness as produced by the giant spider Ungoliant. Rather than simply being an absence of light we have here Corrupted Light or 'Unlight' with a very physical presence of its own. The paper, though often dealing with technical (physical) theory reads well, and it seems to me the re-writing of the piece on the same theme, more or less simultaneously published in *The Hobbit and Tolkien's Mythology. Essays on Revisions and Influences* (ed. Bradford Eden Lee. Jefferson NC: McFarland, 2014), has been worth the trouble.

The penultimate paper by Verlyn Flieger is an investigation into three areas of Tolkien's work that have given rise to contradictory interpretations: his stance on Christianity, Elves and Faërie, and, connected to the second topic, Faërian Drama. Flieger correctly points out that Tolkien often adapted his stance according to the addressees' likely point of view and that it is often difficult, if not impossible, to establish his opinion on these questions (e.g. whether he believed in the existence of Elves or not)—not least since no scholar since Humphrey Carpenter had access to Tolkien's diaries. Flieger's defence of Tolkien's contradictoriness turns the seeming flaw into a strength: "Tolkien's personality allowed him to contain his conflicts without resolving them" (p. 163). You cannot well argue against this. Yet what could (and maybe should) have been taken into account is the chronological dimension of the problem. We know from the rich material documenting Tolkien's work on his Elvish languages that he took the liberty to develop, revise or reject his earlier ideas on any topic, so that if we put early and late items next to each other we often end up with (seemingly) contradictory statements. Maybe we have a similar situation with Tolkien's much less documented ideas concerning the three aforementioned topics.

Lastly, Michael D.C. Drout, Namiko Hitotsubashi and Rachel Scavera provide a comprehensive discussion of the phenomenon of 'textual depth' in Tolkien's work and support their findings, among other things, by means of a lexomic analysis of some selected texts. The textual depth, according to the authors, is due to four major factors: "(1) the vast size and intricate detail of the background Tolkien created for his imagined world; (2) the ways he refers to this background material through seemingly casual and incomplete allusion; (3) the logical gaps and apparent inconsistencies in the stories; and (4) the variations in style within the given texts" (p. 167).

Each of these points is discussed in detail and the numerous versions of the Túrin story are used to exemplify the effects produced by such a rich textual tradition. The impression of depth of such a text—which has gone through numerous stages of revision, re-writing, re-casting and re-editing—is similar to that of many a medieval text. This point is 'proven' by a lexomic analysis of the *Silmarillion* version 'Of Túrin Turambar' which objectifies and renders visible Nagy's (earlier expressed) subjective impression of disunity. In the course of such a lexomic analysis the frequency, distribution, and arrangement of words in large-scale patterns occurring in different 'text-chunks' is compared and their relationship is visualised by means of dendrograms (tree-diagrams). The result is a graphic depiction of the multi-layered and often intricate transmission of Tolkien's texts. Within such a framework, Christopher Tolkien's editorial changes and alterations made to the original documents when preparing *The Silmarillion* are seen in a new light: he is credited as having contributed in a positive way to the creation of depth by stitching together multiple texts written at different times in different styles.

The volume concludes, as usual, with a substantial section containing book reviews and 'The Year's Work in Tolkien Studies 2011'.

Thomas Honegger

Jonathan Witt & Jay W. Richards:
The Hobbit Party
San Francisco: Ignatius Press, 2014, 232 pp.

The blurb claims that this book is the first to link Tolkien's religious faith to his political and economic outlooks as expressed in *The Hobbit* and *The Lord of the Rings*. Indeed it examines questions such as the nature of good and evil, power and authority, and the relationship of law and order to liberty, although often it uses Tolkien merely as a vehicle for these considerations, so its central concern is not literary. Indeed, a large amount of the discussion is derivative, and the populist style does not leave room for much rigorous argument.

What limits the value of this book for anyone interested in Tolkien and his thought is that it is a sermon rather than an analysis. It is certainly not the first book to attempt to enlist Tolkien as an ally in pushing a political programme, but this one is more insidious than most because of its boulevard press style. The problem is not that they get some facts wrong (e.g. Tom Shippey held the same chair as Tolkien at Leeds, not at Oxford (19)), they make false assertions through careless reading of a text, whether primary or secondary (Bilbo does not "sign a contract for adventure" (38) and Old Norse warriors do not fight to the death "for a just cause" (119), which is an anachronistic concept), and their memory of certain scenes owes more to Peter Jackson than to Tolkien (Aragorn does not fight against the Black Riders on Weathertop (112), since that is not unknown in more serious books, too). Witt and Richards both have doctorates and hold, or have held, university positions, so they obviously know how to carry out valid research, but it appears from their brief biographies on the dustjacket that they see themselves more as publicists than as academics.

It is undoubtedly a great skill to be able to explain complex ideas in simple terms, which is ideally what books for the layman do, but it is a clear misuse when over-simplification leads to the argument being biased towards one side. In this book the authors begin by cosying up to their readers by telling something about their everyday lives, and by reaching out to address them directly just like the narrator of *The Hobbit*. They make some valid points in the areas which they set out to investigate, but it is clear that they are starting off with an agenda of their own; they dispose of any interpretations differing from their own by *reductio ad absurdum*, by the use of emotive language, so that for example any regulation by a polity for the benefit of its citizens has to be "in pursuit of some drab workers' paradise of perfect income equality" (67), by citing one eccentric view to discredit a whole critical movement such as environmentalism (133), or by a straightforward appeal to the readers' common sense, which usually means prejudice.

So what is the agenda that they are pushing? The name of the publisher, Ignatius Press, and the Foreword by a Jesuit suggest that the book will be written from a Catholic perspective, which is not unusual in Tolkien studies. However, already on page 17 two popes are cited to establish the "inviolability of private property" and the condemnation of socialism, which suggests a strong connection with American Conservatism. This is soon associated with Tolkien's depiction of the Shire as a land with minimal government, ignoring the differences between an idealised fantasy creation and the complexity of 21st century life. However, lest anyone should be tempted to desire the small-scale local trade practised by the hobbits, we are given a lesson in the benefits of economies of scale, such as the ship that can carry 528,000,000 bananas to guarantee our banana for breakfast (149), thus rescuing international capitalism from the fear that Tolkienites might disapprove of it. We are told that this increases prosperity for the banana-producing countries, disingenuously forgetting that the trade is controlled by multinational companies. This is just one of the many clichés trotted out to make us believe that lack of regulation ensures freedom for everybody (without considering whether they have the financial means to exercise this freedom), and that it is precisely what Tolkien as a Catholic would have desired.

It is not entirely clear whether Witt and Richards are trying to say that ultra-Conservatism is good because it accords with Catholic teaching, or whether Catholicism is good because it supports the self-evident rightness of American ultra-Conservatism, but at any rate they want both to be sanctified by the benediction of St. John Ronald. No-one doubts the sincerity of Tolkien's religious beliefs, but the hi-jacking of his literary creations to bolster this smug political credo is, to say the least, distasteful.   Allan Turner

Edward L. Risden:
Tolkien's Intellectual Landscape
Jefferson NC: McFarland, 2015, 232 pp.

It was the medievalist Tom Shippey who, with *The Road to Middle-earth* (1982), published one of the first important (and, in my opinion, still unsurpassed) academic monographs on Tolkien. Other medievalists followed suit and developed Shippey's argument, so it comes as no surprise that the medievalist Edward L. Risden takes his senior colleague's publications as the starting point and sounding board for ideas of his own.

Risden presents his engagement with Tolkien's central ideas and concepts in a series of eight chapters, with the primary aim to explore the question of "to what human and contemporary issues does Tolkien return, and how does his work treat them?" (7). Yet before doing so, he sketches in his 'Introduction' the most important historical, political and cultural-intellectual developments and events of the 20th century. Although dangerously brief, such a contextualisation of Tolkien and his work within the framework of the 20th century becomes more and more important as the historical distance between our era and Tolkien's time increases.

The first chapter, then, takes a selection of essays from Tom Shippey's *Root and Branches* in order to discuss Tolkien's academic scholarship and to present various approaches towards Tolkien's fiction through his scholarly work on e.g. *Beowulf* or *Sir Gawain and the Green Knight*. Thus Risden's treatment of the academic work becomes (involuntarily?) another example of the strong contemporary tendency to use Tolkien's scholarly publications for a better understanding of his fiction (on this see Honegger). Tolkien's mostly non-linear narrative and his style constitute the other two foci of this chapter. While I found Risden's application of Chaos Theory to Tolkien's non-linear narrative style quite illuminating, I was not equally convinced of his attempt to compare Tolkien's textual structures with that of a Gothic cathedral. The discussion of Tolkien's style, lastly, was a bit short for my taste, mainly summarising the little research that has been done on this topic. I am also not always in agreement with Risden's use of terminology. Thus he writes that people like Elrond, Aragorn, and Boromir speak not different languages but "a dialect" (64). The term 'dialect' can be a bit misleading, not least since Tolkien uses clear and obvious dialect markers to characterise the speech of rural hobbits in the first chapters of *The Lord of the Rings* (see Johannesson). Elrond's (and other characters') stylistically marked use of the Common Speech could be best characterised by terms such as 'register' or 'variety'.

Peter Jackson's *The Lord of the Rings* movies often provide a welcome contrastive foil in the first chapter, e.g. in order to compare the differing narrative structures of film vs. book. This function is taken over in the second chapter by John Boorman's film *Excalibur* (1981). Risden opens this chapter with the generalising observation that medieval literature (and especially medieval romance) is primarily a quest for the 'Heart of Light' (e.g. in the form of the Grail) whereas modern literature often centres on a quest for the 'Heart of Darkness'—which becomes explicit in the fascination with the Dark Side prominent even in archetypical tales such as *Star Wars*. Tolkien's epic romance depicts the quest for the Heart of Light through the Heart of Darkness and the ending is therefore more hopeful than in Boorman's *Excalibur*, which retains much of its ambiguity to the very end. I agree with Risden's claim that *The Lord of the Rings* provides better guidance for modern readers, yet in my mind Boorman's movie, though not providing clear answers, successfully taps directly into the archetypical sphere.

The motif of the Waste Land is at the centre of the third chapter. Risden compares T.S. Eliot's use of the motif with that of Tolkien and notices an additional parallel between the two authors in so far as both reach an ultimately hopeful conclusion and healing: the one in 'Ash-Wednesday' and the other in 'The Return of the King'. It is a pity that Risden did not have access to Nicolay's study where we find an illuminating chapter on the motif of the Waste Land in Tolkien and the modernist writers.

Heroes and heroism is the theme of the fourth chapter in which Risden first discusses the Anglo-Saxon poems *Beowulf* and *The Battle of Maldon* as representatives of the epic-heroic and the historical-heroic modes respectively. He then contrasts Aragorn with Arthur and successfully applies Campbell's monomyth-pattern to both protagonists, arguing that Aragorn is an improved Arthur. This is certainly true in so far as Aragorn succeeds as a *renovator imperii* (which associates him rather with Charlemagne than with Arthur). In my opinion, the two figures of Arthur and Aragorn are related to each other by means of a shared archetype rather than a direct connection. The chapter concludes with an in-depth discussion of the motif of the broken sword. Here Risden's expertise as a medievalist comes to the fore and he regales his readers to a wide-ranging tour through medieval texts that feature 'broken swords'. Tolkien's protagonists, in contrast to their counterparts in medieval literature, reach their goals in spite of the broken weapon—mainly because in Tolkien's world objectives have to be achieved by means of human persistence and courage, and not by trusting in weapons!

This theme is continued in the fifth chapter where, in the first part, Risden explores the encounters with divine powers ('epiphanies') in selected works (most notably *Beowulf* and *The Lord of the Rings*) and reaches the conclusion that Beowulf as well as the hobbits succeed due to their courage and steadfastness rather than thanks to any supernatural help. The supernatural plays a role in the discussion of Faërie as presented in Tolkien's *On Fairy-stories* and Risden investigates not only Tolkien's ideas on Faërie but also the problem of Free Will and Good and Evil in connection with the elves. He correctly points out that Tolkien, in his presentation of the Eldar, continues the medieval tradition of depicting the inhabitants of the Otherworld as (at least) ambiguous. This is not really news to anyone who has paid attention to the discussion about Free Will and predestination in the works of Tolkien (cf. Tolkien, Flieger, and Fornet-Ponse), but may come as a surprise to those readers who have merely seen the movies.

This is symptomatic for the entire volume: I often had the feeling that the target-audience is not too clearly defined. Take, for example, the fascinating problem of the 'conjunction of spirit and flesh' with which Risden engages in the last part of chapter five. He gives his readers truly original insights into the decidedly physical nature of monsters in the Germanic tradition and connects them to Tolkien's approach—yet (astonishingly) without even mentioning the concept of *fëa* (soul/spirit) and *hröa* (body) that play a central role in Tolkien's legendarium. This does not detract from the value of Risden's insights, but if the target audience were to be primarily Tolkien scholars, then this aspect would have to be included.

Chapter six re-visits an old bone of contention among critics: Tolkien's depiction of women and other races and peoples. Taking Edward Said's concept of orientalism as his starting point, Risden analyses Tolkien's strategies of representing 'the Other' in his works and, apart from some minor points, presents two strong arguments in favour of Tolkien: firstly, Tolkien writes about topics (such as mortality or good vs. evil) of interest to humans in general—regardless of their biological sex. Secondly, although he composed his texts as a man of his time and from a specific cultural background, they deal with timeless and universal topics. It is this 'universal and timeless appeal' that makes Tolkien so successful across genres, cultures and generations. Critics who refuse or who are unable to see beyond the surface structure of Tolkien's texts will find fault with many of the narrative elements, yet miss the central themes. I found Risden's argument illuminating as well as refreshingly undogmatic. The second part of chapter six deals with the 'generational succession myths' found in various cultures and the author interprets *The Silmarillion* as a representative of this tradition. Ideas such as the 'handing down' of lore or power could have been additionally linked to Verlyn Flieger's trope of 'Splintered Light' and to the medieval concept of *translatio imperii* and *translatio studii*.

Leadership and how to choose between good and evil are the topics of the seventh chapter. Risden argues that Aragorn and Gandalf, with their dedication to protect and serve, embody and illustrate the essential qualities of leadership as found in contemporary leadership theories. Reading Tolkien (or any author) within a contemporary framework often yields interesting insights, yet I would have liked to see this supplemented by at least a passing reference to medieval leadership theory, as found in the genre of the 'Mirror for Princes'. Connected to the question of 'Which qualities are essential for a good leader?' is the problem of acting correctly, i.e. the ability to discern between good and evil and to choose accordingly. Risden touches upon a question that would ask for a monograph in order to provide a halfway satisfactory answer. His discussion comprising little more than five pages can merely suggest some tentative answers.

The final chapter, then, tackles the question of how and why to teach Tolkien. Here the medievalist comes to the fore and Risden is right in advocating the use of Tolkien's texts as a gateway to medieval literature, which, in turn, contributes towards a better understanding of his works. It is a pity Risden does not mention Stuart Lee's and Elizabeth Solopova's *Keys of Middle-earth* (new expanded and revised edition 2015), which has been written with exactly this aim in mind.

Risden concludes with an 'Afterword' that consists mainly of a list of sixteen Christian themes found in Tolkien. The list is extracted from the works of fellow Tolkien scholars Matthew Dickerson, Paul Kocher and Marjorie Burns and gives food for further thought. However, I personally would have preferred more Risden.

The volume concludes with a bibliography and an index.

All in all *Tolkien's Intellectual Landscape* is worth reading. The text could have done with another round of proofreading (I came across a dozen typos or omissions of words) and one could have included in the bibliography some more titles of relevance for the topics discussed. However, these are in Risden's case minor faults and weigh less than in other cases since this volume is mostly about ideas and concepts. The format in which Risden develops his arguments is sometimes a bit unusual since he often directly engages with the publications of scholars such as Shippey or Flieger. As a consequence, some chapters read almost like commented reviews of some of their works. However, I'd rather have a fellow medievalist developing (often) new ideas by means of a discursive engagement with existing publications than a more comprehensive but in the end merely reproductive presentation of scholarship.

Thomas Honegger

References:

Flieger, Verlyn. 'The Music and the Task. Fate and Free Will in Middle-earth." *Tolkien Studies* VI (2009): 151-181

Fornet-Ponse, Thomas. '"Strange and Free" – On Some Aspects of the Nature of Elves and Men.' *Tolkien Studies* VII (2010): 67-89

Honegger, Thomas. "Academic Writings". *A Companion to J.R.R. Tolkien.* Ed. Stuart Lee. Oxford: Wiley Blackwell, 2014. 27-40

Johannesson, Nils-Lennart. "The Speech of the Individual and of the Community in *The Lord of the Rings".* *News from the Shire and Beyond.* Eds. Peter Buchs & Thomas Honegger. Zurich/Berne: Walking Tree Publishers, 1997. 11-47

Lee, Stuart, & Elizabeth Slopova (Eds.). *The Keys of Middle-earth. Discovering Medieval Literature through the Works of J.R.R. Tolkien.* 2nd ed. London: Palgrave Macmillan, 2015

Nicolay, Theresa Freda. *Tolkien and the Modernists. Literary Responses to the Dark New Days of the 20th Century.* Jefferson NC: McFarlane, 2014

Tolkien, J.R.R. 2009. "Fate and Free Will". *Tolkien Studies* VI (2009): 183-188

Rudolf Simek:
Monster im Mittelalter. Die phantastische Welt der Wundervölker und Fabelwesen

Köln/Weimar/Wien: Böhlau, 2015, 345 S.

We live in a time of monsters.[1] Diese Worte Jeffrey Jerome Cohens sind u.a. treffender Ausdruck einer umfassenden Präsenz des Monströsen in Literatur und Medien unserer Zeit. Rudolf Simek legt hier nun ein Werk vor, das sich gerade nicht hauptsächlich mit unserer, sondern einer lang vergangenen Zeit befasst: Er thematisiert das Monster im Mittelalter. In einem ersten Teil bietet der Verfasser einen Abriss zu Entwicklung und kulturellen Funktion der Monster in der Epoche, um im Folgenden eine lexikalische Zusammenstellung zahlreicher Kreaturen zu präsentieren. Simek, seit 1995 Lehrstuhlinhaber für Ältere Germanistik mit Einschluss des Nordischen an der Universität Bonn, beweist hier eine immense Kenntnis der Materie und bietet eine Zusammenschau von allen in der bekannten mittelalterlichen Literatur erwähnten monströsen Kreaturen.

Der erste Teil schildert zunächst die „lange Geschichte der Monster in der europäischen Kultur" (25), um sich dann speziell dem Mittelalter zuzuwenden. Hier stellt der Autor Kategorien von Wundervölkern vor, die mit Erläuterungen zu Meermonstern und Sonderformen der antiken Mythologie ergänzt werden. Seine Ausführungen bewegen sich durchweg sehr nah an den Quellen, wobei Zitate sowohl im originalen Wortlaut als auch in übersetzter Form wiedergeben werden.

Einen Schwerpunkt legt Simek auf die Abgrenzung des mittelalterlichen Verständnisses von Monster zu einer modernen Definition des Begriffs. So wird plausibel dargelegt, dass erstens jeglichem mittelalterlichen Monster (mit Ausnahme bereits erwähnter Meerwesen) ein gewisser Grad an Menschlichkeit zugrunde liegen musste und zweitens diese meist als nicht gefährlich angesehen wurden, auch weil man sie an der Peripherie des bekannten bzw. des den Menschen zugänglichen Raums verortete. Für die Theologie ergab sich hieraus das Problem, die Monster als teilweise menschlich dem christlichen Glauben zuführen, sie taufen zu müssen. Weiterhin verstand man die Monster als Völker, nicht als einzelne Wesen, wie etwa den Minotaurus. Definiert Simek also einerseits sehr kleinschrittig das mittelalterliche Monster, erscheint die Abgrenzung zu einem modernen Begriffsverständnis als etwas unscharf. Hier

---

1　Cohen, Jeffrey Jerome. "Monster Culture. Seven Theses". *Monster theory. Reading culture.* Hg. ders. Minneapolis: University of Minnesota Press, 1996, S. 3-25, hier: S. 3.

wäre vielleicht die verstärkte Aufnahme verschiedener Definitionsvorschlä-
ge – wie etwa von Hans Richard Brittnacher oder des einführend erwähnten
Cohen – wünschenswert gewesen.

Nach der umfangreichen Präsentation mittelalterlicher Monster sowie deren
Bedeutung in der Kultur der Epoche (siehe hier besonders Kap. 7.3) schlägt
Simek den Bogen hin zur Rezeption der Wundervölker in der Frühen Neuzeit
einer- und in der modernen Phantastik andererseits. Er stellt fest, dass sich
mit der Entdeckung Amerikas am Ausgang des 15. Jahrhunderts der Diskurs
um die Monster zu verändern beginnt. Mit der Rückkehr des Kolumbus aus
der sogenannten Neuen Welt wurde die Auseinandersetzung mit Wundervölkern nicht mehr auf rein theoretischer Ebene geführt, da diese nun konkret
erreichbar schienen. Hier standen vor allem die (wirklichen oder angenommenen) Anthropophagen im Fokus, da diesen – im Gegensatz zu anderen
amerikanisch-indigenen Ethnien – die Menschlichkeit abgesprochen wurde,
sie also rechtmäßig versklavt werden durften.

Im 20. Jahrhundert sieht der Verfasser eine Art Renaissance der Wundervölker in Werken der Science-Fiction und Fantasy. Wären die Monster im
Mittelalter an den Rändern der bekannten Welt angesiedelt worden, so fänden
sie sich nun als Aliens an den Rändern des uns heute bekannten Raums, auf
fremden Planeten. Diese Außerirdischen ähneln in ihren Darstellungsformen
durchaus mittelalterlichen Wunderwesen, wie Simek anhand der sogenannten
„Alien Time Line" belegt. In der Fantasy sieht der Autor einen Trend, das
Monströse nicht von den Wundervölkern, sondern von Figuren der niederen
Mythologie aus zu gestalten. So nimmt beispielsweise Tolkien für seine nach
unserem Verständnis sicherlich monströsen Kreaturen stark auf Letztere Bezug
und bevölkert Mittelerde mit ihnen. Abschließend gelangt Simek zu dem plau-
siblen Schluss, dass es „wohl tatsächlich nur der Abstand vom Zentrum an die
Peripherie einer sich zumindest in Theorie und Phantasie ständig vergrößernden
Ökumene [sei], der im letzten Jahrtausend in Bezug auf die Wundervölker
zugenommen hat" (198).

Der zweite Teil des Werkes widmet sich dem angesprochenen lexikalischen
Überblick aller mittelalterlichen Monster mit Ausnahme der Meerwesen; die
bekannten Amazonen werden ebenso vorgestellt wie beispielsweise die Orestas,
die lediglich in der *Weltchronik* Rudolfs von Ems sowie der *Imago mundi* des
Honorius von Autun Erwähnung finden. Die Ausführungen zu den einzelnen
Lemmata sind meist knapp, dennoch aber informativ gestaltet und bieten eine
kurze Darstellung des jeweiligen Wundervolks, ergänzt durch Hinweise auf
sein Auftauchen in den Quellen sowie einige Literaturhinweise.

Gerade mit diesem zweiten Teil seines Buches bietet Simek der Forschung wie
auch dem interessierten Laien eine überaus wertvolle Handreichung, existiert
eine derartige Zusammenschau doch bislang nicht. Auch der erste Teil weiß

zu überzeugen mit einer sehr gelungenen Darstellung einer umfangreichen Thematik. Hier sind besonders die Erklärungsansätze für die Monster einmal aus mittelalterlicher, einmal aus moderner Sicht hervorzuheben. Rudolf Simek schließt mit dem Band eine jahrzehntelange Auseinandersetzung mit der Thematik ab und diese umfassende Erfahrung merkt man dem Werk an. Der Autor legt hier einen Text vor, der sich sicherlich als ein Standardwerk nicht nur der Mediävistik etablieren wird.   Jan Niklas Meier

Ralph C. Wood (Ed.):
Tolkien among the Moderns

Notre Dame IN: University of Notre Dame Press, 2015, 303 pp.

Tom Shippey is to blame. Ever since his *J.R.R. Tolkien. Author of the Century* (2000), the discussion about Tolkien's relationship and connection with writers of modernity such as Joyce, Eliot or Orwell has grown into an important area of research for Tolkien studies. In addition to individual essays published in journals, e.g. the issue of *Modern Fiction Studies* 50.4 (2004) and collections of papers, we have to date two volumes of essays (Honegger & Weinreich) and two monographs (Hiley and Nicolay) on the topic. Tolkien's relationship with 'modernity' as a cultural-political phenomenon that goes beyond literature has been explored most prominently by Patrick Curry in his book *Defending Middle-earth. Tolkien: Myth and Modernity* and in his various essays on the topic (available in collected form in his volume *Deep Roots*).

The volume of essays edited by Ralph C. Wood can therefore look back onto a critical discourse of almost two decades—if the authors had bothered to take a look, that is. Unfortunately, neither Patrick Curry's ideas on Tolkien and modernity seem to be known (NB: his *Defending Middle-earth* was published in 1998 by HarperCollins, which is no marginal publisher, and carries both 'Tolkien' and 'Modernity' on its cover) nor is Margaret Hiley's monograph mentioned (Nicolay's study would have come out too late for inclusion). Astonishingly, Honegger & Weinreich's volumes make an appearance in Donnelly's essay—which is a laudable exception also in so far as Donnelly gives the reader a definition of what he understands under the term 'modern' and 'modernity' (something that is sadly missing in the rather short introduction). The overall impression after reading the essays is, however, that there was no overall clear focus on 'modernity' as a concept and that they lack a clearly delineated discursive framework. As a consequence, the essays read a bit like a collection of thoughts by experts from different fields with the common denominator 'Tolkien' and 'not the Middle Ages'.

Germaine Paulo Walsh opens with a substantial discussion of Plato's critique of poetry/fiction as deceiving the audience by presenting images instead of giving access to 'real things' and as undermining morality, and Tolkien's 'response' to the Platonic charges in his works of fiction as well as in his more theoretical works (esp. his lecture-cum-essay *On Fairy-stories*). In how far Tolkien's writings are intended to refute Plato's charges remains debatable, though there are sufficient hints that he was aware of and disagreed with the Platonic points of view and the 'parallel reading' of Tolkien and Plato does provide some startling insights (e.g. p. 19 where Walsh describes Gollum's way down to the roots of the Misty Mountains as a reversal of Plato's Allegory of the Cave). However, the fact that Walsh does not even mention Tolkien's poem *Mythopoeia* with its clearly Platonic theme nor Weinreich's essay exploring this very Platonic theme is detrimental to the value of his paper. It is a bit like constructing an argument in court without knowing about the existence of a crown-witness.

Helen Lasseter Freeh's paper on Fate, Providence and Free Will suffers to some extent from a similar flaw. She wisely limits her inquiry to *The Silmarillion* and has read Dickerson's study, which is relevant for her topic, yet does not seem to know either Tolkien's piece on 'Fate and Free Will', edited 2009 by Carl F. Hostetter and published in *Tolkien Studies* VI, or Verlyn Flieger's paper on Free Will in the same issue, or Thomas Fornet-Ponse's informed response in *Tolkien Studies* VII (2010). Her argument, though sound in itself, is thus severely impaired since she does not link it to the current debate on the very topic within Tolkien studies, nor is the connection to the discussion of Fate, Providence and Free Will among 'the moderns' made explicit.

The essays so far have suffered from flaws within a more or less sound structure. Michael D. Thomas' comparison of Cervantes' *Don Quijote de la Mancha* and *The Lord of the Rings*, however, overtaxes even a very tolerant reader's patience. It is an unfortunate and failed example of 'comparative criticism' since the two works chosen have some superficial similarities ("their novels [sic!] both exceed a thousand pages..." (79)) yet are radically different in spirit. And the claim that "the word 'knight' never appears in *The Lord of the Rings*" (82) makes the hackles of any attentive reader rise since it is blatantly false—as proved by a brief look into Richard Blackwelder's *Thesaurus*, where we find at least a score of quotes from *The Lord of the Rings* using the very word that is supposedly non-existent.

'The night is darkest before dawn.' That is also true for this volume. After Thomas' piece things brighten up. Peter M. Candler Jr.'s paper on Tolkien and Nietzsche is an unacknowledged reprint from the volume edited by Caldecott & Honegger (the author seems to have forgotten to mention this—so the reviewer had a Nietzschean moment of 'recurrence' when (re-)reading the paper he had edited eight years ago). Candler compares both Tolkien's and Nietzsche's opposition to modernity and their means to counter the threat posed by the machine. Yet while Nietzsche sees power as the only possible answer to the problem, Tolkien favours a response that relies on the re-enchantment of the world and on sub-creative art.

Candler's discussion of Tolkien and Nietzsche is followed by one of the highlights of the volume: Philip J. Donnelly's investigation of the typical characteristics of modern artists (as seen in Joyce's works—namely the primacy of individual freedom, the detachment of aesthetics from ethics, and the subordination of friendship to artistic freedom) and their contrastive comparison with 'Bilbo the poet'. Donnelly writes persuasively and structures his argument clearly, defines his terminology (as mentioned, he is the only contributor to bother about clarifying what he means by 'modern' and 'modernity'), has 'done his homework' in matters of bibliographical research, and the reader finishes his essay with the feeling that she/he has learnt something more about why Tolkien differs from his modernist contemporaries. The comparison Joyce vs. Tolkien is continued by Dominic Manganiello, who focuses on the depiction of Bloom and Frodo, respectively. While Joyce's isolated hero is striving for a humanistic good in an ironic narrative, the heroism of Tolkien's protagonists is meaningful not so much for them as individuals, but in their support for each other and for offering a "countervision based on a providential hope that exists beyond the void and the walls of the world" (186).

Leaving Joyce behind, we proceed to scholar, writer, critic and avowed Tolkien-afficionado Iris Murdoch. Scott H. Moore outlines some of the biographical points of contact between the two Oxford academics, but the main argument rests on an informed discussion of their respective views of the function of literature and art. As Moore shows, Murdoch's view is often "deeply compatible with Tolkien's vision, however much he might have objected to her use of terms" (204). By the way: Tolkien's essay *On Fairy-stories* was NOT "originally published in the volume *Tree and Leaf* in 1964", as Moore thinks (203) but much earlier (1947).

Joseph Tadie's essay struck me as something of a problem in so far as he levels the big guns of a sophisticated and rhetorically advanced philosophical inquiry (mostly) on *The Hobbit* and reads this children's book through the lens of Emmanuel Levinas' philosophy. As much as I love *The Hobbit* as a tale, I felt that it cannot adequately carry the burden of such a philosophical investigation, let alone language such as "In spite of this… description of the infinite dimension of the ethical relation, Levinas offers an estimable adumbration of Tolkien's appreciation of the release available to the creatures of Middle-earth…" (223). I am therefore not sure whether Tadie's essay was not written tongue-in-cheek—in the tradition of books such as *Pooh and the Philosophers*.

The concluding paper is by Ralph C. Wood, the editor of the volume. It is a well-written theoretical but generally understandable discussion of Tolkien's critique of modernism and how this links him to the phenomenon of post-modernism, without (as Wood rightly stresses) making him into a post-modernist himself. Patrick Curry has put forward similar ideas before, but from a non-Christian point of view, whereas Wood grounds Tolkien's critique of modernity in his Catholic faith. The outcome is the same and both scholars argue that, in contrast to the abstract principles of modernity, Tolkien's ethics are based on very concrete ties of friendship and affection, and truth is not abstract but always storied and concrete. Wood's *interpretatio Christiana* makes him take at face value obviously biased arguments (e.g. Bede's account of the depressingly hopeless pagan view of human life (262), which Bede put into the mouth of one of King Edwin's chief men—a clever piece of Dark Age propaganda that should be seen as exactly that and not as a supposedly authentic depiction of the pagan view of the world) but it also made me see familiar scenes in Tolkien's texts in a new light (e.g. the interpretation of the dialogue between Aragorn and the mortally wounded Boromir as an instance of sacramental penance (271)).

What, then is the final score? In my opinion, it is a volume that offers two excellent papers of general interest (Donnelly, Wood), some that are impaired by oversights of publications in the current discourse and not really connected to modernity, yet will be of interest to researchers in their specific fields of study (e.g. Walsh, Freeh), one I'd call a failure (Thomas), and one that I enjoyed reading yet which I felt must be at least partially tongue-in-cheek (Tadie). The text *per se* is free of spelling mistakes or typos—no matter of course nowadays!

Thomas Honegger

References:

Caldecott, Stratford & Thomas Honegger (Eds.). *Tolkien's The Lord of the Rings. Sources of Inspiration*. Zurich/Berne: Walking Tree Publishers, 2008

Curry, Patrick. *Defending Middle-earth. Tolkien: Myth and Modernity*. Edinburgh: Floris Books / London: HarperCollins, 1997/98 (re-issued 2004 by Mariner Books)

---. *Deep Roots in Times of Frost*. Zurich/Jena: Walking Tree Publishers, 2014

Flieger, Verlyn. "The Music and the Task. Fate and Free Will in Middle-earth." *Tolkien Studies* VI (2009): 151-181

Fornet-Ponse, Thomas. "'Strange and Free' – On Some Aspects of the Nature of Elves and Men." *Tolkien Studies* VII (2010): 67-89

Hiley, Margaret. *The Loss and the Silence. Aspects of Modernism in the Works of C.S. Lewis, J.R.R. Tolkien & Charles Williams.* Zurich/Jena: Walking Tree Publishers, 2011

Honegger, Thomas & Frank Weinreich, Eds. *Tolkien and Modernity.* Two volumes. Zurich/Berne: Walking Tree Publishers, 2006

Nicolay, Theresa Freda. *Tolkien and the Modernists. Literary Responses to the Dark New Days of the 20th Century.* Jefferson NC: McFarlane, 2014

Tolkien, J.R.R. 2009. "Fate and Free Will". *Tolkien Studies* VI (2009): 183-188

Weinreich, Frank. "Metaphysics of Myth. The Platonic Ontology of 'Mythopoeia'". *Tolkien's Shorter Works. Proceedings of the Jena Conference 2007.* Eds. Margarete Hiley & Frank Weinreich. Zurich/Jena: Walking Tree Publishers, 2007. 25-347

Our Authors

Julian Tim Morton Eilmann, Dr. phil., studied History, German Philology, and History of Arts at Aachen and Nottingham and is currently working as a teacher for German, History and Literature at Inda-Gymnasium in Aachen. He conducts advanced training for teachers in films. He is member of the board of editors of *Hither Shore*, publishes since many years on Tolkien's works, and has recently written his dissertation on the topic of *Tolkien as Romanticist and Poet*.
julianeilmann@web.de

Thomas Fornet-Ponse, Dr. theol. Dr. phil., studied Catholic Theology, Philosophy, and Ancient History at Bonn and Jerusalem. He received his PhD in Fundamental Theology and Ecumenics from the University of Salzburg and his PhD in Philosophy from the University of Bonn. He was a committee member of the German Tolkien Society and has been charged with conceptually coordinating the DTG Tolkien Seminars as well as *Hither Shore*.
thomas.fornet-ponse@tolkiengesellschaft.de

Zsuzsa Gáti, Dr. phil., is a lecturer at the Finno-Ugrian Studies Sub-department of the Department of European and Comparative Literature and Language Studies of the University of Vienna. Her research interests include narratology, game studies, storytelling in different media and literary phenomena, especially in fairy tales.
zsuzsa.gati@univie.ac.at

Markus Gut studied German Philology and History in Zurich and is currently working on his PhD thesis at the German Department of the University of Zurich. His research interests focus on semiology, rhetorics and hermeneutics, German literature around 1800 and he published on Middle High German poetry.
markus.gut@uzh.ch

Thomas Honegger received his PhD from the University of Zurich. Apart from his publications on animals (real and imaginary) and Tolkien, he has written about Chaucer, Shakespeare, and medieval romance. He is, since 2002, Professor for English Medieval Studies at the Friedrich Schiller University, Jena.
tm.honegger@uni-jena.de

Gerard Hynes received his PhD from Trinity College, Dublin, where he teaches on the MPhil in Popular Literature and the MPhil in Children's Literature. He is the co-editor of *Tolkien: The Forest and the City* (Dublin: 2013) and has written articles on J.R.R. Tolkien, China Miéville and George R.R. Martin. He has a number of publications forthcoming on the theory and practice of world-building, working towards a monograph on the subject.
ghynes@tcd.ie

Danko Kamčevski has a university degree in English Language and Literature, and has worked as an English teacher and translator. He is currently a doctoral candidate at the University of Kragujevac (Serbia) and in his doctoral thesis he investigates the connections between medieval romance and Tolkien's works. He has written on the Gawain-poet. He is a member of the Tolkien Society. His interests include medieval literature, contemporary fantasy, and philosophy.
dkamcevski@gmail.com

Wilhelm Kuehs, Mag. Dr., studied German Philology and General and Comparative Literature in Klagenfurt. He works as lecturer at the Institut für Kulturanalyse at the AAU Klagenfurt. He has written several novels and non-fictional books.
w.kuehs@gmx.at

Timo Lothmann is a researcher and lecturer of English linguistics at RWTH Aachen where he completed his PhD on the *Tok Pisin Bible* translation in 2006. He has also taught at the universities of Münster and Paderborn. His research interests include reading and translation processing, pidgins and creoles, and post-colonialism. Recent publications comprise a metaphor approach to literary identity. Currently, he focuses on fields of application of conceptual metaphor and blending theory.
lothmann@anglistik.rwth-aachen.de

Marguerite Mouton recieved her PhD in Comparative Literature and Literary Theory from the University Paris 13 (France), where she taught French literature, before teaching at the University of Cergy-Pontoise. Her thesis, to be published by Classiques Garnier Editors, is entitled: *The "Deep Enchantments" of the Epic: Highlighting a New Epic Model with regard to the Powers of Imagination in the Works of Victor Hugo and J.R.R. Tolkien (*Notre-Dame de Paris *and* La Légende des siècles, The Book of Lost Tales, The Lays of Beleriand *and* The Lord of the Rings*).
marguerite.mouton@laposte.net

Anca Muntean studied Comparative Literature in Cluj-Napoca (Romania) and Paris and is currently writing a PhD thesis on the dynamics of the literary genres (fairy tale, romance, novel, fantasy) in J.R.R. Tolkien's work. She has published articles on different topics in Romanian literary journals and several entries in the *Dictionnaire Tolkien* (2012, CNRS Editions), under the supervision of Vincent Ferré.
ancagmuntean@gmail.com

Jonathan Nauman (PhD Duke, 1992) has published papers on the York Cycle of mystery plays, *Macbeth*, T.S. Eliot and W.B. Yeats, and especially the metaphysical poets George Herbert and Henry Vaughan. He lives in Beverly MA and works as an engineering technologist.
jonnauman@hotmail.com

Łukasz Neubauer, Dr. phil., studied English Philology at the Nicolaus Copernicus University in Toruń (Poland) and Scandinavian Literature at the University of Bergen (Norway). He received his PhD in English Philology from the University of Łódź (Poland). He is a member of the British branch of the International Arthurian Society and a conceptual coordinator of the annual Medieval Fantasy Symposium in Unieście (Poland).   lukasz_neubauer@poczta.onet.pl

Friedhelm Schneidewind studied Biology and some terms Computer Science. He is currently working as a free-lance teacher especially for media design and in commercial and economical subjects, as journalist, editor, publisher, musician, and as author of several lexicons and several books on mythology, fantastic literature and Tolkien.   www.friedhelm-schneidewind.de

Janek Scholz teaches in the interdisciplinary branch of the Bachelor course "Linguistics and Literature Studies" at RWTH Aachen. In his PhD project at the Department of Romance Philology he compares texts from Brazil, Italy, Germany, and England to find out how games get out of control. His research interests are aimed at the sociology of space, game, and other inter-spaces in which humans go beyond the ordinary.   janek.scholz@ifaar.rwth-aachen.de

Guglielmo Spirito is a Conventual Franciscan Friar (= Minorit) working and living in Assisi. In Rome he got his PhD in Theology with specialisation in Spirituality at the Antonianum. Since 1994, he is professor at the Theological Institute of Assisi and at the Pontifical Faculty of Saint Bonaventure in Rome. He gave courses of Theology in Canada, Croatia, Romania, Russia, Mexico, Lebanon, and Kenya, as well as lectures on Tolkien in England, Germany, France, and Canada. On J.R.R. Tolkien he had published essays, articles, and books as well as several papers with Walking Tree Publishers and in *Hither Shore*.   fraguspi@gmail.com

Claudio Testi obtained his PhD in Philosophy at the University of Bologna. He is President of the Institute of Thomistical Studies of Modena and Vice President of the Italian Association for Tolkien Studies. He teaches Formal Logic at the Dominican Philosophical Study in Bologna and his publications range from exegetical studies on Aquinas's Metaphysics to essays in logic and epistemology. He is director of the series *Tolkien e Dintorni*, a collection of critical studies and translations concerning Tolkien and the Inklings, and has edited several books on Tolkien. As author he has written several articles and a book on Tolkien.   claudio.testi1967@gmail.com

Allan Turner has recently retired from a career spent as lecturer in English, most recently at the Friedrich Schiller University Jena. He looks forward to being able to spend more time on research into translation studies and stylistics, particularly in relation to Tolkien.   allangturner@aol.com

Christian Weichmann holds a PhD in physics from the university of Bonn. He published diverse papers on Tolkien. He is a member of the board of the German Tolkien Society and is also a member of Unquendor, the Tolkien Society and the Austrian Tolkien Society. He works as technical software developer in Braunschweig.   christian.weichmann@tolkiengesellschaft.de

Frank Weinreich, Dr. phil., studied Communication Science, Political Science and Philosophy and wrote his PhD thesis in Philosophy. His primary research interests with numerous publications are ethics, ontology, media, engineering results assessment, philosophy of science and fantastic. He is currently working as free-lance editor and literary scout for several publishers.

fw@polyoinos.com

Renée Vink has a Masters degree in Scandinavian languages, including Old Norse, and works as a translator from Swedish, Norwegian, Danish, German and English. Among other things, she is the Dutch translator of the poetry in *The Legend of Sigurd and Gudrún*, of *The Fall of Arthur, The Story of Kullervo*, and Tolkien's *Beowulf.*   rvink7@hotmail.com

Unsere Autorinnen & Autoren

Julian Tim Morton Eilmann, Dr. phil., studierte Geschichte, Germanistik und Kunstgeschichte in Aachen und Nottingham und ist gegenwärtig Studienrat für Deutsch, Geschichte und Literatur am Inda-Gymnasium in Aachen. Im Auftrag der Bezirksregierung Köln leitet er Lehrerfortbildungen im Filmbereich. In der Deutschen Tolkien Gesellschaft ist er Mitherausgeber des wissenschaftlichen Jahrbuches *Hither Shore*. Er forscht seit vielen Jahren zu Tolkiens Werk und hat zum Thema *J.R.R. Tolkien - Romantiker & Lyriker* promoviert. Für seine Bemühungen um die Tolkien-Forschung wurde er 2013 mit der Ehrendoktorwürde des Verlages Walking Tree Publishers ausgezeichnet.

julianeilmann@web.de

Thomas Fornet-Ponse, Dr. theol. Dr. phil., studierte Katholische Theologie, Philosophie und Alte Geschichte in Bonn und Jerusalem. Er wurde in Fundamentaltheologie und Ökumenischer Theologie in Salzburg und in Philosopie in Bonn promoviert. Er war Vorstandsmitglied der Deutschen Tolkien Gesellschaft und ist der inhaltliche Koordinater der Tolkien Seminare wie von *Hither Shore*.

thomas.fornet-ponse@tolkiengesellschaft.de

Zsuzsa Gáti, Dr. phil., ist Lektorin an der Abteilung für Finno-Ugristik am Institut für Europäische und Vergleichende Sprach- und Literaturwissenschaft der Universität Wien. Ihre Forschungsinteressen beinhalten Narratologie, Spielstudien, Digital Humanities, Erzählweisen in verschiedenen medialen und literarischen Phänomenen, insbesondere in Märchen.   zsuzsa.gati@univie.ac.at

Markus Gut hat in Zürich Germanistik und Geschichte studiert und arbeitet zurzeit an seiner Dissertation am Deutschen Seminar der Universität Zürich. Seine Forschungsinteressen liegen im Feld der Semiologie, Rhetorik und Hermeneutik, der Deutschen Literatur um 1800. Auch publizierte er zur mittelhochdeutschen Lyrik.   markus.gut@uzh.ch

Thomas Honegger, Prof. Dr. phil., wurde von der Universität Zürich promoviert. Neben seinen Veröffentlichungen über (reale und imaginäre) Tiere und Tolkien, hat er über Chaucer, Shakespeare und mittelalterliche Romanze geschrieben. Seit 2002 ist er Professor für anglistische Mediävistik an der Friedrich-Schiller-Universität Jena.   tm.honegger@uni-jena.de

Gerard Hynes, PhD, wurde vom Trinity College Dublin promoviert, wo er in den Masterstudiengängen Populäre Literatur und Kinderliteratur lehrt. Er ist Mitherausgeber von *Tolkien: The Forest and the City* (Dublin 2013) und publizierte Aufsätze über J.R.R. Tolkien, China Miéville und George R.R. Martin. Eine Reihe von Veröffentlichungen über die Theorie und Praxis der Weltenbildung im Blick auf eine Monographie darüber ist in Vorbereitung.   ghynes@tcd.ie

Danko Kamčevski hat englische Sprache und Literatur studiert und arbeitet als Englischlehrer und Übersetzer. Gegenwärtig promoviert er an der Universität Kragujevac (Serbien) über die Verbindungen zwischen mittelalterlichen Romanzen und Tolkiens Werken. Darüber hinaus schrieb er über den Dichter des Gawain und ist Mitglied der Tolkien Society. Seine Forschungsinteressen beinhalten mittelalterliche Literatur, gegenwärtige Fantasy und Philosophie.
dkamcevski@gmail.com

Wilhelm Kuehs, Mag. Dr., Studium der Germanistik und Komparatistik in Klagenfurt. Er ist Lehrbeauftrager am Institut für Kulturanalyse an der AAU Klagenfurt sowie Autor mehrerer Romane und Sachbücher, zuletzt u.a.: *Mythenweber – Mythos und soziales Handeln.*   w.kuehs@gmx.at

Timo Lothmann lehrt und forscht am Lehrstuhl für Anglistische Sprachwissenschaft der RWTH Aachen, wo er 2006 über die Tok-Pisin-Bibelübersetzung promovierte. Er lehrte außerdem an den Universitäten Münster und Paderborn. Seine Forschungsinteressen beinhalten Lese- und Übersetzungsprozesse, Pidgin- und Kreolsprachen sowie Postkolonialismus. Er legt Gewicht auf eine interdisziplinäre Perspektive. Zu seinen neueren Veröffentlichungen zählt ein metapherbasierter Ansatz zur Erklärung literarischer Identität.
lothmann@anglistik.rwth-aachen.de

Marguerite Mouton, Dr. phil., wurde in vergleichender Literaturwissenschaft und Literaturtheorie von der Universität Paris 13 promoviert, wo sie französische Literatur unterrichtete, bevor sie zur Universität Cergy-Pontoise wechselte. Ihre Dissertation trägt den Titel *Die 'tiefen Verzauberungen' des Epischen: Herausstellung eines neuen epischen Modells mit Bezug auf die Imaginationskräfte in den Werken von Victor Hugo und J.R.R. Tolkien* (Notre-Dame de Paris *und* La Légende des siècles; The Book of Lost Tales, The Lays of Beleriand *und* The Lord of the Rings*).*   marguerite.mouton@laposte.net

Anca Muntean studierte vergleichende Literaturwissenschaft in Cluj-Napoca (Rumänien) und Paris und arbeitet gegenwärtig an einer Dissertation über die Dynamiken der literarischen Genres in Tolkiens Werken (Märchen, Romanze, Roman, Fantasy). Sie veröffentlichte über verschiedene Themen in rumänischen Literaturzeitschriften und verschiedene Beiträge im *Dictionnaire Tolkien* (2012).

ancagmuntean@gmail.com

Jonathan Nauman, PhD, wurde von der Duke University promoviert und veröffentlichte über den York Zyklus der Mysterienspiele, *Macbeth*, T.S. Eliot und W.B. Yeats sowie besonders über die metaphysischen Dichter George Herbert und Henry Vaughan. Er lebt in Beverly, Massachusetts, und arbeitet als Ingenieur.   jonnauman@hotmail.com

Łukasz Neubauer, Dr. phil., studierte Englische Philologie an der Nikolaus-Kopernikus-Universität in Toruń (Polen) und Skandinavische Literatur an der Universität Bergen (Norwegen). Er wurde in Englischer Philologie von der Universität Łódź (Polen) promoviert und ist Mitglied des britischen Zweigs der International Arthurian Society sowie Koordinator des jährlichen Symposiums mittelalterliche Fantasy in Unieście (Polen).   lukasz_neubauer@poczta.onet.pl

Friedhelm Schneidewind studierte Biologie und einige Semester Informatik. Aktuell ist er tätig als freier Dozent vor allem für Mediengestaltung und im kaufmännisch-betriebswirtschaftlichen Bereich, als Autor u.a. mehrerer Lexika und Sachbücher zu Mythologie, zur phantastischen Literatur und zu Tolkien, als Journalist, Herausgeber, Verleger und Musiker.

www.friedhelm-schneidewind.de

Janek Scholz lehrt im interdisziplinären Bereich des Studiengangs „Literatur- und Sprachwissenschaft" an der RWTH Aachen. In seinem Promotionsprojekt am Lehrstuhl für Romanische Philologie vergleicht er Texte aus Brasilien, Italien, Deutschland und England, in denen Spiel außer Kontrolle gerät. Sein Interesse gilt der Spieltheorie, der Raumtheorie und allen Arten von Zwischenräumen, in denen Menschen über das Alltägliche hinausgehen.

janek.scholz@ifaar.rwth-aachen.de

Guglielmo Spirito, Prof. Dr. theol., ist ein Franziskaner-Konventuale (Minorit) und lebt und arbeitet in Assisi. Er promovierte in Rom am *Antonianum* in Theologie mit dem Spezialgebiet Spiritualität und ist Professor am Theologischen

Institut Assisi und an der päpstlichen Fakultät Sankt Bonaventura (Seraphicum) in Rom. Über Tolkien hat er in Italien, England, Deutschland, Frankreich und Kanada Vorträge gehalten und mehrere Essays, Bücher (*Tra San Francesco e Tolkien* und *Lo specchio di Galadriel*) und Aufsätze (bei *Walking Tree Publishers* und *Hither Shore*) veröffentlicht.   fraguspi@gmail.com

Claudio Testi, Dr. phil., wurde von der Universität Bologna in Philosophie promoviert und ist Präsident des Instituts für Thomistische Studien in Modena und Vizepräsident der Italienischen Gesellschaft für Tolkienstudien. Er unterrichtet Formale Logik am Philosophischen Studium der Dominikaner in Bologna und seine Veröffentlichungen reichen von exegetischen Studien über die Metaphysik des Thomas v. Aquin bis zu Beiträgen über Logik und Erkenntnistheorie. Zudem ist er Direktor der Serie *Tolkien e Dintorni*, einer Sammlung kritischer Studien und Übersetzungen über Tolkien und die Inklings und hat mehr als zehn Bücher über Tolkien herausgegeben (zuletzt mit Roberto Arduini: *Tolkien and Philosophy*). Als Autor hat er sich besonders mit der Frage nach dem paganen Charakter des Werkes Tolkiens auseinandergesetzt (*Tolkien Studies* X und eine Monographie *Santi Pagani nella Terra di mezzo di Tolkien* (*Pagan Saints in Tolkien's Middle-earth*).   claudio.testi1967@gmail.com

Allan Turner, Dr. phil., ist kürzlich von seinem Berufsleben als Dozent in englischer Sprache, zuletzt an der Friedrich-Schiller-Universität Jena, in den Ruhestand gegangen und freut sich darauf, mehr Zeit auf die Forschung über Übersetzungsstudien und Stilfragen, insbesondere in Beziehung zu Tolkien, aufwenden zu können.   allangturner@gmail.com

Christian Weichmann, Dr. rer. nat., wurde von der Universität Bonn in Physik promoviert. Er veröffentlichte diverse Beiträge über Tolkien und ist aktuell Zweiter Vorsitzender der Deutschen Tolkien Gesellschaft sowie Mitglied von Unquendor, der Tolkien Society und der Österreichischen Tolkien Gesellschaft. Er arbeitet als technischer Softwareentwickler in Braunschweig.
christian.weichmann@tolkiengesellschaft.de

Weinreich, Frank, Dr. phil., studierte Kommunikationswissenschaften, Politikwissenschaft und Philosophie und promovierte in Philosophie. Seine Forschungsinteressen mit zahlreichen Veröffentlichungen sind Ethik, Ontologie, Medien, Technikfolgeabschätzung, Wissenschaftsphilosophie und Phantastik. Er arbeitet gegenwärtig als freier Lektor und Literaturscout für verschiedene Verlage.
fw@polyoinos.com

Renée Vink hat einen Master in Skandinavischer Sprachwissenschaft, einschließ-
lich Altnordisch, und arbeitet als Übersetzerin für Schwedisch, Norwegisch,
Dänisch, Deutsch und Englisch. Unter anderem ist sie die niederländische
Übersetzerin der Poesie in *The Legend of Sigurd and Gudrún*, *The Fall of Arthur*
und Tolkiens *Beowulf* und *Kullervo*. 2012 erschien ihre Monographie *Wagner
& Tolkien: Mythmakers*.   rvink7@hotmail.com

Siglenverzeichnis

Die Schriften von J.R.R. Tolkien werden im Text jeweils ohne Angabe des Verfassernamens mit den folgenden Siglen zitiert. Die jeweils benutzte Ausgabe findet sich im Literaturverzeichnis.

AI:	The Lay of Aotrou and Itroun
ATB:	The Adventures of Tom Bombadil and other Verses from the Red Book / Die Abenteuer des Tom Bombadil und andere Gedichte aus dem Roten Buch
AW:	Ancrene Wisse and Hali Meiðhad
B:	Die Briefe von J.R.R. Tolkien
BA:	Bilbos Abschiedslied
BB:	Baum und Blatt
BGH:	Bauer Giles von Ham
BLS:	Bilbo's Last Song
BMC:	Beowulf: The Monster and the Critics
BT:	Blatt von Tüftler
BUK:	Beowulf: Die Ungeheuer und ihre Kritiker
BW:	Die Briefe vom Weihnachtsmann
CH:	The Children of Húrin
CP:	Chaucer as a Philologist
EA:	The End of the Third Age (History of Middle-earth 9). Auszug
EW:	English and Welsh / Englisch und Walisisch
FA:	The Fall of Arthur
FC:	Letters from Father Christmas
FGH:	Farmer Giles of Ham
FH:	Finn and Hengest
FS:	On Fairy-Stories
GD:	Gute Drachen sind rar
GN:	Guide to the Names in the Lord of the Rings
GPO:	Sir Gawain and the Green Knight, Pearl, and Sir Orfeo
H:	The Hobbit / Der Hobbit / Der kleine Hobbit
HB:	The Homecoming of Beorhtnoth Beorhthelm's Son
HdR:	Der Herr der Ringe
HdR I:	Der Herr der Ringe. Bd. 1. Die Gefährten
HdR II:	Der Herr der Ringe. Bd. 2. Die Zwei Türme
HdR III:	Der Herr der Ringe. Bd. 3. Die Rückkehr des Königs / Die Wiederkehr des Königs
HdR A:	Der Herr der Ringe. Anhänge
HG:	Herr Glück
HH I/II:	The History of the Hobbit
HL:	Ein heimliches Laster
KH:	Die Kinder Húrins
L:	The Letters of J.R.R. Tolkien
LB:	The Lays of Beleriand (History of Middle-earth 3)
LN:	Leaf by Niggle

LotR:	The Lord of the Rings
LotR I:	The Fellowship of the Ring. Being the first part of The Lord of the Rings
LotR II:	The Two Towers. Being the second part of The Lord of the Rings
LotR III:	The Return of the King. Being the third part of The Lord of the Rings
LotR A:	The Lord of the Rings. Appendices
LR:	The Lost Road and other Writings (History of Middle-earth 5)
LSG:	The Legend of Sigurd and Gudrún
LT 1:	The Book of Lost Tales 1 (History of Middle-earth 1)
LT 2:	The Book of Lost Tales 2 (History of Middle-earth 2)
MB:	Mr. Bliss
MC:	The Monsters and the Critics and Other Essays
ME:	A Middle English Vocabulary
MR:	Morgoth's Ring (History of Middle-earth 10)
My:	Mythopoeia
NM:	Nachrichten aus Mittelerde
OE:	The Old English Exodus
OK:	Ósanwe-Kenta
P:	Pictures by J.R.R. Tolkien
PM:	The Peoples of Middle-earth (History of Middle-earth 12)
R:	Roverandom
RBG:	The Rivers and Beacon-hills of Gondor
RGEO:	The Road Goes Ever On (with Donald Swann)
RS:	The Return of the Shadow (History of Middle-earth 6)
S:	Silmarillion
SD:	The Sauron Defeated (History of Middle-earth 9)
SG:	Der Schmied von Großholzingen
SGG:	Sir Gawain and the Green Knight / Sir Gawain und der Grüne Ritter (Essay)
SK:	The Story of Kullervo
SM:	The Shaping of Middle-earth (History of Middle-earth 4)
SP:	Songs for the Philologists
SV:	A Secret Vice
SWM:	Smith of Wootton Major
SWME:	Smith of Wootton Major Essay
TB:	On Translating Beowulf
TI:	The Treason of Isengard (History of Middle-earth 7)
TL:	Tree and Leaf
ÜB:	Zur Übersetzung des Beowulf
ÜM:	Über Märchen
UK:	Die Ungeheuer und ihre Kritiker. Gesammelte Aufsätze
UT:	Unfinished Tales
VA:	Valedictory Address
VG 1:	Das Buch der Verschollenen Geschichten 1
VG 2:	Das Buch der Verschollenen Geschichten 2
WJ:	The War of the Jewels (History of Middle-earth 11)
WR:	The War of the Ring (History of Middle-earth 8)

Index